# BICENTENNIAL PHILADELPHIA

# BICENTENNIAL PHILADELPHIA

*A Family Guide to the City and Countryside*

*by*

*Ruth L. Gales*
*and Diane F. Loewenson*

*Illustrated by Pamela Johnson*

**J. B. LIPPINCOTT COMPANY**
*Philadelphia and New York*

U.S. Library of Congress Cataloging in Publication Data

Gales, Ruth L
    Bicentennial Philadelphia: a family guide to the city
and countryside.

    1. Philadelphia—Description—1951–      —Guide-
books.    2. Philadelphia region, Pa.—Description and
travel—Guide-books.    I. Loewenson, Diane F., joint
author.    II. Title.
F158.18.G34      917.48′11′044      74–9937
ISBN–0–397–00898–8
ISBN–0–397–01007–9 (pbk.)

*To our husbands and children, who shared many outings—with good humor*

# CONTENTS

# ACKNOWLEDGMENTS

Our special thanks

to our friends who offered suggestions and advice;

to the many people at the institutions and places we visited who gave their time and information: the staff of Independence National Historical Park, especially Martin Yoelson, historian; the professional staff of the Philadelphia Museum of Art; the Philadelphia Department of Recreation; the professional staff of the Free Library; Richard Nicolai of the Fairmount Park Commission; Faye Olivieri of the Greater Philadelphia Chamber of Commerce; Joel Bloom of the Franklin Institute; Joaquin Bowman of SEPTA; Alvin S. Hornstein of the Philadelphia Convention and Visitors Bureau;

to Bernard Albert of Moss Rehabilitation Hospital for his assistance on the chapter for the handicapped;

to those who gave us special help in certain areas of the book: Bernice Chesler of Newton, Massachusetts, for starting us off on the right track; Ellen Feldman; Charles Kahn, Jr.; Betty LeBoutillier; C. Sanford Rector; Lita Solis-Cohn; Molly Stoddard; and Stephanie Wolf.

And to the following for granting permission to use their maps: Independence National Historical Park, Pennsylvania Department of Transportation, Philadelphia Convention and Visitors Bureau, Philadelphia Zoological Gardens, Park House Tours of the Philadelphia Museum of Art.

12

# PREFACE

As the United States approaches its two-hundredth anniversary, it is appropriate that Philadelphia, the birthplace of the nation, be a focal point for the celebration. People from all over the world flock to the Historic Area. But, after the Liberty Bell, where do you begin? Philadelphia is fortunate to have many of the buildings from its Colonial past still standing; you visit the actual places where history was made.

To help residents, visitors, teachers, and group leaders in their explorations of Philadelphia and its environs, here is a guidebook for everyone, with emphasis on the family. Included are history, time schedules, admission fees, what is free, directions on how to get to your destination by auto and/or public transportation, and, for the first time, a list of places accessible to the handicapped. Historic Philadelphia and Germantown, Fairmount Park, and nearby arboretums are covered. There are sections on shops and services; classes, clubs, and hobbies; restaurants; sports. Outings to historic parks and restorations, the Brandywine Valley, Bucks County, and Pennsylvania Dutch Country are included, as well as an annual month-by-month calendar of events.

The trend today is away from "canned" guided tours and museums behind glass. Better to visit at your own pace and experience "living history" at such places as Hopewell Village or Pennsbury Manor—or take an environmental approach by visiting, for example, the Schuylkill Valley Nature Center. Fairs and festivals bring cultural traditions and customs alive. It's more fun to hear the music, see the blacksmith work, and eat the food than just watch a film.

This book explores the city's glorious past as well as its exciting present. Our aim is not to describe in detail but rather to interest you in exploring further, and to make your outings more pleasurable as you discover and rediscover Philadelphia and the surrounding countryside.

# SOME HELPFUL ADVICE

Successful family outings require some thought and planning.

CHECK BEFORE YOU LEAVE. Hours, fees, and other regulations do change. It is best to check before you start out.

DIRECTIONS emanate from Center City or well-known routes.

PUBLIC TRANSPORTATION: SEPTA routes nearest your destination. Call SEPTA (DA 9-4800) for connecting routes from your location.

NEARBY PLACES OF INTEREST. If you want to explore further, we have included other places in the vicinity.

CHECK THE BOOK BEFORE YOU GO. It is frustrating to come back from Washington Crossing State Park and find that you missed the Wild Flower Preserve. We note nearby places at the end of many listings so you *won't* miss them.

AVOID PEAK HOURS IN RESTAURANTS. Plan to eat lunch at 11:45 A.M. and beat the crowds, or have a midmorning coffee break and eat at 2.

PICNIC AREAS AND FACILITIES are emphasized. Eating out can be time-consuming and costly for a family, and picnics are more fun.

MAPS are important in planning your trips. The SEPTA Street and Transit Map of Philadelphia (35¢) is very helpful. It is available at newsstands or from SEPTA, 200 West Wyoming Avenue, Philadelphia 19140. NOTE: Exact change or tokens are needed for buses, trolleys, and subways. For trips outside the city, keep an up-to-date highway map handy, since routes change and are constantly being extended. This may avert many a family squabble.

INFORMATION FOR GROUPS. Some places can be visited without advance notice, but for groups, especially large ones, it is preferable to write or call in advance. This way guides can be provided or areas of special interest incorporated into your visit.

REDUCED ADMISSIONS are available at many places to students with I.D. cards, senior citizens, and servicemen. It is a good idea to come armed with proper identification and ask about reduced admissions, because the information is often not posted.

TELEPHONE NUMBERS are listed as they would be dialed from the Philadelphia Metropolitan area. If no area code appears, it falls in the 215 zone.

IF YOU HAVE A SUGGESTION. It is possible that your favorite place has been overlooked. New restorations are being completed, interesting craft shops open, a park is dedicated. Let us know what you and your family enjoy doing or have discovered. Write to us at: J. B. Lippincott Company, East Washington Square, Philadelphia, Pa. 19105.

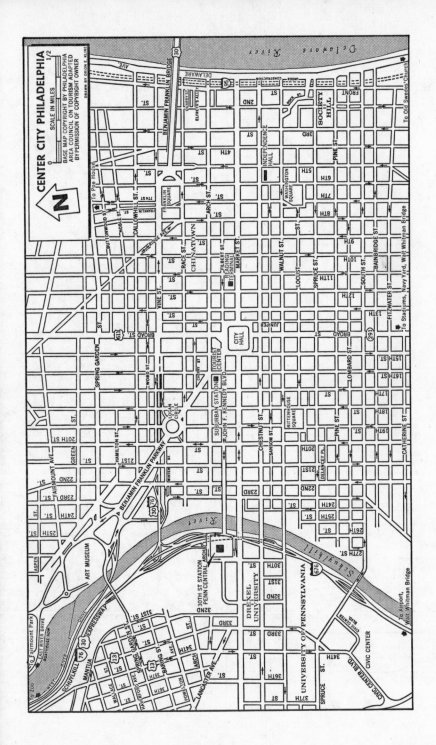

# CENTER CITY PHILADELPHIA

**N**

SCALE IN MILES 1/2

0

BASE MAP COPYRIGHT BY PHILADELPHIA
AREA COUNCIL ON TOURISM ADAPTED
BY PERMISSION OF COPYRIGHT OWNER

DRAWN BY ORION E. KLINE

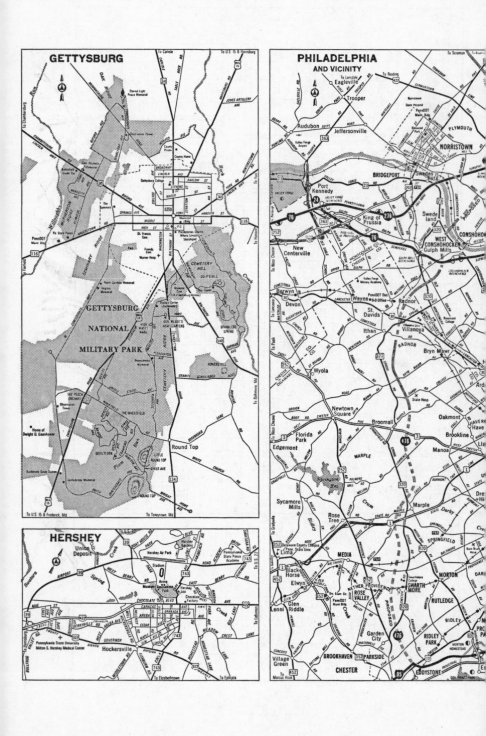

**SCALE OF MILES**

0    1    2    3    4    5

(PHILADELPHIA AND VICINITY ONLY)

# Map of Old Philadelphia

GLORIA DEI (OLD SWEDES') CHURCH
CHRISTIAN & SWANSON STS

1. Independence Hall.
2. Congress Hall.
3. Old City Hall.
4. Independence Square.
5. American Philosophical Society.
6. American Philosophical Society Library.
7. Second Bank of the United States.
8. Carpenters' Hall.
9. New Hall.
10. Pemberton House.
11. First Bank of the United States.
12. The Philadelphia (Merchants') Exchange.
13. Bishop White House.
14. Todd House.
15. Old Saint Joseph's Church.
16. Saint Paul's Church.
17. The Powel House.
18. Saint Mary's Church.
19. Shippen-Wistar House.
20. Philadelphia Contributionship.
21. Penn Mutual Observation Deck.
22. Washington Square.
23. Curtis Building.
24. Philadelphia Saving Fund Society.
25. Walnut Street Theatre.
26. Mikveh Israel Cemetery.
27. Pennsylvania Hospital.
28. Holy Trinity Church.
29. "Mother Bethel" Church.
30. Old Pine Street Church.
31. Hill-Physick-Keith House.
32. Saint Peter's Church.
33. Head House and 2nd Street Market.
34. Gloria Dei (Old Swedes') Church.
35. "A Man Full of Trouble" Tavern
36. Christ Church.
37. Elfreth's Alley.
38. Betsy Ross House.
39. Saint George's Church.
40. Friends Meeting House.
41. Christ Church Cemetery.
42. Free Quaker Meeting House.
43. Atwater Kent Museum.

# INTRODUCTION

In 1776 the Liberty Bell tolled to herald the adoption and public reading of the Declaration of Independence: "When in the Course of human Events..." This was the document that severed all ties with England and proclaimed the right of the colonists to govern themselves. Eleven years later the delegates to the Constitutional Convention drew up and approved the Constitution in the Assembly Room of the Pennsylvania State House, known today as Independence Hall. Through the years this remarkable document has enabled the nation to survive the issue of slavery, sectional rivalries, and economic antagonisms. From 1790 to 1800 Philadelphia served as the capital of the United States, with the Senate and the House of Representatives meeting in the County Court House, now Congress Hall. Here they adopted the first ten amendments to the Constitution, the Bill of Rights. The Supreme Court used Old City Hall for its meeting place and established the role of the judiciary under John Jay.

Philadelphia is unquestionably the birthplace of the nation. Though the area was first settled by the Dutch and the Swedes more than a hundred years before the American Revolution, this great city became a reality in 1681, when William Penn persuaded Charles II to grant him a proprietary province in the New World as payment of a debt to his father. Young Penn envisioned an ideal commonwealth in America, a "Holy Experiment" where people would be free from the religious persecution he had experienced in trying to follow his own Quaker convictions. Penn carefully formulated ideas for a "greene countrie towne"; his plan included streets, statehouses, markets, and private dwellings. The original city had an area of 2 square miles, stretching from the Schuylkill River to the Delaware River, from Vine Street to South Street.

Thomas Holme, Penn's surveyor, did the city planning, laid out the streets on a gridiron plan, and established five parks, which still exist: the center square where City Hall now stands, and squares in the four corners of the city for public parks. They were later named for distinguished eighteenth-century citizens: Washington, Franklin, and Rittenhouse Squares, and Logan Circle. North and south streets were numbered, and streets running east and west were named for trees. Most of them remain today; however, Mulberry became Arch because of a viaduct at Front Street, and Sassafras became Race because of the horse-and-buggy races held there.

From the beginning, the city attracted settlers in great numbers from many different countries because of its reputation for justice and religious freedom. Many of these immigrants were fine craftsmen and carpenters. They left their imprint on the distinguished public buildings, fine homes, and beautiful furniture still highly prized today.

During the Colonial period, Philadelphia was the geographic center of the New World and developed as the center of government, finance, shipping, trade, culture, and the arts. By the time of the Revolution it was, after London, the most important city in the English-speaking world and the largest city in the Colonies. Its leadership in science, industry, and the arts is apparent in the many "firsts" in America it achieved—the first paper mill, botanic garden, waterworks, hospital, medical school, law library, theater, corporate bank, stock exchange, United States Mint, art museum, Naval Academy, zoological gardens—along with the first subscription library in the world. Many of these exist today: John Bartram Gardens, Pennsylvania Hospital, University of Pennsylvania Medical School, Philadelphia–Baltimore–Washington Stock Exchange, Pennsylvania Academy of the Fine Arts, the Zoo, and the Library Company of Philadelphia, not to be confused with the Free Library. Philadelphia, with its great Quaker tradition, became an important station on the Underground Railroad and remained loyal to the Union during the Civil War.

Fairmount Park, one of Philadelphia's greatest assets, is the largest city-owned park in the world. It has facilities for recreation, theater, and concerts, and wild natural areas along the Wissahickon and Pennypack Creeks for hiking, riding, and fishing. The park was the site of the celebration marking the one-hundredth birthday of the United States.

The Centennial Exposition of 1876 took place on 236 acres of Fairmount Park and reflected the change of the country from an agrarian to an industrial nation. Technology was the main focus. Throngs of people marveled at the Corliss steam engine which ran the Fair's machinery and dominated Machinery Hall, along with such marvels as Alexander Graham Bell's telephone and a typewriting machine. The hand and torch of the not-yet-completed

Statue of Liberty were displayed. Memorial Hall housed art and sculpture from around the world. It is the only major building still standing from the Exposition. Horticultural Hall, an ornamental iron-cage greenhouse, featured exotic plant life and continued as a focal point for visitors to the Park until it was damaged during a hurricane in 1954. Regrettably, it was torn down instead of being restored. The Exposition lasted from May to November and was attended by eight million people who celebrated not only the birthday of the original Union but also the reunion following the bitterness of the Civil War.

Following this period population and industry grew, and along with their growth urban problems developed. Many of Philadelphia's wealthy citizens deserted the city for Chestnut Hill and the Main Line, following the tracks of the highly successful commuter rail lines. For the next seventy years or so very little positive action was taken to halt the deterioration and corruption in the city. Finally, in 1951, with creative leadership Philadelphia began an exciting program of restoration and urban renewal. The commercial complex of Penn Center arose. And, with the restorations in Society Hill and the Historic Area, Philadelphia finally realized the obligation of its great heritage and its deep roots in Colonial history. Federal, state, and city organizations, with the help of concerned citizens, have made great strides in preserving the city's past while still giving thought to the present.

# 1
# HISTORIC PHILADELPHIA AND ENVIRONS

## Independence Hall Area

### *Main Attractions*

The Independence Hall area and Society Hill are closely associated with the history of Philadelphia.

When visiting the historic areas, most people head for Independence Hall. Since it is the most important historic shrine in Philadelphia—in fact, in the nation—we have listed it first, along with the adjoining buildings: Congress Hall and Old City Hall. Other historic shrines are listed alphabetically. In addition, we have included museums and restaurants that can be easily combined with your visits in the area.

The places you want to see are not necessarily close together, and parking is a problem. Certain houses are open only for guided tours at specific times, so it is best to try to coordinate what you want to see in advance. You may wish to begin your wanderings at the Visitor Center, located in the First Bank of the United States at 120 South 3rd Street, or, in season, atop the Observation Deck of the Penn Mutual Life Insurance Building, 530 Walnut Street.

Historic churches of all denominations dot the area. William Penn's concern for religious freedom is clearly evident in the diversity of old churches, many of which still have active congregations.

The Society Hill area lies between Walnut and South, Front and 7th Streets. The name is derived from the Free Society of Traders, which was granted a charter by William Penn in 1682. It was a development company whose financial and manufacturing ideas were rarely successful; however, the name continues. Society Hill contains a high concentration of eighteenth-century and early nineteenth-century houses—probably more than any other comparable area in the United States. Many of the buildings have colorful leaded emblems called fire marks. Placed there by the fire insurance companies, these signs alerted the fire fighters to work carefully.

Two of the oldest companies are the Philadelphia Contributionship (1752), which used as its symbol four clasped hands, and the Mutual Assurance Company (1784), formed when the Contributionship ruled that trees were a fire hazard and must be cut down. This company, however, was willing to preserve trees and used as its symbol "The Green Tree."

To fully appreciate and enjoy your visit to the Independence Hall–Society Hill area, you must choose carefully or, better still plan several visits.

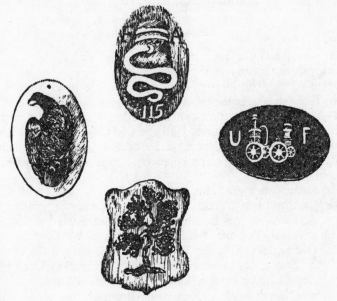

Eighteenth-Century Fire Marks

## INDEPENDENCE HALL
Chestnut Street between 5th and 6th Streets
Philadelphia 19106

**Phone:** MA 7-1776
**Open:** Daily 9 A.M.–5 P.M.; July 1–Labor Day, 8 A.M.–8 P.M.
**Admission:** Free; guided tours only
**Parking:** Public lots in the area and limited street parking
**Public Transportation:** Mid City Loop bus (page 394), Cultural Loop bus (page 394), any bus on Market or Chestnut Streets, Market Street Subway

Independence Hall

Great events took place here, and you can feel it when you enter. On July 4, 1776, the Second Continental Congress met in the Assembly Room of what was then the Pennsylvania State House and adopted the Declaration of Independence—a momentous decision that formally declared the thirteen Colonies free and independent states. In this same Assembly Room eleven years later, the Founding Fathers—fifty-five enlightened and civilized men, the elite of the country—created a nation and drew up the Constitution to govern it. The tables used by such notable delegates as Benjamin

Franklin, George Washington, Alexander Hamilton, and James Madison are here to see, covered in green baize which was purposely left dragging on the floor so that the men could wrap it around their legs on cold days. Inkstands, boxes of blotting sand, and spectacles sit on the tables. The elevated speaker's chair originally used by George Washington is still intact.

The Assembly Room has been restored with utmost care and accuracy by the Independence National Historical Park, which is responsible for preserving Independence Hall and several surrounding historical buildings. This room is considered the most important historic room in the United States. A well-versed guide stands behind a guardrail and relates history, explains the various artifacts, and answers questions.

### LIBERTY BELL

In the stairwell of the main floor stands the famous Liberty Bell, with its inscription from Leviticus, "Proclaim Liberty Throughout All the Land unto All the Inhabitants Thereof." It was cast by Thomas Lester of Whitechapel, London, and arrived here in August, 1752, only to crack while being tested. It was then recast twice by Pass and Stow of Philadelphia and finally hung in the steeple of the Pennsylvania State House (Independence Hall) in 1753 in honor of the fiftieth year of the Pennsylvania Charter of Privileges.

It tolled on special occasions and in times of protest—in 1765 against the Stamp Act; in 1773 for the resolution against landing British tea; in 1774 against the closing of the port of Boston; in 1775 to announce the first hostilities of the Revolution; and in 1776 at the public reading of the Declaration of Independence.

Legend has it that it finally cracked while tolling for the funeral procession of John Marshall on July 8, 1835. Since then it has been silent, but it holds special meaning for Americans as a symbol of freedom. Thousands of visitors come every day to see and touch it.

### THE SUPREME COURT CHAMBER

Across the hall from the Assembly Room is where the Provincial, later the Pennsylvania, Supreme Court met. This room was in continuous service until the middle of the nineteenth century. Now restored, it contains the judge's bench, the lawyer's table, the prisoner's cage, and other legal furnishings.

### UPSTAIRS

The entire Chestnut Street frontage of Independence Hall was designed as one room called the "gallery" or "long room." It measures 100 by 20 feet, and when completed in 1745 it was the largest public room in the Province of Pennsylvania, the scene of suppers, balls, and fêtes. In 1774 the gallery accommodated 500 guests at a sitdown dinner. The simple but unusual proportions of the room, the fine wood moldings, and five chandeliers make this a most impressive room to see. Today evening programs by accomplished musicians are scheduled in Long Gallery.

The Liberty Bell

SOUND AND LIGHT SHOW

*A Nation Is Born.* A dramatic outdoor presentation using lighting effects with a music and voice track to portray scenes of the American Revolution and the signing of the Declaration of Independence. This impressive presentation is one of the city's outstanding summertime attractions. In Independence Square, Tuesday through Saturday 9 P.M., end of June through Labor Day. Free.

HANDICAPPED

Use the entrance at the rear in Independence Square. It is best to call ahead so they can put down a ramp.

VOLUNTEER GUIDE PROGRAM

Summers. Apply at Independence National Historical Park Headquarters, 313 Walnut Street, 597-7132, for further information.

## CONGRESS HALL
6th and Chestnut Streets
Philadelphia 19106

Phone: MA 7-1776
Open: Daily 9 A.M.–5 P.M.
Admission: Free

Philadelphia was the capital of the United States from 1790 to 1800. During that time the House of Representatives and the Senate met in Congress Hall. The building was completed in 1789 and served as a county courthouse until it was needed as a meeting place for the United States Congress. After the national government moved to Washington in 1800, it again became a courthouse. Today it has been restored to its appearance as the meeting place of Congress.

The House of Representatives met downstairs. Continuous semi-circular rows of attached desks fill the room, and you may sit at the desks and listen to the guide. Upstairs the Senate convened. There are thirty-two individual desks—besides the thirteen original states, Vermont, Kentucky, and Tennessee joined the Union while Philadelphia was the capital.

Important events took place here: Washington's Second Inaugural and his last formal message to Congress before he retired; John Adams's first and only inauguration, held in the House of Representatives; and the establishment of the Mint and the Bank of the United States.

## OLD CITY HALL
Southwest corner of 5th and Chestnut Streets
Philadelphia 19106

Phone: MA 7-1776

When Philadelphia served as capital of the new nation from 1790 to 1800, the United States Supreme Court met in this building. Here John Jay presided as the first Chief Justice, and the Court established the framework of the judicial branch of the Federal Government. After the Supreme Court moved to Washington, the building continued in use as the City Hall.

The building is being restored, and the first floor will re-create the appearance of Old City Hall as it was when it served as the meeting place of the first Supreme Court. On the second floor there will be exhibits depicting Philadelphia in the last quarter of the eighteenth century; represented are crafts, the yellow fever epidemic of 1793, the contribution of the black man, and urban problems of the late 1700s as compared to today. This restoration is scheduled to be completed in 1975.

## AMERICAN PHILOSOPHICAL SOCIETY
104 South 5th Street
Philadelphia 19106

Phone: WA 5-3606

You may call for an appointment in advance and be taken through the building, provided that Society meetings are not in session. Benjamin Franklin founded the American Philosophical Society in 1743 "to let light into the nature of things," and it still exists today. It is the oldest learned society in America and is considered among the most exclusive in this country. Membership is limited to 500 Americans and 100 foreigners chosen for their achievements in the physical, biological, and social sciences and the humanities. Benjamin Franklin was a president, and Thomas Jefferson was simultaneously President of the United States and president of the Philosophical Society. Other distinguished members have included Charles Darwin, John James Audubon, Ralph Waldo Emerson, Louis Pasteur, and Madame Marie Curie.

The building, adjacent to Independence Hall, is the second oldest in Independence Square, and has been continuously occupied by the Philosophical Society since 1789. Great treasures lie within the hallowed walls of the Society: the original Charter of Privileges (1701), which was granted by William Penn to the inhabitants of Pennsylvania and which is the forerunner of our Bill of Rights; the original Franklin chair in its unrestored state; Jefferson's chair, in which he wrote the rough draft of the Declaration of Independence; Franklin's original electric battery with which he made early experiments; the astronomical transit telescope made by David Rittenhouse for the observation of the 1769 transit of Venus; busts of famous Colonial figures by William Rush and one of David Rittenhouse by Ceracchi (1794); the only known painting of Deborah Franklin; paintings of Franklin by Peale, Jefferson by Sully, Washington by Stuart; two magnificent Duffield clocks, one a grandmother, one a grandfather, clock.

The publications of the Society are outstanding and reasonably priced. Two notable books are *Historic Philadelphia* and *Historic Germantown*. Ring the outside bell of the Society, then go to the desk to make your purchase.

## AMERICAN PHILOSOPHICAL SOCIETY LIBRARY
5th and Chestnut Streets (across from Independence Square)
Philadelphia 19106

Phone: WA 5-9545
Open: Monday–Friday 9 A.M.–5 P.M.
Admission: Free

The Library of the Philosophical Society contains an awesome collection of books, pamphlets, letters, documents, and journals from the eighteenth century to the present. Topics of special interest include Frankliniana, science in America, Darwin and evolution, American Indian languages, and modern physics and genetics. The library may be used by any serious scholar.

Although the Library is a private organization, visitors are permitted to inspect the exhibits in the display cases in the entrance hall and can look into the scholarly and inviting library.

## BETSY ROSS HOUSE
239 Arch Street
Philadelphia 19106

Phone: MA 7-5343
Open: Daily 9:30 A.M.–5:15 P.M.
Closed: Christmas
Admission: Free
Parking: Nearby public lots
Public Transportation: SEPTA Routes 5, 17, 33, 48

There's a lot of controversy as to whether Betsy Ross really made the first flag or even lived in this house, but it's a legend that children seem to believe and they enjoy a visit here. The only entrance is through a souvenir shop. The house itself is a lovely example of a small, early eighteenth-century dwelling furnished in the period with attention paid to detail. Most of the rooms are fenced off and you can only look in. The stairways are narrow, and even small groups tend to create a traffic jam. Little children (and anyone who has difficulty walking) will find the stairs hard to manage. Nevertheless, this quaint house is worth a visit—whether the legend is true or not.

## BISHOP WHITE HOUSE
309 Walnut Street
Philadelphia 19106

**Phone:** 597-2425
**Open:** Monday–Friday, tours at 11 A.M., 1 P.M., and 2 P.M.
**Closed:** Weekends
**Admission:** Free; guided tours only. Tickets available at Visitor Center, First Bank, 3rd and Chestnut Streets; or at Independence National Historical Park Headquarters, 313 Walnut Street.
**Parking:** On street or in public lots in area
**Public Transportation:** Cultural Loop bus, Mid City Loop bus, D, 50

Bishop William White, first Episcopal Bishop of Pennsylvania, rector of Christ Church, and chaplain to the Continental Congress, built a fine home on Walnut Street near 3rd Street in 1786–1787, and it has been restored to its former elegance. A great family man and a humanitarian, he was a brother-in-law of Benjamin Rush and a good friend to George Washington, who was a frequent visitor.

The first and second floors of this lovely old Colonial residence are open to the public. The house is full of paintings, furniture, and personal possessions of historic significance. The Bishop's books, eyeglasses—even an apple corer—are intact and lend a personal touch to your visit.

Volunteer guides provide history, anecdotes, and a great deal of knowledge about the Bishop, his family, and the era in which he lived.

### GROUP VISITS
Limited to ten people. Tours can be arranged by calling 597-7130.

### NEARBY
A lovely eighteenth-century garden, right next door to the Horticultural Society at 325 Walnut Street. This authentically designed garden with walks and gazebo is planted with attractive flowers, shrubs, and trees.

## CARPENTERS' HALL

320 Chestnut Street
Philadelphia 19106

**Phone:** WA 5-0167
**Open:** Daily 10 A.M.–4 P.M.
**Closed:** Easter, Thanksgiving, Christmas, New Year's Day, and four days when the Carpenters' Company meets: the third Mondays in January, April, July, and October
**Admission:** Free
**Parking:** Nearby public lots
**Public Transportation:** Near Independence Hall

Carpenters' Hall is best remembered as the oldest guildhall in the United States, patterned after the trade guilds of London, and as the meeting place of the First Continental Congress.

The Carpenters' Company of Philadelphia was founded in 1724. Membership was highly selective: the master carpenters who were admitted were not only adept with tools but also more like the architects of today. Many similar organizations existed at the time, but none rivaled the prestige of the Carpenters' Company.

In September, 1774, the First Continental Congress selected privately owned Carpenters' Hall as its meeting place because of the members' sympathies with revolutionary aims. Momentous decisions were made here: grievances against the British government were adopted; the resistance of Massachusetts commended; and an embargo on British goods adopted. When war broke out in the spring of 1775, Congress transferred its sessions to the more spacious State House (Independence Hall).

Over the years Carpenters' Hall has served in many capacities: Land Office, Bank, Customs House, and, since 1857, a patriotic shrine. The Carpenters' Company still exists today and cooperates with Independence National Historical Park in an arrangement that guarantees its future as an historic landmark.

## CHRIST CHURCH

2nd Street above Market Street
Philadelphia 19106

**Phone:** WA 2-1695
**Open:** Daily 9 A.M.–5 P.M.
**Admission:** Free
**Parking:** On street or nearby public lots
**Public Transportation:** SEPTA Routes 5, 17, 33

This lovely old church is an architectural gem with an impressive place in American history. The parish was founded in 1695 and is still active. Fifteen signers of the Declaration of Independence attended services here, and seven are buried in the churchyard or in the burial grounds at 5th and Arch Streets. George Washington Benjamin Franklin, Thomas Jefferson, and Robert Morris were among the famous worshipers here, and some of their pews are marked.

Elfreth's Alley

The chancel is graced with a magnificent Palladian window, the first of this architectural design in America. The "wineglass" pulpit, popular in the eighteenth century, is one of the very few that remain. The gardens in season are also very lovely.

People of all faiths are welcome to visit any day and may attend services on Sundays at 9 and 11 A.M.

GROUP TOURS

No advance notice necessary, but they ask that you not come between 11:45 A.M. and 1 P.M. Christ Church can accommodate groups up to 200.

HANDICAPPED

Enter on 2nd Street. One step. No steps in the church. Off-street parking nearby.

NEARBY

Christ Church Cemetery at 5th and Arch Streets. Benjamin Franklin is buried here.

## ELFRETH'S ALLEY

Between Front and Second Streets, north of Arch Street
Philadelphia 19106

Phone: WA 5-0934
Admission: Free except on Elfreth's Alley Day
Parking: On street nearby or in public lots
Public Transportation: SEPTA Routes 5, 17, 33, 48, Market Street
    Subway

Take a walk down the oldest residential street in Philadelphia. Originally the homes of tradesmen—tailors, pewterers, and cabinet-makers—these houses have been continuously occupied since the early 1700s. You can't go into the homes, but there is a small museum at 126 Elfreth's Alley; the hours vary. The Alley is only 6 feet from curb to curb. Once a year, the first Saturday in June, Elfreth's Alley holds open house and you can see the interiors of many homes. Costumed tour guides demonstrate Colonial crafts, and folksinging and a fife and drum corps are featured.

## FIRST BANK OF THE UNITED STATES

120 South 3rd Street
Philadelphia 19106

Phone: 597-2425
Open: Daily 9 A.M.–5 P.M.
Closed: Christmas, New Year's Day
Admission: Free
Parking: Nearby public lots

This building serves as the Visitor Center and will continue to do so until the new one across the street is completed. A 10-minute slide show about the Revolutionary War period is presented at regular intervals. You can make arrangements here for tours of the Bishop White House. Also check here for information about the Whimmy Diddles Summer Program. Eighteenth-century crafts and games for children aged 7 to 11. It's free. It's fun.

This handsome edifice, built between 1795 and 1797, is the oldest bank building in the United States. The Bank was created by the First Congress of the United States, which granted it a charter from 1791 to 1811: no other similar institution was to be established during that time. When the charter ran out, the Eleventh Congress refused to renew it, and Stephen Girard began his own private bank here in 1812. It was a highly successful venture and remained so until his death in 1831. At that time a group of Philadelphia businessmen began a new state bank known as Girard Bank.

## FRANKLIN COURT
Between 3rd and 4th Streets off Market Street on a little alley
  called Orianna Street
Philadelphia

**Phone:** For information call Independence National Historical Park
  Headquarters, 597-7132

Benjamin Franklin built a house here in 1764 but didn't see it for ten years, for it was during that time that he served in England and France. Franklin was vitally interested in the construction and furnishings, which he followed through correspondence with his wife, Deborah. Franklin did live in the house while he served in the Second Continental Congress and spent the last five years of his life there.

Unfortunately, the house was torn down in 1812. Insufficient evidence remains to restore it; no picture or information can be found to indicate the height of its stories and the pitch of its roof, and the original architectural drawing is likewise gone, although there is a great deal of information about its furnishings and contents. At present the Park Service is working on the site known as Franklin Court, which includes five houses that separated Franklin's house from Market Street. Restoration of these particular houses was decided on because their shells were intact and sufficient evidence was available on them. The archaeology of Franklin's home is there to see. When completed, the whole site will be devoted to Franklin: films, exhibits, slide presentations, and an underground auditorium are in the plans.

## GLORIA DEI (OLD SWEDES') CHURCH
Delaware Avenue and Swanson Street (below Front and Christian
   Streets)
Philadelphia 19147

Phone: FU 9-1513
Open: Daily 9 A.M.–5 P.M.
Admission: Free
Parking: Available
Public Transportation: SEPTA Routes 5, 64

Gloria Dei lies in Southwark, an area originally settled in 1638
by the Scandinavians. The church still has a large active congregation and contains many unusual and priceless religious and historic relics. Built in 1700, it is the oldest church in Philadelphia.
Originally Lutheran, it is now part of the Episcopal Diocese of
Pennsylvania.

The first weekend in June, Gloria Dei features a Colonial Fair—a
smorgasbord of Swedish folk dancing, bands, food, and Scandinavian imports for sale. In December it presents a Lucia Festival—a
candlelight pageant—and the public is welcome to join in the
festivities. It is held for three days in conjunction with Saint Eric's
Fair. There are imports to buy, Scandinavian food, music, and
dancing. Call or watch the papers for the exact weekend in December.

GROUP VISITS
Guided tours available with two or three weeks' advance notice.
Call or write.

NEARBY
The Italian market.


## HEAD HOUSE AND 2ND STREET MARKET
2nd Street from Pine to Lombard Streets
Philadelphia

Public Transportation: SEPTA Routes 5, 40

Middle-of-the-street markets or market houses were common in
Colonial days. Most of them were built on High Street, renamed
Market Street by an ordinance in 1858; one year later another
ordinance abolished middle-of-the-street markets on Market Street,
but many continued in other areas. The 2nd Street Market, built
in 1745, was used continuously until the late 1950s. In 1960 it was

restored to its original appearance of Colonial days. The Head House, circa 1804, was a firehouse for two fire companies.

Today the marketplace with its series of arched openings is busy on summer weekends. Craft groups lease stalls, and food concessions with ethnic fare flourish. See Head House Square Open Air Market (page 262).

Head House

## HILL–PHYSICK–KEITH HOUSE
321 South 4th Street (between Spruce and Pine Streets)
Philadelphia 19106

**Phone:** WA 5-7866
**Open:** Tuesday–Saturday 10 A.M.–4 P.M., Sunday 1–4 P.M.
**Closed:** Mondays, Easter, Christmas, New Year's
**Admission:** Adults $1, children 50¢
**Parking:** Limited; on street
**Public Transportation:** SEPTA Routes 5, 50, 90

This elegant house is among the finest examples of the Federal period that can be seen. The beautiful fanlight over the front door contains the original glass, and the marble entrance floor is also original. The furnishings are lavish, with inlaid woods, Aubusson rugs, pier tables, massive mirrors, and carved chairs, reflecting the Egyptian influence of the Napoleonic era.

The first owner, Henry Hill, was a wealthy wine importer who liked to live well and entertain lavishly, as evidenced by the spacious mansion he built. After Hill's death in 1790, the house was occupied by Dr. Philip Syng Physick, considered the foremost physician in the country. Often called the "father of American surgery," Physick occupied the first chair of surgery established in the United States. His most famous patient was John Marshall, whom he operated on successfully for kidney stones. Marshall gave him a beautiful inscribed silver bowl, which can be seen in the study. The house passed through various branches of the Physick family, and finally to Mrs. Charles Penrose Keith. By then the location was not considered attractive, and the house fell into disrepair. After years of neglect it was restored through a large grant from the Annenberg Fund.

Don't miss the garden. It is laid out in the style popular during the early nineteenth century, complete with serpentine paths, statues, and a natural grotto. The garden is at its height during May.

## "A MAN FULL OF TROUBLE" TAVERN
127–129 Spruce Street
Philadelphia 19106

**Phone:** WA 2-1759
**Open:** April–December, Tuesday–Sunday 1–4 P.M.; December–April, Saturday and Sunday only 1–4 P.M.
**Closed:** Mondays, Easter, Thanksgiving, Christmas
**Admission:** Adults 50¢, children 25¢, under 10 free
**Parking:** On street and in nearby lots
**Public Transportation:** SEPTA Routes 5, 42, 90

Built in 1759, this tavern was used continuously for over 125 years as an inn. Here Philadelphians and travelers met, dined, and discussed the issues of the day. Accommodations were available for overnight guests in the upstairs bedrooms. The tavern and adjoining Paschall House have been restored by the Knauer Foundation as a tavern—museum displaying decorative arts. In the basement is an eighteenth-century kitchen and family dining area. The second floor has a bedroom and a sitting room. On display are American and English pewter and crewelwork, an exceptional collection of English delftware, and fine examples of American pottery and furniture. It takes only about thirty minutes to see this historic eighteenth-century tavern.

GROUP VISITS
Adults 25¢. Minimum number 20. By reservation at least a week

in advance. Written requests preferred, but telephone requests are accepted (NE 7-8111).

## NEW HALL–THE MARINE CORPS MEMORIAL MUSEUM
Chestnut Street between 3rd and 4th Streets
Philadelphia 19106

**Phone:** MA 7-1776
**Open:** 9 A.M.–4:45 P.M.
**Admission:** Free
**Parking:** Public lots in the area
**Public Transportation:** To Independence Hall

The museum, housed in a building used by the War Department in 1791–1792, is devoted to the celebration of the Marine Corps victories in the early Federal period. You can see dioramas of famous Marine Corps battles—the war with the Barbary States (1801–1804), victories at Tripoli (1804–1805), and the like. A Memorial Room contains plaques to Marines who died in World War II.

## MIKVEH ISRAEL CEMETERY
Spruce Street near 8th Street
Philadelphia

This is the oldest Jewish cemetery in the city, founded in 1738, and the burial place of many distinguished people, the most notable being Haym Solomon, revolutionary patriot. Members of the distinguished Gratz family are also here, including Rebecca, who is thought to have been the model for Rebecca in Sir Walter Scott's *Ivanhoe*. The gates are locked.

## OLD SAINT JOSEPH'S CHURCH
Willings Alley near 4th and Walnut Streets
Philadelphia 19106

**Open:** Daily
**Public Transportation:** SEPTA Routes D, 5, 50

Founded about 1732, this is the oldest Roman Catholic church in Philadelphia. At the time it was built, it was the only church in the English-speaking world where public celebration of the Mass was permitted by law, the result of William Penn's Charter of Privileges, which allowed religious freedom to the people of Pennsylvania. It was designated a national shrine in 1959.

Built on the site of the original chapel, the present church building dates back to 1838; the lovely interior is Colonial in style with
fine fluted columns and pilasters. A graceful semicircular gallery is
at the rear of the church, with an impressive organ behind it. The
church borders on Independence National Historical Park.

## PEMBERTON HOUSE—ARMY-NAVY MUSEUM
3rd and Chestnut Streets
Philadelphia 19106

**Open:** Daily 9 A.M.–5 P.M.
**Closed:** Christmas, New Year's Day
**Admission:** Free
**Parking:** Public lots in the area
**Public Transportation:** Cultural Loop bus, Mid City Loop bus,
SEPTA Routes 5, 42, D

For the military and naval history fan. This reconstructed Colonial house contains maps, tapes, dioramas, uniforms, and weapons
tracing the Colonial origins of the United States Army and Navy—
from Rogers's Rangers in the French and Indian Wars to the Navy
on the Barbary Coast. One room re-creates the gundeck of a frigate,
complete with cannon. An elaborate model of the Battle of Saratoga
shows eighteenth-century linear warfare. It helps you understand
the strategy in the battle scenes in historical movies.

The original house was built in 1775 by Joseph Pemberton, a
Quaker merchant.

## PENNSYLVANIA HOSPITAL
8th and Spruce Streets
Philadelphia 19107

**Phone:** 829-3251
**Open:** Historical tour by appointment only
**Admission:** Free
**Parking:** Nearby public lots
**Public Transportation:** SEPTA Routes 47, 90

Pennsylvania Hospital is the oldest hospital in the United States.
It was founded in 1751, after Thomas Bond, an eminent doctor,
convinced Benjamin Franklin of the need of a hospital "for the
relief of the sick-poor and for the reception and cure of lunaticks."
Franklin was largely responsible for the hospital's becoming a
reality. The building is an excellent example of Colonial architecture. The double staircase in the center hall of the central building

is considered one of the finest examples of its kind in the country. Other important things to see are the surgical amphitheater and Benjamin West's famous painting, *Christ Healing the Sick in the Temple.*

### HISTORICAL TOUR

Call 829-3251 at least a week in advance. Mondays and Wednesdays are preferable, but other days can be arranged. This tour is popular with schoolchildren from the 4th grade up. One adult for every 10 children. Length of tour is about 30 to 40 minutes. It includes the famous artwork in the hospital; the medical library, which contains some of the oldest medical books in the world; the surgical amphitheater; and many other fascinating and historic places around the hospital.

## THE POWEL HOUSE
244 South 3rd Street
Philadelphia 19106

**Phone:** MA 7-0364
**Open:** Tuesday–Saturday 10 A.M.–4 P.M., Sunday 1–4 P.M. No advance notice is needed, but the house can be seen only by guided tour; the front door is locked. Ring the bell and you can join a tour in progress or wait until the next tour begins.
**Closed:** Mondays (except holidays) and major holidays
**Admission:** Adults $1; children (12–16) 50¢, (6–12) 25¢
**Parking:** Some on street; local public lots
**Public Transportation:** SEPTA 50, 90

This lovely Georgian-style home deserves a visit not only for its stately proportions and elegant furnishings, but also because its prominent owner from 1769 to 1809, Samuel Powel, was the last mayor of Philadelphia under the British crown and the first mayor under the United States Republic. Mrs. Powel was one of the city's most illustrious hostesses, and George Washington and the Marquis de Lafayette, among other important Colonial figures, were frequent guests at her elaborate receptions. The house is furnished mainly with Philadelphia antiques, many of them from the time the Powels occupied it.

### GROUP VISITS

Telephone about two weeks ahead. Children should have some background in American history. Admission fee for children in groups the same as for individuals. For adults, 10 or more people 75¢.

### SAINT PAUL'S CHURCH
225 South 3rd Street
Philadelphia 19106

**Phone:** WA 5-8110
**Open:** Weekdays 9 A.M.–4:45 P.M.
**Admission:** Free
**Public Transportation:** SEPTA Route 5

Saint Paul's was built in 1761 and altered by renowned architect William Strickland in the Greek Revival style in 1830. Stephen Girard was a congregation member and was married here. The chapel of this lovely Colonial church is still in use. Today the Episcopal Community Services offices occupy part of the church facilities.

### SAINT PETER'S CHURCH
3rd and Pine Streets
Philadelphia 19106

**Phone:** WA 5-5968
**Open:** Daily 9 A.M.–5 P.M.
**Admission:** Free
**Parking:** Public lots
**Public Transportation:** SEPTA Routes 5, 90

This beautiful red brick church with its tall tower and steeple is considered one of the finest Early Georgian churches in the United States. Completed in 1761, it is the work of architect Robert Smith, who also designed Carpenters' Hall, and John Kearsley. It contains the original box pews—George Washington sometimes worshiped here with his friend Samuel Powel, the mayor of Philadelphia—and a handsome wineglass pulpit. Rare Bibles are here, among them a Vinegar Bible, and portraits by Charles Willson Peale, who is buried in the churchyard. Other famous dignitaries' graves include Benjamin Chew, Chief Justice of the Supreme Court of Pennsylvania; Nicholas Biddle, president of the Second Bank of the United States; and the famous naval hero Stephen Decatur.

### SECOND BANK OF THE UNITED STATES
420 Chestnut Street
Philadelphia 19106

**Phone:** 597-7132

**Open:** From early fall, 1974: daily 9 A.M.–5 P.M.
**Closed:** Christmas, New Year's Day
**Admission:** Free
**Parking:** Public lots in the area
**Public Transportation:** To Independence Hall

Designed by Philadelphia architect William Strickland, the Second Bank is considered to be one of the finest and most important examples of Greek Revival architecture in the United States. This noble building was completed in 1824 in the Grecian Doric style, with eight fluted columns on each portico derived from those of the Parthenon. The interior was late Georgian.

Nicholas Biddle presided over this private bank's most successful period, 1823–1832; at that time, because of his concept of democracy, President Andrew Jackson attacked the bank and refused to renew the Federal charter, thus causing its demise. The building was acquired by the Federal Government in 1845, and it became the Customs House, which it remained for almost a hundred years.

The Second Bank has been restored by Independence National Historical Park, and serves as a portrait gallery of important Colonial figures: signers of the Declaration of Independence and the Constitution, prominent military leaders of the Revolution, and important statesmen of Pennsylvania. Many of the paintings are by Peale, and also included are Sharples pastels.

**TODD HOUSE**
4th and Walnut Streets
Philadelphia

**Phone:** 597-7127
**Open:** Tuesday–Saturday 11 A.M.–3 P.M., Sunday 1–4 P.M. Open holidays.
**Admission:** Free
**Parking:** On street or in public lots in the area
**Public Transportation:** Cultural Loop, Mid City Loop, SEPTA Routes D, 50

Built in 1775, this small house was occupied by John Todd, Jr., and his wife, Dolley Payne, from 1791 to 1793, when he died in the yellow fever epidemic. His widow married a rising young Congressman, James Madison, who later became President of the United States. Restored and refurnished, this is a modest Colonial Philadelphia home, in contrast to the more elegant Bishop White House nearby.

## Museums and Other Attractions in the Area

Most of the following are covered in detail in Chapter 2 and are here listed alphabetically. Many fascinating museums lie in the historic area, some, such as the Atwater Kent Museum, directly involved with Colonial history; others, such as the Perelman Antique Toy Museum, with special collections.

### AMERICAN WAX MUSEUM
Independence Hall area
Philadelphia

**Phone:** MA 7-6677
**Closed:** The Museum is temporarily closed. Will reopen at new location. Call for information.
**Admission:** Adults $1.50, children under 14 75¢
**Parking:** Public lots nearby
**Public Transportation:** Cultural Loop bus to Independence Hall, Mid City Loop bus, any bus on Market and Chestnut Streets, Market Street Subway, SEPTA Route 50

Life-size figures in wax, live-action tableaux, and tape narration with music make this a popular tourist attraction. Such historic scenes as *Washington Crossing the Delaware, Grant and Lee at Appomattox, Raising the Flag at Mount Suribachi,* and Dr. Martin Luther King, Jr.'s, "I had a dream . . ." It may not be every adult's idea of living history, but let the kids go through.

#### GROUP RATES

Twenty-five or more: children 55¢, teens 75¢, adults $1. One leader free with each group. Make reservations at least a week in advance by calling MA 7-6677.

### THE ATHENAEUM OF PHILADELPHIA
219 South 6th Street
Philadelphia 19106

**Phone:** WA 5-2688
**Open:** Monday–Friday 9 A.M.–4 P.M.
**Admission:** Free

A proprietary library specializing in nineteenth-century cultural history.

## ATWATER KENT MUSEUM
15 South 7th Street (between Market and Chestnut Streets)
Philadelphia 19106

**Phone:** WA 2-3031
**Open:** Daily 8:30 A.M.–4:30 P.M.
**Admission:** Free

The history of Philadelphia from Colonial times to the present is traced through imaginative exhibits.

## BUST OF BENJAMIN FRANKLIN
4th and Arch Streets
Philadelphia

Huge fiber glass bust, 16 feet high. Conceived and created by Reginald E. Beauchamp, it is covered with 80,000 shiny copper pennies to symbolize the adage "A penny saved is a penny earned."

## EIGHTEENTH-CENTURY GARDEN
325 Walnut Street
Philadelphia

An authentically designed garden featuring walks and gazebo, and planted with flowers, shrubs, and trees characteristic of the Colonial era.

## PENN MUTUAL OBSERVATION DECK
530 Walnut Street
Philadelphia 19106

**Phone:** 629-0600
**Open:** April 1–November 1, weekdays 9 A.M.–4 P.M.; May 15–September 15, Saturday, Sunday, holidays 10 A.M.–6 P.M.
**Admission:** Free
**Parking:** Nearby public lots
**Public Transportation:** Cultural Loop bus to Independence Hall, Mid City Loop Bus, SEPTA Routes D, 42

Three hundred feet above the street is an open observation deck that affords an exceptional view of "the most historic square mile in America." It is atop the home office building of the Penn Mutual Life Insurance Company. This is a good way to begin your visit to the area. A tape recording at each corner describes what you're looking at. Guides are there to give further information. Bring your camera. A larger and more elaborate Visitors' Center with indoor and outdoor exhibits is being built atop their new office building next door.

## PERELMAN ANTIQUE TOY MUSEUM
270 South 2nd Street
Philadelphia 19106

**Phone:** WA 2-1070
**Open:** Daily 9:30 A.M.–5 P.M.
**Admission:** Adults $1, children under 14 55¢

Mechanical toys, dolls, banks in profusion well displayed on three floors.

## PHILADELPHIA FIRE DEPARTMENT MUSEUM
149 North 2nd Street
Philadelphia 19106

**Phone:** 923-9844
**Open:** Tuesday–Sunday 10 A.M.–4 P.M.
**Admission:** Free

Museum of the Fire Department with oldtime engines, fire apparatus, and other memorabilia.

## PHILADELPHIA MARITIME MUSEUM
321 Chestnut Street
Philadelphia 19106

**Phone:** WA 5-5439
**Open:** Monday–Saturday 10 A.M.–4 P.M., Sunday 12 noon–5 P.M.
**Admission:** Donations—adults 50¢, children 25¢

Maritime history from earliest times to *Star I*, a one-man research submarine on display here. And the *Gazela Primeiro*, anchored at the foot of Vine Street on the Delaware River (WA 5-5439), is open Memorial Day to Labor Day, daily 12 noon to 5 P.M. A donation is requested—for adults $1, children under 12 50¢. A chance to explore the last of the Portuguese fishing vessels preserved in sailing condition.

## TIFFANY GLASS MURAL
Lobby of the Curtis Building
6th and Walnut Streets
Philadelphia

**Open:** Monday–Friday 7 A.M.–6 P.M.

Done by Louis C. Tiffany after a painting by Maxfield Parrish, *The Dream Garden,* this mosaic of thousands of hand-fired pieces of glass covers an entire wall. Go see it!

## U.S.S. OLYMPIA
Pier 11 North
Delaware Avenue and Race Street
Philadelphia

**Phone:** WA 2-1898
**Open:** November–Easter, Thursday–Saturday 10 A.M.–4 P.M., Sunday 11 A.M.–5 P.M.; Easter–November 1, Monday–Saturday 10 A.M.–4 P.M., Sunday and holidays 11 A.M.–6 P.M.
**Admission:** Adults $1, children under 12 50¢

Explore Admiral Dewey's flagship from engine room to bridge. Display of naval history and objects.

## UNITED STATES MINT
5th and Arch Streets
Philadelphia 19106

**Phone:** 597-7350
**Open:** Monday–Friday 9 A.M.–3:30 P.M.
**Closed:** Holidays
**Admission:** Free

Fascinating "self-guided" tour with tape explanation of the process of making coins. This is the largest of the three mints in the United States.

### Restaurants in the Area

Unfortunately, there is a dearth of reasonably priced attractive places for lunch in the historic area, and many are closed on weekends. Here is a variety of restaurants with a wide price range, some included because of their proximity to the historic shrines, others because of good food and atmosphere. They range from Levis, a famous standup counter for hot dogs, to Bookbinder's, an old Philadelphia institution noted for its seafood. For details see Chapter 12.

## BOOKBINDER'S, OLD ORIGINAL
125 Walnut Street

A longtime favorite of tourists. Seafood a specialty. Expensive.

## BOURSE CAFETERIA
Basement of the Bourse Building
4th Street between Market and Chestnut Streets

The cafeteria serves sandwiches made to order. Ignore the decor. Close to Independence Hall. Closed weekends.

## THE COLONNADE
Rohm and Haas Building
6th and Market Streets

**Open:** 11 A.M.–2 P.M.
**Closed:** Weekends.

Average cafeteria fare—better than average salads and desserts.

## FAMOUS DELICATESSEN
700 South 4th Street
(4th and Bainbridge Streets)

No atmosphere, but whopping good sandwiches.

## HEAD HOUSE TAVERN
Corner of 2nd and Pine Streets

Lots of Colonial atmosphere in this eighteenth-century alehouse.
Moderate to expensive.

## LAFAYETTE HOUSE
Corner of 5th and Chestnut Streets
(Lafayette Building)

Right across from Independence Hall. Sandwiches, salads, hot dogs,
and hamburgers. Moderate prices. Closed Sunday.

## LERNER'S
134 Market Street
(Below 2nd Street)

Go for good food reasonably priced and forget the surroundings.
Generous portions. Near Christ Church and Betsy Ross House.

## MIDDLE EAST
126 Chestnut Street

For a leisurely lunch; Middle East or American food. No sandwiches. No lunch on weekends. Cheese bar, salad bar. Moderate to
expensive.

## OLD ORIGINAL LEVIS
507 South 6th Street
(6th and Lombard Streets)

Famous standup hot dog counter; cherry soda served from the
oldest working soda fountain in the country.

**SUGAR CONE**
414 South 2nd Street
(Between Pine and Lombard Streets)

Oldtime ice-cream parlor serving soups, sandwiches, and ice-cream specialties. Outdoor dining in summer.

**THE VITTLERY**
(Coffee shop in Holiday Inn)
4th and Arch Streets

Children's portions. Accessible for handicapped.

**H. A. WINSTON**
50 South Front Street
(Front and Chestnut Streets)

Dressed-up hamburgers. Moderate to expensive.

## Special Events in the Area

**A NATION IS BORN**

Sound and Light Show in Independence Square. End of June through Labor Day, Tuesday through Saturday at 9 P.M.

**FOURTH OF JULY CELEBRATION**

At Independence Hall. Special ceremonies, national speaker, bands, parade of flags, children in foreign costumes, and a reading of the Declaration of Independence. 11 A.M.–3 P.M.

**HEAD HOUSE SQUARE OPEN AIR MARKET**

Weekends in the summer at 2nd and Pine Streets. Crafts of every variety to buy, ethnic food, great fun.

**PHILADELPHIA FLEA MARKET**

Occasional Sunday afternoons at Independence Mall, May through September. Antiques, bric-a-brac, food, entertainment. Admission charge. (Page 266.)

**SOCIETY HILL WALKING TOURS**

The "18th-Century Towne and Countrie Tour" is a two-hour guided walk with stops at historic houses, inner courtyards, and walkways—and then a two-and-a-half-hour drive through Fairmount Park visiting Colonial mansions (page 129). Call Park House Office of Philadelphia Museum of Art, PO 3-8100.

Check the month-by-month Calendar of Events in back of book for additional activities in the area.

## *South Street Renaissance*

Handicrafts, health foods, ethnic restaurants, theater and street people. It's all very friendly and fun to wander in the area around South Street from 2nd to 7th Streets. Meander in and out of the imaginatively named stores: Eyes, The Painted Bride (puppet shows here on Sunday afternoon once a month), Essene, The Works. New ones keep opening.

# Germantown

When Germantown was first settled in 1683, the Main Road, now Germantown Avenue, was little more than an Indian trail to the interior—to Bethlehem and the rich farmland of up-country Pennsylvania. One hundred years later there were elegant mansions along the road for almost 5 miles. In 1969, Germantown Avenue (from Apsley to Phil-Ellena Streets) was designated a Registered Historic Landmark. It is considered "one of the two most historic streets in America." The Main Road witnessed many of the city's most important events, from its earliest days on.

Germantown was founded by Francis Daniel Pastorius and a small group of Quakers from Holland. The early settlers were artisans and craftsmen rather than farmers. Consequently, the village quickly acquired a unique urban character. It developed not as a farming community—not around a square—but as a single street village of crafts and industry. Acreage was carefully measured in long narrow lots extending back from the Main Road. Tanners, millers, spinners, weavers, carpenters, coopers, butchers, bakers, tailors, and tavern keepers came here to live and work. In 1690 the first paper mill in British America was established by William Rittenhouse (whose house still stands in Wissahickon Park next to Wissahickon Drive at Rittenhouse Street). Germantown remained the center of the paper-making, ink, and typefoundry industries until the mid-nineteenth century. The Saur Press, one of the largest in the colonies, turned out an endless stream of publications from Bibles to almanacs and periodicals.

Just two hours from Philadelphia, Germantown also became a favorite spot for Philadelphians during the summer—particularly after the Revolution and during the yellow fever epidemics of the 1790s. Washington and Jefferson lived here for a time, as did Charles Willson Peale and Gilbert Stuart. Prominent Philadelphians, including Benjamin Franklin's granddaughter, slipped into Germantown for quick and secret marriages.

Many of the historic places can still be seen. Many are unfortunately merely a number on a map. Some have been remodeled beyond recognition. Nevertheless, it is interesting to see where an event occurred or someone lived. Historic Germantown, however, is not an easy place for sightseeing, nor can it all be seen or enjoyed in one visit. Don't be put off by areas of urban blight. Pick out one or two houses, depending upon the children's—and your—interests. All houses have guided tours lasting about half an hour and include much detail about furniture and architecture mingled with the history. Recently there has been an attempt to coordinate visiting hours at the various houses. As interest in this treasure trove of Colonial America increases, the Germantown Historical Society, Cliveden, and some of the other mansions have begun the complex plans of arranging combination visits and tours. Also, group visits can usually be arranged to any of the houses on other than specified days by calling about two or three weeks in advance. For more information call the Germantown Historical Society (VI 4-0514). You might also consider taking the 23 trolley along Germantown Avenue. There aren't many trolleys around anymore, so it can be a special treat. As you ride along, look above the storefronts of the buildings—something one rarely does—and you'll spot the older buildings.

We have included the houses that are open to the public, starting with Stenton and going north along the avenue. Stenton, the Germantown Historical Society, Clarkson-Watson Costume Museum, the Deshler-Morris House, and Cliveden are probably of most interest to children. Two other places worth mentioning, off Germantown Avenue, and not generally open to visitors are: (1) Germantown Lutheran Academy, School House Lane and Greene Street, built in 1760 as a school and still a school today. George Washington's adopted son attended school in these buildings. (2) The Ebenezer Maxwell Mansion, 200 West Tulpehocken Street (at Greene Street), built in 1859. It is on the National Register of Historic Places as an outstanding example of castellated Victorian Gothic. It is opened annually for a Dickens Christmas Party (page 408). *The Mystery of the Square Tower,* by Elizabeth Honness, a popular children's mystery book, was set here.

For those interested in Victorian architecture, the area from Germantown Avenue to Wayne Avenue, from Tulpehocken to Harvey Streets, contains many private homes in this style.

The Germantown Historical Society (VI 4-0514) sponsors house tours: a spring tour of Colonial Germantown, a fall tour of Victorian Germantown. *Historic Germantown* by Harry M. and Margaret B. Tinkcom and Grant M. Simon (American Philosophical Society, $5) has a marvelous map and is an excellent source of information about the area.

One block south of Chelten Avenue (between Germantown Avenue and Greene Street) is Maplewood Mall. This attractive new pedestrian mall has among other things a fascinating kite store, a cheese shop (offering light lunches featuring—cheese), and a plant store.

Continue north on Germantown Avenue to Chestnut Hill, a lovely residential section of Philadelphia and a veritable wonderland of small, quality shops: cheese shops, dress shops, toy stores, bookstores, florists, kitchenware shops, antique shops, and restaurants. This beautifully planned area is the very antithesis of a large suburban shopping center. Two good restaurants there are: 21 West at 21 West Highland Avenue, and The Green Pepper, 8515 Germantown Avenue.

For a quick bite there are Gino's and McDonald's along the Avenue. For a leisurely meal in Germantown, with typical American tearoom menus, there are Boswell House, 5920 Greene Street (VI 3-1525), and Greene Hedges, 6020 Greene Street (VI 4-8956).

## STENTON
18th and Courtland Streets
Philadelphia 19140

**Phone:** DA 9-7312
**Open:** Tuesday–Saturday 1–5 P.M.
**Admission:** 50¢, children under 12 10¢. Guided tours only. Go to the Log House where the custodian lives. School groups free.
**Directions:** Schuylkill Expressway to Roosevelt Boulevard (U.S. Route 1 north) to Broad Street exit, left on 15th Street, left on Courtland Street, right on 18th Street, entrance on the right
**Parking:** Available on the grounds
**Public Transportation:** Reading Railroad to Wayne Junction. Walk: Windram Avenue to Courtland Street to 18th Street. *Or:* SEPTA Route 23 trolley on Germantown Avenue to Courtland Street.

At the edge of Germantown—amid factories, railroad tracks, trolleys, and city traffic—is a 5-acre oasis of eighteenth-century

American elegance: Stenton, the country residence of James Logan, Secretary of State for William Penn and the guiding hand in the establishment of Pennsylvania. This large brick mansion, built in 1728 on a simple early Georgian plan, has an inner court, gardens, and outbuildings. Logan's astounding library of over 2,000 books reflecting his scientific and scholarly interests is no longer housed here but is now contained in the Library Company of Philadelphia (page 99). The house is furnished with beautiful period pieces, some of which belonged to Logan, so that Stenton, like the Park Houses and the historic mansions along Germantown Avenue, presents an authentic picture of upper-class life in Colonial America.

One of the most impressive features of this house is the spacious entrance hall with its brick floor. The large upstairs sitting room was also known as a lodging room. It provided much-needed sleeping space for travelers and guests. On the second floor there is also a child's room with toys, chairs, and blocks and a dollhouse built into a closet dating from 1848.

The outbuildings attached to the main house by a covered walkway contain the kitchen (now a small souvenir shop), the orangery, and the spinning room. The custodians live in the Log House next to the barn. The Log House was not part of the original estate. Built in 1790, it was moved here from the Benjamin Franklin Parkway when Friends Select School expanded. Visit on a bright day; the electricity at Stenton is for all practical purposes nonexistent.

Stenton is maintained by the National Society of the Colonial Dames of America in the Commonwealth of Pennsylvania. Guided tours with hostesses in Colonial dress by advance reservation.

## LOUDOUN
4650 Germantown Avenue
Philadelphia 19144

**Phone:** 842-2877
**Open:** Tuesday and Thursday 1–4 P.M. For a special appointment call VI 3-3388.
**Admission:** 25¢; children under 12 free when accompanied by adult. Guided tours only. Allow about an hour.
**Directions:** Broad Street (Pa. Route 611) north, left on Windram Avenue (beyond Roosevelt Boulevard), right on Germantown Avenue
**Parking:** On the grounds
**Public Transportation:** SEPTA Route 23 trolley on Germantown Avenue

Standing on a hill overlooking Germantown is Loudoun. With its columned portico, this large white mansion set in 8½ acres could easily be in Loudoun County, Virginia, for which it was named. The house and furniture reflect the five generations of Armats who lived here. From the basement kitchen, built about 1800, with its fine pewter collection, enormous fireplace, spinning wheel, and child's rocker to the Victorian back parlor and library, the house is filled with the same furnishings, paintings, crystal, and silver that were used by the Armat family.

Since 1967 a dedicated group of volunteers, the Friends of Loudoun, have been busily restoring the house and its impressive contents. They will be happy to show you the house, relate its history, and tell you all sorts of anecdotes about the family—even about the family ghost.

## GERMANTOWN HISTORICAL SOCIETY
5214 Germantown Avenue
Philadelphia 19144

**Phone:** VI 4-0514
**Open:** Tuesday, Thursday, Saturday 1–5 P.M.
**Closed:** Holidays
**Admission:** Free
**Directions:** Broad Street (Pa. Route 611) north, left on Windram Avenue (beyond Roosevelt Boulevard), right on Germantown Avenue
**Parking:** Metered, on street
**Public Transportation:** SEPTA Route 23 trolley

The Germantown Historical Society administers a complex of buildings along Germantown Avenue. The Conyngham Hacker House at 5214 Germantown Avenue is a museum with a collection of old fans, bells, Germantown Bibles, fire marks, helmets and pumpers, surgeons' instruments, carpenters' tools, household items, flags from Colonial days to the present, clocks, china used by Lafayette, surveyors' instruments—in short, a wondrous assortment of artifacts representative of everyday life in Germantown from its earliest times on through the years, all displayed in old-fashioned cases which add to the aura of yesteryear. The Von Trott Annex in the rear houses a giant dollhouse and a craft exhibit, both from Colonial times.

**HOWEL HOUSE,** next door at 5218, contains the Society's collection of quilts, fabrics, and old toys.

**BAYNTON HOUSE,** at 5208, is the Library of the Germantown
Historical Society

**Phone:** VI 4-0514
**Open:** Tuesday 1–5 P.M.
**Admission:** Free

For those doing any research on the Germantown area, this is
the place to start—manuscripts, newspapers, maps, books, old tracts,
pictures. The librarian is on duty to lend a hand.

NOTE: For Germantown history buffs, the Germantown Historical
Society has for sale a map of Germantown as it looked during the
Battle of Germantown. Black and white $5, color $25.

**GRUMBLETHORPE**
5267 Germantown Avenue
Philadelphia 19144

**Phone:** VI 3-4820
**Open:** Tuesday–Saturday 2–5 P.M.
**Closed:** Sundays, Mondays, and holidays
**Admission:** Adults 50¢; children to 15 25¢, under 15 free. Guided
    tours only. Group tours by advance reservation. Minimum num-
    ber 10. School groups free.
**Directions:** Broad Street (Pa. Route 611) north, left on Windram
    Avenue (beyond Roosevelt Boulevard), right on Germantown
    Avenue
**Parking:** Metered, on street
**Public Transportation:** SEPTA Route 23 trolley

Grumblethorpe, with its brown stonework and dark red trim,
stands out prominently on Germantown Avenue. John Wister, a
successful Philadelphia merchant and uncle of David Deshler, the
owner of the Deshler-Morris House just up the street, built this
home in 1744 of locally quarried stone. Its use as a summer residence probably explains the simplicity and impression of age when
compared with the more pretentious Stenton, built in 1728.

Behind the house is the summer kitchen kept just as it was in
the eighteenth century. John Wister was an avid horticulturist, and
a few of the trees and bushes he planted and cared for still remain in the garden. During the Revolution the house was occupied
by the British. Other than this brief period, the Wisters lived here
until 1910. In 1940 the Philadelphia Society for the Preservation
of Landmarks acquired the house and has been restoring and re-
furnishing it.

## CLARKSON-WATSON COSTUME MUSEUM
5275 Germantown Avenue
Philadelphia 19144

**Phone:** VI 4-0514 (Germantown Historical Society)
**Open:** Tuesday, Thursday, Saturday 1–5 P.M.
**Closed:** Most holidays
**Admission:** Free
**Directions:** Broad Street (Pa. Route 611) north, left on Windram Avenue (beyond Roosevelt Boulevard), right on Germantown Avenue
**Parking:** Metered, on street
**Public Transportation:** SEPTA Route 23 trolley

Most museums display formal gowns, but few have ordinary everyday clothes. This small museum, opened in May, 1971, contains mostly nineteenth-century clothes: not only fine silks from Paris, simple Quaker garments, and children's outfits in room settings but, more important, housedresses of the era. One of the displays is set in the Victorian kitchen found in the house. There are a cast-iron stove, a metal-lined wood sink, laundry drying on racks. It's an interesting era—often neglected in our preoccupation with Colonial times. You can see it all in about fifteen minutes, but do go.

NOTE: Thomas Jefferson lived here in 1793 when the United States Government moved to Germantown during the yellow fever epidemic.

## DESHLER-MORRIS HOUSE
(Independence National Historical Park)
5442 Germantown Avenue
Philadelphia 19144

**Phone:** 597-2747
**Open:** Tuesday–Sunday 1–4 P.M.
**Closed:** Mondays, most holidays
**Admission:** 25¢ Guided tours only. For groups of 15 or more, call two or three weeks in advance for reservations.
**Directions:** Broad Street (Pa. Route 611) north, left on Windram Avenue (beyond Roosevelt Boulevard), right on Germantown Avenue
**Parking:** Metered, on street
**Public Transportation:** SEPTA Route 23 trolley

The Deshler-Morris House, the farthest outpost of Independence National Historical Park, was for a short time the residence of President George Washington. Built in 1772 by David Deshler, a wealthy Philadelphia merchant, as a summer home, it became Washington's temporary home when the Government moved to Germantown to escape the yellow fever epidemic of 1793. Other members of the Cabinet also moved to the area, and they held their meetings here; thus this house became the seat of the United States Government. Washington also spent the following summer here with his family to escape the oppressive heat of the city.

The gracious house has been restored and furnished with period pieces by the Germantown Historical Society. It is interesting to see the rooms where Washington not only slept but held his Cabinet meetings, worked, and entertained—and where he took tea with Martha Washington, in the oddly shaped tearoom over-looking the garden in the rear.

There is also a roomful of toys and dolls and a dollhouse on the second floor from the Lincoln period.

## WYCK HOUSE
6026 Germantown Avenue
Philadelphia 19144

**Phone:** For information call Germantown Historical Society, VI 4-0514

Built in 1690, this is the oldest house in Germantown still standing and was occupied by a member of the original owner's family until 1973. It is an example of the eighteenth-century Quaker homestead and emphasizes the "plain" side of Philadelphia life, in contrast to the more sumptuous mansions such as Cliveden, Stenton, and Deshler-Morris.

## CLIVEDEN
6401 Germantown Avenue
Philadelphia 19144

**Phone:** VI 8-1777
**Open:** Daily 10 A.M.–4 P.M.
**Closed:** Christmas
**Admission:** Adults $1.25, students 50¢. Guided tours only.
**Directions:** East River Drive to Wissahickon Drive to Johnson Street, right to Germantown Avenue, left to entrance in middle of the block on your right
**Parking:** On grounds or street
**Public Transportation:** SEPTA Route 23 trolley

At the time of its construction in 1763, Cliveden was one of the largest and most magnificent houses in North America. Today it is considered an outstanding example of Georgian architecture. The balanced proportions of the mansion, its simple lines, the urns on the roof, and the statuary in the 6-acre garden reflect an elegance, grace, and luxury in keeping with the style of the interior. It was built as a summer residence by Benjamin Chew, Attorney General and later Chief Justice of the Pennsylvania Supreme Court. The spacious hallway and rooms furnished with fine Philadelphia eighteenth-century pieces were the scene of many important social events, including a gala for Lafayette upon his return to this country in 1824. There is a painting in the hall depicting this occasion.

Perhaps the most important historical event occurred on October 4, 1777, during the Battle of Germantown when George Washington attempted unsuccessfully to dislodge the British troops barricaded in the house. Bullet marks, cannonball holes, and chipped and headless statuary are still visible. From here Washington retreated to Valley Forge.

One of Cliveden's unusual features is that it was for over six generations home to one family, until its recent acquisition by the National Trust for Historic Preservation in the United States. The Chews had lived here continuously, except for a brief period immediately after the Revolution. As you drive through the gate into the gardens of Cliveden, you have a true sense of historical continuity.

## UPSALA
6430 Germantown Avenue
Philadelphia 19144

**Open:** Tuesday and Friday 1–5 P.M.
**Admission:** 50¢. Guided tours only.

Built in 1798 and considered one of the finest examples of Federal architecture in Germantown, this house is maintained by the Upsala Foundation.

## CONCORD SCHOOLHOUSE
6313 Germantown Avenue
Philadelphia 19119

To visit this old schoolhouse, just stop in at Kirk and Nice, Undertakers (since 1761—and the first funeral parlor in America), on the corner of Germantown Avenue and Washington Lane and ask for the key. Someone is always in the office. If planning to bring a group, it would be a good idea to call GE 8-6328 in advance. The schoolhouse was built in 1775 because the Germantown Union School (now Germantown Lutheran Academy) was too far away to be convenient. Everything is very well preserved. There is a pump in the yard, and the classroom still has desks and blackboards.

## Historic Parks and Restorations

Many historic sites surrounding Philadelphia preserve and commemorate important events in the nation's development: Valley Forge, where Washington's troops wintered and survived; Old Fort Mifflin, a Revolutionary defense post; and Hopewell Village, an iron-making community that supplied ammunition to the Continental Army.

The "living history" sites that follow provide you with a vivid picture of the past.

### BATSTO HISTORIC SITE
R.D. 1
Hammonton, N.J. 08037

**Phone:** 1-609-561-3262
**Open:** April–October, Monday–Friday 11 A.M.–5 P.M., weekends 11 A.M.–6 P.M.; remainder of the year, 11 A.M.–5 P.M.
**Closed:** Christmas, New Year's Day
**Admission:** No charge to walk the grounds, see the Nature Center, Blacksmith Shop, or general store. For tour of mansion and carriage house, adults $1; children 12–17 25¢, 5–11 10¢.
**Directions:** U.S. Route 30 across Benjamin Franklin Bridge, south to N.J. Route 542 (Hammonton), 7 miles east on N.J. Route 542
**Parking:** Parking area adjacent to Batsto Visitors Center at entrance to village
**Picnicking:** Grove with tables; no fires permitted. There's a large meadow—fine for badminton, kite flying, or a fast game of frisbee.

Just a little over an hour's drive from Philadelphia in the Jersey Pine Barrens is the pre-Revolutionary town of Batsto. Cannon and cannonballs were manufactured for the Continental Army at the iron foundry here. Restored by the state and opened to the public in 1962, the village offers a glimpse of an earlier, more leisurely era. There are a gristmill, a blacksmith shop, an icehouse, a carriage shed, and a working sawmill, powered by water, which clearly demonstrates the principle of "gearing down" because all the wheels are visible. The mansion on the hill—guided tours only—has a collection of antique kitchen utensils, always of great interest to children. And further down the road, in front of a worker's cottage, is a hand pump with drinking water. Great sport for kids accustomed to faucets! A horse-drawn stagecoach tours the village (35¢), but it's pleasant and more interesting to walk.

Summer days draw the crowds. If possible, go in the spring or fall. Batsto Village is in Wharton State Forest—155 square miles of wilderness for camping, canoeing, swimming, riding, fishing, and hiking (page 211).

SPECIAL EVENTS

Annual Arts and Crafts Day in June. Call for exact date.

GROUP VISITS

Admission: Adults 50¢, others 10¢. Minimum number 20. About 4 weeks' notice required for group rate. Guided tours available by advance reservations preferably in writing to Batsto Visitors Center. Minimum number: 20. Maximum number: 100. One adult for every 6 children. Suggested minimum age: 4th grade. Length of tour: Approximately 1½ hours.


**BRANDYWINE BATTLEFIELD STATE PARK**
U.S. Route 1
Chadds Ford, Pa. 19317

**Phone:** 459-3342
**Open:** Park open daily 8 A.M.–dusk; buildings open 10 A.M.–5 P.M. Memorial Day–Labor Day, remainder of the year weekends only; April–October 10 A.M.–5 P.M., standard time 9 A.M.–4 P.M.
**Closed:** Thanksgiving, Christmas, New Year's Day
**Admission:** Free
**Restrictions:** Pets on leash. No food or unaccompanied children in buildings.
**Directions:** Schuylkill Expressway to U.S. Route 1 south (City Avenue) to Chadds Ford. Entrance to park on the right. Less than an hour's drive.
**Parking:** Four lots; facilities for six buses
**Picnicking:** Wooded picnic groves, tables, charcoal grills, soda machines

When the weather is warm, this beautifully kept shady park of about 50 acres is a delightful place for a family picnic, with hills for climbing, lots of space for running and games, and some American history to interest almost everyone. It's great for an all-day outing or a short visit.

It is hard to imagine this peaceful rolling countryside as the scene of an important battle of the American Revolution in September, 1777. From here the victorious British moved on to a comfortable winter in Philadelphia; Washington and his defeated troops to their ordeal at Valley Forge. Both Washington's and Lafayette's headquarters have been restored and furnished, including appropriate wax figures. Lafayette's carriage, a Conestoga wagon, an icehouse with a rather immaculate Hessian prisoner, and two elaborately decorated bronze cannons offer interesting and easy sightseeing.

GROUP TOURS

Guided tours of buildings for school groups by advance reservation weekdays during the winter.

NEARBY

Brandywine River Museum and Longwood Gardens. The picnic facilities at Brandywine Battlefield State Park are more extensive than those at Longwood, should you be planning to attend a special event at Longwood.

## GETTYSBURG NATIONAL MILITARY PARK
Gettysburg, Pa. 17325

**Phone:** 1-717-334-1124
**Open:** Daily all year round. Visitor Center closed Christmas and New Year's Day.
**Admission:** Free. Cyclorama 50¢ for 16 and up.
**Directions:** Pennsylvania Turnpike to Gettysburg Interchange (17); U.S. Route 15 south to Park (about 140 miles from Philadelphia)
**Parking:** In designated areas
**Picnicking:** Areas available; fires and public camping prohibited

In spite of creeping commercialism and the pseudo-shrines all around it, the Gettysburg National Military Park is carefully maintained by the National Park Service. This was the scene of a furious battle between General Robert E. Lee's Confederate forces of the South and Brigadier General George G. Meade's Union Army on July 1, 2, and 3, 1863. It was the turning point of the Civil War, from which the South never fully recovered. After Pickett's charge failed, the Confederate forces retreated across the Potomac.

Battle casualties on both sides were enormous. Four months later, President Abraham Lincoln came to Gettysburg to deliver "a few appropriate remarks" at the dedication of the National Cemetery, the immortal Gettysburg Address directed to both the North and the South.

### VISITING THE BATTLEFIELD

Gettysburg National Military Park covers more than 6,000 acres. Start at the Visitor Center. Here you will see a film, *These Honored Dead*, exhibits, and the famous Gettysburg Cyclorama, a 356-foot-long painting with the sound–light story of Pickett's charge. There are self-guided auto tours, bus tours, and walking tours of the battlefield that start from the Visitor Center—or you can arrange for licensed guides, highly knowledgeable, to accompany you in your car for a complete two-hour tour ($7) or to accompany bus groups ($15). Arrangements can be made with the Superintendent. This service is offered year-round.

Commercial ventures surround the Park: helicopter tours, electric map, wax museum, Charlie Weaver's American Museum. They vary in quality, so visit these according to your time and inclination.

### HANDICAPPED

Practically the entire park can be seen from your car. A guide can join you.

## GRAEME PARK
County Line Road (1 mile west of Pa. Route 611)
Horsham. Pa. 19044

**Open:** Hours vary. Call Montgomery County Tourist Bureau, 275-0525
**Admission:** 50¢
**Directions:** Route 611 north (Broad Street) to County Line Road (the first street past Willow Grove Naval Air Station), then turn left to Park (1 mile)
**Parking:** On grounds

The buildings in Graeme Park were erected by Provincial Governor of Pennsylvania William Keith in 1721–1722. He did not intend to use the property for his residence but for the manufacture of alcoholic beverages. After William Penn removed Keith from office, however, he lived there in the "Long House" before returning to England in 1728.

Dr. Thomas Graeme, who married Keith's stepdaughter, took over the property and used it for a summer residence. Although he could not change the outside, which reflected its industrial origins, the interior was modified into a gracious Georgian house. Fine paneling extends from floor to ceiling in the parlor, and the dining-room fireplace is covered with imported English marble. Graeme was a respected physician, a judge of the Supreme Court, and a surgeon at the Pennsylvania Hospital.

For a glimpse of how an eighteenth-century "country gentleman" lived, a visit to the lovely restoration at Graeme Park is a rewarding experience.

The Park is administered by the Pennsylvania Historic and Museum Commission.

Waterwheel at Hopewell Village

## HOPEWELL VILLAGE NATIONAL HISTORIC SITE
R.D. 1
Elverson, Pa. 19520

**Phone:** 1-582-8783
**Open:** March 1–October 31, 9 A.M.–6 P.M. daily; November–February, 8 A.M.–5 P.M. daily
**Closed:** Christmas, New Year's Day
**Admission:** Free
**Directions:** Pennsylvania Turnpike to Morgantown exit. Follow signs for about 8 miles to Hopewell Village on Pa. Route 345. About a 1½-hour drive from Philadelphia

**Parking:** Plenty, and it's free

**Picnicking:** A very small picnic grove is adjacent to the village; no cooking permitted. If you want more elaborate facilities, use nearby French Creek State Park.

Here is an authentic picture of an iron-making community in early America. Hopewell Village, founded by Mark Bird in 1770, supplied cannon and shot for the Revolutionary armies. Until replaced by more modern methods, cold-blast charcoal-burning furnaces such as Hopewell's supplied all the iron to the growing nation. In 1883 the furnace was shut down for the last time, and the Village fell into disrepair until 1938 when the National Park Service took it over.

Today you can visit this magnificent restoration and see the old iron-making village as it was when it stood at the height of its glory from 1820 to 1840.

VISITORS CENTER

Start here with an illustrated color slide and tape narration which tells the background of the village. Proceed down the village road and see the restored charcoal hearth, blacksmith shop, company store, Big House, and a rare operating waterwheel. At each stop on this self-guided tour, you can push a button and hear a descriptive tape. In the summer costumed craftsmen are busy weaving, making soap, charcoal, and iron molds, and demonstrating fireplace cooking. They'll even offer you samples of what they've cooked.

SPECIAL EVENTS

*Wagon rides:* July and August and weekends in September and October. Adults 75¢, children 50¢. It takes about half an hour, and it's an interesting way to see Hopewell Village.

*Candlelight Program:* One in July, one in August. All personnel are in Colonial garb, and the whole village is lit by candlelight —a beautiful sight. For date call 1-582-8773.

*Establishment Day:* First Sunday in August. The charcoal pile is ignited in the morning (also on the Fourth of July), and in the afternoon many craftsmen join the Hopewell regular staff in demonstrations.

GROUP VISITS

Can be arranged, preferably by telephone or by writing to the Superintendent a week in advance. No minimum age.

HANDICAPPED
Special tours can be arranged through the Superintendent's office.

NEARBY
French Creek State Park (page 197) with marvelous facilities for picnicking, swimming, fishing, boating, and hiking. Daniel Boone Homestead (page 242).

PENNSBURY MANOR
Route 9 (Pennsbury Lane)
Morrisville, Pa. 19067

Phone: 1-946-0400
Open: All year. April–October, weekdays 8:30 A.M.–5 P.M., Sundays 1–5 P.M.; November–March, weekdays 9 A.M.–4:30 P.M., Sundays 1–4:30 P.M.
Closed: Good Friday, Easter, Primary and General Elections, Thanksgiving, Christmas, New Year's Day
Admission: Adults 50¢, children under 12 free
Directions: Take U.S. Route 1 or 13 north and follow state signs for Pennsbury Manor. About 30 miles from Philadelphia.
Parking: Adjacent to Reception Center
Picnicking: In pavilion area. Tables and benches at pavilion only. No cooking permitted. Spread a blanket under the trees and watch the guinea fowl go by.

On the Delaware River is the meticulously reconstructed country estate of William Penn. Rebuilt on its original foundations, Pennsbury Manor has been furnished much as it would have been in 1700 and contains the largest collection of seventeenth-century antiques in Pennsylvania. This self-contained plantation contains a barn, an icehouse, a smokehouse, a bake-and-brew house, and a plantation office, all carefully restored. There are a boathouse and a replica of Penn's barge on the banks of the river—the quickest and most comfortable way to travel to Philadelphia about 25 miles away.

Behind the bake-and-brew house is a seventeenth-century herb and vegetable garden with everything clearly labeled and neatly planted along brick paths. The barnyard has been stocked with turkeys, hens, sheep, goats, geese, and horses. Guinea fowl, chattering incessantly, chase each other around the grounds. There's a small museum at the Reception Center. You may wander through the buildings, grounds, and manor house at your own pace. Industrial New Jersey and Pennsylvania are all around, but at Pennsbury Manor it's still the seventeenth century—almost.

### Group Visits

Admission 35¢. Minimum number 10. Reservations should be made as far in advance as possible. Check must accompany advance reservations for group rate.

*Guided tours:* for school groups. Monday through Friday throughout the year. Reservations may be made by telephone or in writing six months in advance. Minimum age suggested: 4th grade. Minimum number 10, maximum number 150. Adults required: Teachers. If no reservation is made, the group must wait until all other groups are finished. Tour: Approximately 1½ hours; includes history of manor, tour and explanation of the grounds, buildings, boat and living conditions (cooking, etc.).

### Strictly for Adults

Two annual seminars on decorative arts, with lectures by leading authorities in the field. For information write: Dewey Lee Curtis, Curator, Pennsbury Manor, Route 9 (Pennsbury Lane), Morrisville, Pa. 19067.

### Nearby

Historic Fallsington, a pre-Revolutionary village in Bucks County where William Penn used to worship (page 224).

## OLD FORT MIFFLIN
Island Avenue South near Airport Circle
Philadelphia

**Phone:** WA 3-8299

Administered for Philadelphia Department of Recreation by The Shackamaxon Society, Inc. (P.O. Box 1777, Philadelphia 19107)

**Open:** Daily Memorial Day to Labor Day, 10 A.M.–4 P.M.; balance of the year, Sunday 10 A.M.–4 P.M.

**Admission:** Adults $1, children under 12 50¢ (tickets tax deductible)

**Directions:** Schuylkill Expressway east, follow signs to Airport. At Airport Circle follow signs to Island Avenue South, then follow signs to Old Fort Mifflin.

**Parking:** At entrance

**Picnicking:** Pick your spot inside the walls of the fort: under the trees? near the commandant's house? on the embankments? Hoagies and sodas also sold in souvenir shop.

Next door to the airport and right in the flight pattern of in-coming jets is Old Fort Mifflin, an important landmark of the American Revolution—part of the chapter on the Battle of Brandy-wine and the winter at Valley Forge. Put on good climbing shoes and drive down to this historic spot on the Delaware River, which is slowly being restored by the imaginative, spirited group of men, The Shackamaxon Society. Devoted to stirring up greater interest in and enthusiasm for Philadelphia's historical heritage, they have taken their name from the place where William Penn allegedly met the Indians under that great elm in 1683. The resto-ration of Old Fort Mifflin and the lively activities there are the result of the dedication of the Society, which mans the fort ex-clusively with volunteers.

Whenever the fort is open, you will find them—the Old Fort Mifflin Guard—resplendent in their Revolutionary War uniforms presenting militia muster, demonstrating the arts of the Revolu-tionary soldier (making uniforms, cartridge boxes, bullets, belts), raising the Colonial flag, shooting their muskets and cannons, and happily answering questions visitors ask. If you want a guided tour, one of the "militia" will oblige, but visitors are encouraged to ramble all over the place independently. You can go from the top of the embankments (to check for an incoming "British" fleet) to the underground bombproofs where the garrison lived during the bom-bardment of the Fort. Today, some archaeological "digs" are going on there by the men of Fort Mifflin.

SPECIAL EVENTS

Washington's Birthday Observance; Colonial Field Days (chil-dren's games played during Colonial times) during Freedom Week; Independence Day; Mifflin Day (free admission to anyone living on Mifflin Street or with the name Mifflin) in July; Penn's Landing Observance; Anniversary of the Battle of Fort Mifflin (Sunday closest to November 16).

OLD FORT MIFFLIN GUARD

Boys twelve years and up interested in becoming part of this "living history" program and learning Colonial military crafts can get more information from the Shackamaxon Society. This program almost becomes a way of life.

GROUP VISITS

By advance reservations in writing to the Shackamaxon Society. Minimum number: 25. Admission: Half-price.

HANDICAPPED

Call in advance to make arrangements.

## VALLEY FORGE STATE PARK
Valley Forge, Pa. 19481

**Phone:** 783-0177
**Open:** Daily 9 A.M.–5 –P.M.
**Closed:** Christmas Day
**Admission:** Free
**Directions:** Schuylkill Expressway to Valley Forge, or Pennsylvania Turnpike to Valley Forge exit; then Pa. Route 363 north to Pa. Route 23 to park
**Parking:** Ample and free
**Picnicking:** Many areas—some with grills, shelters, tables, and benches—abound. The largest one adjoins Fort Huntingdon. Restroom facilities at convenient locations.

This sprawling 2,255-acre state park is both an historic and a recreational marvel. The Valley Forge Park Commission is restoring the area to show it as it was during Washington's encampment. Your tour of the park grounds can begin at any point. The buildings, statues, and points of interest are easily reached on paved roads. The whole area is well marked, and parking places are available in many areas.

A good idea is to start at the Reception Center at the juncture of Pa. Routes 23 and 363. Here you will receive background information and can pick up a map. You may also rent a cassette for your car for $5 for two hours. If you prefer to let someone else do the driving, arrange for a bus tour by calling 265-6466. Daily tours leave on the hour from the King of Prussia Motor Inn, Pa. Route 202 North and Schuylkill Expressway, from April to November and weekends during the rest of the year. Adults $3.50; children 6–12 $1.50, under 6 free if not occupying a seat.

Valley Forge was the quarters of George Washington's Continental Army from December, 1777, to June, 1778. While General Howe and the British occupied Philadelphia, the 11,000 Revolutionary troops staggered into Valley Forge and entrenched themselves. During the encampment over 3,000 soldiers died of sickness and starvation. The area was chosen after Washington's Army failed to stop the British at Brandywine Creek, Paoli, and Germantown. It had a strategic location, allowing surveillance of the British from the western approaches to the city of Philadelphia, where the enemy had comfortably settled in for the winter.

The entire camp and fortifications were laid out by Brigadier General Louis DuPortail, a Frenchman whose terminology— "abatis," "redan," "lunette"—still identifies the fortifications and ramparts. Replicas of the huts used by the soldiers dot the Valley Forge landscape. A number of the buildings used to house Washington's staff—the bakehouse, the hospital, and Washington's headquarters—as well as statues and memorials to the brave dead are scattered throughout the park.

Although the war went on for four more years, it was here at Valley Forge that the Revolution held. After the long bitter winter, an alliance with France was established and the tide turned.

Valley Forge is one of the most sacred spots in American history. A visit at any time of the year will afford great satisfaction and pride.

### SOME POINTS OF INTEREST

*Washington Memorial Chapel:* The cornerstone of this impressive Gothic-style building was laid in 1903. Each pew is dedicated to a Revolutionary war family. Flags of historical symbolism adorn the chancel. The brilliantly colored stained-glass windows depict the early history of the country. The Chapel building is considered one of the finest memorials to George Washington anywhere.

*The Chapel Cabin Shop*, manned by parishioner volunteers, is located directly behind the Washington Memorial Chapel. It sells delicious homemade jellies, jams, bread, pies, and cakes. Many of the jams and jellies are family recipes. All the food is prepared and wrapped there in the kitchens. The Cabin Shop is open 10 A.M.–4:30 P.M. on weekdays, 10 A.M.–5:30 P.M. on Saturdays, and from 12 noon–6 P.M. on Sundays.

*Museum of the Valley Forge Historical Society.* Open Monday–Saturday 9 A.M.–4:30 P.M., Sunday 1–5 P.M. Priceless relics are on display, the most famous of which is Washington's marquee, or field tent. Also see the original Commander-in-Chief's flag, fine examples of old china, paintings, rifles, and an excellent large contour map of the encampment grounds. The layout is complete with push buttons illuminating troop locations and showing the defenses of the camp.

*Valley Forge Memorial Belltower.* The Belltower houses the Washington Memorial National Carillon, which consists of fifty-six bells. The Carillon is played at intervals throughout the day. Carillon recitals are scheduled every Sunday afternoon at 4 P.M.

*Washington's Headquarters.* A simple stone Colonial house, owned by Isaac Potts, is open to the public. It served as Washington's headquarters from Christmas Day, 1777, until the following June. His office, reception room, kitchen, and bedrooms are open to visitors.

*The Mount Joy Observatory.* Seventy-five feet high. The climb is

well worth the effort. It affords a magnificent view of the surrounding countryside.

*The Bakehouse.* A room on the first floor re-creates the setting of
a military court-martial. In the basement are the huge ovens used
for making bread for the soldiers during the encampment.

### RECREATION IN THE PARK

Valley Forge Park has wide open fields for romping and games,
sledding in winter, bicycling, wooded trails to wander and explore
in good weather. On the hottest day cool breezes blow in the forest
area. Valley Forge is famous for its magnificent groves of dogwood
trees, which are at their height of bloom in early May.

If you are a history enthusiast, or if you just want to find a lovely
area to play and picnic, visit Valley Forge Park again and again.

### HANDICAPPED

You may rent a tape cassette at the Reception Center and tour
the Park in your car.

## WASHINGTON CROSSING STATE PARK
Washington Crossing, Pa. 18977

**Phone:** 1-493-4076
**Open:** Park is open 365 days a year. Buildings open daily
9:30 A.M.–5 P.M.
**Closed:** Easter, Primary Election Day, Election Day, Thanksgiving,
New Year's Day
**Admission:** Free, except for entrance to the few buildings noted
**Directions:** I-95 to Pa. Route 32, north to Park. *Or* Pa. Route 611
(Broad Street) to Willow Grove, Pa. Route 263 north to New
Hope, then take the River Road (Pa. Route 32) 2 miles south
to Park.
**Parking:** Free, at various locations

It's history, nature, and a great place for a picnic. This 500-acre
park along the Delaware River just outside New Hope commemorates the famous crossing of the Delaware by George Washington and his troops on Christmas night, 1776. It was the turning
point of the American Revolution and made the Declaration of Independence a reality by his defeat of the British.

The park is divided into two separate parts. Three miles separate
the two areas. Our personal preference for picnicking is the Lower
Park. Both areas are historic and filled with natural rustic beauty.
Don't miss either one.

UPPER PARK (BOWMAN'S HILL AREA CLOSER TO NEW HOPE)

*Bowman's Hill Tower.* Heavily wooded Bowman's Hill served as a lookout station during the Revolutionary War. It afforded Washington and his men a view of enemy activity across the Delaware. In 1930 a tower was erected to commemorate the historic crossing. Climb the steps to the top of the stone observatory, and you will be rewarded with a magnificent view of the rolling countryside, farmland, and river.

*Bowman's Hill State Wild Flower Preserve:* Phone: 1-862-2924. Daily 9:30 A.M.–5 P.M. Children under 12 must be accompanied by an adult.

Adjacent to Bowman's Hill Tower are 100 acres that have been developed into a sanctuary for flowers, trees, shrubs, and ferns native to Pennsylvania. Wander down any one of fifteen nature trails marked with such names as "Medicinal," "Gentian," "Aster Walk," "Bluebell," and "Azalea." The paths vary in length from 150 to 1,250 feet.

From March through November there are always some flowers in bloom, but the peak is April through June. The best time to visit the fern trail is June through August.

FOR GUIDED TOURS: Call Preserve Headquarters or write to the Park Botanist, Washington Crossing, Pa. 18977. Make your reservation for groups at least thirty days in advance; for May allow two months or more. Minimum age: 4. Minimum number 6, maximum 50. One adult for every 10 children. The tour includes a 15-minute orientation at Preserve headquarters and a trail walk of about 40 minutes.

SUMMER NATURE CLASSES: Free, ages 8–12, on ecology.

CHILDREN'S WALK, first Saturday of the month 10 A.M. to noon except January, February, and August.

You cannot picnic in the Preserve, but there are plenty of nearby areas for just that purpose.

The tour of the Preserve is easy to do on your own, and even on a hot day it is cool on the trails.

*Thompson-Neely "House of Decision": Open:* Daily 9:30 A.M.–5 P.M. *Phone:* 1-862-2915. *Admission:* 50¢, including admission to Old Ferry Inn

Just before Washington crossed the Delaware, he held important strategy conferences here with Brigadier General Lord Stirling, Captain James Moore, and Lieutenant James Monroe, later President of the United States.

It's a beautiful Colonial house, with period furnishings.

*Picnicking:* There are lots of picnic tables and a few grills in some of the areas of the Upper Park, and three large covered pavilions that can accommodate groups of fifty or more. If you wish to reserve one, call the Reservation Clerk at 493-4076. No reservations on holidays.

LOWER PARK (WASHINGTON CROSSING AREA)

*Washington Crossing Memorial Building. Open:* Daily 9:30 A.M.– 5 P.M.

Here is displayed an exact copy of the huge world-famous painting *Washington Crossing the Delaware.* A narration with musical background is played every half hour. In front of the building is a statue of George Washington. Stairs lead down to the point of embarkation from where the famous attack on the British was launched on Christmas night, 1776.

There is a reenactment of this famous event annually on Christmas Day at 2 P.M. Two Durham boats, the type Washington used, cross with about thirty men in each boat dressed in Colonial garb. Come early for parking and a good vantage point to watch the "crossing."

*Taylor House: Open:* 8:30 A.M.–5 P.M. weekdays. *Closed:* Saturdays, Sundays, and holidays

The administrative offices of the park are contained in this spacious mansion, built by Mahlonk Taylor in 1812.

*Lagoon:* This lovely area is perfect for a picnic. It is a bird sanctuary and, in the winter, a popular skating center.

*Old Ferry Inn: Open:* Daily. Gift shop and snacks. Here Washington Punch is sold. *Admission:* 50¢, including a visit to the Thompson-Neely House

# 2
# MUSEUMS, LIBRARIES, THE ZOO

If you hear someone say he is going to the museum, most likely he is referring to the renowned Philadelphia Museum of Art on Benjamin Franklin Parkway. However, don't overlook the many other fascinating museums, large and small, all around you; they make the Philadelphia area one of the great cultural centers of the world.

Although every institution is not mentioned, we have included general and specialized museums in the Delaware Valley which appeal to a wide range of ages and interests.

## THE ACADEMY OF NATURAL SCIENCES
19th Street and Benjamin Franklin Parkway
Philadelphia 19103

**Phone:** 567-3700
**Open:** Monday–Saturday 10 A.M.–4:30 P.M., Sunday 1–4:30 P.M.
**Closed:** Thanksgiving, Christmas, New Year's Day
**Admission:** Adults $1.00; children to 12 50¢, under 5 free
**Parking:** On the street or in public lots nearby
**Public Transportation:** SEPTA Routes A local, 33, Cultural Loop bus, Penn Central train to Suburban Station at 17th Street and the Parkway and walk two blocks
**Eating Facilities:** Small cafeteria with vending machines. The Free Library cafeteria across the street has a wider selection.

Dina, the two-story-high dinosaur, is probably the star at this Philadelphia landmark, even though the Academy has recently been emphasizing its ecology and drug programs. But where else in the city can you see such a monster? Tableaux of mounted animals are now considered a bit outmoded; nevertheless, the animals from Africa, Asia, and North America exhibited here stand still, giving young naturalists ample opportunity to study not only the animals themselves, but also the insects, birds, and vegetation of their natural habitats.

75

For those who have progressed beyond tigers and zebras, there are fossil and rock and gem exhibits; the John Audubon Hall, including a section on birds common to the Philadelphia area; and the most recent addition: a hall devoted exclusively to shells. The Academy contains one of the largest and most important shell collections in the world, and one exhibit shows the economic importance of shells—their use in making buttons, decorations, and jewelry. There is also an exhibit contrasting the Schuylkill River of 200 years ago with that of today.

Plan a leisurely half-day visit. Be sure to check the Live Animal Show schedule at the entrance.

### Live Animal Shows

Generally daily 10 A.M. and 12:30 P.M., Saturday 11 A.M. and 2 P.M., Sunday 2 P.M., holidays 11 A.M. and 2 P.M. Subject to change. It's a good idea to call in advance. Geared to younger children (up to 9), these popular shows demonstrate how animals interact, how they adapt to their environment, how and where they find food, where they live. An assortment of live animals—snakes, opossums, porcupines, owls—are present, and children answer questions, ask some, and have a chance to participate generally.

### Film Series

One-hour nature films fall and winter. Saturday at 11 A.M. Free. Use 19th Street entrance. Sunday once a month at 1:30 P.M. Free with admission to museum. Call Academy for program or check local papers.

### Museum Shop

Postcards, rocks, jewelry, Eskimo sculpture, nature hobby kits, and books.

### Workshops and Classes

Saturday workshops for grades 5 to 8, restricted to residents of Philadelphia, or nonresidents with Junior or Family Membership. For further information call: LO 7-3700, ext. 287. Summer courses: weekly sessions by grade levels from 1 to 7. Call for information.

### Group Visits

Adults 75¢, children 30¢. Minimum number 10. Preferably with advance reservations.

### Volunteer Program

High-school students with a particular interest call Public Relations Department.

SPECIAL EVENTS

*Expeditions for Everyone:* Year-round program of weekend expeditions open to members and nonmembers: fossil hunting, bird-watching, canoeing, nature hikes in the Pine Barrens. For more information call Membership Office, Field Trips.

HANDICAPPED

One step at 19th Street entrance. Elevator available inside building. Mineral and gem collections inaccessible. Call in advance so 19th Street entrance can be opened for you.

MEMBERSHIP

Student (including college level) $7.50, individual $5, family $20. Additional categories on request.

*Benefits:* Free admission to museum and film programs. Publications, field trips, and classes. Special events. Discount at museum shop.

## AMERICAN SWEDISH HISTORICAL MUSEUM
19th Street and Pattison Avenue
Philadelphia 19145

**Phone:** FU 9-1776
**Open:** Tuesday–Friday 10 A.M.–5 P.M., Saturday and Sunday 12 noon–5 P.M.
**Closed:** Mondays and all major holidays
**Admission:** 25¢; children 12 and under must be accompanied by an adult
**Directions:** Schuylkill Expressway east. Watch for Walt Whitman Bridge turn and exit on Broad Street ramp. Continue south on Broad Street to Pattison Avenue, turn right, and continue to 20th Street, which is the motorists' entrance to the museum.
**Parking:** Free
**Public Transportation:** Broad Street Subway extension to Pattison Avenue stop, then walk west for 4½ blocks (across from the Naval Hospital). *Or* SEPTA Route 17, or C and G during peak periods.

Forty years before William Penn began his "Holy Experiment," Swedish settlements existed in what are now Philadelphia and Chester. The Swedes made the first permanent settlement in the area in 1638.

Swedish customs and traditions are kept alive in this museum, which is owned and operated by the American-Swedish Historical Foundation, a national nonprofit institution. In the various rooms are exhibitions of Swedish heritage and accomplishments. Changing exhibits and events on Swedish past and present throughout the year. Call or write for information.

### GROUP VISITS

Contact the museum by phone or preferably in writing two weeks in advance. Children with adequate supervision are admitted free. Minimum age suggested: 10 years. Maximum number: 30–40 children accompanied by 2 or 3 adults.

### SPECIAL EVENT

Lucia Festival in early December. Crafts, folk dancing, Swedish foods for sale. Two performances, including the lovely Lucia procession sung by costumed girls as they descend a double staircase carrying lighted candles, and climaxed by "Lucia" with a traditional crown of candles on her head. Annual traditional welcome to spring: Valborgs celebration, last Saturday in April.

### NEARBY

Franklin D. Roosevelt Park—picnicking; paddle boats, rowboats, and canoes for hire.


## THE ATHENAEUM OF PHILADELPHIA
219 South 6th Street
Philadelphia 19106

**Phone:** WA 5-2688
**Open:** Monday–Friday 9 A.M.–4 P.M.
**Closed:** Weekends and holidays
**Admission:** Free
**Parking:** Street parking or public lots in the area
**Public Transportation:** SEPTA Routes D, 42 on Chestnut Street, 50, Cultural Loop bus to Independence Hall, Mid City Loop

Founded in 1814, the Athenaeum is a proprietary library (members pay annually to belong and borrow books). However, the public is welcome to visit and may use the books for reference purposes on the premises. The library specializes in nineteenth-century American cultural history and is especially strong in art and architecture, early travel books, and American fiction of the nineteenth century.

Students are welcome and encouraged to use these excellent facilities for research projects. You may not take the books out, but the quiet, dignified surroundings are conducive to research and study.

The periodical table contains current special-interest magazines as well as the more popular ones, and these can be perused at any time: *Illustrated London News, Audubon, Antiques, Smithsonian, American Book Collector,* along with *Harper's, Time,* and *Newsweek.*

From time to time special literary exhibits are held in the upstairs hall. These are free and open to the public.

Cigar Store Indian at Atwater Kent Museum

## ATWATER KENT MUSEUM
15 South 7th Street (between Market and Chestnut Streets)
Philadelphia 19106

**Phone:** WA 2-3031
**Open:** Daily 8:30 A.M.–4:30 P.M.
**Closed:** Good Friday, Thanksgiving, Christmas, New Year's Day
**Admission:** Free
**Parking:** Public parking lot next door
**Public Transportation:** Any bus or subway on Chestnut Street or Market Street, Mid City Loop bus, Cultural Loop bus to Independence Hall

History comes alive in this exciting museum, which traces the growth of Philadelphia from earliest times. Scenes of life long ago on the Delaware and Schuylkill Rivers, samplers, frakturs, Liverpool jugs and pitchers, cigar-store Indians, and scrimshaw can be seen here. There is a display of old guns, and there are push-button dioramas of Indian and Colonial life. Children love the re-created old toy store full of games and books for the young.

GROUP VISITS

Call and make a reservation. No minimum age—from nursery school on up.

HANDICAPPED

Accessible with one step through the rear entrance. All but one section of the museum can be reached by elevator. Restrooms totally accessible.

NEARBY

Right up the street at 34 South 7th Street is Lore's Chocolate Spot. Good homemade ice cream and tasty chocolates. Take a cone out.


## ALVERTHORPE GALLERY
511 Meetinghouse Road
Jenkintown, Pa. 19046

**Phone:** TU 4-0466
**Open:** Monday–Friday 9 A.M.–5 P.M., by appointment
**Closed:** 1–2 P.M. for lunch; August
**Directions:** Pa. Route 611 north (Broad Street), right on Meetinghouse Road. Entrance to museum will be on your right.

This small private gallery contains Mr. Lessing J. Rosenwald's collection of over 25,000 rare prints, engravings, woodcuts, and illuminated books dating from the fourteenth century to the present. It is not for the casual outing; but, for the individual or group with special interests, it offers a unique and unforgettable experience. You cannot wander through the gallery exploring its treasures. When you call for an appointment, explain your particular area of interest. When you arrive, a staff member will be ready to show you this exquisite collection: fifteenth-century German woodcuts, Brueghel prints, Rembrandt etchings, Goya lithographs. Are you fascinated by rare books? Here is the greatest private collection of illustrated books by Blake—not just one early illustrated Book of Hours, but shelves of them. And there is also an incredible selection of unusual and extravagant bindings which are works of art in themselves.

# BARNES FOUNDATION
300 North Latches Lane
Merion Station, Pa. 19066

**Phone:** MO 7-0290
**Open:** Friday and Saturday 9:30 A.M.–4:30 P.M., Sunday 1–
4:30 P.M.
**Closed:** Legal holidays; July, August
**Admission:** $1; Friday and Saturday visitors limited to 200 (100
by advance reservation and 100 without), Sundays 50 with and
50 without.
**Restrictions:** No children under 12 admitted to either gallery or
arboretum. Children 12–15 admitted when accompanied by an
adult.
**Directions:** Schuylkill Expressway to City Avenue (U.S. Route 1),
south to Old Lancaster Road, right to Latches Lane, left to
museum
**Parking:** On street
**Public Transportation:** SEPTA Route 44 stops at Latches Lane on
Old Lancaster Road

It is hard to believe that an ugly-tasting, dark-brown patent
medicine, Argyrol, could have led to a magnificent art collection—
but it did. Dr. Albert C. Barnes invented the medicine, amassed
a fortune, and collected paintings, priceless masterpieces—mod-
erns, impressionists, and Old Masters. For many years the collection
was not open to the general public, only to students of his art
course. But since the early 1960s, after a prolonged taxpayers' suit,
the Foundation opened its doors on a limited basis. The gallery is
set in a 12-acre arboretum of rare trees, shrubs, and flowers, all
carefully labeled—but visitors are not encouraged to inspect any of
this carefully. A guard checks your name at the gate, and you
check everything you're carrying (coats, pocketbooks, cameras).
You can barnstorm through the gallery or plan to spend the day.
(Go out for lunch and return.) Either way you'll be a bit over-
whelmed by what is there. Over 1,000 paintings floor to ceiling,
wall to wall. You almost don't know where to look first: Degas,
Seurat, Picasso, Utrillo, Modigliani, Klee, Rouault, El Greco,
Titian, Tintoretto, Corot, to mention a few, represented not singly
but in goodly numbers. You can see more Renoirs, Cézannes, and
Matisses here than almost anywhere else.

In spite of the restrictions imposed—all part of the "Barnes experience"—it's really worth a visit. Works of art at the Barnes may
appear in books, but they don't travel to other museums.

For information about art appreciation classes and classes in botany and horticulture for adults, write the Barnes Foundation.

NEARBY

For lunch:
Hymie's Merion Delicatessen
342 Montgomery Avenue
Merion, Pa.
MO 4-3544

## BRANDYWINE RIVER MUSEUM
U.S. Route 1
Chadds Ford, Pa. 19317

Phone: 1-388-7601
Open: Daily including holidays 9:30 A.M.–4:30 P.M.
Closed: Thanksgiving, Christmas
Admission: Adults $1.50, students 12–18 75¢. children 6–12 50¢
Directions: Schuylkill Expressway to City Line Avenue (U.S.
   Route 1), then south to Chadds Ford. Museum is on the left.
Parking: Free

This is Wyeth country, and the museum is a celebration of the Brandywine School of Artists—Howard Pyle and his pupils N. C. Wyeth, Andrew Wyeth, James Wyeth, and other members of the clan. An old gristmill has been restored and transformed into an extraordinary showcase for these artists, with curved glass walls overlooking the Brandywine Creek. There are three floors of galleries. In addition to a permanent collection, exhibitions change in the spring, summer, and fall, and A *Brandywine Christmas* is a marvelous way to start the holidays. Each year the museum comes up with a unique concept for the Christmas season.

Special events take place all through the year—Sunday concerts, a Harvest Market and Antique Show weekends in the fall. Call the museum for the schedule of events.

Volunteers from the museum go out on request to schools and present a program on *The Brandywine Artists.* Mile-long river trail to John Chad House open.

MUSEUM BOOKSTORE

Wyeth reproductions, children's classics, art and environmental books, and ecology kits.

TEAROOM

Attractive place for lunch and snacks overlooking the Brandywine Creek.

GROUP VISITS

Guided tours can be arranged with one week's notice. Children should be of school age. Minimum number: 10 children with 1 adult. Group rate: 50¢. The tour can include gallery talks, slide lecture, ecology information, and nature tours at Ridley Creek State Park and on the museum's nature trail.

HANDICAPPED

Special parking and entrance. Restrooms are accessible but booth doors are narrow; there is an elevator. Handicapped groups are requested to call in advance so that every effort can be made to insure an easy and comfortable visit.

## BUTEN MUSEUM OF WEDGWOOD
246 North Bowman Avenue
Merion, Pa. 19066

Phone: 664-9069
Open: October–May, Tuesday, Wednesday, and Thursday 2–5 P.M.
Admission: Free. Guided tours only.
Directions: Schuylkill Expressway to U.S. Route 1 (City Avenue) south to Montgomery Avenue, west on Montgomery to Bowman Avenue
Parking: On street
Public Transportation: SEPTA Route 44 to Bowman Avenue

This museum is devoted exclusively to the exhibition of Wedgwood, from its earliest examples to the most contemporary products. There are over 10,000 pieces here, illustrating the different varieties, glazes, colors, and patterns. A special museum for a very special interest.

MUSEUM SHOP

Wedgwood of all varieties on sale here: jasperware, queensware, bone china. Special items such as medallions and cameos are sold exclusively here. Seconds of odd pieces are also available.

## CAMPBELL MUSEUM
Campbell Place
Camden, N.J. 08101

Phone: 1-609-964-4000 or WA 5-4003, ext. 2688
Open: Monday–Friday 9:30 A.M.–5:00 P.M.
Closed: Weekends and legal holidays
Admission: Free

**Directions:** Benjamin Franklin Bridge, U.S. Route 30, Admiral
Wilson Boulevard, right on Memorial Avenue, right on Eleventh
Street, bear left to Tenth Street to Campbell Place
**Parking:** In front of museum

Where else but at the Campbell Soup Company would you find a
museum devoted to a collection of tureens, bowls, and ladles
from 500 B.C. to the present? The collection has been exhibited at
the Smithsonian Institution in Washington and at the Art Institution
of Chicago. The tureens are bizarre, unusual, imaginative to say the
least. Some are exquisite, some are just the opposite. For the
"student"—casual or serious—of the decorative arts.

GROUP VISITS

Group tours by appointment only. Call for reservation. Minimum number 4, maximum number 50. Length of tour: 45 minutes.

PLANT TOURS

For children over 10 and groups of more than 10 but less than
40. For information call Mr. Zelley.

## CHAPEL OF THE FOUR CHAPLAINS
1855 North Broad Street
Philadelphia

**Phone:** CE 6-6394
**Public Transportation:** Broad Street Subway to Columbia station
*or* SEPTA Route C
**Tours:** Weekdays by appointment. Services Sundays at 4 P.M.

Located on the Temple University campus, this interfaith chapel
was built in 1951 in memory of the four young army chap-
lains who went down with the troopship S.S. *Dorchester* during
World War II. The building contains paintings of the *Dorchester*
and artifacts donated by the survivors.

## CHILDREN'S MUSEUM OF PHILADELPHIA—"TOUCH AND LEARN"

This new organization is planning to move into the Monastery
in the Wissahickon Creek area of Fairmount Park. Meanwhile, it
has developed a special exhibit, *It's About Your Size*, designed
especially for children 4 to 8. Anyone interested in borrowing this
exhibit for use in a community center or school, or in obtaining
more information about the Children's Museum, can write to:
417 East Durham Street, Philadelphia 19119.

## CHINESE CULTURAL CENTER
125 North 10th Street
Philadelphia 19107

**Phone:** WA 3-6767
**Open:** For tours. Call for information.
**Public Transportation:** SEPTA Routes 23, 47, 61

You really can't miss it. It has dragons atop the flyaway roof and multicolored tiles up and down the front of the building. Inside are Oriental exhibits, statues, musical instruments, a gift shop, and the dragon used to celebrate the Chinese New Year in Philadelphia. Courses given in Chinese cooking, brush painting, calligraphy, and languages. Call for information.

## DELAWARE MUSEUM OF NATURAL HISTORY
Del. Route 52
Greenville, Del. 19807

**Phone:** 1-302-658-9111
**Open:** Wednesday–Saturday 9 A.M.–4 P.M., Sunday 1–5 P.M.
**Closed:** Mondays, Tuesdays, and all national holidays
**Admission:** Adults $1.25, children 4–16 75¢
**Restrictions:** No cameras
**Directions:** Schuylkill Expressway to City Line Avenue (U.S. Route 1), south to Pa. Route 52, left 2.3 miles beyond Pennsylvania–Delaware border. Museum entance on right. *Or* I-95 south to Del. Route 52, then northwest on Del. Route 52 past Greenville Shopping Center. Entrance to museum on left about 2 miles beyond railroad crossing. About an hour's drive.
**Parking:** On museum grounds
**Picnicking and Eating Facilities:** None at museum. Picnicking at Brandywine Battlefield State Park. Restaurants at Henry Francis duPont Winterthur and Brandywine River Museums nearby.

Founded by Mr. John E. duPont, the marine biologist, the Delaware Museum of Natural History is the newest natural history museum in the area. Divided into three sections—Sky, Land, and Sea—it contains 100 exhibits of birds, shells, and small mammals, all lavishly and dramatically mounted. A glass floor in the World of Shells covers a section of the Great Barrier Reef of Australia. Other displays show the growth and development of shells and their use in art, medicine, heraldry, and religion. Or you can just enjoy the beauty of the whole collection.

In the Hall of Birds the exhibit of large bird eggs from around the world—for example, the penguin, ostrich, ibis, and the extinct elephant bird—is startling, accustomed as most of us are to the eggs of robins, wrens, and jays. Some of the birds are mounted a bit high for careful inspection, but does one ever really come eye to eye with an owl?

### NATURE FILMS SERIES
Weekdays at 10, 12, and 2. Sundays at 1:30 and 3 P.M. They change every two weeks for six months; then the series is repeated.

### SHELL CLUB
Meets first Monday of the month at 8 P.M. Membership fee: $5 for an adult, $1 for each additional family member. Junior membership (under 16) $2. For information and application call museum office.

### GROUP VISITS
Scouts and schoolchildren 50¢. By reservation only.

### HANDICAPPED
Museum has a ramp at the entrance. Exhibits all on one floor.

## DUKE GARDENS FOUNDATION
Somerville, N.J. 08876

Across the border, beyond Princeton, are a museum and garden well worth a special trip: the Southeast Asian Art Collection and glass-enclosed gardens of Doris Duke, tobacco heiress, horticulturist, and art collector (see page 195).

## EDGAR ALLAN POE HOUSE
530 North 7th Street (near Spring Garden Street)
Philadelphia 19123

**Phone:** MA 7-1364
**Open:** Monday–Friday 10 A.M.–5 P.M., Saturday and Sunday 2–5 P.M.
**Closed:** Easter, Thanksgiving, Christmas, New Year's Day
**Admission:** Adults $1; children 12–17 50¢, under 12 free when accompanied by an adult. Guided tours only.
**Parking:** On street.
**Public Transportation:** SEPTA Routes 43, 47

Edgar Allan Poe lived in Philadelphia for six years, from 1838 to 1844. It was here that he wrote "The Raven," "The Gold Bug," and "The Tell-Tale Heart"—those nightmarish creations which are still told around campfires and continue to fascinate and horrify. The house has been restored and designated a National Historic Landmark, and a small museum has been added. Some first editions, manuscripts, and mementos are here, but the major portion of the Poe collection is in the Free Library at Logan Square. Anyone who has recently survived a retelling of "The Tell-Tale Heart" might enjoy a brief visit here.

GROUP VISITS

Minimum grade: 11th. Special rates. Call for information.

## FRANKLIN INSTITUTE
Benjamin Franklin Parkway at 20th Street
Philadelphia 19103

**Phone:** 448-1000. For current schedule information call LO 4-3838.
**Open:** Monday–Saturday 10 A.M.–5 P.M., Sunday 12 noon–5 P.M.
**Closed:** July 4, Labor Day, Thanksgiving, Christmas Eve, Christmas, New Year's Day
**Admission:** Adults $1.50; children 6–12 $1, under 5 free. Planetarium 25¢ additional; children under 5 not admitted.
**Parking:** Weekends and evenings: Free parking at the Institute lot at rear of building, entrance on 21st Street. Municipal parking lot: Callowhill Street between 19th and 20th Streets (behind Free Library). Some metered and street parking.
**Public Transportation:** SEPTA Routes A local, 7, 33, 48; Cultural Loop bus
**Eating Facilities:** It's a McDonald's! There is a cafeteria at the Free Library across the Parkway.
**Membership:** Individual $15; family memberships: resident $25; nonresident (50 miles or more) $10; educator (active faculty members, elementary schools through university levels) $12.50; student membership (8–25) $6.

*Benefits:* Free admission to Institute and Planetarium, science workshops, discount at Ben's Shop, subscription to quarterly publication. For additional information call Membership Office: 448-1231.

The Franklin Institute is one of the giants of Philadelphia in more ways than one: That colossal building on the Parkway has something for everyone. Plan to spend the better part of a day and/or come back often—in which case you should consider a family membership. Pick up a floor plan and directory at the entrance; it will tell you not only where exhibits are, but also what, when, and where the demonstrations are.

And "demonstrations" is the name of the game at the Institute. There are more buttons to push, levers to pull, and wheels to go around than almost anywhere else in town. Sometimes you make it happen, sometimes you watch; but it's always fun—and educational.

There are optical illusions, distortion mirrors, a telescope on the top floor (used on sunny days only), paper-making demonstrations, and a pendulum that continues to prove the earth rotates on its axis. The development of the steamboat is shown in a series of working models—just push the buttons. Have you ever wanted to see the light on a lighthouse but were too lazy to climb to the top? How about man-made lightning?

You can walk through a giant heart, hear your voice on a telephone, and take a "ride" on a 350-ton locomotive. This 16-foot journey has been delighting children since the engine arrived at the Institute in 1933 (before the building was completed, if you wonder how it got inside). It's one of the highlights of the Train Section. What would you like to know about the Apollo capsules and space flights—or airplanes? There are exhibitions on energy, computers, and bicycles, and there are special exhibits that come and go periodically.

Franklin Memorial Hall contains a 20-foot statue of Benjamin Franklin, the founder of the Institute, and assorted artifacts and memorabilia to this giant of eighteenth-century America. Admission is free. Children must be accompanied by an adult.

Somewhere in all this activity, rest your feet and gaze at the stars in the Fels Planetarium (page 89). No children under 5 admitted, but they may go to the free films.

### FILM SERIES

Free. Saturday and Sunday afternoons for various age levels. Check the newspapers or call for further information. You might catch a classic W. C. Fields the whole family would enjoy.

### FAMILY NIGHTS

Once a month, September through May. Free to members and their guests by reservation. If space is available, these very popular programs are also open to nonmembers with payment of regular admission charge. Geared to children (minimum age 5), these programs are scheduled at 7:30 and 8:30 P.M. in the Lecture Hall and Planetarium. If you make your reservation for 7:30, you can attend both programs; at 8:30, only one. The program may be a demonstration; it may be a discussion of an exhibit. The program varies, but there's always time for questions. For information and reservations call 448-1254.

## GROUP VISITS

Advance reservations must be made for all groups by telephone or mail to Museum Reservations Office (448-1201). Include name of organization, date and time of arrival, person in charge, whether group will attend Planetarium, whether group will use lunchroom. Facilities are available for those bringing lunch. Minimum number 10. Group rate 85¢ per person; adult free with every 15 children.

## HANDICAPPED

Entrance at 21st and Winter Streets. Elevators to all floors, but only a portion of each floor accessible to person in wheelchair because of steps. Restrooms accessible, but booth doors are narrow. Planetarium accessible, and person may remain in wheelchair. Parking lot adjacent. Guided tours for the blind can be arranged, preferably in the afternoon. Minimum number: 6. For information call 448-1111 or 448-1346.

## JUNIOR VOLUNTEER PROGRAM

All year. Minimum age 16. It's a flexible program adapted to the interests of the individual and needs of the museum: Some youngsters help set up exhibits, some do research for new exhibits, some act as guides for individuals or groups, some give demonstrations. For information and application call 448-1288.

## SCIENCE WORKSHOPS

Spring and fall on Saturdays, summer weekdays. Kindergarten through 12th grade and preschool. Electricity, chemistry, ham radio, photography, and more—for many age and grade levels. The model airplane course includes radio-controlled airplanes. For brochure and information call Workshop Registrar, 448-1287.

## BEN'S SHOP

Books, models, gifts, toys, hobby kits, chemistry sets, magnets, telescopes, and gyroscopes.

**FELS PLANETARIUM at the Franklin Institute**
Benjamin Franklin Parkway at 20th Street
Philadelphia 19103
(Entrance on Winter Street)

**Phone:** LO 4-3838 for current schedule information

**Admission:** General admission to Franklin Institute (adults $1.50, children $1) plus 25¢
**Restrictions:** No children under 5 admitted
**Planetarium Shows:** Monday–Friday 3 P.M. (and 12 noon during the summer), Saturday 11 A.M., 1, 2, 3 P.M., Sunday 2, 3, 4 P.M. Friday evenings 8 P.M. (except Family Nights 8:30 P.M.). For information and reservations call 448-1292.

Shows change periodically and wander all over the universe and seasons—from *Once Around the Sun* to *Spring, Summer,* or *Autumn Constellations* to *The Christmas Sky (Past and Present)*. In clear weather, shows are followed by observatory visits. All those streetlights and smog make it difficult even to locate real stars these days, so this is a good way to see them.

HANDICAPPED

Entrance at 21st and Winter Streets. Persons may remain in wheelchairs.

**THE FREE LIBRARY OF PHILADELPHIA**
The Central Library
Logan Square
19th and Vine Streets
Philadelpha 19103

**Phone:** MU 6-5322 (Departments of the Central Library and all branches have individual listings in telephone book under Free Library of Philadelphia)
**Open:** Monday–Wednesday 9 A.M.–9 P.M. Thursday and Friday 9 A.M.–6 P.M., Saturday 9 A.M.–5 P.M.; also Sunday 2–6 P.M. (October–April) Call General Information (MU 6-5322) for branch hours and to find out what's going on.
**Closed:** The Library System is closed on President's Day, Good Friday, Easter, Memorial Day, Independence Day, Labor Day, Columbus Day, Veteran's Day, National Election Days, Thanksgiving, Christmas, New Year's Day.
**Parking:** Like many of the buildings along the Parkway, the library seems inaccessible. However, there is a municipal parking lot on Callowhill Street, directly behind the library. Some metered space is available on the street, or you might be lucky enough to find free space nearby.
**Public Transportation:** SEPTA Route A local, Cultural Loop bus

Anyone who lives in Philadelphia, studies at a Philadelphia school or college, belongs to the immediate family of a Philadelphia taxpayer, or is willing to pay an annual fee of $3 may obtain a library card after showing proper identification (children need a parent's signature) and may borrow books and materials from the library system, usually for 21 days. There are special extended summer loan privileges.

But the Library is more than just a place for borrowing books. It's a concert hall, a movie theater, an art gallery—and an inexpensive restaurant along the Parkway, where not many restaurants exist. The Monthly Calendar of Events is your guide to what is going on in the library system. Pick it up at any of the branches. All events are free: There are story hours, book concerts for children, chamber music concerts, films for the whole family, and a lecture series that is mainly for adults but possibly of interest to high-school students, depending on interests and subject matter.

A trip to the Logan Library should always include a visit to the main lobby and the gallery, both on the first floor, to see what little-known treasures have been put on display. The opening of the fishing season may be celebrated with an exhibit of seventeenth-century angling prints, Christmas with medieval illuminated manuscripts (an annual event), or the Library may feature a tribute to Hollywood greats, from Valentino to Chaplin, Gable, or Monroe. Exhibits are changed every six weeks, so you'll almost always find something new to look at. Drop in, or check the Monthly Guide.

THE CHILDREN'S DEPARTMENT

Monday–Friday 9 A.M.–6 P.M., Saturday 9 A.M.–5 P.M.; also Sunday 2–6 P.M. (winter). Phone: MU 6-5364. Conveniently located on the ground floor with a separate entrance on the 20th Street side. Its large pleasant rooms are filled with books, magazines, reference books, phonographs with earphones, and records for listening and borrowing. There is also a collection of children's books in foreign languages. Materials are geared to children from preschool age through the 8th grade, and there are tables, chairs, benches—and a friendly helpful staff. Unaccompanied children are not permitted to wander through the building. Therefore, those old enough to enjoy browsing independently might appreciate these larger facilities.

From mid-June to the end of August, the Children's Department holds its *Vacation Reading Club* for children entering grades 4 through 9. Groups meet weekly with the librarian for informal discussions of the books read. Usually activities related to the reading are included in the program: craft projects, trips to a summer theater, a museum, a historical site. All in all it's much livelier than writing book reports. Vacation Reading Clubs are held in the local branches as well. Watch for the announcements or call Office of Work with Children (MU 6-5372). The Library for the Blind and Physically Handicapped, 919 Walnut Street (WA 5-3213), conducts a Vacation Reading Club by mail. Children are sent four books (talking books, Braille, tape, or large print) and may write their reviews or telephone free of charge to report. If at all possible, however, they are urged to attend the local meetings and materials are sent from the Library for the Blind and Physically Handicapped for them to read.

Happily, the ancient art of storytelling is being kept alive by the talented storytellers in the Children's Department. Story hours for preschool children (ages 3 through 5) require preregistration; those for school ages (kindergarten through 6th grade) do not. Parents are not permitted to attend. The program generally lasts about an hour. Check the Monthly Calendar, your local branch, or call Office of Work with Children (MU 6-5372).

*Book Concerts for Children* are held six or seven times during the year, from mid-October through April, Sundays at 2:30 in the Lecture Hall at the Central Library. Doors open at 2 o'clock, and seating is on a first come, first served basis. The programs are primarily for children and are very popular with family groups. All are welcome, but a word of caution: To minimize distractions, there is generally a no-return policy if you leave the concert hall with a younger child. Programs last about an hour and have included chamber music, ballet, puppets, magicians, and folksingers. A reading list of related books is distributed at each concert. For more information, call Office of Work with Children (MU 6-5372). Schedules are also available at the branches.

EVENING CHAMBER MUSIC CONCERTS

These concerts are presented by the Friends of Music of the Free Library of Philadelphia at the Central Library. A reserved section is set aside until ten minutes before concert time for Friends donating $5 or more (it's tax deductible). The Curtis String Quartet, the American Society of Ancient Instruments, the Philadelphia Woodwind Quintet, and the Juilliard String Quartet have appeared in the past. For information, call the Music Department (MU 6-5316), or pick up a schedule at any of the branches or at the Tourist Center.

RARE BOOK DEPARTMENT

The Rare Book Department is one of the largest in a public library in this country. Visitors are always welcome (Monday–Saturday 9 A.M.–5 P.M.). Ring the bell on the third floor and sign in. Tours can be arranged by calling MU 6-5416. If there's something special you'd like to see, it can probably be arranged by calling a day or two in advance. The Monthly Calendar will describe the current exhibit. The collections include Sumerian cuneiform tablets of 5,000 years ago (those first "books" written on clay), medieval and Oriental manuscripts, early hornbooks, Bibles, and books printed in Europe as long ago as the fifteenth century, as well as charming Pennsylvania Dutch frakturs.

For the more whimsically minded, there are the collections of original drawings, watercolors, and sketches by those favorites of all generations: Beatrix Potter, Kate Greenaway, and Arthur Rackham.

Probably of more interest to adults than children are the Rosenbach Collection of Early American Children's Books from 1682 to 1836. The Historical Collection of Children's Literature from 1837 to the present can be found in the Children's Department.

If you prefer the less delicate and fanciful, ask to see the Gimbel Collection of Edgar Allan Poe, limited editions of lithographs for *Moby Dick* by Benton Spruance, and original drawings for Dickens's *David Copperfield* and *Dombey and Son*.

While you're in the Rare Book Department, you might take a look at the charming greeting cards and notepaper and the amusing literary map of Philadelphia—all for sale at reasonable prices. And then continue further down the corridor to the Elkins Room. This beautifully paneled delightful library room with all its furnishings and books was taken from Mr. William M. Elkins's home in Whitemarsh and installed on the third floor of the Central Library. It contains his Dickens collection (including Dickens's desk and candle holder), Goldsmith collection, and Americana with maps, original early narratives about the New World, and two prints by Paul Revere. A guide in the department will be happy to show you this magnificent library within a library.

Outside the Children's Department the Library has collected and hung its set of National Book Week posters from 1909 to the present. One of two complete sets in the country, it contains works of some well-known illustrators and is an interesting commentary on changing art styles. Find the poster for a birthday year. . . . Then go on to the Newspaper Room with its microfilm file of old newspapers. Discover what was happening in the world on the day you were born. For 45¢ a page you can have a Thermo-Fax copy immediately. It makes a good birthday present.

MAP ROOM

The Map Room contains maps, globes, and atlases, old and new, factual and fictional. Ask the librarian in charge to see their maps of fantasyland: Treasure Island, Sherwood Forest, the Argonauts' travels, and science fiction places.

### PRINT AND PICTURE COLLECTION

This collection is the basis for many of the exhibits and displays mounted by the library, and it also has an interesting circulating collection. Prints can be borrowed for three weeks, just like books.

And for families who are thinking of college the Education, Philosophy, and Religion Department (MU 6-5392) has an extensive collection of college and university catalogues.

### CAFETERIA

The Cafeteria on the fourth floor is open to the public. It's a pleasant spot, with reasonably priced salads and sandwiches. In the summer there's an open terrace for outdoor dining. A welcome, relaxing change from the vending machines found elsewhere in the area.

### FILM DEPARTMENT

Library card holders are eligible to borrow films; there is an annotated film catalogue here and at all library branches of 16 mm. sound films available free of charge. Films range from *Blueberries for Sal* to *The Phantom of the Opera*, from nature and music to the life of Benjamin Franklin and *Alistair Cooke's America*. Phone: MU 6-5367.

### THEATER COLLECTION

The second largest in the country, this is a noncirculating collection. It consists primarily of newspaper clippings, posters, old lithographs, programs, pictures, reviews. Call MU 6-5327 if you want to know who played what role when and where.

### BRANCH FACILITIES

The Library System has forty-five branches throughout the city. They generally have the same facilities and many of the same activities—albeit on a smaller scale—as the Central Library. Check the calendar, the local branch, or General Information (MU 6-5322). A free film, a concert, or a play may be just around the corner. In addition, there are some branches offering special collections or facilities. Because of private funds, the Philadelphia City Institute Library (19th and Locust Streets, PE 5-9137) and the Roxborough Branch (Hermitage Lane and

Ridge Avenue, IV 3-7107) have more extensive book collections. The Roxborough Branch also has a circulating library of records for both children and adults.

*The Northeast Regional Library,* Cottman Avenue and Oakland Street, (MU 6-3930). Parking: On lot. Public Transportation: SEPTA Route 4 on Cottman Avenue at Gimbels Northeast, 59B at Bustleton and Cottman Avenues. Larger than a branch, but somewhat smaller than the Central Library, this regional library is readily accessible to the Northeast section of the city.

*The Library for the Blind and Physically Handicapped,* 919 Walnut Street, Phone: WA 5-3213, is described in detail in Chapter 11.

The library staff is friendly and helpful—whether suggesting a book, finding a specific title, or offering you their vast array of brightly colored reading lists for any age. There's even a list of books to help parents cope with children.

## SAMUEL S. FLEISHER ART MEMORIAL
715–721 Catharine Street
Philadelphia 19147

**Phone:** WA 2-3456

**Open:** October–April, Monday–Friday 10 A.M.–4 P.M. and 7–9:30 P.M., Saturday 1–3 P.M.; June and July, Tuesday and Thursday 7–9:30 P.M. Classes for adults (over 18). Museum open also in May, August, and September 10 A.M.–4 P.M.; visit by appointment.

**Closed:** Sundays, most major nationally observed holidays, May, August, and September

**Admission:** Free

**Restrictions:** No cameras

**Directions:** South on Broad Street, left on Bainbridge Street, right on 6th Street, right on Catharine Street

**Parking:** Museum parking lot across the street for classes only; also street parking

**Public Transportation:** SEPTA Route 47 to 8th and Catharine Streets

**Picnicking and Eating Facilities:** Small park next door; Italian Market nearby

The Samuel S. Fleisher Art Memorial contains an art school, two galleries, and a collection of Romanesque and medieval art. Founded in 1898 as the Graphic Sketch Club, to bring art to depressed neighborhoods, it still maintains the same policy of free classes to which people come from all over the city. There are no registration fees, no enrollment requirements. The only charge is for materials used. Classes ranging from sketching and portraiture to sculpture and ceramics are held in the evenings for adults, and on Saturday afternoons for children (5–17) and for the parents of these children, October to April 1. Registration early in the fall. Call for information. There is also a six-week summer session in landscape painting for adults.

In the galleries is a collection of contemporary art, including works by Baskin, Calder, Shahn, and Spruance. Several times during the year special exhibits are hung here: photography and painting, American nineteenth-century painting and literature, animals in contemporary art.

The quiet of the Romanesque sanctuary provides a startling change of pace. You'll find a collection of ikons, medieval sculpture, primitive painting under glass, and an exquisite eighteenth-century Portuguese chapel. This is one of the loveliest spots in town. Try it before or after a visit to the Italian Market. You'll almost forget you're in Philadelphia.

The Fleisher Art Memorial is administered by the Philadelphia Museum of Art.

## HERITAGE HOUSE EDUCATIONAL AND CULTURAL CENTER
1346 North Broad Street
Philadelphia 19121

Phone: CE 2-1700
Open: Monday–Friday 9 A.M.–5 P.M.
Closed: Weekends and holidays
Admission: Free by appointment; guided tours only, about 30 minutes
Public Transportation: SEPTA Routes 15, C, Broad Street Subway to the Girard stop

This old mansion has been converted to a museum of black history, art (there is an exhibit entitled *400 Black Builders of American Heritage*), dance, drama, and music, as well as a cultural center with related programs and classes.

## HISTORICAL SOCIETY OF PENNSYLVANIA
1300 Locust Street
Philadelphia 19107

Phone: 732-6200

**Open:** Monday 1–5 P.M. (library open until 9 P.M.), Tuesday–Friday 9 A.M.–5 P.M.

**Closed:** August to the second Monday in September; weekends; and legal holidays

**Admission:** Free (but $1 per day library use fee for nonmembers)

**Parking:** Public lots in area

**Public Transportation:** SEPTA Routes A, C, 23, 38, 90, Broad Street Subway to Walnut–Locust stop

**Membership:** $15. *Benefits:* Stack privileges, meetings, teas, and the magazine

Founded in 1824, this is the first historical society in Pennsylvania and among the first in the nation. It contains manuscripts covering three centuries of American history. The Pennsylvania Historical Society Library is an excellent research center for the serious student of American affairs.

In the museum are outstanding paintings of important Colonial patriots and scenes of Pennsylvania, early furniture, Philadelphia silver, and many possessions of William Penn, Benjamin Franklin, George Washington, and Thomas Jefferson.

SCHOOL GROUPS

To arrange a visit, write to Nicholas B. Wainwright, Director, or call 732-6200 a few days in advance.

## ILE-IFE MUSEUM OF AFRO-AMERICAN CULTURE
2300 Germantown Avenue (7th and Dauphin Streets)
Philadelphia 19133

**Phone:** 684-0352

**Open:** Tuesday–Sunday noon–9 P.M.

**Admission:** Adults $1, children under 12 50¢; guided tours only

**Parking:** Difficult

**Public Transportation:** SEPTA Routes 39, 47

This museum is run by the touring Arthur Hall Afro-American Dance Ensemble. When they are in town they will give you a guided tour which includes their African and Haitian art collection, drums, and dancing. There is no minimum number required for a group visit, but the more people there are the more the discussion develops. Minimum age suggested: 4–5.

The Ile-Ife Humanitarian Center, 2544 Germantown Avenue (BA 5-7565), also run by Arthur Hall, has a cultural arts program for children and adults, with classes in African and modern dance, music, drama, and the arts.

## INSTITUTE OF CONTEMPORARY ART
Fine Arts Building
University of Pennsylvania
34th and Walnut Streets
(Entrance on Locust Walk)
Philadelphia 19174

**Phone:** 594-7108
**Open:** Monday–Friday 9 A.M.–5 P.M. (except Wednesday 9 A.M.–
9 P.M.), Saturday and Sunday 12 noon–5 P.M.
**Closed:** Mid-May–mid-September
**Admission:** Free
**Parking:** Parking lots on campus, 34th and Spruce Streets, and
Franklin Field
**Public Transportation:** SEPTA Routes D, D-1 from the Penn Cen-
tral 30th Street Station, 42

The Institute of Contemporary Art, a fairly new and welcome
addition to the Philadelphia art scene, presents many fine changing
exhibitions throughout the year of works not yet considered "safe"
by the older established museums. The collections—four different
ones a year—are exciting, diverse, and well worth a visit.

Children, armed with a natural curiosity, are better viewers of
contemporary art than most adults. They don't feel they have to
understand it to enjoy it. Their involvement in art is encouraged
here. Four Saturday mornings during the year at 11 A.M., the
Institute schedules programs aimed at the 5-to-10-year-old set.
Learning is fun, and each session becomes a visual treasure hunt.
Sixty children can participate, and they all have a marvelous time.
Part of the morning the children create their own artwork with a
variety of materials supplied by ICA. Refreshments are served,
and altogether it's an enjoyable and rewarding experience. For further information and the Saturday morning schedule, call the ICA
office (594-7108).

You may visit the Institute any time, but it is best to call ahead.
The museum closes for ten days while new exhibits are being
installed.

GROUP VISITS

Call for reservation. Gallery talks can be arranged.

## THE LIBRARY COMPANY OF PHILADELPHIA
1314 Locust Street
Philadelphia 19107
**Phone:** KI 6-3181

**Open:** Monday–Friday 9 A.M.–4:45 P.M.
**Closed:** Weekends and major holidays
**Admission:** Free
**Parking:** Public lots in the area
**Public Transportation:** SEPTA Routes A, C, 23, 38, 90, Broad
Street Subway to Walnut–Locust stop

Founded by Benjamin Franklin and his friends in 1731, the
Library Company was the first circulating library in America. Today, at its present location, it contains the largest and most valuable
rare book collection in Philadelphia—over 100,000 volumes of
American history and culture providing background from Colonial
times to the Civil War.

It had many locations since its founding; for the longest period
(1790 to 1880) it was in a beautiful building known as Library Hall
across from Independence Square, now the home of the American
Philosophical Society Library. In its present attractive and modern
location the Library's valuable materials can be preserved under
proper temperatures and kept in maximum security. Two handsome rooms to see:

### LOGAN MEMORIAL ROOM

James Logan (page 55) had the finest collection of books in
Colonial America. In 1792 the Library Company received in trust
the Loganian Library, an extraordinary collection embracing volumes on history, philosophy, mathematics, linguistics, geography,
classics, and astronomy. The richly furnished room contains William Penn's desk and clock, a Meschianza mirror from the Wharton
House (1778), a music stand, and a fine Georgian breakfront.

### RUSH MEMORIAL ROOM

Named after Benjamin Rush for his great donations to the Library
Company, this room has a bust of Minerva, a monument by
Ceracchi, two marine pictures by Birch, Windsor chairs, and a
facsimile of Benjamin Franklin's machine for creating static
electricity.

The Library is open to the public and may be used by any serious
scholar and researcher. Housed among its rare books is Franklin's
original *Pennsylvania Gazette*, printed in 1729, a rare treat to see.
This can be brought down on request. Anyone may walk in to
see the Memorial rooms and browse in the Library. The rare books
are kept above in special temperature-controlled areas.

Edwin Wolf II is the knowledgeable librarian and inspiration of
the present Library Company.

## MERCER MUSEUM
Pine and Ashland Streets
Doylestown, Pa. 18901

One of the world's finest collections of Early American tools
and artifacts. See page 221.

## MUETTER MUSEUM
19 South 22nd Street
Philadelphia 19103

**Phone:** 561-6050
**Open:** Tuesday–Saturday 10 A.M.–4 P.M. Summer hours vary; call
ahead.
**Closed:** Sundays, Mondays, holidays
**Admission:** Free. Minimum suggested age: 9.
**Parking:** Nearby public lots
**Public Transportation:** SEPTA Routes 7, 12, buses on Chestnut or
Market Street. Penn Central train to Suburban Station.

Housed in the dignified Old World surroundings of the College
of Physicians and Surgeons is a highly unusual, macabre, and
fascinating museum. Here you will see hundreds of skulls, ribcages,
skeletons (one of a giant 7 feet 6 inches, the largest one known to
have existed in America), kidneys in jars, a plaster cast of Siamese
twins, plus cases full of surgical instruments. Its main appeal may
be for future scientists and doctors; it's definitely not for the
squeamish or delicate of nature, but the two-floor display is unique
and bears inspection. Don't miss the herb garden in season.

### GROUP VISITS
For the scientifically minded student—preferably junior and
senior high-school level. Call or write in advance.

### VOLUNTEER PROGRAM
Junior high school and up—guiding, cataloguing, museum exhibit
maintenance. Call for information.

## MUSEUM OF THE PHILADELPHIA CIVIC CENTER
34th and Civic Center Boulevard
(Below Spruce Street)
Philadelphia 19104

**Phone:** EV 2-8181
**Open:** Tuesday–Saturday 9 A.M.–5 P.M., Sunday 1–5 P.M.
**Closed:** Mondays, all legal holidays

**Admission:** Free

**Directions:** Exit 3 on Schuylkill Expressway, turn west on South Street to 34th Street, south to Civic Center

**Parking:** 1,000-car parking garage $1.25; street parking allowed when all lots are filled

**Public Transportation:** SEPTA Routes D-1 from the Penn Central 30th Street Station, 40, 42

This museum is part of the vast and varied complex known as the Civic Center, Philadelphia's showcase for regional, national, and international exhibitions. The impressive fountain in front is by Harry Bertoia.

### PERMANENT EXHIBITIONS

On any visit you may go to the ground floor and see a dramatic and fascinating presentation entitled *Philadelphia Panorama: Philadelphia as it was, as it is, and as it will be in the 1980s.* A large-scale animated model flips over and lights up, accompanied by an integrated tape narration with music. The Philadelphia City Planning Commission is responsible for the displays and regularly updates them.

### INTERNATIONAL FESTIVALS

For over ten years the Civic Center has been presenting International Festivals. They occupy several floors of the Museum and last for a month or more. These festivals, which in the past have included Great Britain, Canada, Brazil, France, and Denmark, focus attention on all aspects of the country through arts, crafts, food, dance, and exports. Watch the newspapers for announcements, or call the Museum for information.

### CONTEMPORARY EXHIBITIONS OF CRAFTS

Regional, national, and international shows in the fields of fine arts, crafts, industrial design, and architecture are on display in everchanging exhibitions. Community clubs such as the Philadelphia Watercolor Club, School Art League, and the Children's Art Exhibition in spring have temporary exhibits here. International exhibitions have included *Crafts of Finland, Soviet Graphic Arts,* and *Contemporary and Swedish Design.* To be put on the mailing list for these craft shows, write the Civic Center Museum, 34th and Civic Center Boulevard, Philadelphia 19104.

### EDUCATIONAL PROGRAMS

On the second floor of the Museum are "living classrooms"— areas that are set aside to convey the feeling and atmosphere of different parts of the world. Through panoramas, models, products, and artifacts, such areas as the Port of Philadelphia, Japan, India, Pennsylvania farms, and Africa are created. Films about the region are often included, and teachers are on hand to offer their special knowledge to the students. Public, parochial, private, and out-of-town schoolchildren are eligible to attend these classes. Reservations are required. Local public schools call Board of Education, Division of Museum Education. Private, parochial, and suburban schools make reservations directly by calling MU 6-1776 (ask for Civic Center Museum).

SPECIAL EVENTS FOR CHILDREN

From September through June a fine variety of programs—children's film classics, ballet, theater, concerts, and lectures—takes place on Saturdays. (Films at 1 and 3 P.M.; other programs at 11 A.M. and 1 P.M.) There is no charge for tickets. In the past such film classics as *Meet Me in St. Louis, King Solomon's Mines,* and *Teahouse of the August Moon* have been shown. Send requests for the calendar of events and tickets along with a stamped self-addressed envelope to Tickets, Civic Center Museum, 34th Street and Civic Center Boulevard, Philadelphia 19104. Separate requests are required for each event. Write about three weeks in advance.

EATING FACILITIES

University Museum restaurant; University Hospital snack bar and cafeteria. Or walk up to 38th and Walnut Streets, and you will find a variety of places on the University of Pennsylvania campus.

CONVENTION AND TRADE SHOW DIVISION

The Boat Show, Folk Fair, Ice Follies, Philadelphia String Bands Annual Show of Shows, and Flower Show make annual appearances at the Civic Center. These are always popular family events. Check newspapers or Civic Center for schedule of events.

HANDICAPPED

There is a side door and restroom facilities on the ground floor. Elevators can accommodate wheelchairs.

# NEW JERSEY STATE MUSEUM
205 West State Street (Cultural Center Complex)
Trenton, N.J. 08625

**Phone:** 1-609-292-6464 (a recorded message tells you exactly what's going on when and where throughout the museum)

**Open:** Monday–Saturday including holidays 9 A.M.–5 P.M., Sunday 2–5 P.M.
**Closed:** Fourth of July, Thanksgiving, Christmas, New Year's Day
**Admission:** Free
**Directions:** U.S. Route 1 into New Jersey (Calhoun Street), first right to Cultural Complex
**Public Transportation:** From Trenton railroad station, a short bus ride on West State Street

Three distinct facilities are housed here: the museum, the auditorium, and the planetarium. They are all part of the State Cultural Center Complex featuring astronomy, natural history, and fine arts. Within this fine Complex is a Natural Science Hall with exhibits of New Jersey mastodons, lifesize dioramas of the Pine Barrens and Island Beach areas, and artifacts relating to the Lenni-Lenape Indians. At the planetarium gallery you can see a 6-foot model of the near side of the moon and lunar material brought back by the astronauts of *Apollo 11*. There are changing exhibitions of American and European painting and sculpture and the decorative arts of New Jersey. Throughout the year this active museum features film series, many aimed especially at children, moon talks, and art gallery walks with a discussion of current exhibitions. Write to the Reservation Desk for School Groups for further details and information on group visits, or call 1-609-202-6347.

HANDICAPPED
Museum and restroom accessible.

**PEALE HOUSE**
1811 Chestnut Street
Philadelphia 19103

**Phone:** LO 4-0219
**Open:** Tuesday–Saturday 10 A.M.–5 P.M., Sunday 1–5 P.M.
**Closed:** Mondays
**Admission:** Free
**Public Transportation:** SEPTA Routes D, 17. 42, Suburban Station, Market Street lines

Part of the Pennsylvania Academy of the Fine Arts, Peale House has changing exhibits of contemporary art throughout the year.

## PENNSYLVANIA ACADEMY OF THE FINE ARTS
Broad and Cherry Streets
Philadelphia 19102

**Phone:** LO 4-0219
**Closed:** The Academy is closed for renovation until February 1976.
During this time exhibitions will be mounted at the Peale House,
1811 Chestnut Street; the Civic Center Museum; and other lo-
cations throughout the city. Call for information.
**Admission:** Free
**Parking:** Public lots nearby
**Public Transportation:** SEPTA Route C, Broad Street Subway to
Race–Vine stop, Cultural Loop bus (also a short walk from City
Hall)

Founded in 1805, this is the oldest art institution in the United
States. It's worth a visit for the building alone, even though it's
closed for renovation at present. A superb example of high Victorian architecture designed by Frank Furness and completed in
1876, it caused a sensation during the Centennial Exposition. The
collection contains masterpieces of American art from the Colonial
period to contemporary times, including the works of Stuart, Sully,
West, Peale, Cassatt, Eakins, Shahn, and Andrew Wyeth. In addition to its regular exhibitions, the Academy has been presenting
chamber music concerts for over twenty years.

MUSEUM SHOP

Art books and posters, interesting puzzles and games.

TOURS

By appointment only from September to July. Written requests
are preferable, but telephone reservations are accepted. Contact
Information on Guided Tours. No minimum number, maximum
number 80; 1 adult for every 10 children. Length of tour:
30–45 minutes.

MEMBERSHIP

Individual members receive notices of all Academy activities—
concerts, lectures, and motion pictures. Contributing membership
entitles you to club privileges at Peale Club, 1819 Chestnut Street.

## PENNSYLVANIA HORTICULTURAL SOCIETY
325 Walnut Street
Philadelphia 19106

**Phone:** WA 2-4801

**Open:** Weekdays 9 A.M.–5 P.M.
**Closed:** Weekends, all major holidays
**Admission:** Free
**Public Transportation:** SEPTA Routes D, 42, 50, Cultural Loop
bus, Mid City Loop bus

The Horticultural Society, the oldest society of its kind in America, founded in 1827, is a nonprofit organization of individuals interested in horticulture. They presented the magnificent Azalea Garden in Fairmount Park just west of the Art Museum to the city, and they sponsor the annual Philadelphia Flower and Garden Show in the spring at the Civic Center, the largest and finest flower show anywhere. Recently it has revived the Harvest Show in the fall at Memorial Hall in Fairmount Park. During December it has a display of spectacular Christmas decorations.

### SUMMER PROGRAMS FOR CHILDREN

A nine-week garden workshop at Morris Arboretum for children 10–14. Each child has his own garden to tend. Modest fee. The Society has also recently inaugurated a series of summer gardening programs for children 7–14 in all parks of the city. For further information call the Horticultural Society.

### SHOP

Books and assorted items, all related to horticulture; also a map of the Wissahickon, for which the Shop will accept telephone orders.

### MEMBERSHIP

A fee of $12.50 entitles you to monthly publications, use of the library, lectures, and a Flower Show ticket.

## PERELMAN ANTIQUE TOY MUSEUM
270 South 2nd Street
Philadelphia 19106

**Phone:** WA 2-1070
**Open:** Daily 9:30 A.M.–5 P.M.
**Closed:** Thanksgiving, Christmas, New Year's Day
**Admission:** Adults $1, children under 14 55¢
**Parking:** Street parking
**Public Transportation:** SEPTA Routes 5, 42

The world's largest collection of mechanical and still banks is here to see, along with massed displays of early tin toys, dolls, cap pistols, lead soldiers, the history of American transportation in toys, and a collection of marbles from all over the world. The toys are housed in well-lit glass cases on three separate floors. Visually the museum is a treat, but it would be more exciting to see the toys in operation.

GUIDED TOURS

Can be arranged for groups with a few days' notice. Write or call in advance. Minimum number for tour: 25; maximum number: 75. One adult for every 25 children. Group rate: Adults 75¢, children 40¢. Length of tour: About one hour.

HANDICAPPED

One step to enter. Elevator to upper floors and to restrooms. Handicapped groups have enjoyed visits here.

## PHILADELPHIA AQUARIUM

Philadelphia once had an aquarium—in those pseudo-Greek temple buildings of the old waterworks behind the Art Museum at the Schuylkill dam. The Philadelphia Aquarium Society (225 Port Royal Avenue, Philadelphia 19128) has been working to restore and reopen it. Until that's accomplished, you will find a collection of freshwater and saltwater fish at Martin's Aquarium (page 392).

## PHILADELPHIA ART ALLIANCE
251 South 18th Street
(Rittenhouse Square)
Philadelphia 19103

**Phone:** KI 5-4302
**Open:** Monday–Friday 10:30 A.M.–5 P.M., Saturday and Sunday 1–5 P.M.
**Closed:** Saturdays and Sundays in the summer, 2 weeks before Labor Day, major holidays
**Admission:** Free
**Parking:** Some street parking; public lots
**Public Transportation:** SEPTA Routes D, 17, 42, 90 to Rittenhouse Square

A nonprofit cultural and educational institution housed in a turn-of-the-century mansion, the Philadelphia Art Alliance presents changing exhibits in all the visual arts, crafts, and jewelry as well as performing arts events. The artists and craftsmen whose works are on exhibit come from all over the world; especial notice is given to those from the Philadelphia area. Exhibitions range from oils, watercolors, photography, and pottery to sculpture, weaving, and

American Indian designs and crafts. The Art Alliance is always worth a visit. The wide variety of exhibits almost guarantees something of interest for gallery-hoppers ages 10 and up.

Special programs for advanced high-school art students. Call for information.

Composers, authors, musicians, dancers, and theater personalities regularly appear at the Art Alliance's free evening lecture series. Call for information.

For a unique gift, check the Gallery Shop.

## PHILADELPHIA FIRE DEPARTMENT MUSEUM
149 North 2nd Street
Philadelphia 19106

**Phone:** 922-9844
**Open:** Tuesday–Sunday 10 A.M.–4 P.M.
**Closed:** Mondays, Good Friday, Labor Day, Thanksgiving, Christmas, New Year's Day
**Admission:** Free
**Parking:** On street
**Public Transportation:** SEPTA Route 5

This building was the original headquarters of Engine Company 8, the oldest continuously active fire company in the United States. Now it serves as a museum to preserve the colorful history and tradition of the Fire Department. It houses hand- and horse-drawn fire apparatus dating back to 1799, oldtime fire engines, uniforms, fire hats, and other displays relating to fire fighting. Future firemen will have a grand time visiting here.

GROUP TOURS

Telephone or write a few days in advance. Minimum number: 8–10; maximum number: 50. One adult for every 10 children. Length of tour: 30 minutes.

## PHILADELPHIA MARITIME MUSEUM
321 Chestnut Street
Philadelphia 19106

**Phone:** WA 5-5439
**Open:** September 15–June 15, Monday–Saturday 10 A.M.–4 P.M., Sunday 12 noon–5 P.M.; June 16–September 14, Monday–Saturday 10 A.M.–5 P.M., Sunday 12 noon–5 P.M.
**Closed:** Christmas, New Year's Day
**Admission:** Donations: adults 50¢, children under 12 25¢

**Restrictions:** Children must be accompanied by an adult
**Public Transportation:** SEPTA Routes 5, 42, Cultural Loop bus to
Independence Hall

Here is a fine collection of nautical history and maritime material
from the time of early sailing to modern vessels. Collections of
scrimshaw, old paintings and prints, ship's figureheads, models,
flags (including a reproduction of the Grand Union flag George
Washington raised in Boston in 1776), marvelous Liverpool jugs
and pitchers, and ship's logs are among the many artifacts on
display. An underwater museum gallery covers exploration of the
depths, and on exhibit is *Star I,* the one-man research submarine.

MUSEUM SHOP
Interesting seafaring memorabilia. Original scrimshaw.

SCHOOL GROUPS
Call in advance for reservation. Admission free. Maximum number: 40. Call WA 5-5440 from 1–4 P.M. Mondays and Tuesdays for
reservations. Length of tour: 1 hour. Lecturer for different grade
levels.

## *GAZELA PRIMEIRO*
Foot of Vine Street on the Delaware

**Phone:** WA 5-5439
**Open:** Memorial Day–Labor Day daily 12 noon–5 P.M.
**Closed:** Winters
**Admission:** Adults $1, children 50¢
**Parking:** At the river

See the last of the Portuguese fishing vessels, built circa 1883,
with its impressive rigging and white sails. It is preserved in sailing
condition by the Philadelphia Maritime Museum in memory of
Portuguese seamen and all other seamen who have gone "down to
the sea in ships."

## PHILADELPHIA MUSEUM OF ART
Benjamin Franklin Parkway at 26th Street
Philadelphia 19130

**Phone:** PO 3-8100; or PO 5-3800 for a recorded message of current
exhibits and events
**Open:** Tuesday–Sunday 9 A.M.–5 P.M.
**Closed:** Mondays, all legal holidays

**Admission:** Adults $1, children (to 18) 25¢, students with I.D. card free; free Sunday until 1 P.M. and all day Tuesday

**Restrictions:** Cameras permitted, but no tripods or flash

**Parking:** Free. Entrance to parking area on East River Drive. Parking also permitted in Thomas Eakins Circle in front of the Museum on the Gene Davis street painting. Billed as the world's largest painting, this design of multicolored stripes measures 414 feet × 76 feet. It's probably the most colorful parking lot in the world and is best viewed from the East Terrace of the Art Museum.

The Philadelphia Museum of Art

**Public Transportation:** SEPTA A local to 25th Street (entrance at ground level through the tunnel), or Cultural Loop bus.

**Picnicking and Eating Facilities:** Picnicking permitted in Fairmount Park directly behind the museum. Restaurant (Phone: PO 3-1600), with Bauhaus-inspired decor and expensive menu, open Tuesday–Friday 11:30–3:30, Wednesday–Saturday 5–10 P.M. for dinner; cafeteria, pleasant and with reasonable prices, open daily, except Monday.

**Membership:** Individual $15, family $25. Higher categories of membership available. Any amount of membership over $15 is tax deductible. *Benefits:* Free admission to Art Museum, Rodin Museum, Cedar Grove, and Mount Pleasant; invitations to pre-

views; discounts at Museum Shop; adult and children's workshops; rental of original works from Art Sales and Rental Gallery; publications. For more information call Membership Office,
PO 3-8100.

Overlooking the Benjamin Franklin Parkway to the east and the
Schuylkill River to the west rises the Philadelphia Museum of Art,
an imposing Greco-Roman structure first opened to the public in
1928. It offers fascinating views of the city and art treasures from
the pre-Columbian and early Renaissance periods to the modern
masters, from the Far East to the Pennsylvania Dutch. One of the
leading art museums in the country, it covers 10 acres and should
be visited for more than just a morning. Those living in the area
return to it regularly. For, in addition to its prized permanent collection, its temporary exhibitions, either on loan or mounted by the
museum staff, offer a variety of subjects—and you never know what
will fascinate a given age group.

Where you start your visit will probably depend on your interests and whether a gallery is open on that particular day. If you're
heading for a specific gallery, it might be wise to call in advance.
Unfortunately, lack of funds and personnel has forced the museum
to close sections on a rotating basis. In any event, pick up a semi-
helpful map at the Information Desk. It will tell where the Medieval
art is—but not that you'll find an eleventh-century Romanesque
cloister there, that the Japanese Art section has a ceremonial teahouse, that the John G. Johnson Collection spans the fourteenth to
the nineteenth centuries and includes early Renaissance paintings,
or that you will find an elaborate fifteenth-century Italian choir
screen on the second floor. If it's the history of Western art you're
after, just keep going through the Johnson Collection to the Renoirs,
Manets, Rouaults, Matisses and on to the Louise and Walter
Arensberg Collection of Dali, Duchamp, Brancusi, Miró, and Arp.
It's really not imperative to know whose collection you're viewing,
but that's the way most of the works are displayed—for obvious
reasons. The Eakinses, Sargents, and Peales, however, hang logi-
cally in the section labeled "American Painting."

The period rooms—French, English, American, Medieval, and
Renaissance—the Pennsylvania Dutch Galleries, the Fashion Wing,
and the Decorative Arts Galleries are always popular with children
(but are also the ones most often closed). Tapestries are more
interesting when you realize they were functional as well as decorative; elaborate candelabra are more meaningful when seen in an
eighteenth-century room. The simple Quaker outfits and elab-

orate Colonial costumes almost always provoke the same comment: "How small the people were!" (And the 1930s fashions don't look so strange any more.)

In the Great Stair Hall you can stand under the enormous Alexander Calder mobile, and look down the Parkway to the Swan Fountain in Logan Square done by his father, Alexander Stirling Calder, and on to the 37-foot statue of William Penn atop City Hall, done by his grandfather, Alexander Milne Calder. Also in the Great Stair Hall is the Saint-Gaudens statue of Diana, the Huntress, which once stood on top of Madison Square Garden in New York City. Philadelphia has rejected suggestions by New York City that it be returned.

Ask one of the attendants for directions to the Wintersteen Student Center Gallery with its changing exhibits. Though it is theoretically geared for the 12-year-old, those much younger and much older have been equally fascinated by such exhibits as *The Mind's Eye, Impact Africa, 1492* (a look at seven civilizations around the world at the time of Columbus's voyage), and *The Invisible Artist*.

### VOLUNTEER GUIDES

A group of highly trained, well-informed people who provide free one-hour gallery tours several times a day. Check the bulletin board or at the Information Desk for the schedule. If you're interested in a specific gallery and want to be certain it is open, call the Volunteer Guides Office (PO 3-8100) and arrange a tour for a group (minimum number: 5). They prefer a week's notice, but it can be done with less if necessary. With advance notice a Volunteer Guide will take you through even though the gallery is closed that day. Special group tours of the permanent collection as well as current special exhibitions and foreign-language tours can also be arranged. For more information call Volunteer Guides Office.

The Volunteer Guides will also take the museum to your group, club, hospital, school, or organization. With their projector and slides, they will present a 45-minute program about the Museum and its collections, period rooms, and conservation work. No charge; minimum number: 10. For more information on their mini-tours call the Volunteer Guides Office (PO 3-8100).

### COLONIAL MANSIONS IN THE PARK

Six of the Colonial mansions in Fairmount Park are open to the public and can be seen either independently or on a tour. To those interested in the eighteenth century these homes present a marvelous picture of Colonial life and architecture. Children enjoy Cedar Grove, Mount Pleasant, and Strawberry Mansion the most. For a more detailed description see Chapter 3. Call Park House Office (PO 3-8100) for information on tours to suit your particular group or interests. It's a great idea for a birthday party activity.

CONCERTS

Sundays at 3:30 P.M. in the Van Pelt Auditorium (not held in summer). Free with admission to the Museum. Not for all ages but for those who enjoy concert-going. This series of professional string ensembles, woodwind quintets, and soloists has been a popular attraction over the years. The Museum is free on Sundays until 1 P.M., so plan to get there early and see one or two exhibits beforehand.

FILMS

Saturdays at 10 A.M. and 2 P.M. Free with admission to the Museum. It can be anything from Tom Mix (with piano accompaniment) to W. C. Fields, *A Member of the Wedding, The Yellow Submarine,* or a Katharine Hepburn retrospective. Call the Museum for current listing.

SHOPS

*Museum Shop.* East Entrance. Books on art and architecture around the world including folk art, crafts, and decorative arts. An excellent selection of art books for children. You'll also find jigsaw puzzles, embroidery kits, postcards, jewelry, sculpture, and posters—and Christmas cards in season.

*Art Sales and Rental Gallery.* Balcony off West Foyer. Open 10:30 A.M.–12 noon, 1–4:30 P.M. Paintings, prints, photographs, sculpture by Chagall, Shahn, Baskin, Motherwell, Davis, to name a few. For sale to the general public. Members may rent works and apply rental fee to purchase price.

*Children's Shop.* Adjacent to Student Center. Open Monday–Friday 9:30 A.M.–4:30 P.M. Thoughtful selection of books, prints, craft projects, and gifts items priced for a juvenile's budget.

WORKSHOPS

For ages 6–15. Winter sessions Saturdays; summer sessions weekdays. Students have an opportunity to work in various media: painting, printmaking, sculpture, drawing. Filmmaking for ages 14–22. Summer Talk and Sketch program for groups only includes a guided gallery tour and an afternoon art class. Workshops for adults also. For more information on workshops and programs call the Division of Education, PO 3-8100.

DEPARTMENT OF URBAN OUTREACH

Rather than wait for children to come to the Art Museum, this dynamic group has been taking the museum out into the community. Those colorfully decorated SEPTA buses and many of the exciting wall murals around the city are a few of the projects created by the workshops in art, music, dance, and film set up in various sections of the city and suburbs. For more information on their work and locations call Department of Urban Outreach, PO 3-8100.

GROUP VISITS

Adults 75¢, children 15¢. Minimum number 20. By advance reservation through Volunteer Guides office.

HANDICAPPED

Entrance at tunnel on East River Drive side. Drive in to passenger elevator. Museum accessible by elevator. Restrooms near restaurant accessible. Guides for the blind can be arranged through the Division of Education, for the deaf through Volunteer Guide Office.

## PHILADELPHIA ZOOLOGICAL GARDEN
34th Street and Girard Avenue
Philadelphia 19104

**Phone:** BA 2-5300
**Open:** Daily 9:30 A.M.–5 P.M. (later on weekends and holidays during warmer months)
**Closed:** Thanksgiving, Christmas Eve, Christmas, New Year's Day
**Admission:** Adults $1.75, children 2–11 50¢, under 2 free. Extras: Children's Zoo, 25¢ per person; Hummingbird Exhibit, 25¢ per person (free during winter months); Monorail, adults $1, children 50¢ (operates April–November).
**Restrictions:** No strollers or carriages in Reptile, Small Mammal, and Hummingbird Houses. No pets.
**Parking:** Free parking areas: Two on 34th Street, two on Girard Avenue; bicycle rack at North Gate
**Directions:** Schuylkill Expressway to Girard Avenue exit. Or West River Drive to Sweetbrier cutoff and follow signs to zoo.
**Public Transportation:** SEPTA Routes 15 trolley, 38 bus to Zoo stop, Cultural Loop bus
**Picnicking:** There's a pavilion and picnic ground with tables and benches near the Children's Zoo, additional tables near Sea Lion Pool. Both operate on a first-come, first-served basis. No fires or

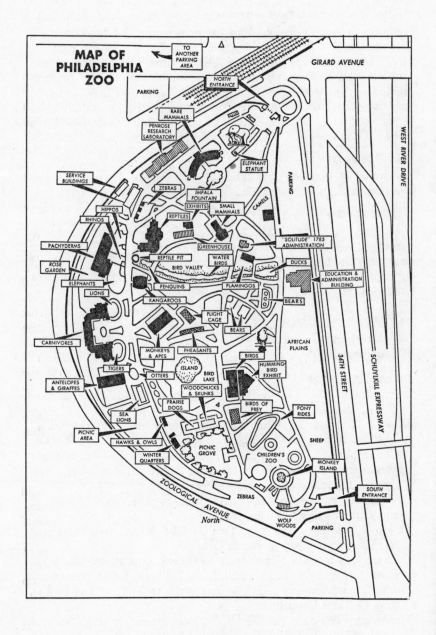

The Philadelphia Zoo

alcoholic beverages. Refreshment stands throughout the zoo, but only one open during winter.

The Philadelphia Zoo covers 42 acres in Fairmount Park, which means there's a lot to see in one day. So put on your walking shoes and go early, particularly during the warmer months: A visit to the Zoo is one of the more popular places for a family outing, even though the cost climbs steadily. Eighty percent of the zoo is indoors, and all ten buildings are open throughout the year, though most people limit their trips here to warm, sunny weather. Try it in the winter. It's especially lovely after a snowstorm. The tigers and lions may be indoors, but deer, wolves, and seals will be out, as will many of the other 1,400 birds, mammals, and reptiles living here.

Everyone has his own favorite animals here. However, in addition to seeing the elephants, rhinos, kangaroos, flamingos, orangutans, and trumpet swans, visit the naturalistic habitat exhibits of the Wolf Woods and the Reptile House; the latter contains everything from crocodiles and Galapagos tortoises to the snakes you might meet in the Pine Barrens, plus an electronically controlled tropical thunderstorm (stand at the center window for the best view). Unfortunately, many of the exhibits of snakes are a bit high for small children, so be prepared to do some lifting. Don't miss the exquisite Hummingbird Exhibit. These tiny, brightly colored creatures fly freely among the flowers, trees, ferns, and waterfalls within inches of your head as you follow the walkway through the tropical American jungle setting. Bring your camera and plan to linger.

The African Plains Exhibit is the newest project to provide naturalistic settings for compatible species such as zebras, giraffes, antelopes, ostriches, and cranes.

### CHILDREN'S ZOO

The Zoo's touch-it museum. Barnyard animals and baby wild animals can be petted, studied, fed, and admired at close range. It's also a good spot for a brief rest while watching an animal demonstration. Sort of show-and-tell in reverse: This time the children listen while one of the hostesses introduces and talks about some of her "friends"—snakes, opossums, monkeys.

And then there's that Monorail constantly circling at treetop level. The twenty-minute ride, which operates from April to November, gives you a passing glance at the whole area.

A good souvenir for everyone is the Storybook Key (50¢). It turns on taped descriptions of the animals at various places and can be used on return visits. For the smaller children bring your own stroller or rent one at the Main Gate (no charge to members of the Zoo).

The feeding schedule for some of the favorites: lions and tigers, 3 P.M.; hippos, 4 P.M.; sea lions and otters, 11 A.M. and 4 P.M.; bears 3:30 P.M.

The Philadelphia Zoo is also a fine horticultural garden. The trees and flowers are all clearly labeled.

### ADDITIONAL INFORMATION

*High-School Students:* High-school girls are employed as hostesses at the Children's Zoo. They must be willing to handle small reptiles and mammals and able to speak to groups. It's a fulltime job (40 hours each week) during the summer months. Training program includes how to handle both animals and presentation material. Apply early in February to Superintendent at Children's Zoo.

### SPECIAL EVENTS

Monkey Island Day: A Sunday in May; contests and prizes to celebrate the monkeys' move to their summer residence.

### GROUP VISITS

Rates: Monday–Saturday. Minimum number 15; adults 75¢, children 2–11 35¢. No advance reservations for groups under 50. One person should pay at gate. Monorail: Minimum number 15; adults 65¢, children 35¢.

### TOURS

September–May. Call Zoo Docent Council.

### HANDICAPPED

Many buildings have ramps. Wheelchairs available for small fee at Main Gate. Restrooms have one step; booth doors are narrow. Parking adjacent.

### MEMBERSHIP

Various classifications from $20. *Benefits:* Free admission to Main Zoo, Children's Zoo, Hummingbird Exhibit. Book of twenty free tickets for friends and guests. Subscription to Zoo magazine.

## THE PRINT CLUB
1614 Latimer Street
Philadelphia 19103

Phone: PE 5-6090

**Open:** Wednesday after Labor Day–June 15, Monday–Friday
10 A.M.–5 P.M.; October–May, Saturday 12 noon–4 P.M.
**Closed:** Sundays, mid-June to Wednesday after Labor Day, most
national holidays
**Admission:** Free
**Parking:** Public lots nearby
**Public Transportation:** SEPTA Routes 2, 90
**Membership:** Annual single $15, family $20, artist $10, student $5.
*Benefits:* Lectures, receptions, discounts, advice on collecting

Changing exhibits of contemporary prints, graphics, and photography are on display and for sale at this unique house on Latimer Street. The established printmakers—Daumier, Rouault—are here as well as new discoveries.

### PRINTS IN PROGRESS

These programs work with young people in the inner city to encourage their participation in the arts and prepare them for future careers in the field. At the various workshops children learn the art of print-making, such as silkscreen, etching, lithography, and woodcut. For information on locations and hours, call the Print Club.

Prints in Progress maintains a booth at Head House Square Open Air Market (page 262), where you can see and purchase their cards, prints, and fabrics.

## RODIN MUSEUM
Benjamin Franklin Parkway and 22nd Street
Philadelphia 19130

**Phone:** PO 3-8100 (Rodin is administered by the Art Museum)
**Open:** Tuesday–Sunday 9 A.M.–5 P.M.
**Closed:** All legal holidays, Mondays
**Admission:** Adults 50¢; children under 18 25¢; students with I.D.
card free. Combined Art Museum and Rodin Museum ticket
$1.25. Free Sundays until 1 P.M. and all day Tuesday; free to
members of Philadelphia Museum of Art.
**Restrictions:** Cameras permitted but no tripods or flash
**Parking:** Small lot behind Rodin Museum, entrance on 22nd
Street; no sign. Free parking also at Art Museum at 26th and
Parkway. Street parking sometimes available.
**Public Transportation:** SEPTA Route A bus stops at 22nd and
Pennsylvania Avenue just behind the museum, Cultural Loop
bus stops directly in front of museum

**Picnicking:** In Fairmount Park behind the Art Museum
**Eating Facilities:** At the Art Museum and the cafeteria in the
  Free Library at 20th Street

This small museum, given to Philadelphia by Jules E. Mastbaum,
contains the largest collection of Rodin works outside Paris, many
of them cast especially for Mr. Mastbaum. In addition to the
bronzes, there are drawings and prints by Rodin. Recently paintings
and sculptures by friends and contemporaries of Rodin have been
added.

Just as *The Thinker* dominates the entrance, so Rodin's monumental *Burghers of Calais* dominates the main room. But his studies
of hands, his animals and smaller statues are all fascinating—and all
touchable. It's a serene, rather elegant spot and rarely crowded.
On a bright day it is a good place for photographers—both indoors
and out.

### GROUP VISITS

By appointment only two weeks in advance. Group rate:
adults 25¢, children 15¢; minimum number 20. For guided tours call
Volunteer Guides Office at Art Museum (PO 3-8100). Schools
call Division of Education at Art Museum. Minimum age: 4th
grade. Maxmum number 20.

### THE ROSENBACH FOUNDATION MUSEUM
2010 Delancey Place
(Between Spruce and Pine Streets)
Philadelphia 19103

**Phone:** 732-1600
**Open:** September–May, Tuesday–Sunday 2–5 P.M.; June and July,
  Monday–Friday 2–5 P.M. Open to groups between 10 A.M. and
  5 P.M. by appointment only.
**Closed:** Mondays, weekends in June and July, all of August, legal
  holidays
**Admission:** Adults $1, students and under 18 free
**Parking:** Street parking scarce, public lots nearby
**Public Transportation:** SEPTA Route 17 to 19th Street (between
  Spruce and Pine)

In a nineteenth-century townhouse on Delancey Place is an
incomparable and unique museum emphasizing rare books and
manuscripts, but here also are fine antiques, rugs, and paintings—
and the house is indeed a beautiful showcase for the priceless
treasures displayed. Bibliophiles from around the world come to
visit. It is the inspiration of two Rosenbach brothers: Philip H., who

collected antiques; and Dr. A. S. W., the dean of rare book collectors.

In this peerless collection you can see over a hundred letters written by George Washington, the finest known first edition of Cervantes' *Don Quixote,* and Dickens's manuscripts for *Pickwick Papers* and *Nicholas Nickleby*—as well as manuscripts of Scott, Wordsworth, Lamb, Shelley, and Keats. Hundreds of letters of Lewis Carroll are here, and a copy of the first edition of *Alice in Wonderland,* with original drawings by John Tenniel, that Lewis Carroll kept for his own use. The manuscript of James Joyce's *Ulysses* has been in the collection since 1924. Twentieth-century poetry is well represented, with great masses of Dylan Thomas, Pound, and Eliot. Don't miss seeing the Marianne Moore Room on the third floor; it contains her entire literary effects, furnishings, library, and her famous black cloak and three-cornered hat.

If you call ahead and state your interest, highly knowledgeable people will gather together the material. Children are welcome, but the collections are geared more to adults, with the exception of original Maurice Sendak drawings. The Rosenbach Museum is the sole repository for all of Sendak's manuscripts and drawings. You can purchase highly amusing and distinctive holiday greeting cards by Maurice Sendak and Marianne Moore. If books are your interest, don't miss a visit here.

GROUP VISITS

High School age suggested. Minimum number for guided tour: 8; maximum: 25 with two adults. Telephone requests are accepted with at least a week's notice. Group rate 50¢.

*U.S.S. OLYMPIA* (Admiral Dewey's Flagship)
Pier 11 North
Delaware Avenue and Race Street
Philadelphia 19106

**Phone:** WA 2-1898
**Open:** Easter–November 1, Monday–Saturday 10 A.M.–4 P.M., Sundays and holidays 11 A.M.–6 P.M.; November–Easter, Thursday–Saturday 10 A.M.–4 P.M., Sundays and holidays 11 A.M.– 5 P.M.
**Closed:** Thanksgiving, Christmas, New Year's Day
**Admission:** Adults $1, children under 12 50¢
**Directions:** It's right under the Benjamin Franklin Bridge.
**Parking:** Free on Delaware Avenue
**Public Transportation:** SEPTA Routes 17, 33 to Front and Market

Streets, then one block east to Delaware Avenue and two blocks
north

The *U.S.S Olympia* is the last survivor of the Spanish-American
War fleets. On this flagship Admiral Dewey said, "You may fire
when ready, Gridley." This is definitely a spot for active kids. They
can climb all over the ship from the engine room to the crew's
quarters to the captain's cabin to the bridge. There's a display of
Naval artifacts and history from *Old Ironsides* to World War II.
Wear sturdy shoes, because there are lots of steep metal stairs.
Don't take very small children who can't manage all the ladders.
And don't forget it's on the waterfront, where it is even colder in
cold weather.

SHIP'S STORE

For snacks and souvenirs.

GROUP VISITS

Adults 75¢, children under 12 35¢. Minimum number 15. At least
one week's advance notice. Written requests are preferable, but
telephone reservations are accepted. Minimum age suggested: 8
years. One adult for every 15 children. Length of tour: 1 hour.

NEARBY

Pier 11 North is also home port for the Police Marine Unit, Fire-
boat Engine 15, and the Philadelphia Harbor Tours (page 291).
The Portuguese square-rigger *Gazela Primeiro* is docked a block
away (page 108). And Downtown Airlines has it   ield" at Delaware Avenue near the foot of Walnut Street. Or just go out on the
jetty and watch the freighters go by.

## THE UNIVERSITY MUSEUM OF THE
## UNIVERSITY OF PENNSYLVANIA

33rd and Spruce Streets
Philadelphia 19174

**Phone:** EV 6-7400
**Open:** Tuesday–Saturday 10 A.M.–5 P.M., Sunday 1–5 P.M.
**Closed:** Mondays, all legal holidays
**Admission:** Free. Children under 12 must be accompanied by an
adult.
**Directions:** Schuylkill Expressway to South Street exit. Turn west
one block. Museum is on the left.
**Parking:** $1.25 next door, or on the street in the University area
if you can find a spot

**Public Transportation:** SEPTA Routes D, D-1 from Penn Central 30th Street Station, 40, 42

**Eating Facilities:** Potlatch Restaurant, open Tuesday–Saturday 10 A.M.–4 P.M. Cafeteria style. In the new wing overlooking the garden.

The University Museum contains one of the largest and finest archaeological collections in the country. The permanent collection is attractively displayed, presenting a choice exhibition of the life

Ceremonial Masks at University Museum

and art of ancient and primitive civilizations–the Indians of the Americas (from the Eskimos of Alaska to the Indians of Chile), the Islands of the Pacific, Africa, the Classical World, Egypt, China, and the Lands of the Bible.

Pick up a floor plan at the entrance. It will help you with your own "digs" in this unique museum. Anyone from the ages of 6 or 7 on up with an inquiring mind can find much that is fascinating. Children will enjoy seeing the jewelry of a queen of Mesopotamia in 500 B.C. and the full-length feather cloak of a Hawaiian high chief. Indian arrowheads, a Colt pistol, and African drums and nail fetishes will undoubtedly intrigue them also. The Ancient American Gold Room, with its priceless collection of crowns, necklaces, figurines, breastplates, pendants, and bracelets, is a dazzling display for everyone. These are samples of the gold the Spaniards were seeking in Central and South America during the sixteenth century. The Charles H. Curtis Hall containing the China exhibit and the

Egyptian mummies is often closed for luncheons and receptions. If you are planning to visit this section, it would be wise to check ahead of time. Special exhibits are mounted during the year. Call for information or check the papers.

### THE NEVIL GALLERY FOR THE BLIND AND SIGHTED

A permanent section of archaeological exhibits for the visually handicapped, it's definitely "touch-it" style. The emphasis is on texture, contour, and sound. Braille and large-type labels along a railing identify the objects, which are on revolving pedestals. It's a fascinating gallery even for those with no sight problems. You suddenly "see" another world.

### CHILDREN'S PROGRAMS

On Saturday mornings during the winter there is a film program for children at 10:30 A.M. in the museum auditorium. Admission is free. Films in the past have included *Nanook of the North, White Mane, Island of the Blue Dolphin.*

### ADULT PROGRAMS

On Sundays at 2:30 the museum presents a film and concert series. Children are admitted with an adult. No groups of children or teenagers. Admission is free. A guided gallery tour at 1:30 is offered covering related material. Some of these films might also be of interest to children. *Aku-Aku* (about Easter Island), *Elizabethan England and the Spanish Armada,* and *Drums Along the Mohawk* have been presented in the past. For information on the series call the Education Section or send a 10-inch stamped, self-addressed envelope for the schedules.

### MUSEUM SHOP

The Museum Shop at the Main Entrance sells reproductions from casts made in their workshops. Prices range from 25 cents for an ancient Carthaginian coin to whatever your pocketbook permits for books, exquisite jewelry, rugs, and original items of sculpture. You can shop around the world: from Bali, to Ethiopia, to Guatemala, and on to Thailand.

### THE PYRAMID SHOP

Open Tuesday–Friday 10:30 A.M.–4 P.M., Saturday 11 A.M.–3 P.M., this cheerful shop is meant for children. Prices start at 1¢ for a marble and go on up, with a wide selection under and around $1. Tomahawks, design-your-own kite kits, Indian masks, arrowhead jewelry, puzzles, tops, and games. Everyone is encouraged to touch, feel, and see how it works.

WORKSHOPS

Recently the Museum's Department of Education has been developing Saturday programs in archaeology and anthropology for children and teenagers. Open to members of the Museum only. (Junior membership for ages 8 to 16 is $4.) Workshops for ages 8 to 15 have included making pottery as the ancient Egyptians did, a visit to a "dig" in the Society Hill area, and woodcarving sessions with Northwest Coast Indians. High-school students have been learning archaeological techniques by establishing sites at Valley Forge and in the Wissahickon. For more information call the Department of Education.

The Ethnic Arts Division uses the Museum's collection of costumes, masks, and ancient instruments for its program. High-school and college students with a serious interest in musical instruments are restoring antique gongs, guitars, drums, and chimes to playing condition. Children study the music, dance, and ceremonies of Asia, Africa, India, and the Middle East and present a concert in costume at the end of the six-week session. Ethnic groups may also use the facilities of this department. For more information call the Ethnic Arts Division, ext. 309.

GROUP VISITS

By appointment only. Telephone secretary of Education Department Tuesday–Friday 10 A.M.–12 noon, 1–4:30 P.M. Minimum number: 10; maximum number: 40.

HANDICAPPED

Entrance through Kress Gallery (school bus entrance). If you will announce yourself at the yellow barrier, they will open the gate to admit your car. Attendants will tell you which are the best elevators. Wheelchair available.

MEMBERSHIP

Junior (8–16) $4, individual $20, family $25. Additional categories. *Benefits:* Workshops, publications, discount at Museum Shop, special events.

## WAR LIBRARY AND MUSEUM
1805 Pine Street
Philadelphia 19103

**Phone:** PE 5-8196
**Open:** Monday, Wednesday, Friday 12 noon–4 P.M.; other times by appointment
**Closed:** Weekends, holidays

**Admission:** Free; guided tours only
**Parking:** On street
**Public Transportation:** SEPTA Routes 2, 17, 90

Don't be put off by the name. This is an interesting place. In an old house on Pine Street in what at first appears to be a repository of old war relics is quartered a marvelous collection of memorabilia for Civil War and Lincoln buffs. The rooms get better as you wander through the Confederate, Grant, and Navy Rooms, and then upstairs to the Lincoln Room with life masks of Mr. Lincoln, the Relics Room full of unusual medals, holsters, and garb of the soldiers, and finally to the Weapons Room with an astounding arsenal of pistols, swords, muskets, shells, and powder flasks. Throughout the halls are colorful lithographs and handbills of the period. A knowledgeable guide takes you through with or without prior appointment.

GROUP VISITS
Call in advance. They prefer groups of 10 with 1 adult.

## THE HENRY FRANCIS DU PONT
## WINTERTHUR MUSEUM
Del. Route 52
Winterthur, Del. 19735

**Phone:** 1-302-656-8591
**Restrictions:** Guided tours a must in Museum; you can wander on your own in gardens
**Open:**

MAIN MUSEUM
By advance reservations only. No children under 16. Tuesday–Saturday 9:30 A.M.–4:00 P.M.

SOUTH WING
No reservations needed. Children accompanied by adults permitted. Tuesday–Saturday 9:30 A.M.–4 P.M. Also open Sunday mid-April through October. Adults $1; children 6–16 50¢, under 6 free. Tour approximately 1 hour long.

SEASONAL TOURS
Gardens and portions of the Museum. No reservations needed.
*Spring:* Spring Flower and Azalea Gardens and thirty period rooms in the museum. Mid-April to late May. Tuesday–Sunday 10 A.M.–4 P.M. Admission: Gardens $1; Main Museum (16 rooms) $1.50; South Wing (14 rooms) $1. Children under 16 with

adults 50¢. Under 6 free. Tour of thirty rooms takes about two hours. Allow about 1½ hours for a stroll through the gardens.

*Summer:* Gardens and fourteen rooms of South Wing, June through September, Tuesday–Sunday 10 A.M.–4 P.M. Admission: Gardens $1. Fourteen rooms: $1. Children under 16 with adult 50¢. Under 6 free. Allow an hour for tour of rooms and 1½ hours for a stroll through the gardens.

*Autumn:* Gardens, five rooms of H. F. Du Pont House and fourteen rooms of South Wing. October. Tuesday–Sunday 10 A.M.–4 P.M. Admission: Adults $3. Children under 16 with adult 50¢. Under 6 free.

**Closed:** Mondays, July 4, Thanksgiving, December 24, Christmas, New Year's day; also Sundays, November–mid-April. Main Museum also closed week preceding and following special spring tour.

**Directions:** Schuylkill Expressway to City Line Avenue (U.S. Route 1) south, left on Pa. Route 52. Entrance to museum on left 2.3 miles beyond Pennsylvania–Delaware state line. *Or* Route 291 to north of Chester, then I-95 to Route 52. Entrance on right 2 miles beyond railroad crossing at Greenville Shopping Center.

**Restrictions:** Cameras permitted outdoors only. No narrow heels in Museum.

**Parking:** Ample facilities

**Eating Facilities:** No picnicking permitted. Luncheon served cafeteria style in the delightful Garden Pavilion 11 A.M.–2 P.M. Sandwiches, desserts, and beverages until 4 P.M.

Mention the name "Winterthur" to anyone interested in American decorative arts and you're bound to get a very special, very positive response. For here is one of the finest collections of American antiques from the seventeenth to the early nineteenth century. Formerly the residence of Henry Francis Du Pont, the Museum was opened in 1951 and contains over 100 period rooms with exquisite examples of architecture, furniture, textiles, silver, ceramics, paintings, and prints. The rooms—bedrooms, parlors, drawing rooms, dining rooms—are carefully furnished to the smallest detail, as they might have been originally used. Colonial arrangements of fresh flowers and fruits are in appropriate spots.

It's definitely not a touch-it museum. Even the guides are not permitted to touch anything; they are, however, extremely well trained and informative. Children under 10 may not be too much interested in the museum, but there are plenty of winding paths in the gardens.

In the sixty acres of the Winterthur Gardens are almost every species of flower, tree, and shrub that will grow in Delaware— naturalized plantings, formal gardens, wooded paths, open lawns and hillsides, and tall trees. Just follow the arrows or wander as you please. It's especially beautiful in spring and fall.

GROUP TOURS

*Main Museum.* Minimum age 16. Forty-eight people for each half-day tour, divided into groups of four. Individual visitors join other groups. By advance reservation only. Write Reservations Office and include alternate date.

*Regular Tours:* One half of the museum in the morning; one half in the afternoon. Fee: $4 each half-day tour.

*Special Subject Tours* also available. Write for brochure.

*Junior Student Tour Program.* Grades 5–9. Life in the early American home. Tour and touch-it session.

*Senior Student Tour Program.* High-school, college, and adult education groups. Tailored to needs and interests of group. For further information write Education Division. Fee for student tours: 25¢.

**WISTAR INSTITUTE OF ANATOMY AND BIOLOGY**
36th and Spruce Streets
Philadelphia 19104

**Phone:** EV 7-6700
**Open:** Monday–Friday 9 A.M.–4 P.M.
**Closed:** Saturdays, Sundays, all legal holidays
**Admission:** Free
**Directions:** Schuylkill Expressway to South Street exit, then west to 36th Street (South Street becomes Spruce Street at 33rd Street)
**Parking:** Metered and street parking, particularly if University is not in session; parking lots in the area
**Public Transportation:** SEPTA Routes D, D-1 from Penn Central 30th Street Station, 40, 42

Definitely not for a casual museum visit. But if you've ever wondered why an infant's head must be protected, or how the human skull develops, or how to tell a female skeleton from a male skeleton, the answers are probably all here at the Wistar Institute. Founded in 1891, it is the oldest biological research institution in the United States.

It's ideal for children aged 10 and up with a question or two about the bone structure of the body, its development, and related subjects. There are Lucite models and embalmed exhibits as well.

GROUP VISITS

Call a day in advance. Minimum age 10; 1 adult for every 15 children. No fee. No guided tour. Allow about ½ hour for your visit.

NEARBY

International House, 3701 Chestnut Street. Pleasant cafeteria and an architecturally interesting building.

## WOODMERE ART GALLERY
9201 Germantown Avenue
Philadelphia 19118

Phone: CH 7-0476
Open: Monday–Saturday 10 A.M.–5 P.M.; summers 10 A.M.–4 P.M., Sunday 2–6 P.M.
Closed: All legal holidays
Admission: Free
Restrictions: Children under 14 must be accompanied by an adult. No strollers. Cameras permitted.
Directions: East River Drive to Lincoln Drive to Allens Lane, right to Germantown Avenue, left on Germantown Avenue
Parking: On gallery grounds or on street
Public Transportation: SEPTA Route 23 trolley *or* Reading and Penn Central trains to Chestnut Hill Station; then 6 blocks to gallery.

Exhibitions feature area artists and some craft displays. This community art center also contains a permanent collection housed in the Victorian mansion—the former home of Charles Knox Smith, who on his death left his valuable collection of paintings, furniture, magnificent Persian rugs, ivories, and all for the public to see. The house is a Victorian delight—it is elaborately furnished and features a Meissen chandelier and mirror frame, and bell jars made entirely from shell.

There are Saturday-morning classes for children as well as classes for adults in drawing and painting. The Philadelphia Guild of Handweavers holds classes here for beginners as well as more advanced students.

# 3
# FAIRMOUNT PARK

Fairmount Park is the largest city-owned park in the world. Its four thousand acres contain recreational facilities, a theater, picnic areas, woods for hiking, sculpture, outdoor concerts, the first zoological gardens in this country, the site of the Centennial Exposition, and an outstanding group of Colonial mansions.

Its name is derived from the hill, Faire Mount (the site of the Art Museum), mentioned in the survey made for William Penn. Faire Mount lay beyond the 2-square-mile city plan and was originally intended for Penn's use. In the early nineteenth century it became the location of the city's reservoir and water supply. In 1812 the city bought 5 acres of Faire Mount and built the reservoir for the Philadelphia waterworks where the Art Museum now stands. The neoclassical buildings built along the river to house the pumping station are still standing.

In 1822 a dam across the Schuylkill River was completed for the purpose of increasing the water supply, and the river became much wider. The area around the pumping station became so popular with the residents that the city fathers had it landscaped for a park. A Sunday stroll in the gardens along the river and in Laurel Hill Cemetery was the fashionable activity of the early nineteenth century. Additional land along the river was acquired to preserve the purity of the water. But it was the city's purchase of Lemon Hill, Robert Morris's estate, in 1844 that set the pattern for Fairmount Park. A city ordinance was passed in 1855 placing the land in trust for Philadelphia citizens, and in 1867 the Fairmount Park Commission was established. Since then the park has been expanded to its present size by purchase or donation.

Fairmount Park has withstood many attempts to convert its land to other uses. Generations of Philadelphians have cherished and enjoyed this remarkable park. It is indeed an outstanding feature of Philadelphia.

## Colonial Mansions

The Fairmount Park mansions offer visitors and residents a rare treat, quite unique to Philadelphia: beautiful examples of Colonial architecture and interiors in a country setting within the city limits. Overlooking the Schuylkill River, these homes were the country seats of the prosperous Philadelphia gentlemen who also maintained townhouses near the State House (now Independence Hall), the focal point of power and politics.

Philadelphia in the mid-eighteenth century was the geographical and trade center of the Colonies, as well as the center for banking, finance, publishing, and the arts. By 1775 the city had grown to 20,000 and was the largest city in the Colonies and one of the largest cities in the British Empire as a whole. It was the center of all activities for the Colonies during the Revolution—both the First and Second Continental Congress met here—and it was the capital of the United States from 1790 to 1800. It is, therefore, not at all surprising that these Colonial homes were built here.

The typical Philadelphia merchant of this time acquired his wealth from Indian trade, Army contracts, Western land, shipping, export and import, trade and finance. He had business correspondents in London and Dublin and close family and professional ties with England, and he often sent his sons abroad to study law or for the clergy. He thought of himself as an English gentleman and, like the London merchants, considered his country seat his real home. A great deal of thought, time, and effort went into its planning and decoration. All of this is immediately evident on viewing any one of these homes.

Fairmount Park has over twenty eighteenth- and nineteenth-century homes. Some are now municipal buildings. Some are occupied by Park House guards. Six are open to the public and can be visited either independently or on a tour. However, this is one of the few instances when a guided tour is probably better. You will learn more about the houses from a Park House Guide, and you can be certain the houses will be open when you get there. Dates and times seem to change a bit or sometimes just aren't followed.

Call the Park House Office at the Museum of Art (PO 3-8100) and they will be happy to arrange a tour for a group from 2 to 20. (They can even arrange for up to 200 on simultaneous tours.) The Park House Guides are a knowledgeable group, trained by the Museum in the history, architecture, and decorative arts of the

# FAIRMOUNT PARK

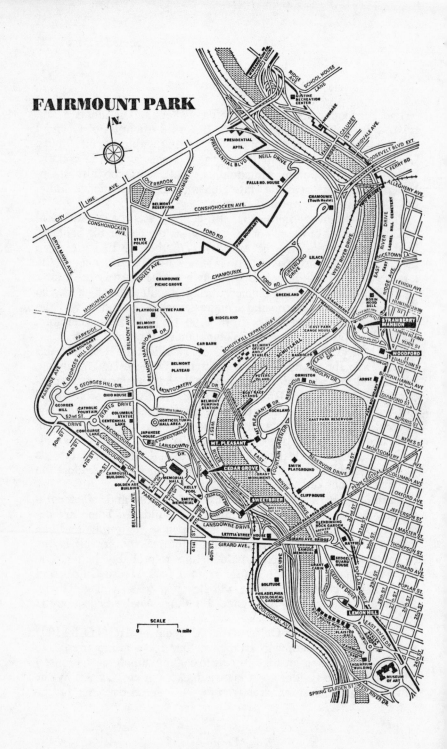

period. They do not give the usual "canned" speech but will adapt their tour to the age, size, and interests of the group, and include delightful anecdotes about the occupants of the various houses (one house supposedly has a resident ghost). All the houses are furnished and fascinating to anyone interested in eighteenth- and early nineteenth-century Colonial and social history and architecture. Three of them, however, are more appropriate for children: Cedar Grove, the Quaker farmhouse; Mount Pleasant; and Strawberry Mansion with its display of toys in the attic. The Japanese House, not part of this group, can nevertheless be included in a tour and is a delight.

## COLONIAL MANSIONS IN THE PARK
Philadelphia Museum of Art
Benjamin Franklin Parkway at 26th Street
Philadelphia 19130

**Phone:** PO 3-8100 (Park House Office)
**Open:**

### CEDAR GROVE
Daily 10 A.M.–5 P.M. except Monday and legal holidays. Adults 25¢, children under 18 10¢.

### MOUNT PLEASANT
Daily 10 A.M.–5 P.M. except Monday and legal holidays. Adults 25¢, children under 18 10¢.

### LEMON HILL
Thursday 11 A.M.–4 P.M., also second and fourth Sundays in July and August. Also on requested dates for private tours. Adults 50¢, children under 12 25¢.

### STRAWBERRY MANSION
Daily 11 A.M.–5 P.M. Closed Monday and month of January. Adults 50¢, children under 12 25¢.

### SWEETBRIER
Daily 10 A.M.–5 P.M. Closed Sunday and month of July. Adults 25¢, children under 12 10¢.

### WOODFORD
Daily 1–4 P.M. Closed Monday and month of August. Free. Prefer no children under 18.

### JAPANESE HOUSE
Tuesday–Saturday 10 A.M.–4 P.M. Admission, 25¢.

### Length of Tour
Half-day tour of three houses is usually recommended, morning or afternoon. *Fee:* $10 for a guide, plus admission to houses.

### Special Tours
*18th Century Towne and Countrie Tour:* A 2-hour walking tour through Society Hill with stops at historic buildings and restored houses and a 2½-hour drive through Fairmount Park with visits to several country estates. A Park House Guide accompanies the group. The tour can be arranged for two half days or one full day.

*Afternoon Auto Rambles:* May through October. Three houses. Fee including professional guide and house admissions, $4 per person, children under 12 $3, under 7 free. Transportation not included. Private cars go in caravan. Reservations: Call any day before noon. Advance reservations for groups at special rates also available.

*Regular Bus Tours:* To Fairmount Park and some of the historic houses in the park are available from the Art Museum.

*Christmas Tours:* Feature Colonial floral arrangements and decorations, usually early in December. For information call Park House Tours Office at Art Museum.

*Pennsylvania Schoolchildren:* Groups admitted to Cedar Grove, Mount Pleasant, and the Japanese House free of charge and guided free too.

### Transportation for Tours
The Park House Office will advise about chartered buses or private cars, but will not make arrangements. When cars are used, the guide will ride in the lead car.

### Cedar Grove
Cedar Grove is a simple-elegant Quaker stone farmhouse, unique among the Colonial mansions in Fairmount Park. It is the only house of this group moved to the Park, as well as the only house to contain the original Morris family furnishings, from William and Mary through the Federal period. It had been the summer home of five generations of Paschalls and Morrises from 1746 to 1888 when the Frankford area became too industrialized and the family moved to Compton (now Morris Arboretum) in Chestnut Hill. During these years the size of the house was doubled to accommodate a family of eleven children (you can see the center seam on the exterior of the house), and a piazza similar to porches on Friends' meetinghouses was also added.

Cedar Grove makes eighteenth- and nineteenth-century country living come alive; doors opening from every room to the outside, an herb garden, small closets for candles at the stairway on the first and second floors, children's furniture and toys, a pewter "welcome bowl" kept under the pump, and "breakneck stairs" (no bannister) from the parents' bedroom to the children's sleeping quarters in the attic. In one of the bedrooms is a "field" bed with canopy—the kind of bed that could be taken apart for use by an Army officer in the field; in another, writing scratched by a guest on a windowpane. In the kitchen are many cooking utensils of the period—a rotisserie, a griddle, a toaster, a built-in oven, even a hot-water heater (an enormous copper caldron set in the top of an oven). The blue-and-white Canton porcelain on the counters adds to the general feeling that the family will shortly arrive from Philadelphia for the summer.

The Philadelphia Museum of Art maintains Cedar Grove.

### LEMON HILL

As previously noted, Fairmount Park started with the purchase of Lemon Hill by the city in 1844. Originally the property was part of the "northern liberties"—land outside the city limits given to purchasers of lots in town. In 1770 Robert Morris, a signer of the Declaration of Independence and a man who exercised influence on George Washington to make Philadelphia the capital, built a farm and greenhouses, including the first lemon trees in Philadelphia—from which the name Lemon Hill came. In 1798 he went to debtor's prison, and the property was sold to a merchant, Henry Pratt, who built this elegant Federal-style house. His extensive gardens and greenhouses became such a popular tourist attraction that admission was charged. After Lemon Hill was purchased by the city, it became a beer garden and restaurant. In 1926 it was renovated to its original dignity by Fiske Kimball, the director of the Art Museum, as his residence. From its upstairs oval room, he could watch the construction of the museum. A unique feature of Lemon Hill, the elegant oval salons on three floors with matching curved doors and fireplaces were popular in France and are also found in the White House. The furnishings of Lemon Hill reflect the grace and charm of the Federal and Empire periods. Children's toys and furniture are scattered throughout, but it is hard to visualize youngsters racing through this elegant house.

Lemon Hill is maintained by the Colonial Dames of America.

### MOUNT PLEASANT

This mansion is one of the finest examples of classical Georgian architecture in America. It was built in 1761 by a Scottish sea captain, John Macpherson, who had been given a writ of marque by George I for privateering and had made his fortune during the French and Indian War preying on enemy ships as a "legalized pirate." According to the custom of the day, he did not hire an architect for his house, but studied design books and made his own plans. With no architectural training, Macpherson built a home described by John Adams in 1775 as "the most elegant country seat in the northern colonies." It is still considered a masterpiece.

Everything is symmetrical and in balance, including the two outbuildings. The house was entered either from a long driveway on one side or from the river on the other side. Windows balance front and back. None were placed on the sides, however, because there was no view. The symmetry is continued on the interior. Entranceways are balanced by false doors on the opposite side; outside ornate window decorations and columns appear inside as well. This elaborate country home was obviously furnished with great care for the time when its occupants would entertain. The antique period furnishings from the Art Museum collection enhance the atmosphere of Chippendale elegance and help portray the customs and life of an eighteenth-century country gentleman. Tobacco jars rest on the windowsills in the upstairs hall; the men chose their favorite blend for smoking in the upstairs parlor. In the great chamber is a portrait of a lady holding an orange, a symbol of great wealth. Beds are shorter not only because people were smaller, but they slept sitting up. Clothes were too heavy to hang, so closets were built with shelves. And in the hall the fire buckets stand ever ready.

The various owners and residents of Mount Pleasant were as interesting as the mansion itself. John Macpherson lectured on astronomy, designed a vermin-free bed, and compiled the first city directory—with editorial comments. In 1779 Benedict Arnold purchased the house but never lived there. It is said, however, that his ghost does. In 1792 it was sold to Jonathan Williams, grandnephew of Benjamin Franklin and first superintendent of West Point.

Mount Pleasant was a beer garden in the 1850s, became part of Fairmount Park in 1868, and was restored in the 1920s to its original magnificence. The Philadelphia Museum of Art maintains Mount Pleasant and furnishes it from its extensive collection of eighteenth-century treasures.

*Touch-It Museum.* Specially arranged for children, this small museum in one of the outbuildings contains Colonial household items and toys. Arrangements can be made for school groups or individuals by calling Park House Office (PO 3-8100).

## STRAWBERRY MANSION

Strawberry Mansion was known as Somerville when it was built by Judge William Lewis in the late 1790s. The center portion of this imposing mansion is the original house. It reflects the light Federal architecture popular at the time. The two wings in the heavier classical style were added in the 1820s by the Hemphill family: the south wing by a son, Alexander, for a ball while his parents were in Europe, and the north wing by the parents to restore some architectural balance to the house. The other son, Coleman, was very successful growing strawberries from roots imported from Chile; thus the name Strawberry Mansion.

The house now contains a collection of Federal and Empire period rooms. An Empire ballroom is resplendent with furniture imported from Paris. A rose velvet circular sofa (causeuse) in the center makes the French influence very apparent. The kitchen has a collection of interesting cooking utensils as well as a valentine and pictures made of shells by sailors as gifts to their wives and girl friends at home. The bedrooms on the second floor were built in the front of the house, away from the Schuylkill, because of the fear of the "River disease." The attic contains a marvelous assortment of toys and everyday household objects: a Quaker dollhouse, wooden ice skates, a sit tub for bathing (it looks difficult to use), a Victorian dollhouse, spinning wheels. If you leave the attic for the last, allow plenty of time.

The house is maintained by the Committee of 1926.

## SWEETBRIER

Built in 1797, Sweetbrier is the first of the Fairmount Park mansions planned and built not merely as a summer home, but as a year-round residence where the owner and his family could escape the yellow fever epidemics. This exquisite house with the lighter Federal architecture and delicate furnishings of that period is an interesting example of an elegant aristocratic home of the early 1800s. Its owner, Samuel Breck, was a Federalist who disliked Jacksonian democracy. He was active in the affairs of the city, in politics and the arts, and he entertained many fashionable and famous people, including Lafayette and Talleyrand. On the wall in the study is a framed letter of introduction for Talleyrand and an invitation to a party at Sweetbrier. Above the center hall is a music balcony where Samuel Breck and his only daughter, Lucy, practiced. Only the first floor is open, but there are many interesting items to linger over: pictures by Samuel Breck's friend Audubon, Birch prints of nineteenth-century Philadelphia, Breck family jewelry, mother-of-pearl loo counters. The Venetian blinds in the salon look quite modern, but belong to their period as well. In fact, they have been used in the West ever since Marco Polo first brought them to Venice from Persia.

The Brecks sold the house in 1839 after the death of their daughter of the "dread River disease" from the damming of the Schuylkill River. It became part of Fairmount Park in 1867 and was used as a restaurant. In 1927 it was restored by the Junior League to its original dignity and charm. The Modern Club maintains Sweetbrier.

Sweetbrier—Colonial Mansion in Fairmount Park

## WOODFORD MANSION

Woodford is a handsome example of Georgian architecture and contains the Naomi Wood Collection of Colonial furnishings. Built originally in the 1750s by Judge William Coleman, a friend of Benjamin Franklin's, as a one-story home, it was enlarged in 1771 and again at the turn of the century. These changes can be seen most readily on the outside. Its occupants have included David Franks, whose ship brought the Liberty Bell to Philadelphia from England. The family entertained Lord Howe and the British, and Franks was arrested by Benedict Arnold for treason. Judge William Lewis lived at Woodford while supervising the building of Strawberry Mansion. Abandoned in the 1830s because of yellow fever, it became part of Fairmount Park and was used as a police station. It is difficult to imagine the drawing room of this exquisite mansion as a courtroom.

In 1928 the house was restored for the Naomi Wood Collection: furniture of the William and Mary, Queen Anne, and Chippendale periods and a completely equipped kitchen with a toaster, a roaster, lighting devices, pewterware, a Delft trick drinking mug. You can almost see the servants working and talking in the kitchen while the family was busy upstairs sewing, playing checkers with the carved set on display, listening to the music box, using the spectacles which now lie open on the desk, and waiting for tea to be served. It's all there to see, even to the pewter toddy warmer. Each room deserves a leisurely examination. The Trustees continually add to the Naomi Wood Collection. Please: no children under 18.

## Fairmount Park Landmarks

### JAPANESE HOUSE

Not far from Cedar Grove and Sweetbrier is a glimpse of another world—the Japanese House and garden. Originally sent by the Japanese Government to the Museum of Modern Art in New York City, it was presented to Philadelphia in 1957 and erected on the site of the Japanese House built for the Centennial Exposition. This typical seventeenth-century home of a scholar and intellectual presents quite a contrast to the Colonial mansions, not only in its architecture, but also as a picture of a different culture and way of life.

Its architecture is a beautiful blend of the practical, the symbolic, and the aesthetic. The flyaway cypress roof is an important aspect of Japanese architecture. The curving path to the front door guards the house from evil spirits, which were thought to travel in a straight line. Because of the rainy climate Japanese houses were built on stilts, thus allowing the air to circulate and preventing mildew. And here the roof extends over the veranda to provide cover during bad weather. Sliding doors change the upper level of the veranda into a hall and permit the people to move from room to room during a storm. Rooms were meant to be used for many different purposes—sleeping, eating, study. Furniture consisted of cushions, low tables, boxes, screens, chests, or drawers. Bedding (there were no beds) was simply put away when not in use. The sliding screens you see here were also used to change the size of the various rooms, depending upon the needs of the family on different occasions. The garden, with representations of trees, mountains, rivers, forests, and waterfalls, is a viewing garden used for nothing but contemplation and inspiration. The sound of running water near the teahouse added to this serenity and was considered an important aspect of Japanese life. The tea ceremony is often demonstrated here during the afternoon. Call the Fairmount Park Commission (MU 6-9700) for times and dates. Visit this lovely spot and you will have taken a brief trip out of Philadelphia. Public transportation provided by SEPTA Route 38 to Belmont and Parkside Avenues.

## MEMORIAL HALL
42nd Street and Parkside Avenue
Philadelphia

**Phone:** MU 6-1776 (ask for Memorial Hall)
**Directions:** At the Art Museum pick up the West River Drive to the Sweetbrier cutoff and follow signs to Sweetbrier and Memorial Hall.
**Public Transportation:** SEPTA Route 38 to Belmont and Parkside Avenues

The physical remains of the Centennial Exposition of 1876, held in Fairmount Park to commemorate the nation's one hundredth birthday, are all but extinct. Of the more than 200 buildings constructed for the occasion, Memorial Hall is the only major building still intact. Erected for the Exposition as an art gallery and intended to be permanent, this massive granite building surmounted by a giant glass and iron dome was considered in its day the height of artistic elegance, and housed the city's art treasures until the present Art Museum was built in 1928. Memorial Hall stands high on a plateau overlooking the river, and it is still impressive to see.

Fortunately, a large-scale model of the entire Exposition was made in 1890 while all the information was still available. It can be seen in the basement of Memorial Hall by appointment only (call MU 6-1776, ext. 81216). Richard Nicolai of the Fairmount Park Commission, a knowledgeable and enthusiastic admirer of the Centennial Exposition, will explain this large, fascinating display.

Today, after years of neglect, the Great Hall has been restored to its original appearance. Part of the building serves as headquarters for the Fairmount Park Commission. Another is a recreation center with an indoor swimming pool and a basketball court.

In early fall Memorial Hall is the site of an annual Harvest Show. It's a magnificent display of fall flowers and harvest crops.

TOURS

By appointment only. Call Park House Office at the Art Museum (PO 3-8100).

## SMITH CIVIL WAR MEMORIAL

The large impressive columns at the entrance to Memorial Hall are not in any way related to the Centennial Exposition. This monument was constructed in 1890, twenty-five years after the war, to honor its heroes. It was endowed by Richard Smith, a philanthropist and printer, who also gave Smith Memorial Playground (see below) to the city. He is there in his printer's apron among the generals.

The large curved benches close by are known as whispering benches because if you sit at one end and whisper your voice can be heard at the other end.

Near Memorial Hall you will encounter an imposing group of statues known as the "Temperance Fountain" or "Moses Fountain," erected by the Catholic Total Abstinence Union of America at the time of the Centennial. It's interesting only because it's so large that you wonder, "What is it?"

## SMITH MEMORIAL PLAYGROUND
East Fairmount Park
Philadelphia 19121
(Near 33rd and Oxford Streets entrance)

**Phone:** PO 9-0902
**Open:** Grounds daily 9 A.M.–5 P.M., building daily 1–4 P.M.
**Closed:** Sundays, Good Friday, Thanksgiving, Christmas Eve, Christmas, New Year's Day.
**Admission:** Free
**Restrictions:** No children over elementary school age admitted except in a family group. When school is in session children over 6 not allowed until after school hours, except on school holidays.
**Directions:** From the East River Drive turn into the Park at Grant's Statue, then take the next three right-hand turns (streets unmarked).
**Parking:** Ample facilities
**Public Transportation:** SEPTA Route A to 33rd and Oxford. Follow signs to playground (about ⅛ mile). *Or* SEPTA Route 3 on Columbia Avenue to 33rd Street and Columbia Avenue. Short walk. Follow signs.
**Picnicking:** Good spot with outdoor cooking facilities, picnic tables, and benches. Snack bar also available.

This large Victorian building with spacious porches and grounds has been a favorite spot for generations of Philadelphia children, the gift of Richard Smith, philanthropist, printer, and typefounder —the same man depicted on the Civil War Memorial in West Park. He left his estate in trust for the operation of the playground.

There are toys, games, and space for all kinds of play, and a staff to go with it. Once inside the main house, head for the basement and a door marked "Entrance to the Village." Inside are cars and fire trucks for the kids to drive, parking meters, gas pumps, angle and parallel parking indicated on the "streets"—it's all scaled for small ones and guaranteed to delight them. Outdoors there are 6½ acres full of playground equipment, swings and seesaws, baseball facilities, a basketball court, and the highlight: a giant slide wide enough for ten children to go down side by side!

When there's snow on the ground, Smith Playground provides the sleds, flying saucers, and hot chocolate and cookies to warm up, all free. In warm weather the Strawbridge Memorial Pool is available for group swimming by appointment only. Call PO 9-0902. Children under 6 require a parent. Locker rooms for changing are available.

NURSERY SCHOOL

On Monday and Wednesday mornings from 10 A.M.–12 noon. For 3- to 5-year-olds. Free with $2 registration. No transportation.

GROUP VISITS AND BUS ARRANGEMENTS

Smith Memorial Playground offers bus transportation on a partial-pay basis to all kindergarten and nursery groups who would like to visit. The charge is 50 cents per person. If the group is less than 35 in number, a minimum charge of $18 is required. Call or write for additional information.

BIRTHDAY PARTIES

The large upstairs room in the main building can be reserved for Saturday afternoons from 1 to 4 P.M. for parties. No children over 5 admitted. No charge. You bring your own decorations and refreshments. Have refreshments and then use all the other facilities.

## Entertainment in the Park

## JOHN B. KELLY PLAYHOUSE IN THE PARK

Belmont Mansion Drive
West Fairmount Park
Philadelphia

This is the first city-owned and operated theater in the United States. Originally started as a tent theater, it is now a permanent air-conditioned structure offering theater-in-the-round from late spring to early fall (see page 162).

## REGATTAS

Almost every weekend from spring into the fall something is going on along the Schuylkill River. High-schools, colleges, and rowing clubs compete in the various regattas during the season. These events attract thousands of spectators. Stands are set up along the East River Drive at the Columbia Avenue Bridge and the finish for some of the big races—or you can just sit on the banks of the river. It's fun and free. For information on sculling events call PO 9-2068. Some of the major events are listed in Chapter 14.

### THE SCHUYLKILL NAVY

Philadelphia is considered the "sculling capital of America." The Schuylkill Navy is made up of the representatives of the clubs in Boat House Row on the East River Drive behind the Art Museum. They sponsor various national and international rowing competitions during the year, the highlights being the Dad Vail Regatta, the largest collegiate regatta in the country, and the Independence Day Regatta.

## ROBIN HOOD DELL
Near Huntingdon Street and Ridge Avenue
East Fairmount Park
Philadelphia

**Phone:** LO 7-0707
**Open:** Concerts in June and July
**Admission:** Free tickets can be obtained three weeks prior to a concert by writing the Department of Recreation (call or watch newspaper for the post office box number which must be included); enclose self-addressed stamped envelope. Two tickets are issued for each request. There are also coupons appearing in the daily newspapers that can be clipped and sent in for tickets. Children under 12 not permitted at evening concerts.
**Parking:** Facilities available
**Public Transportation:** SEPTA Route A from Center City; *or* special SEPTA buses marked "Robin Hood Dell" from various locations in the city (call DA 9-4800 for further information)

Since 1930 the Dell has offered outdoor concerts in the summer. Renowned soloists and guest conductors perform in a natural amphitheater with the Philadelphia Orchestra. It's a lovely setting. Seats are provided for those who get there early. Better still, bring a blanket and picnic supper and sit on the hill among the trees.

### CHILDREN'S CONCERTS

There are three morning concerts from 10:30 to 11:30 A.M. especially arranged for children. These include a child soloist chosen from auditions by the Philadelphia Orchestra. Sit under the trees if it is a hot day.

### AFTER-SEASON CONCERTS

After the regular season, the Department of Recreation sponsors a full schedule of events called the August Festival. On Tuesday and Thursday nights popular bands perform, and there are ballet and opera and ethnic programs: Greek Night, Italian Night. Teenagers might especially enjoy this fare.

## Recreation in the Park

### BICYCLING

Starting at the Aquarium, behind the Art Museum, is an 8¼-mile bicycle path, from the Art Museum, up the East River Drive, across Falls Bridge, down the West River Drive, and back to the Museum—all with no intersections. Bicycles can be rented there for 75¢ an hour ($5 deposit and driver's license necessary), spring, summer, and fall. The path is especially beautiful in April during cherry blossom season.

### BOATING

You can rent a sailboat, rowboat, or canoe from the East Park Canoe House, below Strawberry Mansion Bridge, East River Drive.

**Phone:** BA 8-9336
**Open:** April–October 11:30 A.M.–8 P.M. Rowboats $3 per hour, 1 or 2 people. Canoes $3 per hour, 1 or 2 people. Sailboats $5 per hour, 2–4 people. Life jackets provided. Paddle boats for rent at Franklin D. Roosevelt Park, 20th Street and Pattison Avenue.

# FISHING

**Regulations:** No fishing license required for residents age 16 and
under. For ages 16–64 license $5.20, over 65 $2.20, obtainable
at Municipal Services Building, 15th Street and John F. Kennedy
Boulevard.

### Wissahickon Creek

From mid-April to September the creek is stocked with trout.
Areas to fish: Valley Green, Bells Mill Road, and Thomas Mill
Road. Don't miss seeing the only covered bridge in Philadelphia
just below Bells Mill Road. Originally built in 1737, the Thomas
Mill Bridge is the only one remaining of the six covered bridges
over the Wissahickon. It is 97 feet long and 14 feet wide and can
be reached on foot or on horseback.

### Pennypack Creek

Both sides of the creek from State Road to Pine Road. Trout
fishing in season.

### Concourse Lake

At 44th Street and Parkside Avenue. Only children under 16.

### Schuylkill River

From Manayunk through Fairmount Park to Southwest
Philadelphia.

# GOLF COURSES

There are six public eighteen-hole golf courses in Fairmount
Park: Cobbs Creek, 72nd and Lansdowne Streets; Karakung, 72nd
and Lansdowne Streets; Juniata, "M" and Cayuga Streets; John F.
Byrne, 9500 Frankford Avenue; Walnut Lane, Walnut Lane and
Henry Avenue; Franklin D. Roosevelt Park, 20th Street and
Pattison Avenue.

**Rates:** $2 weekdays for residents of the city, $2.50 for nonresidents;
$3 weekends and holidays for residents, $3.50 for nonresidents.
Reservations needed on weekends and holidays. Tournaments
for Junior Golfers. For further information call MU 6-1776, ext.
81221.

### Driving Ranges

At 52nd Street and Parkside Avenue, 79th Street and City Line
Avenue, and Central and Cottman Avenues.

## HORSEBACK RIDING

The Wissahickon and Pennypack Park offer over 100 miles of bridle paths. Nearby riding academies rent horses by the hour, and you can use the Fairmount Park paths. One of the most beautiful and popular bridle paths in the country is Forbidden Drive in the Wissahickon.

Riding Stables: It is best to call for reservations. Academy Riding Club, 617 Rector Street, IV 2-9834; Al's Riding Academy, 605 Gorgas Lane, IV 2-9810; Rock Hill Farm Stables, 641 East Dupont Street, IV 2-9858; Courtesy Horse Farms, Cathedral Road, IV 2-9955.

## ICE SKATING

Designated areas are carefully flagged to indicate dangerous spots. Flags remain until ice measures 3½ inches. HUNTING PARK LANE, 9th Street and Hunting Park Avenue; GUSTINE LAKE, Ridge Avenue and School House Lane; FRANKLIN D. ROOSEVELT LAKE, Broad Street near Pattison Avenue; CONCOURSE LAKE in West Park; VALLEY GREEN in the Wissahickon; PENNYPACK CREEK, several locations. For skating conditions call MU 6-1776, ext. 81324. NIGHT SKATING: Hunting Park pool and Gustine Lake.

## JOGGING

Six jogging trails, varying in length from 1 to 5 miles, are laid out in various park areas. Colored distance markers are placed at half-mile intervals. East River Drive, West River Drive, Wissahickon at Valley Green.

Cross-Country Courses are located at Belmont Plateau in West Park and at the Edgely area in East Park.

## PICNICKING

There are many picnic areas in Fairmount Park, some with tables and fireplaces. If you do not require either of these, your choice is even wider. BARTRAM PARK (fireplaces), Southwest Philadelphia on the west bank of the Schuylkill River, 53rd to 56th Streets. BURHOLME PARK (fireplaces), Fox Chase, Central Avenue to Fillmore Street, Shelmire Avenue to Cottman Avenue. CARPENTER'S WOODS, Mount Airy, east of Wissahickon Avenue, north of Sedgwick Street (also a bird sanctuary). COBBS CREEK PARK (fireplaces), West Philadelphia, extends along Cobbs Creek from Manoa

Road to Woodland Avenue. FERNHILL PARK, lower Germantown, Abbottsford Road to Roberts, Wissahickon Avenue to Morris Street. FISHER PARK, Olney, Nedro Avenue to Spencer Street. HUNTING PARK (fireplaces), North Philadelphia, Old York Road to 9th Street, Lycoming Street to Wingohocking Street. FRANKLIN D. ROOSEVELT PARK (fireplaces), South Philadelphia below Pattison Avenue, west of Broad Street. MORRIS PARK (fireplaces), West Philadelphia, north of Lansdowne Avenue to City Line, west to 60th Street. PENNYPACK PARK (fireplaces), Northeast Philadelphia, extends along both sides of Pennypack Creek from State to Pine Roads. TACONY CREEK PARK, Northeast Philadelphia, extends along Tacony Creek from Wyoming to Cheltenham Avenues. VALLEY GREEN in Chestnut Hill. Wissahickon in Roxborough and Germantown (fireplaces). WOODWARD MEADOW (fireplaces), Cresheim Drive off Germantown Avenue.

## SKIING

There are natural ski areas throughout the park for beginners and novices.

## SLEDDING

Throughout the park in designated areas. Lighted areas for night sledding at Walnut Lane Golf Course, Henry Avenue and Walnut Lane; Driving Range at 52nd Street and Parkside Avenue.

## SWIMMING

There are five outdoor swimming pools and one indoor pool throughout the park fully staffed with lifeguards. Lockers for changing clothes are available. No fee.

### INDOOR

At Memorial Hall, 42nd Street and Parkside Avenue in West Fairmount Park. Open Labor Day to Memorial Day. Instruction can be arranged through Fairmount Park Recreation Division, MU 6-1776, ext. 81221.

### OUTDOOR

All these are open from Memorial Day to Labor Day daily. Instruction can be arranged.

*John B. Kelly Pool,* adjacent to Memorial Hall, West Fairmount Park, 42nd Street and Parkside Avenue.

*Hunting Park Pool* 9th Street and Hunting Park Avenue. For children up to 14.

*Gustine Lake,* Ridge Avenue and School House Lane, children all day, adults after 4 P.M.

*Franklin D. Roosevelt Pool,* Broad Street near Pattison Avenue.

*Cobbs Creek Recreation Center,* 63rd and Spruce Streets.

*Strawbridge Memorial Pool* (page 140).

## TENNIS

Fairmount Park boasts seventy-seven all-weather courts at various locations. Free instruction during the summer at special courts. For further information call MU 6-1776, ext. 81222. No reservations necessary.

# Organized Recreation

## ARCHERY

Cedar Park Archery Range, Edgely Road east of Belmont Avenue. Organized competition by the Philadelphia Archery Association. Call TR 7-9774 for information.

## BASEBALL

Seventy-five ball diamonds are scattered throughout the Park. There are also facilities for soccer, cricket matches, rugby, archery, and lawn bowling. For information and reservations call MU 6-1776, ext. 81221.

## BOCCE

Organized activity at Cedar Park, Edgely Road east of Belmont Avenue. For further information call Mr. Jeshon, TR 7-9774.

## CRICKET

League matches at Cedar Park Cricket Field, Edgely Road east of Belmont Avenue, and cricket field next to Memorial Hall. Call TR 7-9774 for information.

# Pennypack Park

Sprawling through the crowded Northeast suburbs of Philadelphia is a beautiful oasis—1,334 acres of natural woodland bordering Pennypack Creek. Pennypack Park was created by city ordinance in 1905 as a haven for city-dwellers. It is part of the Fairmount Park System.

The Park, similar in atmosphere to the rugged Wissahickon Valley, contains bridle paths, trails to walk, picnic areas (some with fireplaces), a bird sanctuary, and an environmental center. Pennypack Creek offers canoeing, boating, fishing, and skating (no swimming).

## ENVIRONMENTAL CENTER

Verree Road and Pennypack Creek. Nature walks, lectures and films on ecology on Sunday afternoons. Picnic groves, trails for hiking and leisurely walks.

# The Wissahickon

**Public Transportation:** SEPTA Routes A, E, H, L, R, 61; trolleys 23 and 53. For further information call SEPTA: DA 9-4800.

The Lenape Indians named it; poets and writers have extolled its beauty. Our advice: Take a hike, take a bike, go on horseback, use public transportation, or take your car, but do become acquainted with this vast wild natural area known as the Wissahickon. The 1,372-acre park follows the winding creek. Rising up from the water are heavily wooded and rocky banks. There are excellent bridle paths, jogging and bicycle runs—and it's a great place if all the exercise you want is a Sunday stroll or picnic.

The Wissahickon can be entered at several points. An excellent map showing all the entrances and places of interest has been put out by the Friends of the Wissahickon. You can pick one up at the Valley Green Inn, or at the Pennsylvania Horticultural Society, 325 Walnut Street, Philadelphia 19106 (they will also accept telephone orders if you phone WA 2-4801).

Picnic areas abound. Those with fireplaces are at Northwestern Avenue, Thomas Mill Road, Blue Bell Meadows, and Cresheim Valley.

*Some Places of Interest*

## CARPENTER'S WOODS

Wissahickon Avenue and Sedgwick Street. A small scenic extension of the Wissahickon with a bird sanctuary, bridle paths, and picnic groves.

## CLIMBERS' ROCK

A short distance from Livezey House is a rock often used by rock-climbing groups to practice rope work.

## FORBIDDEN DRIVE

So named because it is closed to automobile traffic. This gravel road runs from Wissahickon Drive to Northwestern Avenue; it's one of the loveliest bridle paths in America—and an ideal place for a leisurely walk.

## FORMER VINEYARD

Close to Henry Avenue and Gorgas Lane. Baseball, football, and playground areas are here in a flat area of the park.

The Inn at Valley Green

## LIVEZEY HOUSE AND MILL RUINS

Follow Allens Lane to Livezey Lane into the Park. The mill was built in 1717 and is known to have been one of the largest in the Colonies. The house (not open) dates back to 1683.

## MONASTERY

At the bottom of Kitchens Lane off Wissahickon Avenue is one of the loveliest entrances to the park. Several times in the spring horse shows are held here on Sunday afternoons.

## VALLEY GREEN in Chestnut Hill

**Directions:** Henry Avenue to Wise's Mill Road, *or* Willow Grove Avenue, left on Cherokee Street, left immediately over the bridge on Springfield Avenue, and a sharp left on Valley Green Road

**Public Transportation:** SEPTA Route A to Wise's Mill Road

If you would like a hike in the woods but don't want to leave the city, Valley Green provides just about everything: miles of wooded trails for horses, bicycles, and walkers, rocks and fallen trees for climbing, hidden streams for leaping over. Stay as long as you like. Be as active or lazy as you like. Bring a bag of bread to feed the ducks on Wissahickon Creek. Wear rubber-soled shoes for climbing, take a hiker's picnic lunch, and climb the Valley wall to a comfortable boulder. There are a covered bridge, waterfalls, and, in winter, skating on Wissahickon Creek. It's an unbelievable rural setting—right in the city. Should you wish to include country dining, try the Valley Green Inn.

## VALLEY GREEN INN
Valley Green Road and Wissahickon Creek

**Phone:** CH 7-3450

The Inn serves breakfast, lunch, and dinner and is open every day from 10:30 A.M. to 8 P.M. This charming inn set in the Valley resembles an old farmhouse. In summer you can dine on the porch and watch the horses, hikers, and ducks meander by. Old prints, kitchen utensils, farm tools, and glassware decorate the pleasant dining rooms and should help keep children interested during the meal. The menu ranges from sandwiches and salad plates to lobster and steak dinners, all moderately priced. There is also a children's menu, as well as special holiday dinners.

NOTE: The Inn has no liquor license, but will supply an ice bucket and glasses free of charge if you bring your own bottle.

Attached to the Inn is an outdoor snack bar (open 9 A.M.–9 P.M.) with several picnic tables. Here you can get hot dogs, beverages, pretzels, etc.

NOTE: Public toilets and drinking water only at Valley Green.

## *Special Events*

### DOGSLED RACES

Usually once in January and February dogsled teams compete. If there's no snow, they use wheels on their sleds, which are pulled by Siberian huskies. There are both junior and senior competitions. It's a popular annual event. Watch the papers for announcements. At Valley Green.

### FROSTBITE SAILING COMPETITION

Beginning in late January and running eight consecutive Sundays. Races take place between the Columbia Avenue railroad and Dauphin trolley bridges along the Schuylkill River.

### WISSAHICKON DAY

A Sunday in May. A colorful parade of horses—hunters, Arabian horses, wagons, and pony carts. All children participating in the parade get a ribbon. Spectator stands are set up at Valley Green. Activities from 1 to 3 P.M.

# 4
# THE PERFORMING ARTS

Philadelphia has a long tradition in the performing arts. The first permanent theater in the United States, the Southwark, was built here in 1766; the Walnut Street Theatre, circa 1809, is the oldest surviving theater in the English-speaking world. Producers have continually brought "tryouts," classics, and old favorites to Philadelphia audiences over the years.

The Academy of Music with its peerless acoustics is the home of the world-renowned Philadelphia Orchestra. The Pennsylvania Ballet, a first-rate resident company, performs during the year, and leading dance companies such as the Stuttgart and Alvin Ailey appear regularly in Philadelphia.

Films both old and new, classics and revivals, can be seen at first-run and neighborhood theaters. Special series designed for movie buffs thrive. Many films are presented free and aimed at the young set. Area colleges and universities sponsor cultural events, a great number open to the public.

To keep up with current happenings check the local newspaper, especially on Friday; the Sunday entertainment sections list future events. *Philadelphia* Magazine has an excellent schedule of entertainment. Other sources: *Metropolitan* Magazine and the *WFLN Guide*.

For education, culture, or just plain fun, there is a world of entertainment available every day of the year.

## Music

**ACADEMY OF MUSIC**
Broad and Locust Streets
Philadelphia 19102

**Phone:** PE 5-7379

**Box Office Information:** Tickets to performances are on sale from

*151*

the Box Office three weeks prior to event. Mail orders accepted one month prior to event. The Box Office is open 10 A.M.– 9 P.M. or until 5:30 P.M. when there is no evening performance. Sundays only when a performance is scheduled. Mail orders should be addressed to the Academy of Music Box Office, Broad and Locust Streets, Philadelphia, Pa. 19102, accompanied by a stamped self-addressed envelope. Checks and money orders should be made payable to the Academy of Music Box Office.

The Academy of Music opened its doors in 1857. It is patterned after the famous La Scala of Milan and has the finest acoustics in the world outside of La Scala. In 1963 the Academy was designated a Registered National Historic Landmark.

TOURS OF ACADEMY OF MUSIC

Monday afternoons 2–4 P.M., 75¢; groups of 25 or more, 50¢. Advance reservation necessary; call Academy office, KI 5-1535. For further details see page 289.

## ALL STAR–FORUM–MOE SEPTEE
1530 Locust Street
Philadelphia 19102

**Phone: PE 5-7506**

Moe Septee, Philadelphia impresario, consistently brings outstanding talent to the city. There are different series, some devoted to dance, others primarily to music. For further information write to All Star–Forum. Single tickets to events included in Forum are available three weeks prior to the event at the Academy of Music.

## AMERICAN SOCIETY OF ANCIENT INSTRUMENTS
7445 Devon Street
Philadelphia 19119

**Phone: CH 7-7823**

For over forty-five years this dedicated group has been presenting concerts on its outstanding collection of ancient instruments: viola d'amore, harpsichord, viola da gamba, baroque flute. Their annual concert at Saint Clement's Episcopal Church, 20th and Cherry Streets, offers a unique opportunity to hear the music of five centuries written for these instruments. Performances throughout the year at other locations. Write or call for information.

## BOOK CONCERTS FOR CHILDREN
Free Library
19th and Vine Streets
Philadelphia 19103

**Phone:** MU 6-5372
**Open:** Occasional Sunday afternoons at 2:30 P.M. Schedules available at all branches. For more information see page 92.
**Admission:** Free

## EVENING CHAMBER MUSIC CONCERTS
Free Library
19th and Vine Streets
Philadelphia
(See page 92.)

## FRANKLIN CONCERTS, INC.
1904 Chestnut Street
Philadelphia 19103

**Phone:** LO 7-4230

Diversified concerts at the Civic Center Museum, 34th Street and Civic Center Boulevard; Moore College of Art, 20th and Race Streets; and various other places in the community. Accomplished young artists perform. At Moore College they give debut concerts. For further information call or write.

## LYRIC OPERA COMPANY
1518 Walnut Street
Philadelphia 19102

**Phone:** PE 5-7572

Call or write for schedule and ticket information. Performances at Academy of Music. Guest soloists.

## MENDELSSOHN CLUB
P.O. Box 288
Radnor, Pa. 19087

**Phone:** 688-8858

Long-established 220-voice choir under the direction of Robert Page, conductor. Two or more performances a year. For further information write or call. Special student rates.

## PHILADELPHIA CLASSICAL GUITAR SOCIETY
28 South 18th Street
Philadelphia 19103

Phone: LO 7-2972

Concerts held in Jefferson Hall, 1020 Locust Street, the fourth
Sunday of every month at 8 P.M.

## PHILADELPHIA FOLK FESTIVAL

Annual event held the last weekend in August. Folksongs, ballads,
workshops, concerts. See page 266.

## PHILADELPHIA GRAND OPERA COMPANY
1422 Chestnut Street
Philadelphia 19102

Phone: LO 7-1048

Performances are held at Academy of Music. Guest soloists. For
information and schedule write or call.

## PHILADELPHIA MUSEUM OF ART
Van Pelt Auditorium
26th Street and Benjamin Franklin Parkway
Philadelphia 19130

Sundays during the season professional string groups, woodwinds,
soloists. See page 112.

## PHILADELPHIA MUSICAL ACADEMY
313 South Broad Street
Philadelphia 19107

Phone: 735-9635

Concert series: orchestra, jazz groups, woodwind ensembles, and
opera performed by students and faculty. Many free and open to
the public. For further information write or call.

## THE PHILADELPHIA ORCHESTRA

This world-acclaimed orchestra is one of the city's—and country's
—finest assets. Under the leadership of Eugene Ormandy and guest
conductors, its varied concerts are the best evening's entertainment

around. Various subscriptions or single performance tickets are available. Write to Philadelphia Orchestra Office, 230 South 15th Street, Philadelphia 19102, or call KI 5-3830. During June and July the orchestra performs at Robin Hood Dell (page 141).

### CHILDREN'S CONCERTS

Six Saturday mornings during the winter from 11 A.M. to 12 noon. Send requests for information and subscriptions to Academy of Music, Broad and Locust Streets, Philadelphia, Pa. 19102. In addition, three concerts are held during the summer at Robin Hood Dell (page 141).

### AMPHITHEATER

Known as "student heaven," this section has reasonably priced seats. Friday and Saturday performances, $3.25; Tuesday and Thursday, $3. Rush seats: one hour before Friday afternoon and evening performance and Saturday performance, $2.

## ROBIN HOOD DELL
East Fairmount Park

Evening concerts during June and July by the Philadelphia Orchestra. Three morning concerts for children during the summer at 10:30 A.M. for one hour. After-season concerts in August. See page 141.

## TEMPLE UNIVERSITY MUSIC FESTIVAL
Meetinghouse Road and Butler Pike
Ambler, Pa. 19002

**Phone:** CE 5-4600. Tickets available at box office and all Ticketron locations. Group rates on orders of forty or more tickets to any single performance. Phone 787-8318 or CE 5-3352.

A six-week summer festival that brings a wonderful potpourri of dance, opera, jazz, and noted soloists to the Philadelphia area. The surroundings include ten acres of gardens and orchards plus a sculpture garden. Come early for a snack—hamburgers, hot dogs, hand-dipped ice cream. Weekends: Special suppers, reasonably priced. Informal live performances each evening at 6:30. Handicapped: Call ahead and appropriate tickets will be issued. Nearby: Formal gardens on Ambler campus (see page 208).

# Films

## ACADEMY OF NATURAL SCIENCES

19th Street and Benjamin Franklin Parkway
Philadelphia 19103

**Phone:** LO 7-3700. Saturdays, October to April at 11 A.M.

One-hour nature films. Free. Sundays once a month at 1:30 P.M. family nature film. Museum admission also covers movie. Call or watch newspapers for listings.

## BANDBOX THEATRE

30 Armat Street
Philadelphia 19144

**Phone:** VI 4-3511

The best of foreign films and cinema classics. Write to be put on mailing list.

## CIVIC CENTER MUSEUM

34th Street and Civic Center Boulevard
Philadelphia 19104

**Phone:** EV 2-8181

Children's film classics at 1 and 3 P.M. one Saturday a month. Write for schedule or watch for listing in local papers. Send self-addressed stamped envelope for free tickets. Separate request necessary for each event. For further information on Civic Center activities see page 100.

## EXCEPTIONAL FILM SOCIETY

725½ North 24th Street
Philadelphia 19130

**Phone:** 978-4202

Private screenings at the Van Pelt Auditorium, Philadelphia Museum of Art, on Friday evenings. Excellent foreign films and the best of American movies. For information write to Exceptional Films.

**FRANKLIN INSTITUTE**
Benjamin Franklin Parkway at 20th Street
Philadelphia 19103

**Phone:** LO 4-3838

Free films Saturday and Sunday afternoons for various age levels.
Check newspapers or call for further information.

**FREE LIBRARY**
19th and Vine Streets
Philadelphia 19103

**Phone:** MU 6-5322

Films throughout the year at various locations. Pick up monthly
schedule at main library or any branch. A catalogue of films for
rent (to be used for entertainment only) available at all branches
of the library.

**MONTGOMERY COUNTY–NORRISTOWN PUBLIC LIBRARY**
542 DeKalb Street
Norristown, Pa. 19401

**Phone:** 277-3355

Wide selection of movies for preschool and elementary-school children. Free. 11 A.M. to 12 noon every Saturday year-round.

**PHILADELPHIA MUSEUM OF ART**
Van Pelt Auditorium
26th Street and Benjamin Franklin Parkway
Philadelphia 19130

**Phone:** PO 3-8100

Children's film classics free with admission to Museum. Call for
schedule.

**TLA CINEMA, INC.**
334 South Street
Philadelphia 19147

**Phone:** WA 2-6010 for recording of week's schedule.

The finest variety of film classics old and new, experimental, or just good flicks. Children's matinees. For yearly listings and information on group rates, call the office, WA 2-6011.

**UNIVERSITY MUSEUM**
33rd and Spruce Streets
Philadelphia 19174

Children's film series October–May, Saturday morning at 10:30. A mix of children's classics and educational shows: *Treasure Island, Born Free,* Jacques Cousteau. Free, no tickets necessary. Every Sunday, family films at 2:30 P.M. (About once a month a live concert replaces the film.) Children must be accompanied by an adult. In the past such films as *To Kill a Mockingbird, African Queen,* and fine historical movies have been shown. January and February: Archaeological Film Series. Saturday and Sunday at 2:30 P.M. For all events write for a program, enclosing a stamped, self-addressed 10-inch envelope. Or pick up a program at the Museum.

# Dance

**AFRO-AMERICAN DANCE ENSEMBLE**
Ile-Ife Humanitarian Center
2544 Germantown Avenue
Philadelphia 19133

**Phone: BA 5-7565**

Arthur Hall, founder and director. This group goes into the community and performs a wide range of dance—ballet, jazz, and modern—but principally African dances. Young Professional Group (ages 10 to 12) and a Junior Company of teenagers also perform. For information call or write the Center.

**BALLET DES JEUNES**
7596 Haverford Avenue
Philadelphia

**Phone: GR 3-2253**

Ursula Melita, director. This ballet company of young dancers performs at the Civic Center's children's programs and other places in the community.

## GERMANTOWN DANCE THEATER
5555 Germantown Avenue
Philadelphia 19144

Phone: VI 3-4797

The company is a member of the National Association of Regional Ballet. They perform at the Civic Center and in the community, and have performed in New York City. Most local performances are free.

## PENNSYLVANIA BALLET COMPANY
2333 Fairmount Avenue
Philadelphia 19130

Phone: 232-1500

Classical and contemporary ballet performed by this nationally acclaimed company at the Academy of Music. Every Christmas a sparkling rendition of *The Nutcracker*. For information write or call. Yearly subscriptions available. School of the Pennsylvania Ballet: professionally oriented, by audition only from age eight. For serious students of the ballet. Call for information. Barbara Weisberger, Director.

## PHILADELPHIA CIVIC BALLET COMPANY
277 South 11th Street
Philadelphia 19107

Phone: WA 5-4405

Directors: Alicia Dakerian and husband, Norman Craig. The Philadelphia Civic Ballet goes out into the community and can be seen in such diverse places as in the Art Museum, on city streets, in Pennypack Park, and in Rittenhouse Square. Their objective is to bring dance to audiences not familiar with it in order to whet their appetite for ballet.

## PRINCETON REGIONAL BALLET
McCarter Theater
Princeton, N.J. 08540

Phone: 1-609-921-8700

Performances during the season and *The Nutcracker* at Christmas.

# Theater

## ABBEY STAGE DOOR
6615 Rising Sun Avenue
Philadelphia 19111

**Phone: PI 2-8324**

Summer workshop for teenagers: 6 weeks, Tuesday, Wednesday, and Thursday, 10 A.M.–3 P.M. Ages 12–19 may apply. All aspects of theater. In November and December Abbey Players stage a children's show.

## ALLENS LANE ART CENTER
Allens Lane and McCallum Street
Philadelphia 19119

**Phone: CH 8-0546**

Children's theater; matinees once a month. Café Theater: subscription or individual seats at 8:30 P.M. Write to be put on mailing list. Special student rates. Classes in children's drama available with an annual production one week in February. For further information on the many activities at Allens Lane call or write.

## THE ANNENBERG CENTER
University of Pennsylvania
3680 Walnut Street
Philadelphia 19174

Includes the Zellerbach Theater, Harold Prince Theater, Studio Theater, and Annenberg Auditorium. Phone 594-6791 for information and reservations. Telephone reservations accepted for all tickets except Student Discount Tickets.

This complex contains four uniquely designed areas encompassing all aspects of the performing arts: theater, dance, films, concerts, and panel discussions. Some of the most exciting entertainment events in Philadelphia are presented here. There are many subscription series available, depending upon your interest.

HANDICAPPED

Theaters and restrooms accessible. Assistance available. Call in advance.

**BUCKS COUNTY PLAYHOUSE**
New Hope, Pa. 18938

Phone: 1-862-2041

One of America's oldest summer theaters. Approximately one hour's drive from Philadelphia. Call for information and reservations.

**CHELTENHAM PLAYHOUSE**
439 Ashbourne Road
Cheltenham, Pa. 19012

Phone: ES 9-4027

Four adult productions during the year plus a children's play. Student rates for all performances. Special group rates available.

**CHILDREN'S REPERTORY THEATER**
1134 Western Savings Bank Building
P.O. Box 1222
Philadelphia 19105

Phone: LO 3-2050

Children's Repertory Theater performs at the Mandell Theater of Drexel University (32nd and Chestnut Streets) and in the community October through May. Summer Festival at Drexel during July and August. Call or write for schedule and for information about their workshop programs for children 8 through 14. Watch newspapers for notice of auditions. Paid apprenticeship programs.

**CIVIC CENTER MUSEUM**
34th Street and Civic Center Boulevard
Philadelphia 19104

Phone: EV 2-8181

Children's theater on Saturdays at 11 A.M. and 1 P.M. Free. For information and tickets, send stamped self-addressed envelope to "Tickets" at above address. See page 161.

**GERMANTOWN THEATER GUILD**
4821 Germantown Avenue
Philadelphia 19144

Phone: VI 9-9799

Dance, puppet theater, and plays. Auditions for children and adults; anyone interested may apply. Call for free tickets to productions.

## HEDGEROW PLAYHOUSE
Rose Valley Road
Moylan, Pa. 19065

**Phone:** 565-4855

Children's theater programs. Write or call for information. Special group rates for schools. Adult theater year round, Thursday, Friday, and Saturday evenings at 8:30 P.M. Productions of classics and old favorites, plus many original scripts.

## IMMACULATA COLLEGE
King Road
Immaculata, Pa. 19345

**Phone:** NI 7-4400

The Children's Theatre Department produces one play a year, usually in April.

**Admission:** Adults $1.50, high-school and college students $1, children 50¢.

Write for information: Children's Theatre, Immaculata College.

## JOHN B. KELLY PLAYHOUSE IN THE PARK
Belmont Mansion Drive
West Fairmount Park
Philadelphia 19131

**Phone:** GR 7-1700 for information and tickets. Mail orders accepted.
**Open:** late spring to early fall, Monday–Saturday (Saturday performances at 6 and 9 P.M.) Twice-a-week children's musicals, two performances each day, morning and early afternoon. Reasonable admission. Group rates.
**Directions:** West River Drive to Belmont Pumping Station, left on Montgomery Drive, and right on Belmont Mansion Drive.

This first city-owned and operated theater in the United States presents theater-in-the-round in a permanent, air-conditioned building. During the season Belmont Mansion (TR 7-4830) serves lunch and dinner. Refreshment stand. Inquire about box lunches.

HANDICAPPED

Ramps and special seating when necessary. Outdoor restroom accessible. Parking adjacent. Call ahead.

## LA SALLE MUSIC THEATRE
La Salle College
20th Street and Olney Avenue
Philadelphia 19141

**Phone:** VI 8-8300, ext. 308

Summer theater. July and August. Two musicals; special student and group rates. This is a fine company offering Broadway-proven musicals and brand new productions. Write for brochure.

## MANNING STREET THEATRE
1520 Lombard Street
Philadelphia 19146

**Phone:** 732-5430

Several productions a year by Philadelphia's only resident company. The Children's Touring Company of the Manning Street Theatre takes shows into the community at a nominal cost. All are original adaptations available for any interested schools or groups in Philadelphia and the outlying areas. For further information call or write. Acting classes for 14 years and up.

## McCARTER THEATER
Princeton, N.J. 08540

For ticket information: 1-609-921-8700. Children's theater, films, and *The Nutcracker* ballet at Christmas.

## PERFORMING ARTS FOR CHILDREN
P.O. Box 265
Plymouth Meeting, Pa. 19462

**Phone:** 828-7088

Directors: Rennie and Cy Cohen. Live theater for children. Three traveling children's productions from the New York area are presented at Plymouth–Whitemarsh High School each year. Call or write for information.

## SOCIETY HILL PLAYHOUSE
507 South 8th Street
Philadelphia 19147

**Phone: WA 3-0210**

Wednesday through Saturday performances at 8:30 P.M. Original scripts and recognized contemporary plays. Small and intimate theater. Reasonably priced tickets; student rates. Philadelphia Youth Theater: workshops for 15- to 18-year-olds (page 308).

## THEATER ARTS FOR YOUTH (TAFY)
1636 Walnut Street
Philadelphia 19103

**Phone: KI 6-2263**

Three or four times a year this professional group, the inspiration of Laurie Wagman, presents plays for children. Their aim is to provide the same elements of good adult theater for a younger group. Productions run approximately one week, and each one is for a different age, from the youngest up to junior high level. Performances are mostly for school groups, and tickets are reasonably priced. Student discount rates: minimum number 20; one free adult with twenty tickets. Children's productions at Playhouse in the Park in the summer. Ask to be put on their mailing list or watch for ads in paper.

## VALLEY FORGE MUSIC FAIR
Routes U.S. 202 and Pa. 363
Devon, Pa. 19333

**Phone: 644-5000**

Year-round permanent theater. Successful Broadway musicals with name performers, "star" concerts, contemporary music, and rock concerts. Children's Theater: July and August once a week at 11 A.M. and 2 P.M. Admission: $1.75; special group rates for twenty-five or more tickets, $1. Children's classics set to music are performed.

## YMHA ARTS COUNCIL
Broad and Pine Streets
Philadelphia 19146

**Phone: KI 5-4400**

Every year the "Y" Arts Council brings imaginative programs to Philadelphia audiences, many of them "firsts" for the city. To be put on their mailing list, write or call.

## Colleges and Universities

The colleges and universities in the Philadelphia area offer a
wide variety of cultural and sporting events—many open to the
public, and many free. Theater ranges from classical to contemporary. Films can be anything from old favorites to a "noncommercial" success. Art and music are likely to be just as selective. As for
sports, in addition to the usual basketball and football there are
soccer, wrestling, fencing, and lacrosse. Write or call about specific
events, or ask to be put on their mailing list.

**BEAVER COLLEGE**
Easton and Church Roads
Glenside, Pa. 19038

**Phone: TU 4-3500**

**BRYN MAWR COLLEGE**
Bryn Mawr, Pa. 19010

**Phone: LA 5-1000**

**DREXEL UNIVERSITY**
32nd and Chestnut Streets
Philadelphia 19104

**Phone: 895-2000**

**HAVERFORD COLLEGE**
Box Office
Haverford, Pa. 19041

**Phone: MI 2-7644**

**IMMACULATA COLLEGE**
Immaculata, Pa. 19345

**Phone: NI 7-4400**

**LA SALLE COLLEGE**
20th Street and Olney Avenue
Philadelphia 19141

**Phone: VI 8-8300**

La Salle Music Theatre—summer.

**PHILADELPHIA COLLEGE OF TEXTILES AND SCIENCE**
School House Lane and Henry Avenue
Philadelphia 19144

Phone: VI 3-9700

**SAINT JOSEPH'S COLLEGE**
54th Street and City Line Avenue
Philadelphia 19131

Phone: 879-1000

**SWARTHMORE COLLEGE**
News Office
Swarthmore, Pa. 19081

Phone: KI 4-7900, ext. 456

**TEMPLE UNIVERSITY**
Philadelphia 19122

Phone: 787-7000; School of Communication and Theater, 787-8422

**UNIVERSITY OF PENNSYLVANIA**
Philadelphia 19174
Department of Public Relations
3451 Walnut Street

Phone: 594-8448

**URSINUS COLLEGE**
Collegeville, Pa. 19426

Phone: 1-489-4111

**VILLANOVA UNIVERSITY**
Villanova, Pa. 19085

Phone: 527-2100

**WEST CHESTER STATE COLLEGE**
West Chester, Pa. 19380
Office of Cultural Affairs: phone 1-436-1000

# 5
# SPORTS

## Active Sports

If you would rather "do it" than "see it," Philadelphia and the surrounding areas offer almost any form of recreation imaginable, and much of it is free. The Philadelphia Department of Recreation, MU 6-3600, is a good source for what is available in the city. The nearby counties all have Departments of Parks and Recreation, and a call or letter will provide you with information on their facilities.

**DEPARTMENT OF RECREATION**
1450 Municipal Services Building
Philadelphia 19107

**Phone:** MU 6-3600

Philadelphia's Department of Recreation ranks among the best in the country in providing sources of entertainment, sports, cultural activities, and playgrounds for people of all ages.

The Department oversees thirty-eight recreation centers, ninety-seven parks and squares, seven outdoor basketball courts, and eighty-four tennis courts, and the list of facilities grows every year. In addition, the Department runs two day camps, a camp for the retarded, a Summer Arts camp, and an overnight camp in the Poconos, William Penn by name.

It is responsible for such varied places as Robin Hood Dell, the Atwater Kent Museum, Old Fort Mifflin and the former Pennsylvania State Fish Hatchery with its fishing ponds and boat ramps, and more.

### PHYSICAL RECREATION

Philadelphia is divided into twelve recreational districts. Each district contains large recreation centers, numerous playgrounds, parks and squares, and swimming pools. For information on your particular district call MU 6-3600.

A wide variety of sports programs is run all year at the recreation centers and on the playgrounds: outdoor basketball is played year round; baseball is extremely popular, with about 10,000 engaged in organized leagues and countless others in free play. The Department operates bocce courts, soccer leagues, and volleyball and badminton programs; tennis is played on eighty-four courts with free instruction offered in summer; track and field are conducted both indoors and out, along with track meets; gymnastics, foul-shooting tournaments, table tennis, golf, boating, judo, and karate are among other sports available.

### CULTURAL ACTIVITIES

In the field of the arts the Department offers a wide range of programs covering arts and crafts, music, drama, and dance. There are summer art camps, and almost every recreation center has a dramatic group that stages several productions a season. Dance of all kinds—modern, tap, ballet, and folk—are offered, and musical concerts from firemen's bands to symphonic music and opera are available.

### SPECIAL EVENTS

In addition to the fine job of supplying recreation through playgrounds and recreation centers, the Department is responsible for many exciting events, such as the Mummers' Parade and the Soap Box Derby.

### WANDERLUST WALKS

Every weekend throughout the year a two-hour hike to interesting spots around the town and country. Free.

Each year, depending on the budget, the Department comes up with original ideas for starting new projects and expanding existing ones that help to enrich the leisure hours of people of all ages. Watch the papers for announcements of the various activities, or call the office for specific information.

## Bicycling

In Fairmount Park the popular bicycle route takes you from the Art Museum up the East River Drive to Falls Bridge, over to the West River Drive, and back to the Art Museum. Every Sunday at 2:15, groups meet on the Art Museum steps before starting their bicycle trip into the park. You can pick up a map of bicycle paths in Fairmount Park at the Fairmount Park Commission office in Memorial Hall or at the Fairmount Park bicycle rental concession located behind the Art Museum at the site of the old Aquarium. This concession is open 11 A.M.–7 P.M. weekdays, 10 A.M.–6:30 P.M. weekends (phone: 765-9076).

The Department of Recreation sponsors rides on the East and West River Drives, and to New Hope, Atlantic City, and Cape May. They are usually during the week at 7 P.M. or Saturday mornings at 11 A.M. Call MU 6-3616 and ask them to send you a cycling schedule. Also inquire about the Fairmount Park Invitational Bicycle Race in August, open to all, and the Annual Safety Bicycle Rodeo Program, open to children up to 14. Four categories: straight-line riding, maneuvering, balance, and stopping. Twelve district champions from neighborhood recreation centers compete in city finals. Call MU 6-3616 for further details.

**AMATEUR BICYCLE LEAGUE OF AMERICA** sponsors bicycle races in front of Memorial Hall every Sunday in March and into April. All classes. Call MI 9-3209 or write to C. J. Harper, Jr., 921 Delmont Drive, Wynnewood, Pa. 19096, for further information.

**AMERICAN YOUTH HOSTELS (AYU)** (4714 Old York Road, Philadelphia 19141; phone: GL 7-5700) offers short and long trips with various degrees of difficulty. You can tour Society Hill or Valley Forge State Park, or take a 30-mile trip along the Horseshoe Trail.

There are many lovely areas to bicycle in and around the city. Pack your bicycle in your car and try Valley Forge Park, the towpath in New Hope, or Valley Green in the Wissahickon.

## *Boating*

### SAILING

The Schuylkill River is a good place to begin sailing, since it is protected from strong winds. Starting in the spring on weekends and in the summer seven days a week, canoes, rowboats, and sailboats are available for rent from the East Park Canoe House, East River Drive below the Strawberry Mansion Bridge. Call BA 8-9336 for further information.

Another popular local sailing place, open all year, is on the Delaware River at a city-owned launching site located at Torresdale Street off Linden Avenue. The Delaware, the experts say, is not for beginners because of the tides and the debris in the water.

## CANOEING

Right here in the city is a very active club, the Philadelphia Canoe Club (4900 Ridge Avenue, Philadelphia 19127; phone: IV 2-9785). Anyone may participate in their varied trips and training sessions. White-water canoeing available at Fat Rock Lake, head of Manayunk Canal, said to be the only such access to a section of river rapids within a large U.S. city. Call or write for further information.

**Kittatinny Canoes,** Silver Lake Road, Dingman's Ferry, Pa. 18328. Phone: 1-717-828-2700. Saturday, Sunday, holidays, $9 for single-day rental; Monday–Friday $8 for single-day rental. This includes paddles, two life vests, and delivery and pickup service. Canoe trips on the Delaware River—quiet trips for the beginner, white water for the expert, and overnight trips. Call in advance for reservations.

**Canoe Trips on the Raritan River.** Ten-mile canoe trip down the sparkling and scenic south branch of the Raritan River through the forest and farmland of Hunterdon County, New Jersey. These trips are led by veteran canoeist Peter F. Buell, member of the American Canoeist Association. For trip reservations write or call Mr. Buell, R.D. 1, Lebanon, N.J. 08833 (phone: 1-201-236-2716).

Many local townships and counties have parks with fine boating facilities. Some of these, such as the Bucks County parks, are open to the public. Write to Bucks County Department of Parks and Recreation, Box 358, R.D. 1, Langhorne, Pa. 19047, or phone 757-0571 for information. Also try Wharton State Forest, Batsto R.D. 1, Hammonton, N.J. 08037, phone: 1-609-561-0024; French Creek State Park, phone: 1-582-8125; or write to Pennsylvania State Parks, Department of Environmental Resources, Feller Building, Harrisburg, Pa. 17101.

### *Camping*

## NEW JERSEY STATE PARKS

**Wharton State Forest** (see page 211), U.S. Route 206 at Atsion, 155 square miles in the Pine Barrens of central New Jersey. Hiking, fishing, hunting, boating.

For information on other sites write: Bureau of Parks, P.O. Box 1420, Trenton, N.J. 08625.

# PENNSYLVANIA STATE PARKS

Pennsylvania state parks do not accept advance reservations. They are administered by the Department of Environmental Resources. Write to them and they will furnish a list of parks and available facilities, rules, locations, and maps: Pennsylvania Department of Environmental Resources, Feller Building, Harrisburg, Pa. 17101.

## *Fishing*

Pack a picnic lunch and take your rod. Fishing enthusiasts have a wealth of places to choose from in the Delaware Valley. Try Fairmount Park, the Wissahickon Creek, the Roxborough–Germantown area (trout fishing in season), and Concourse Lake, 44th Street and Parkside Avenue, which is only for children under 16.

### FISHING REGULATIONS

Residents 16 to 64 years of age require a $5.20 license, those 65 and over a $2.20 license, both good for one year. Those 16 and under do not require a license. A nonresident license for those 12 years old and over costs $9.70, also good for one year, and a nonresident tourist license covering five days of the season costs $5.20. Licenses are obtainable at Concourse, Municipal Services Building, 15th Street and John F. Kennedy Boulevard, Philadelphia.

Some nearby good places for fishing:

## FORMER PENNSYLVANIA STATE FISH HATCHERY
8900 Delaware Avenue
Philadelphia

**Phone: DE 2-7458**

Fishing for young children. The area around the hatchery has a park with picnic facilities. Open all day and free.

## FRENCH CREEK STATE PARK
Stocked with brown and rainbow trout in season (page 197).

## GREEN LANE RESERVOIR
Hill Road near interesection of Pa. Routes 29 and 63
Green Lane, Pa. 18054

**Phone: 234-4863**

Fishing for bass, pike, and trout at an 815-acre reservoir maintained by the Philadelphia Suburban Water Company. Boat rentals available, or fish from the banks. Fee: Adults $1, children under 16 free.

## NEWLIN MILL PARK
U.S. Route 1
Glen Mills, Pa.

**Phone:** GL 9-2359

Ponds heavily stocked with rainbow and brook trout in spring, brown trout in summer. No license required. You pay by the fish. If you want to be sure of a "catch," try here (page 236).

## PERKIOMEN CREEK

From Perkiomenville to Oaks. Bass and muskies.

## RIDLEY CREEK STATE PARK
Media, Pa.

Good for trout April through Labor Day (page 204).

## SPRINGTON RESERVOIR

Between Media and Newtown Square off Pa. Route 252. Bass (June to March), all year for pan fish.

## VALLEY FORGE STATE PARK

Schuylkill River; muskies, May through March (page 70).

## WHARTON STATE FOREST
See page 211.

For a free complete fisherman's guide to Pennsylvania waters and access areas, write: Fish Commission, P.O. Box 1673, Harrisburg, Pa. 17105. The waters are listed alphabetically and by county, with the nearest towns, route numbers, and size in mileage or acreage.

For a list of fishing locations and species of fish in New Jersey's many lakes and ponds, write: Division of Fish and Game, Department of Environmental Protection, Box 1809, Trenton, N.J. 08625.

## *Hiking*

### AMERICAN YOUTH HOSTELS, INC.
4714 Old York Road
Philadelphia 19141

**Phone:** GL 7-5700

AYH offers many varieties of hikes—long, short, easy, difficult.
Some in the past have been to the New Jersey Pine Barrens and
along the Horseshoe Trail. Write or phone for further information
on the club's activities.

Two of the best-known hiking trails anywhere lie within easy
reach of Philadelphia. They are the Appalachian and Horseshoe
Trails.

### APPALACHIAN TRAIL

Pennsylvania is fortunate that, of the 214 miles of the Appalachian Trail that go through Pennsylvania, only about 40 miles of
the trail are on privately owned land. The rest is park and game
lands. For information and publications on hiking the 2,000-mile
Appalachian Trail, from Mount Katahdin in Maine to Springer
Mountain in Georgia, write: Appalachian Trail Conference, P.O.
Box 236, Harpers Ferry, West Virginia 25425. For local information
write or call Kenneth Graham, 320 Merion Avenue, Narberth,
Pa. 19072 (MO 4-8530).

### HORSESHOE TRAIL

The trail begins at the intersection of Pa. Routes 23 and 252
in the heart of Valley Forge State Park. Yellow blazes of paint on
trees and rocks and an occasional yellow horseshoe pinned to
trees mark the trail for you. The path at times turns into suburban
roads but then plunges back into the woods. You go through rolling
Chester County countryside, back country roads, and cornfields
to Chester Springs. This will cover about 15 miles of the 120-mile
Horseshoe Trail, which extends to Harrisburg. For further information contact the Horseshoe Trail Club, John Goff, Chairman, 623
Righter's Mill Road, Narberth, Pa. 19072. For a map of Horseshoe
Trail, enclose $2.

## SIERRA CLUB

This is a very active club offering activities almost every weekend of the year. The local branch of the nationwide famous Sierra Club offers hikes and canoe trips. They explore Valley Forge, the Horseshoe Trail, and Brandywine Creek, as well as longer trips. Membership is not required to join in the local explorations. For information on activities and membership write Albert C. Gerould, 6923 Greene Street, Philadelphia 19119, or call VI 8-3268.

## WANDERLUST WALKS

Now sponsored by the Philadelphia Department of Recreation, this hiking program has attracted followers for over sixty years. Every Saturday (fifty weeks of the year) hikers meet at a spot accessible to local transportation and explore such places as Morris Arboretum, the Wissahickon, and Tookany Creek Park. The average hike is about 4 miles. Call MU 6-3616 for schedule.

### Horseback Riding

The bridle paths in Fairmount Park, especially the Wissahickon and Pennypack Park are hard to beat. See page 147.

### Hosteling

**AMERICAN YOUTH HOSTELS, INC.**
4714 Old York Road
Philadelphia 19141

**Phone: GL 7-5700**

AYH is a nonprofit association for the purpose of encouraging people of all ages to enjoy the out-of-doors by cycling, hiking, skiing, sailing, canoeing, and riding, and to travel inexpensively by staying in hostels, which are simple overnight accommodations in scenic, historic, and cultural areas.

The Delaware Valley Council of AYH carries on a vast program all year, including ski trips, hikes in the Wissahickon, sailing on the Chesapeake, bicycling (one- and two-day trips), exploring the local countryside around Philadelphia, and canoeing on the Schuylkill, in New Jersey's Pine Barrens, on the Delaware Canal near New Hope, and on the Brandywine River. There is also white-water canoeing near Hickory Run State Park. Hiking trips take you through the Pine Barrens, the Horseshoe Trail, and the Appalachian Trail. You do not have to be a member to join in their many and varied trips.

Write or call for further information on this most worthwhile organization that in a very real sense offers recreation for the whole family.

## Ice Skating

Here is a list of the principal skating rinks in Greater Philadelphia and their public skating hours. Check in advance; sometimes the schedule is altered because of special events or hockey games.

**BOULEVARD ICE RINK**
Roosevelt Boulevard and Princeton Avenue
Philadelphia

**Phone:** MA 4-1133

Open every evening 6–11 P.M. Public hockey sessions daily 3:30–5 P.M.

**CHERRY HILL ARENA**
Brace and Berlin Roads
Cherry Hill, N.J.

**Phone:** 1-609-795-1275

Public skating times vary. Call for information.

**GRUNDY RECREATION CENTER**
700 Jefferson Avenue
Bristol, Pa.

**Phone:** 788-3311

Open until April 15. Skating every Tuesday through Sunday at various hours during day and evening. Call for information.

**MELODY BROOK ICE SKATING RINK**
Pa. Route 309 and Lenhart Road
Colmar, Pa.

**Phone:** 1-822-3613

Monday, 12:30–2:30 P.M. and 3–5 P.M.; Wednesday–Sunday 12:30–2:30 P.M., 3–5 P.M., 8–10:30 P.M.

## PENN CENTER RINK
17th Street and John F. Kennedy Boulevard
Philadelphia

**Phone:** LO 4-4430

Winter months, day and night.

## RADNOR RINK
789 Lancaster Avenue
Villanova, Pa.

**Phone:** 527-1230

Sunday–Friday, mornings and afternoons; Saturday afternoons; Wednesday, Friday, and Sunday evenings.

## SCANLON RECREATION CENTER
"J" and Tioga Streets
Philadelphia

**Phone:** RE 9-5515

## SIMONS RECREATION CENTER
Walnut Lane and Rodney Street
Philadelphia

**Phone:** HA 4-9359

## TARKEN RECREATION CENTER
Frontenac and Levick Streets
Philadelphia

**Phone:** PI 3-3266

The three rinks listed above are all under the aegis of the Philadelphia Department of Recreation. Open winter months after school, evenings, all day Saturday, and part of Sunday, all school and major holidays.

## UNIVERSITY OF PENNSYLVANIA CLASS OF 1923
### ICE SKATING RINK
3130 Walnut Street
Philadelphia

Open all year. Public skating every day. Call 594-6607 for tape recording of hours open. Group rate and instruction available.

## Public Skating at Private Clubs

### OLD YORK ROAD SKATING CLUB
Old York and Church Roads
Elkins Park, Pa.

**Phone:** ME 5-0331

October 15–April 15. Monday and Friday afternoons 3:30–5 P.M.;
Saturday mornings 10:15 A.M.–12 noon; Friday, Saturday, and Sunday evenings 8:30–10:30.

### PHILADELPHIA SKATING CLUB
Holland Avenue and County Line Road
Ardmore, Pa.

**Phone:** MI 2-8700

Mid–October to mid–May. Friday evening, 8–10:30 P.M.; Saturday evening, 7:30–10 P.M.

### SKATING CLUB AT WILMINGTON
Weldin Road off Foulk
Wilmington, Del.

**Phone:** 1-302-656-5005

Open all year except May and September. Friday and Saturday evenings 8:00–10:00, Saturday 1:30–3:30 P.M., Sunday, 4:00–6:00 P.M.

### WINTERSPORT SKATING ARENA OF WILLOW GROVE
551 York Road
Willow Grove, Pa.

**Phone:** OL 0-6976

All year. Weekdays 10 A.M.–12 noon; Saturday 10:30 A.M.–12 noon; Friday and Saturday 8–10:15 P.M.

### WISSAHICKON SKATING CLUB
Willow Grove Avenue and Cherokee Street
Chestnut Hill, Philadelphia

**Phone:** CH 7-1907

Open all year except September to mid-October. Public sessions: Friday, Saturday, Sunday 8:30–10:30 P.M. Summer figure-skating school, hockey clinic; skate shop.

## Skiing

For the novice, intermediate, or expert, there are many ski areas close to Philadelphia that will provide a pleasant day on the slopes. Some places offer nursery schools for the very young while parents ski, others run ski schools for children aged four and up. Many of these resorts are in the Poconos: for complete information on their winter activities write to Pocono Mountain Vacation Bureau, 1004 Main Street, Stroudsburg, Pa. 18360, or call 1-717-421-5791.

The following is a good sampling of ski areas in Pennsylvania, New Jersey, and Delaware. They are listed alphabetically and are included because of proximity or excellent facilities. Unless otherwise noted, the areas are in Pennsylvania.

### APPLE HILL

Fifty miles northwest of Philadelphia; three miles from Lehigh Valley interchange on Northeast Extension of Pennsylvania Turnpike; turn left at blinker in Orefield. Phone: 1-395-4241. Terrain: five slopes and trails; vertical drop 240 feet. Lifts: one T-bar, three rope tows. Lodge facilities: cafeteria, ski sales and rental shop. Instruction: children's learn-to-ski classes. Special for children: nursery open daily. Special ski races and contests.

### BIG BOULDER

Ninety miles northwest of Philadelphia at Lake Harmony, 10 miles east of White Haven off Pa. Route 903 via Pa. Routes 940 and 115; off Pocono exit 35 of Northeast Extension of Pennsylvania Turnpike. Phone: 1-717-722-0101. Terrain: seven slopes, four trails; vertical drop 475 feet. Lifts: three double chairs, two T-bars, one J-bar, one rope tow. Lodge facilities: cafeteria, ski sales and rental shop. Special for children: children's nursery, student rate for junior season ticket.

### BUCK HILL

North of Philadelphia, 110 miles, 15 miles from East Stroudsburg off Pa. Route 191. Take Northeast Extension of Pennsylvania Turnpike to exit 34, U.S. Route 209 east to Stroudsburg and Pa. Route 191 north. Phone: 1-717-595-7441. Terrain: twelve slopes and trails; vertical drop 300 feet. Lifts: two poma lifts. Lodge facilities: snack bars, rental shop. Special for children: 22,000-square-foot skating rink and special sledding slopes. Snowmobiling, cross-country skiing, and rentals available.

## CAMELBACK

Ninety-five miles northwest of Philadelphia in Tannersville 18372, northwest of Stroudsburg. Take Northeast Extension of Pennsylvania Turnpike to Interstate 80; exit 45 off Interstate 80. Phone: 1-717-629-1661. Terrain: three slopes, thirteen trails; vertical drop 750 feet. Lifts: two chairs, two T-bars, one J-bar. Lodge facilities: ski sales and rental shop, snack bar. Special for children: nursery is open daily 9:30 A.M.–4:30 P.M., Friday 6–9:30 P.M.; ski school for 4-year-olds and up.

## CHADDS PEAK

Eighteen miles south of Philadelphia on U.S. Route 1, Chadds Ford, Pa. 19317. Phone: 1-388-7421. Weekends and holidays 9 A.M.–5:30 P.M., nights 6:30–10:00. Terrain: vertical drop 283 feet. Lifts: poma lift, three ropes. Lodge facilities: snack bar, complete rental shop. Special for children: ski school for 6- to 12-year-olds.

## DOE MOUNTAIN

Fifty miles northwest of Philadelphia off Pa. Routes 29 and 100, 12 miles south of Allentown, via Northeast Extension of Pennsylvania Turnpike. Phone: 1-682-7107. Terrain: two slopes; vertical drop 367 feet. Lifts: two double chairs, one T-bar, one rope. Lodge facilities: ski school, ski rentals.

## ELK MOUNTAIN

. . . is 160 miles northwest of Philadelphia, R.D. 2, Union Dale, Pa. 18470, 9 miles east of I-81 via Northeast Extension of Pennsylvania Turnpike. Phone: 1-717-679-2611. Terrain: vertical drop 1,000 feet. Lifts: three chairs, one J-bar. Lodge facilities: ski school, ski rental, cafeteria, and shack where you can bring your own lunch or grill over an indoor fire. It's a long trip for a day of skiing, but it offers the finest skiing facilities if you're more than a novice skier.

## FERNWOOD

At Bushkill, Pa. 18324, 115 miles from Philadelphia. Phone: 1-717-588-6661. Pennsylvania Turnpike, Northeast Extension to exit 34, Route U.S. 209 north to Stroudsburg bypass (I-80 East) to exit 52, then U.S. Route 209 north to Fernwood. Terrain: four slopes and trails; vertical drop 200 feet. Lifts: one rope. Lodge facilities: rental shop, ski school. Special for children: sledding and tobogganing; nursery; ice skating; ice fishing; children free midweek. Snowmobile rental.

## GREAT GORGE

In McAfee, New Jersey 07428, 115 miles northeast of Philadelphia. New Jersey Turnpike to Route I-80, west to N.J. Route 23, north to N.J. Route 94, east for 3 miles. Phone: 1-201-827-2000. Terrain: twenty trails; vertical drop 1,033 feet. Lifts: eight double chairs, two ropes for beginners. Lodge facilities: quick snacks or full meals; the dining rooms offer a special children's menu. Special for children: ski instruction for toddlers; also nursery for 2- to 6-year-olds while parents ski. Emphasis on kids' learn-to-ski programs and racing events for youngsters.

## HONEY BROOK HILL

Fifty miles west of Philadelphia on Pa. Route 10, 10 miles south of Morgantown Interchange of Pennsylvania Turnpike in Honey Brook, Pa. 19344. Phone: 1-717-273-3248. Terrain: ten trails; vertical drop 240 feet. Lifts: one funicular, one rope. Lodge facilities: ski school, ski rentals.

## JACK FROST MOUNTAIN

Ninety miles northwest of Philadelphia on Pa. Route 940 in Whitehaven, Pa. 18661, via Northeast Extension of Pennsylvania Turnpike to exit 35. Four miles from Big Boulder (offer combines lift ticket with Big Boulder). Phone: 1-717-443-8425. Terrain: eleven slopes; vertical drop 500 feet. Lifts: five chairs, one J-bar. Lodge facilities: summit lodge, cafeteria.

## MOUNT AIRY LODGE

One hundred miles north of Philadelphia at Mount Pocono, Pa. 18344. Take Northeast Extension of Pennsylvania Turnpike to I-80, east to U.S. Route 380, north to Pa. Route 940. Phone: 1-717-839-7133. Terrain: vertical drop 230 feet. Lifts: one double chair. Special facilities: cross-country skiing over miles of country trails along with rental equipment. Mount Airy also has a team of Alaskan huskies to pull sleds; snowmobiles available for rent; indoor and outdoor ice skating.

## POCONO MANOR

. . . is 105 miles northwest of Philadelphia, 15 miles northwest of Stroudsburg off Pa. Route 611, Pocono Manor, Pa. 18349; travel via Northeast Extension of Pennsylvania Turnpike to I-80, east to U.S. Route 380. Phone: 1-717-839-7111. Terrain: four slopes and trails; vertical drop 250 feet. Lifts: J-bar and rope tow. Lodge facilities: ski school, rental shop. Special for children: sledding slopes, 1,000-foot toboggan chute. Snowmobile rentals.

## POCO-NORTH

North of Philadelphia 135 miles, 2 miles west of Hawley off U.S. Route 6, Hawley, Pa. 18428. Travel via Northeast Extension of Pennsylvania Turnpike to exit 38. Phone: 1-717-226-4595. Terrain: six slopes and trails; vertical drop 417 feet. Lifts: double chair, T-bar, double rope tow. Lodge facilities: lounge-restaurant, ski shop. Special for children: kiddie ski school.

## SKI ROUNDTOP

. . . is 95 miles west of Philadelphia off Pa. Route 177 in Dillsburg, Pa., 3 miles north of Pinchot Park near Harrisburg and York; travel via Pennsylvania Turnpike to exit 18, south on I-83 to Pa. Route 177. Phone: 1-717-432-9631. Write R.D. 1, Dillsburg 17019. Terrain: vertical drop 550 feet. Lifts: three chairs, two ropes.

## SPRING MOUNTAIN

Twenty-eight miles northwest of Philadelphia on Pa. Routes 29 and 73, Schwenksville, Pa. 19473; take Pa. Route 309 to Pa. Route 73, west to Schwenksville. Phone: 1-287-7900. Operates daily until 11 P.M. Terrain: two slopes, five trails; vertical drop 410 feet. Lifts: two double chairs, three rope tows. Lodge facilities: ski rental and ski school. Good place close to Philadelphia for children to start.

## TIMBER HILL

Ninety-five miles from Philadelphia off Pa. Route 447, 10 miles north of East Stroudsburg, Pa. 18301; via Northeast Extension of Pennsylvania Turnpike to I-80, east to Stroudsburg. Phone: 1-717-595-7571. Terrain, six slopes and trails; vertical drop 400 feet. Lifts: two T-bars and a poma lift. Lodge facilities: cafeteria, ski and rental shop. Special for children: ski-jumping school, 15 and 30 meters; free skiing during first hour of operation.

## Swimming

Philadelphia and its surrounding counties operate a multitude of pools all summer for recreation, competition, and instruction. For information on the pools run by the Philadelphia Department of Recreation call MU 6-3615; also, see page 145 for information on pools in Fairmount Park. Memorial Hall indoor pool is open all year, Monday through Saturday. Call for hours.

## Tennis

In recent years interest in tennis has grown to unbelievable proportions, and this is reflected in the number of facilities, public and private, that have mushroomed all over the city and suburbs. The advent of indoor tennis facilities, allowing the game to be played year round, has added to the popularity of the sport—and to the proficiency of the players. There are over 1,000 public outdoor courts in parks, recreation centers, and schools available to the public free or for modest charges. Call your local Department of Parks and Recreation for location of courts. There are over 100 courts in Fairmount Park and 125 scattered throughout the city. For locations call MU 6-1776, ext. 81204.

Private indoor tennis clubs are often open to the public. The great advantage of indoor courts is controlled weather and lighting conditions. The courts are open seven days a week with evening hours. The usual season is October to May. Each club offers different plans. Rate schedules are usually divided into prime and nonprime times depending on the time of day and day of the week. Some offer clinics for children and special rates for juniors. There are approximately fifty indoor clubs in the Delaware Valley. For further information consult "Tennis Clubs" in the yellow pages of the phone book.

## Spectator Sports

Philadelphia is one of the foremost centers of amateur and professional sports in the United States. In all seasons of the year you can watch top athletes and contests, be it ice hockey, track and field, professional and amateur tennis, basketball, football, rowing regattas, or horse shows. The sports complex of Veterans Stadium and the Spectrum offers fans comfortable seating and fine viewing. If large crowds aren't for you, try a polo match at Toughkenamon, or a sailing regatta on the Schuylkill River.

## *Baseball*

**THE PHILLIES**
Veterans Stadium
Broad Street and Pattison Avenue
Philadelphia 19148

**Phone:** General ticket information: HO 3-1000; inclement weather and game information: HO 3-5300; season tickets, group rates, and birthday parties: HO 3-5000
**Admission:** Field box seats, $4.50, terrace and loge box seats, $4, reserved seats, $3.25; general admission, $2.25 (under 14, 50¢)
**Directions:** Schuylkill Expressway east to Stadium exit (Broad Street); *or* south on Broad Street to Veterans Stadium
**Public Transportation:** By subway (the fastest): Broad Street Subway south to Pattison Avenue stop

The Phillies have been drawing crowds of sports fans for over ninety years. Now they are playing in the new Veterans Stadium with an animated electronic scoreboard, comfortable seats, and lots of concessions for eating. The Phillies sponsor many special events —family night, teen night, cap day, bat day, and fireworks displays. At any game you can run into some highjinks dreamed up by their promotion department.

## *Basketball*

**THE '76ERS**
The Spectrum
Broad Street and Pattison Avenue
Philadelphia 19148

**Phone:** HO 3-1776
**Admission:** $3 to $6
**Directions:** Schuylkill Expressway to Stadium exit (Broad Street); or south on Broad Street to Spectrum
**Public Transportation:** Broad Street Subway south to Pattison Avenue stop

Our local professional basketball team's season extends from October to March. Call to inquire about special promotions—"ladies' night" and "shirt night" are two examples—and group rates.

**THE BIG FIVE** (La Salle, Saint Joseph's, Temple, Villanova, and the University of Pennsylvania)
The Palestra
33rd Street near Spruce Street
Philadelphia 19174

**Phone:** 594-6151 for ticket information
**Admission:** $3 and $4; group rate for 25 or more seats, phone 594-4747
**Directions:** Schuylkill Expressway to South Street exit; right on 33rd Street to the Palestra
**Public Transportation:** SEPTA Routes D, D-1 from the Penn Central 30th Street Station, 42

Philadelphia is an enthusiastic collegiate basketball town and always comes up with teams to justify the fans' excitement. There is great spirit (and a high noise level) for all the Big Five games. These teams compete with each other and outside schools.

## Boating and Sailing

**ROWING REGATTAS**
On the East River Drive
Philadelphia

**Phone:** PO 9-2068
**Admission:** Free

From April to September you can watch sculling on the Schuylkill. For over a hundred years Philadelphia has been active in competitive rowing. There are local, national, and international regattas. Amateur, scholastic, and collegiate classes compete on weekends in April and May. Check the dates of the Philadelphia Scholastic Championship and the largest college regatta in the country, the Dad Vail. The University of Pennsylvania holds its annual Skimmer Day, an Ivy League rivalry, here.

The boat club competitions include the famous biennial American Henley Regatta for colleges and clubs in June, the Independence Day Regatta, and the Middle States Regatta on Labor Day. Check for dates and information with the National Association of Amateur Oarsmen (PO 9-2068).

## SAILING REGATTAS

Sailing races are held most of the year, including the winter months when the Frostbite Sailing Competition is held. Best vantage point is from the East Park Canoe House at the Strawberry Mansion Bridge. Many local colleges compete on weekends. Call PO 9-2068 for schedule.

## Bocce

The Italian version of lawn bowling. You can watch this at Columbus Square Park, 12th and Wharton Streets, or in Fairmount Park, Edgely Road east of Belmont Avenue. For information call TR 7-9774.

## Football

**ARMY–NAVY GAME**
John F. Kennedy Stadium
11th Street and Pattison Avenue
Philadelphia

This annual classic is played late in November in mammoth John F. Kennedy Stadium (formerly Municipal Stadium), built for the Sesquicentennial Exposition of 1926 with a seating capacity of over 102,000. There are great tradition and excitement attached to the Army–Navy Game. No matter what the team records are at the time, something unexpected can happen—and often does. Write for tickets to U.S. Military and Naval Academies. A limited number of tickets available at ticket agencies, and some are sold at the stadium on the day of the game, as well as at the Convention and Visitors Center.

**PHILADELPHIA BELL**
John F. Kennedy Stadium
11th Street and Pattison Avenue
Philadelphia

**Phone:** KI 6-2300 for ticket and schedule information
**Admission:** $4, $6, $8

Philadelphia's new pro football team, a member of the World Football League, plays July through November.

**PHILADELPHIA EAGLES**
Veterans Stadium
Broad Street and Pattison Avenue
Philadelphia 19148

**Phone:** HO 3-5500 (ticket office)
**Admission:** $5, $6, $7, $8, and $12.50
**Directions:** Schuylkill Expressway to Stadium exit (Broad Street);
   *or* Broad Street south to Stadium
**Parking:** Available for a fee at stadium lots
**Public Transportation:** Broad Street Subway south to Pattison
   Avenue; special "Sportsmen's Buses" from the outlying suburbs.
   Call SEPTA (DA 9-4800) for schedule.

Loyal fans continue to pack Veterans Stadium for every home
game. Many of the seats go to season-ticket holders, but there are
always some available.

## *Horse Shows*

### DEVON HORSE SHOW AND COUNTRY FAIR
Devon Horse Show Grounds
Devon, Pa. 19333

In late May and early June the finest equestrians in the country
come to Devon to compete for one week in various events (see
page 260).

### THE MORGAN HORSE SHOW AND COUNTRY FAIR
Devon Horse Show Grounds
Devon, Pa. 19333

Held in August. Three days of events demonstrating the skills of
the highly prized Morgan horse (see page 265).

### PENNSYLVANIA HUNT CUP

In November near Unionville, Pa. Post time 2 P.M. Features cross-
country races over fences and hedges. Here you can see racing
silks, great horses, and old carriages. Go early and take your
camera. Bring a folding chair. Food tent. For further information write Pennsylvania Hunt Cup Committee, Brooklawn Farm,
Unionville, Pa. 19375.

### PHILADELPHIA HORSE SHOW AND
   JUMPING COMPETITION
The Spectrum
Broad Street and Pattison Avenue
Philadelphia 19148

**Admission:** For ticket information call Episcopal Hospital, GA 6-8000, and ask to be connected with the Philadelphia Horse Show office.
**Directions:** Schuylkill Expressway to Stadium exit (Broad Street); *or* south on Broad Street to Spectrum
**Parking:** Available; fee
**Public Transportation:** Broad Street Subway south to Pattison Avenue stop

In a few short years this has become one of the largest indoor horse shows in the country, with champions from all over the world competing. Held in October, the Philadelphia Horse Show combines rodeo, high jumpers, and dressage. The beneficiary is Episcopal Hospital.

## *Ice Hockey*

**THE FLYERS**
At the Spectrum
Broad Street and Pattison Avenue
Philadelphia 19148

**Phone:** HO 5-4500
**Directions:** Schuylkill Expressway south to Stadium exit (Broad Street); *or* south on Broad Street to Spectrum
**Public Transportation:** Broad Street Subway south to Pattison Avenue stop

The Flyers (Stanley Cup champions) and ice hockey are extremely popular with Philadelphia sports fans. This fast-moving game plays to capacity crowds. Many season tickets are sold; call the box office (389-5000) for information on single tickets, priced $4.50 to $8.50.

## *Lacrosse*

**PHILADELPHIA WINGS**
The Spectrum
Broad Street and Pattison Avenue
Philadelphia

**Ticket information:** FU 9-5000. For group rates and season tickets call MO 7-0880.
**Admission:** $2, $3, $4, $5.

The North American Indians developed this rough-and-tumble sport, named lacrosse by the French settlers. The Wings, a professional team, now play this exciting fast game here, May through August.

## Polo

There's lots of action when two teams of four men on horseback using long-handled mallets try to hit a wooden ball into the opponents' goal. A good spectator sport.

### BRANDYWINE POLO CLUB
U.S. Route 1 between Kennett Square and Avondale
Toughkenamon, Pa.

**Phone:** 1-268-8692
**Directions:** Schuylkill Expressway to U.S. Route 1 south

Wednesday nights at 8 P.M. and Sunday afternoons at 3 P.M., weather permitting. Admission is $1, children under 12 free. Open June to October. Pack a picnic lunch or supper and eat on the "tailgate." Bring field glasses. Stands for viewing.

### CHUKKER VALLEY POLO CLUB
Chukker Valley Farms
Gilbertsville, Pa. 19525

**Phone:** 1-754-7261

It's on Pa. Routes 663 and 73, 5 miles north of Pottstown; travel via Pa. Route 611 to Pa. Route 309 to Pa. Route 73. About an hour's drive from Center City. Open June to October, Sunday afternoons at 3 P.M., weather permitting. Admission: $1, children under 12 free. Stands provided for viewing, but many people prefer to bring a folding chair or blanket. Teams from all over the Eastern Seaboard compete. Luncheon available at the Chukker Valley Golf Club. Write for schedule.

## Soccer

### THE ATOMS
Veterans Stadium
Broad Street and Pattison Avenue
Philadelphia 19148

189

**Ticket information:** 542-7799. Call for information about season tickets.

**Admission:** Reserved seats $4; general admission $2.50; students (with I.D. card) $2; senior citizens and children (under 15) $1. Group rates available.

**Directions:** Schuylkill Expressway east to Stadium exit (Broad Street); *or* south on Broad Street to Spectrum

**Public Transportation:** Broad Street Subway south to Pattison Avenue stop; *or* call SEPTA, (DA 9-4800) for information on special buses.

This new and highly successful professional soccer team, the Philadelphia Atoms Club, is a member of the North American Soccer League. During their season from May through August they play at least once a week, Fridays at 8:05 P.M. (and some Wednesdays). Junior teams often play in preliminary and halftime games.

## THE UKRAINIAN NATIONALS

The "Ukes," a semiprofessional team, play from September to December and March to May at the Central High football field, 5400 North Broad Street, Philadelphia. Admission: Adult men $3, ladies and students $1, children under 14 free. For further information call LI 9-8529. Public transportation: Take the Broad Street Subway to the Olney stop; *or* SEPTA Route C.

## *Tennis*

Tennis as a spectator sport is enjoying tremendous popularity all over the country, and Philadelphia is a leader in both amateur and professional tournaments, indoor and outdoor.

## PENNSYLVANIA LAWN TENNIS CHAMPIONSHIPS

Held in August at Merion Cricket Club. Grass court tennis championship featuring international stars and top college players (men and women). For ticket information call Merion Cricket Club (MI 2-5800).

## PHILADELPHIA FREEDOMS
The Spectrum
Broad Street and Pattison Avenue
Philadelphia

Phone: 265-6400 or 265-3800
Admission: $4, $5, $6. For group rates and further information call or write: P.O. Box 132, King of Prussia, Pa. 19406.

Sixteen teams throughout the country compete in singles and mixed doubles. Billie Jean King and Fred Stolle headline the Philadelphia team. May through August 7:30 P.M. at the Spectrum.

## PHILADELPHIA VIRGINIA SLIMS TENNIS CLASSIC

Held in April at the Palestra, 33rd and Walnut Streets (University of Pennsylvania campus). Women's professional tournament. Singles and doubles. Admission: $4 to $8. Student and group rates available. All proceeds to benefit free public tennis programs for children. Call 949-2530; or write Philadelphia Indoor Tennis Corporation, 536 Moredon Road, Huntingdon Valley, Pa. 19006. Directions: Schuylkill Expressway to South Street exit. Public Transportation: SEPTA Routes D, D-1 from Penn Central 30th Street Station, 42.

## UNITED STATES PROFESSIONAL INDOOR TENNIS CHAMPIONSHIPS

All of the world's top professional male tennis players of World Championship Tennis compete in singles and doubles for top prize money at the Spectrum, Broad Street and Pattison Avenue, Philadelphia, in late January. Admission: $5 to $8. Student and group rates available. All proceeds benefit free public tennis programs for children in the Delaware Valley. Directions: Schuylkill Expressway to Stadium exit (Broad Street); *or* south on Broad Street to Spectrum. Public transportation: Broad Street Subway south to Pattison Avenue. For information call 947-2530; or write Philadelphia Indoor Tennis Corporation, 536 Moredon Road, Hunting-don Valley, Pa. 19006.

## THE USLTA NATIONAL–GIRLS 18 (GRASS)

Held in August at the Philadelphia Cricket Club. Singles and doubles. For information call the Philadelphia Cricket Club (CH 7-6001).

## Track and Field

**PENN RELAYS**
Franklin Field
33rd Street below Walnut Street
Philadelphia

**Phone:** 594-6154
**Public Transportation:** SEPTA Routes D, D-1 from Penn Central
30th Street Station, 40, 42

For over seventy-five years this major classic of track and field events has attracted top high-school and college athletes from all parts of the country. Last full weekend in April. Admission: Friday all seats $3; Saturday box seats $8, reserved $7, general admission $5. Handicapped: general admission ticket. Wheelchairs may be brought in at west end of stadium.

**PHILADELPHIA TRACK CLASSIC**
The Spectrum
Broad Street and Pattison Avenue
Philadelphia

**Admission:** For ticket information call MU 6-3597 or 563-1242.
**Directions:** Schuylkill Expressway to Stadium exit (Broad Street);
  *or* south on Broad Street to Spectrum
**Public Transportation:** Broad Street Subway south to Pattison
  Avenue stop

Annual event Friday evening in early February. This international track meet is sponsored by the Philadelphia Department of Recreation. Top track stars from around the world compete, including local high-school and college athletes by invitation. New records are often set at this meet. An 11-lap track is put down for this event. Master's Mile for 40-year-olds and over.

Most of the local colleges support active sports programs which are open to the public. The University of Pennsylvania football games on Saturday afternoons in the fall are a Philadelphia institution. The "Big Five" basketball games attract large, enthusiastic crowds in the Palestra. See page 165 for a list of local colleges and write and ask to be put on their mailing lists for sporting events.

# 6
# ARBORETUMS, SANCTUARIES, AND PARKS

## Plant and Wildlife Sites

Within the city and surrounding areas lie many arboretums, sanctuaries, and parks—refuges from the pressures of twentieth-century living. Quiet and green, they offer a place to study and enjoy nature, or just "to get away." You will find only winding paths, towering trees, bushes and shrubs, meandering streams, wildlife, and flowers—no swings or baseball diamonds. They are the woods and meadows of this era of urban encroachment. The Delaware Valley has some of the oldest, most famous arboretums in the United States—and in greater numbers than almost anywhere else. The many arboretums included vary in size and sophistication; some carefully label the trees and shrubs, contain exotic specimens, or have special trails; others are primarily a way of preserving lovely wooded areas for future generations.

## JOHN BARTRAM HOUSE AND GARDENS
54th Street and Elmwood Avenue
(On the west bank of the Schuylkill River)
Philadelphia 19143

**Phone:** SA 9-5281
**Open:** Daily 8 A.M.–4 P.M.
**Closed:** Christmas, New Year's Day
**Admission:** 25¢
**Directions:** Schuylkill Expressway to University Avenue exit, left on Woodland Avenue to 54th Street, left to Bartram Estate
**Parking:** On premises
**Public Transportation:** SEPTA Route 36 trolley

In the midst of smokestacks, oil refineries, housing projects, and general urban sprawl lies a quiet rural area from another era. It is the home and gardens of John Bartram, naturalist, botanist, plant collector, and proprietor of the first botanical garden in the New World. The oldest part of the house dates back to 1683; John Bartram bought and added to it in 1728. It is furnished in Colonial style.

Bartram explored the wilderness from New York to Florida, and west to the Ohio Valley and Lake Ontario. He brought back previously unknown seeds, roots, and herbs and planted them in his garden. The first hybrids of azaleas and rhododendrons were developed by Bartram. It is said that Benjamin Franklin, while ambassador to France, sent Bartram rhubarb, and that Bartram was, therefore, the first to grow it in America. Many early specimens from his planting remain.

The grounds slope down to the river, and you can follow several paths to the edge—only to be jarred by puffs of smoke from the oil refineries. The custodians will answer questions, and, if you're lucky, you'll run into Leonard Silverstein, a custodian who knows a wide range of facts about the Bartram family, the house, and the gardens. He's usually there Tuesday through Sunday. A small area with tables and benches is available for picnicking.

GROUP VISITS

Call in advance. Reservations are not necessary but suggested. Organizations such as school groups and Scout troops are admitted free.

## BRIGANTINE NATIONAL WILDLIFE REFUGE
P.O. Box 72
Oceanville, N.J. 08231

**Phone:** 1-609-641-3126
**Open:** Sunrise to sunset every day
**Admission:** Free
**Directions:** I-676 over Walt Whitman Bridge to Atlantic City Expressway (N.J. Route 42) to U.S. Route 9 north to Oceanville, turn east at Leed's Market
**Parking:** In refuge
**Picnicking:** Picnic tables near entrance

Just 10 miles north of the boardwalk at Atlantic City—but light-years away—is the Brigantine Wildlife Refuge, a 20,000-acre oasis of salt marshes, tidal bays, and freshwater pools for waterfowl using the Atlantic flyway. Depending upon the season, you might see flocks of dappling ducks, herons, osprey, teals, skimmers, Canada geese, warblers, ibis, and perhaps eagles or a whistling swan if you're lucky. Any day of the year is a great day to go. The 8-mile road around the refuge has stopping points, observation towers —even a section reserved for camera buffs.

So pack your picnic lunch, cameras, binoculars, sketch pads, and bird books. Pick up the auto tour map that serves as your guide at the entrance and spend the day where the loudest noise you hear may be the flapping of wings or the honking of geese. If you go during the summer (June 20–September 10), take insect repellent: the insects are plentiful, and those biting flies come in August.

### SEASONAL EVENTS

To help you plan your trip, we include a general calendar of seasonal events at the Refuge. Because of weather, there may be variations of one to two weeks.

*January and February:* Best during thaws. Diving ducks, rough-legged hawks, short-eared owls, bluebirds, and maybe a bald eagle or a snowy owl.

*March 20–April 15:* Peak of northbound waterfowl migration.

*April 20–May 30:* Shorebirds and wading birds. Glossy ibis peak about April 28. Canada geese hatching, usually feeding on dikes by May 20.

*First week in May:* Warblers best on bright, warm days.

*May and June:* Horseshoe crabs spawning; ruddy turnstone migration.

*About June 20:* Annual Canada goose roundup, at sunrise.

*June 15–July 15:* Ducks hatching.

*August:* Shorebirds and warblers return. Wading birds gather.

*September:* Ducks gathering in flocks. Teal migration. Terns and skimmers flocking to Holgate Unit on Long Beach Island.

*October:* Canada goose migration begins about the eighth and peaks about the twenty-fifth. Brant arrive about the nineteenth and peak about the twenty-fifth.

*November 1–10:* Spectacular concentrations of ducks, geese, brant in pools, exceeding 100,000 birds on 1,600 acres. Snow geese begin stopping.

*November 15–December 15:* Peak snow goose numbers. Ducks and geese moving south. Most likely to see bald eagle in December.

### GROUP VISITS

By advance reservation only, preferably two weeks in advance if it is to be a guided tour.

HANDICAPPED

Most of the Refuge can be seen from the car. Restrooms have one step at entrance. Booth doors about 28 inches wide.

NEARBY

Smithville Inn in Historic Smithville, 2 miles north of refuge.

## CROSSWICKS WILDLIFE SANCTUARY
Delene and Crosswicks Roads
Jenkintown, Pa. 19046

**Open:** Daylight hours
**Admission:** Free
**Directions:** Broad Street (Pa. Route 611) to Old York Road to Meetinghouse Road, right to Delene Road, right to entrance
**Parking:** On street

Crosswicks Wildlife Sanctuary is composed of 16 acres, mostly wooded, with several small streams. The public is welcome, and nature walks are conducted at intervals throughout the year. The property was donated to the National Audubon Society so that its unspoiled state could be permanently preserved.

Over a hundred species of birds have been observed. Many winter here because of the feeding stations maintained by the Wyncote Bird Club, which is responsible for the Sanctuary.

## DUKE GARDENS FOUNDATION
Somerville, N.J. 08876

**Phone:** 1-201-722-3700
**Open:** Daily; winter hours 12 noon–4 P.M., spring and fall 1 P.M.– 5 P.M.
**Closed:** July and August, Christmas, New Year's Day; by advance reservation only
**Admission:** Museum, $2.50; Gardens, $1.75, children under school age free
**Directions:** I-95 north to U.S. Route 206 to Somerville
**Parking:** Parking area free—bus takes you to Museum and Gardens without charge

Behind stone gates on a 4,000-acre preserve lies the estate of Doris Duke, tobacco heiress, horticulturist, and collector. Her magnificent collection of Southeast Asian art and incomparable 1-acre glass-enclosed gardens are open to the public.

SOUTHEAST ASIAN ART AND CULTURE FOUNDATION MUSEUM

Over the years Miss Duke collected more than 1,400 treasures of Thai and Burmese art. Included are Buddha heads, Thai porcelain and altars, gold lanterns inlaid with multicolored glass, elephant chairs, scroll boxes, colorful masks, and paintings. Guides are on hand to explain the exhibition and answer questions.

THE GARDENS

This is one of the most unique and exciting gardens in the world— 1 acre of plantings under glass representing eleven countries, among them China, Japan, England, Colonial America, and Indo-Persia. You move from one garden setting to another, each totally different in approach, each capturing the flavor of the country. Knowledgeable guides will answer questions about this astounding conservatory. The gardens took six years to construct and require the services of thirty-five people for maintenance.

GROUP VISITS

For information write or call Duke Gardens Foundation. Groups of 10 or more: admission $1.50.

NEARBY

Somerville Inn, U.S. Routes 22 and 206, for lunch. *Or* Turntable Junction, Flemington (page 220).

## FORT WASHINGTON STATE PARK
Militia Hill Road off Bethlehem Pike
Whitemarsh, Pa. 19034

**Phone:** MI 6-2942

**Directions:** East River Drive to Wissahickon Drive to Lincoln Drive to Allens Lane, right to Germantown Avenue, left to Bethlehem Pike (at top of Chestnut Hill). Continue (right) through Erdenheim and Flourtown to Pa. Route 73, left to park.

Steeped in Revolutionary history, the Park was once the scene of intense fighting during the British occupancy of Philadelphia. Little evidence remains today, but the Park is a delightful spot for hiking, picnicking, and relaxing.

GROUP VISITS

Call about a week in advance.

NEARBY

Hope Lodge, on Bethlehem Pike, Fort Washington, Pa. 19034; phone 646-1595. Open Saturday and Sunday 1–4:30 P.M. Admission, adults 50¢ children under 12 free. This graceful Colonial mansion is a fine example of eighteenth-century Georgian architecture. Set well back from the road, Hope Lodge is a beautifully preserved and furnished country home with a general air of elegance and serenity. Not only does it present a picture of Colonial America, but it is another link in Washington's march from Brandywine to Germantown and finally to Valley Forge. It is administered by the Pennsylvania Historical and Museum Commission. Guided tours only.

## FRENCH CREEK STATE PARK
R.D. 1
Elverson, Pa. 19520

**Phone:** 1-582-8125
**Open:** All year round
**Admission:** Free
**Directions:** Schuylkill Expressway to Pennsylvania Turnpike west to Morgantown exit; follow signs to Hopewell Village and French Creek State Park

Over 7,000 acres in this preserve surrounding the National Historic Site of Hopewell Village (page 65). Here are excellent facilities for swimming (Memorial Day to Labor Day), picnicking (grills and open fires), hiking, fishing, boating, bicycling, and camping. (No reservations. Call for information.) It's close enough to Philadelphia to attract crowds on the weekends. Best to go early or on weekdays. No boat rentals.

## HAWK MOUNTAIN SANCTUARY
R.D. 2
Kempton, Pa. 19529

**Open:** Daily 8 A.M.–5 P.M.
**Closed:** Christmas
**Admission:** Adults 55¢, children under 12 30¢
**Restrictions:** No trash barrels: bring trash back to trail entrance. No pets or radios.
**Directions:** Pennslyvania Turnpike Northeast Extension to I-78 west to Route 143 north. Follow signs to Hawk Mountain. Driving time under two hours from Philadelphia.
**Parking:** Can accommodate about 175 cars; they try to limit the number of visitors to the capacity of the parking lot
**Picnicking:** Permitted on rocks in lookout areas only, so pack your lunch in a knapsack or something equally portable

September, October, and November are the most popular months of the year to visit Hawk Mountain Sanctuary. Depending upon weather conditions, hawks, bald eagles, and osprey fly over this unique sanctuary dedicated to the preservation of birds of prey. This privately maintained wildlife sanctuary contains about 2,000 acres of rugged terrain on Blue Mountain. Its beautiful forests rise more than a thousand feet to the rocky outcroppings where visitors literally spend the day patiently waiting for those migrating broad-winged birds. Pack a "hiker's" picnic, put on sturdy shoes, take your binoculars (if possible, more than just one for the whole group), your bird books, and your cushions (the lookouts are very rocky). And don't forget to bring something to drink: There are no soda machines along the nature trails or at the lookouts. At the entrance to the Sanctuary is a sign reading, "DON'T DO IT IF YOU DON'T LIKE TO HIKE." But it's really an easy climb of just under a mile to the highest spot, where in clear weather you'll have a spectacular 70-mile view of the valley. Elderly hikers, teenagers, even five-year-olds enjoy the trail through the woods, climbing about the rocks, and checking the birds and the sights through binoculars.

Restroom facilities along the trails are neat, clean, and ecologically acceptable.

GROUP VISITS

School groups free on written request for reservations two weeks in advance to Office of Environmental Education. *Tours:* December–August: every day. September–November: weekdays only. 8 A.M.–5 P.M. Reservations in writing two weeks in advance. Maximum number: 1 adult to 15–20 students. Length of tour adapted to group.

NEARBY

Crystal Cave, Kutztown (page 246).

MEMBERSHIP

Various classes, including $5 family membership. *Benefits:* Fees help support a private wildlife foundation and are tax deductible. Free admission to Sanctuary. Newsletter and special privileges at Sanctuary. For further information write Hawk Mountain Sanctuary Association at above address.

**ISLAND BEACH STATE PARK**
Seaside Park, N.J. 08752

**Phone:** 1-201-793-0506

**Open:** All year
**Admission:** Recreation area (effective entire year) $1 for each car plus 25¢ for each person over 12; under 12 free
**Directions:** Benjamin Franklin Bridge to N.J. Route 70 to N.J. Route 37 to Seaside Park, then south to park entrance
**Parking:** In specified areas; space for 2,000 cars
**Picnicking:** In bathing areas and adjacent beaches. Cooking devices and fires permitted 50 feet east of dunes. No tables; no fireplaces provided

This narrow 1-mile-wide, 10-mile-long strip of land between the Atlantic Ocean and Barnegat Bay is one of the few remaining expanses of natural barrier beach in the East. Because of this, use of the Park is carefully controlled. The area is divided into three sections: a botanical zone, a recreational zone, and a wildlife sanctuary. Nature trails have been laid out for guided and "self-guided" tours through the botanical and wildlife preserves. During the summer season guided tours are available daily at 3 P.M. The wildlife sanctuary is also open to fishermen.

A 1-mile stretch of beach in the center has been reserved for ocean swimming, surfing, and picnicking, or just strolling along the shore. Bathing is permitted from the second Saturday in June through Labor Day (10 A.M.–6 P.M.). There are lifeguards, bathhouses, and refreshment stands in this area. If you plan to swim, get an early start from Philadelphia. When the parking lots are full (often by 11 or 12), you simply have to wait until someone leaves.

GROUP TOURS

By appointment only, two weeks in advance. Minimum age: 9. Maximum number: 20. One adult for every 8 children. Length of tour 1½ hours, includes native vegetation and wildlife, history, and an explanation of dune stabilization.

**LONGWOOD GARDENS**
Kennett Square, Pa. 19348

**Phone:** 1-388-6741
**Open:** Every day of the year: greenhouses 10 A.M.–5 P.M.; outdoor gardens 8 A.M.–sunset
**Admission:** Weekdays 50¢, weekends and holidays $1; children 6–12 50¢, under 6 free
**Restrictions:** Proper attire (shoes and shirt); no dogs or other pets; no food, alcoholic beverages, firearms, sports equipment, radios, phonographs, or tape recorders. Strollers permitted.

**Directions:** Schuylkill Expressway to U.S. Route 1 south to intersection with Pa. Route 52 north, then follow signs to Longwood Gardens. About a 1-hour drive from Philadelphia.

**Parking:** Area adjacent to entrance

**Public Transportation:** SEPTA Bus Rambles schedules trips here (DA 9-4800)

**Picnicking:** Area adjoins Gardens. Open April through October, 11 A.M.–7 P.M. to guests of Longwood. Tables and benches in a wooded grove. Take a left turn just before entrance to main parking area.

Longwood Gardens is one of the outstanding display gardens in America. This former Du Pont estate contains almost 1,000 acres of incredibly beautiful trees, flowers, and bushes—all magnificently maintained. The thought and care given by the staff are evident as soon as you enter: a sloping lawn was constructed to hide the parking area. Once inside your pace slows. There are winding paths, shaded benches, a forest walk, an Italian Renaissance Water Garden, a rose arbor, a wild-flower garden, a bridge over a waterfall, a topiary garden, and more. It is an endless flowering display, outdoors and in. The conservatories have a tropical forest, orchids, banana trees, ferns, houseplants, and palm trees. It's flower-show time at Longwood every day of the year. Don't wait for warm weather and the sun. A rainy day or winter visit to the conservatories is great fun. Walk among the cactus plants while it's snowing outside.

During the summer months June through September on Tuesdays, Thursdays and Sundays, rain or shine, there are half-hour colored fountain displays as soon as it's dark. Fountain displays fascinate all ages. You may wander through the conservatories on these evenings for an hour after the display.

Take a picnic supper and spend the evening. Picnicking also at nearby Brandywine Battlefield State Park (page 62) and Newlin Grist Mill Park (page 236). On summer weekends and holidays, there are also afternoon fountain displays at 2 and 4 P.M. Theater, ballet, and music performances are sponsored by outside nonprofit organizations in the Open-Air Theater. Ticket information and a schedule of public events are available from the Information Center, as well as detailed information about flowering dates of the plants.

GROUP VISITS

Tours available for groups all year, Monday through Friday. One-month advance notice required. Telephone Tour Coordinator's

Office (1-388-6741). Minimum age suggested: first grade. Minimum number: 12; maximum number: 200. One adult for every 10 children. Tour lasts 90 minutes and includes outdoor gardens, conservatory, and greenhouses. Public tours are conducted during the week. Times depend on time of year. Check at the Information Center. Guide maps available at the Center.

HANDICAPPED

Wheelchairs available on a first-come, first-served basis at the security office. No charge. Gardens and restroom accessible.

*Garden for the Blind:* Just next door to the building with the scale model of Longwood is a very small garden for the blind. From mid-April through the summer there are about twenty different kinds of plants with a distinctive smell—mint geranium, licorice, and so forth—all with labels in Braille. It might be a bit warm in the summer. Nearby, Ridley Creek State Park (page 204) and John J. Tyler Arboretum have large facilities (page 209).

## MILL GROVE (AUDUBON WILDLIFE SANCTUARY)
Box 25
Audubon, Pa. 19407

**Phone:** 666-5593
**Open:** Tuesday–Sunday and legal holidays that fall on Monday 10 A.M.–5 P.M.
**Closed:** Mondays, Thanksgiving, Christmas, New Year's Day
**Admission:** Free
**Restrictions:** No dogs, picnicking, bicycles, or picking of flowers or shrubs
**Directions:** Schuylkill Expressway to Valley Forge exit, Pa. Route 363 north across Betzwood Bridge to second traffic light. Turn left on Audubon Road and follow it to the gates of Mill Grove.
**Parking:** Free
**Picnicking:** None on the grounds. Valley Forge State Park nearby *or* Lower Perkiomen Park (for Montgomery County residents only)

High on a hill overlooking the Perkiomen Creek stands Mill Grove, the 130-acre estate where John James Audubon hunted, observed, and sketched wildlife that was to bring him enduring fame. Audubon, of course, is best remembered for his *Birds of America,* magnificent life-sized paintings of North American birds.

Today Mill Grove is beautifully maintained and preserved as a permanent memorial to Audubon by the Montgomery County

Commissioners. The mansion, originally built in 1762, contains murals by George M. Harding depicting scenes of bird life and Audubon's adventures. Many Audubon paintings and books are displayed.

Nearly 6 miles of trails wind through the sanctuary. Over 175 species of birds have been identified, drawn to the area by feeding stations, nesting boxes, trees, and shrubs attractive to them. The area has astounding natural beauty and should be visited in spring or fall, or any fair day, when you can wander down to the creek and through the trails. May brings the height of bloom.

The site also includes an old copper mine. Mineral collecting is permitted in the Mine Dump Area.

GROUP VISITS

By advance reservation in writing to Edward W. Graham, Curator–Director, at least two weeks in advance at Mill Grove. Maximum number of 30 may tour the house at one time. Suggested minimum age: 9.

BOOKSTORE

Bird and nature guides, prints, books, and materials pertaining to Audubon's life.

**MORRIS ARBORETUM**
9414 Meadowbrook Avenue
(Off Stenton Avenue)
Chestnut Hill
Philadelphia 19118
(Entrance on Hillcrest Avenue)
**Phone:** CH 7-5777
**Open:** Weekdays 9 A.M.–4 P.M., weekends 9 A.M.–5 P.M. No one admitted 30 minutes before closing time.
**Closed:** Christmas, New Year's Day
**Admission:** Free
**Restrictions:** Children under 14 must be accompanied by an adult. Dogs must be on leash. No picnicking.
**Directions:** East River Drive to Wissahickon Drive to Lincoln Drive to Allens Lane, right on Allens Lane to Germantown Avenue, turn left and continue through Chestnut Hill to Hillcrest Avenue on your right.
**Parking:** Along Hillcrest Avenue
**Public Transportation:** SEPTA Route L stops at Hillcrest Avenue along either Germantown Avenue or Bethlehem Pike; *or* SEPTA Route 23 trolley on Germantown Avenue

The Morris Arboretum has one of the oldest tree collections in the country. When the Morris family moved from their Cedar Grove home (page 132) to Chestnut Hill in the 1880s, they began collecting and planting rare and beautiful trees and shrubs from all over the world. The resulting gardens contain those species which grow hardily in this area. The rolling 175-acre arboretum overlooking Whitemarsh Valley provides not only some delightful paths for wandering—you'll even find a lake with a Greek temple —but also an opportunity to learn what might grow in your own backyard. Pick up a map at the main building on Meadowbrook Road, or Arbor Shop in the Hillcrest Pavilion. Wear comfortable shoes.

The Morris Arboretum was given to the University of Pennsylvania and was opened to the public in 1933. It is administered by the Department of Biology.

PROGRAMS

A summer garden workshop (ages 10–14) at the Arboretum is sponsored by the Pennsylvania Horticultural Society. In addition to planting, growing, and harvesting vegetables and plants, the children are taught propagation and drying of flowers, houseplant care, flower arranging, and making terraria. For more information write: Pennsylvania Horticultural Society, 325 Walnut Street, Philadelphia 19106; or call: WA 2-4801. A 4-H Club (4th–7th grades) meets at the Arboretum. Call for information.

GUIDED TOURS

Minimum number: 10. By advance reservation.

ANNUAL EVENT

December: Fresh holly and Christmas greens sales. Plant distribution and sale early in May. For exact date call Arboretum.

ARBOR SHOP IN HILLCREST PAVILION

Open: Weekends 10 A.M.–4 P.M. Books, magazines on gardening and related subjects; plants propagated from arboretum's unusual specimens.

MEMBERSHIP

Various categories starting at $10.
*Benefits:* Tax deductible. Receive Arboretum bulletin. Share of yearly distribution of unusual trees or shrubs. Courses, lectures, trips. For more information call or write the Associates of the Morris Arboretum at above address.

## RIDLEY CREEK STATE PARK
Main entrance on West Chester Pike (Pa. Route 3)
Media, Pa. 19063

**Phone:** LO 6-4800
**Open:** Daily 8 A.M.–sunset
**Restrictions:** No swimming
**Directions:** Schuylkill Expressway to U.S. Route 1 south, right on
West Chester Pike (Pa. Route 3); *or* continue south on U.S.
Route 1, right on Pa. Route 252 (becomes Providence Road) 4
miles to Gradyville Road, left into Park
**Parking:** In the Park in designated areas

Ridley Creek gurgles through this newest state park, 2,500 acres
of wooded rolling hills and open meadows, most of them still in
their wild state. You can hike over 10 miles of nature trails, ride
horseback on the 7 miles of bridle paths (horses for hire by advance reservation), bait and fly-fish in specially stocked streams,
bicycle on 6 miles of special trails, and picnic in any one of
several picnic areas with tables and barbecue grills. And, for those
who enjoy a bit of history, there is a restored working farm of
the early 1800s. Visitors may participate in weaving, candlemaking,
etc.

Just 20 miles from Center City, Ridley Creek State Park is one
of the most conveniently located state parks for Philadelphians.
They try to limit the capacity of the Park to the capacity of the
parking lots, so on a lovely warm day start out early.

### HANDICAPPED
There's a special mile-long nature trail especially designed for
the handicapped—handrails and Braille labels for the blind, paths
for wheelchairs.

## SCHUYLKILL VALLEY NATURE CENTER
8480 Hagys Mill Road
Philadelphia 19128

**Phone:** 482-7300
**Open:** Monday–Saturday 8:30 A.M.–5 P.M., Sunday (October–June)
1–5 P.M.
**Closed:** Sundays (July–September), Washington's Birthday, Good
Friday, Easter, Memorial Day, Fourth of July, Labor Day,
Thanksgiving, Christmas, New Year's Day
**Admission:** Adults $1, children under 18 50¢

**Restrictions:** No pets, food, or collecting. Terrain and paths too hilly for strollers.

**Directions:** Benjamin Franklin Parkway, East River Drive to Nicetown cutoff at Laurel Hill Cemetery; at second traffic light take a left on Henry Avenue to Port Royal Road (almost at city limits); left to Hagys Mill Road, right to Nature Center

**Parking:** On the grounds

**Public Transportation:** SEPTA Route A (marked Barren Hill, Andorra, or Ridge and Summit) to Port Royal Road. *Or* Shawmont Station on Reading Railroad and walk to Hagys Mill Road. A mile walk from either stop.

**Picnicking:** No picnicking or eating facilities. Valley Green nearby (page 149).

There are 360 acres of open fields, woodlands, streams, and ponds at the Schuylkill Valley Nature Center in upper Roxborough, just about 12 miles from Center City. It's a place for city-dwellers to enjoy and study nature. You can follow 6 miles of trails, investigate their small weather station, and poke around the nature museum, where almost everything is meant to be examined closely and touched. Maps and booklets for "self-guided" tours help you discover the names and habits of local plants, insects, and animals. At every time of the year there's something interesting going on outside. Don't wait for the warm weather. At the Nature Center they'll show you what to look for. You can learn to identify animals and birds by their tracks in the snow. Wear good walking shoes and take your camera.

### SPECIAL EVENTS AND PROGRAMS

The "Spider's Web": family-oriented Saturday and Sunday nature walks and programs. Free to members; for others, general admission rates. Held every few weeks regardless of the weather and related in some way to the time of year—"What's happening outdoors in winter?"—films, bird walks, night sounds in spring, local pollution, making pictures from pods. Similar workshops held for adults weekday mornings. For information call Nature Center.

### NATURAL HISTORY STORE

Natural well water, nature-oriented items, books, games.

### GROUP VISITS

Admission: 50¢ per person by advance reservation only. Guided tours: Minimum age: 5. No minimum number; maximum number: 60. One adult (free admission) to 10 children. There's a 1½-hour nature walk, by appointment only. Spring and fall reservations a month or more in advance for school classes.

VOLUNTEER PROGRAM

For teenagers and adults interested in natural history, ecology, and environment. Call for information.

HANDICAPPED

A new self-guided nature trail for the blind and physically handicapped meanders through a portion of the Nature Center. Parking, restrooms, the museum, bookstore, and auditorium are all accessible.

MEMBERSHIP

Family $15, individual $10, junior (to 18) $5 (limited privileges). *Benefits:* Free admission, guest passes, special events and programs, newsletter, discount in shop and on courses, use of library.

## ARTHUR HOYT SCOTT HORTICULTURAL FOUNDATION
Swarthmore College
College Avenue
Swarthmore, Pa. 19081

**Phone:** KI 3-5380
**Open:** All week during daylight hours
**Closed:** Fourth of July, Labor Day, Thanksgiving, Christmas
**Admission:** Free
**Directions:** Schuylkill Expressway to U.S. Route 1 (City Avenue) south to Pa. Route 320 south, right onto College Avenue
**Parking:** Available on campus
**Public Transportation:** Penn Central to Swarthmore; SEPTA Red Arrow Bus O from 69th Street Station

The Scott Foundation encompasses the entire Swarthmore campus. Here they are constantly experimenting to find the best plants for this area—and they seem to have been very successful. Anywhere you wander you will find some special display: lilacs, a 2,000-plant rhododendron collection, flowering cherry trees, magnolias, 100 varieties of day lilies, daffodils. Stop in at the office or write for a map and descriptive folder. Then you can wander about anytime during daylight hours. Be sure to wear comfortable shoes.

GUIDED TOURS

Spring, fall, and winter: Monday–Friday 10 A.M. and 2 P.M. By appointment only, three weeks in advance. Minimum age

suggested: 6. Minimum number: 10; maximum number: 40. One
adult to 20 children. Length of tour: 1 hour.

HANDICAPPED
Asphalt paths throughout campus, hills not too steep.

NEARBY
Ingleneuk Tearoom, 120 Park Avenue, Swarthmore, Pa.,
KI 3-4569 (page 337).

## SWISS PINES
Charlestown Road
R.D. 1
Malvern, Pa. 19355

Phone: 1-933-6916
Open: March 15–December 15 weekdays 10 A.M.–4 P.M., Satur-
days 9 A.M.–12 noon
Closed: Sundays, holidays
Admission: Free
Directions: Schuylkill Expressway to Valley Forge interchange, Pa.
Route 202 south to Great Valley exit (Pa. Route 29), then Pa.
Route 29 north. At first stop sign where Route 29 turns off, go
straight onto Charlestown Road, and proceed 1.6 miles to Swiss
Pines. Entrance on the right, parking area on the left.
Parking: Free

Acres to roam and explore—or just sit on one of the many benches
and relax and enjoy the beautiful, serene surroundings. This lovely
preserve is the inspiration and creation of Arnold Bartschi, a Swiss-
born retired manufacturer. The eleven acres contain Japanese
gardens encompassing a Zen and Polynesian setting. There are also
rhododendron, herb, fern, and wild-flower gardens. Visit the Japanese teahouse, walk over the trellis bridge and stepping stones.
It's a pleasant way to unwind and forget the pace of twentieth-
century living. Children will enjoy the foreign atmosphere. Swiss
Pines is associated with the Academy of Natural Sciences.

GROUP VISITS
Guided tours can be arranged with three weeks' notice, preferably in writing. Minimum age: 6. Maximum number of children: 20 with 2 adults. Cost of a guide: $10.

SHOP
Open Monday, Wednesday, and Friday. Specializes in gift items
from Japan, including a selection for children.

## TEMPLE GREENHOUSES
Ambler Campus of Temple University
Butler Pike and Meetinghouse Road
Upper Dublin, Pa.

**Phone:** 643-1200
**Open:** 9:30 A.M.–4 P.M. daily
**Admission:** Free
**Directions:** Pa. Route 611 (Broad Street) north to Pa. Route 309
   north to Butler Pike exit, ½ mile north on Butler Pike to Meeting-
   house Road, east on Meetinghouse Road past Temple Music
   Festival amphitheater to main campus and greenhouses on the left

The Temple Greenhouses grow almost anything at any time of
the year and contain, among other things, tropical foliage plants,
potted banana trees, a coffee tree, and beautiful begonias. There
is an orchid room, and there are many unusual cacti. In the spring
and summer don't miss the formal gardens. They are planted to
bloom continuously and as the weeks pass achieve many different
effects. Visit the gardens when you go to the Temple University
Music Festival (page 155).

## TINICUM WILDLIFE PRESERVE
87th Street and Lyons Avenue
(1 mile west of Philadelphia Airport)
Philadelphia

**Open:** Daily during daylight hours
**Closed:** Christmas
**Admission:** Free
**Restrictions:** No picnicking. Children's fishing permitted.
**Directions:** Schuylkill Expressway, follow signs to the airport, con-
   tinue past Airport Circle to 84th Street and follow signs to Tini-
   cum Wildlife Preserve (right on 86th Street, left on Lyons
   Avenue)
**Parking:** Near observation deck

Near the Airport and Industrial Highway seems an unlikely place
for a wildlife preserve, but there it is! These 250 acres of marshland
are an important resting and feeding place for waterfowl on the
Atlantic Flyway and a haven for marsh plants and animals.
   The approach to this place may be somewhat less than inviting. The area resembles an abandoned Midwestern farm community. But keep going—over unpaved and sometimes unimproved

roads (it really still is Philadelphia!) to the entrance to the preserve. Park your car, take your binoculars and bird book, and wander over the quiet trails, along the marshes. Planes may be overhead, and there are highways all around—as well as an occasional beer can—but you'll be more aware of the wild flowers, trees, and shrubs and the sights and sounds of the animals and birds. Almost 300 different species of birds have been observed here. Your luck depends on the day and the season—spring and fall are obviously best.

There is also an observation deck should your preference lean toward looking rather than walking. Skating in the winter and canoeing if weather conditions are favorable.

## TREXLER–LEHIGH COUNTY GAME PRESERVE
U.S. Route 1
Schnecksville, Pa. 18078

**Phone:** 1-799-3611
**Open:** July and August Monday–Saturday 10 A.M.–6 P.M., Sunday 10 A.M.–7 P.M.; April–June and September–November, Saturdays, Sundays, holidays 12 noon to dusk
**Closed:** Mid–November to early April
**Admission:** 50¢ per car, plus 50¢ for each adult and child over 12 (under 12 free)
**Directions:** Northeast Extension of Pennsylvania Turnpike to Allentown exit (33), Pa. Route 309 north 5.6 miles to Ye Olde Ale House in Schnecksville, then west (left) 2.1 miles to entrance
**Parking:** Free
**Picnicking:** Free picnic area

On the Game Preserve are free-ranging herds of buffalo, North American elk, white-tailed deer, and palomino horses. In the main zoo are hoofed animals from all over the world: guanaco from South America, zebu (the sacred cow of India), Scotch Highlands cattle, aoudad from North Africa, pigmy donkey from Persia, water buffalo from Indochina. A children's zoo has baby animals to feed and pet. You can drive your car over a 4-mile hardtop road past the preserve.

## JOHN J. TYLER ARBORETUM
515 Painter Road
Lima, Pa. 19060

**Phone:** 566-5431

**Open:** Every day dawn to dusk
**Admission:** Free
**Restrictions:** No picnicking except with permission. Dogs must be on a leash. No bicycles or motorcycles.
**Directions:** Schuylkill Expressway to U.S. Route 1 (City Avenue), south to Pa. Route 352, right to Forge Road, right to Painter Road, right on Painter. Entrance on your left.
**Parking:** At Arboretum

Barn at John J. Tyler Arboretum

Wander through acres of dogwoods, past Chinese, English, Japanese, and American holly, a hill of mountain pinks, 25 acres of conifers, and some very special trees: the famous 90-foot giant sequoia, a cedar of Lebanon, a 100-foot Southern bald cypress with its many "knees." You'll find the unusual, the rare, and an enormous collection of plants native to the area.

The Arboretum contains approximately 700 acres of open fields, woods, steep slopes, and level spots. There are 20 miles of trails, including a 10-mile wilderness trail for hikers, and a scenic circle for the less rugged taking forty-five minutes. At the entrance is a Fragrant Garden especially for the blind, containing flowering shrubs, plants, bulbs, and herbs selected for scent and texture. There is a guide rail for blind visitors, and plants have both Braille and printed labels. It is a fascinating experience for everyone.

Nature rambles are held during spring and fall months. Check the Arboretum bulletin board at Lachford Hall near the entrance or write for information.

## WHARTON STATE FOREST
(In the Pine Barrens)
Batsto
R.D. 1
Hammonton, N.J. 08037

**Phone:** 1-609-561-0024
**Directions:** U.S. Route 30 to N.J. Route 542 to Batsto. U.S. Route 206 passes through portions of the forest.

Just a little over an hour's drive from Philadelphia you will find 155 square miles of wilderness in the Pine Barrens of New Jersey. This beautiful forest provides facilities for camping, canoeing, riding, boating, fishing, swimming, picnicking, and nature trails. There's something for everyone here—from Batsto Village (page 62) to wilderness camping. Write for a map before you go; they reply promptly.

Detailed information on camping facilities (cabins available April through October) and use, stables, canoe rentals, etc., may be obtained at Batsto Visitors Center, or by writing Superintendent, Wharton State Forest, Batsto, R.D. 1, Hammonton, N.J. 08037.

SUGGESTED RIDING ACADEMIES

Bass River Ranch, West Bank Road, New Gretna, N.J. 08224, 1-609-296-4488

Rolling Acres Riding School, Atsion Road, Indian Mills, N.J. 08088, 1-609-268-0414

PRIVATELY OWNED CANOE RENTALS

Bell Haven Lake, Green Bank, R.D. 2, Egg Harbor, N.J. 08215, 1-609-965-2031

Micks Canoe Rental, Route 563, Chatsworth, N.J. 08019, 1-609-894-8511

Mullica River Boat Basin, Green Bank, R.D. 2, Egg Harbor, N.J. 08215, 1-609-965-2120

Picalilly Canoe Rental, Lake Road, Atsion, Vincentown Post Office, N.J. 08088, 1-609-268-9831

## Amusement Parks

For those who want manmade entertainment in their parks, here are the amusement parks in the area.

### DORNEY PARK
3830 Dorney Park Road
Allentown, Pa. 18104

Phone: 1-395-3724
Open: Weekend after Easter to Labor Day, Tuesday–Sunday 12 noon–11 P.M.
Closed: Mondays
Directions: Northeast Extension of the Pennsylvania Turnpike to U.S. Route 222 and follow signs

It isn't a Disneyworld or Disneyland, but this amusement park, not more than an hour's drive from Philadelphia, will provide a fun-filled day. Bring your own picnic lunch and eat at the vast family picnic groves provided. There are thrills and excitement— roller coasters, an oldtime "paddle wheeler" showboat, and a section of amusements devoted to the very young. The Park is well maintained, spacious, and able to accommodate the crowds.

GROUP VISITS
Picnic and bus reservations should be made in advance.

### DUTCH WONDERLAND
U.S. Route 30 in Lancaster County, Pa.

See Pennsylvania Dutch Country (page 246).

### GREAT ADVENTURE
Prospertown, New Jersey 08514

Phone: 1-609-758-3301
Open: June–September daily 10 A.M.–10 P.M. May and October weekends only. Safari Park open 9 A.M. to ½ hour before sundown; also open weekends in April and November.
Admission: Amusement Park (including all rides and entertainment): Adults $6.50, children $5.50. Safari Park: Adults $2.50, children $2. Combination Tickets: Adults $7.50, children $6.50.
Parking: Free

**Directions:** U.S. Route 30 across Benjamin Franklin Bridge to New Jersey Turnpike, north to exit 7, east on N.J. Route 68, north on N.J. Route 537. Entrance to park is at the intersection of 537 and N.J. Route 576.

This is the newest and probably the largest recreational complex in the area: 1,500 acres. What makes this place different from all the other amusement areas is the drive-through Safari Park with about 2,000 wild animals.

## HERSHEYPARK
Hershey, Pa.

See page 252.

## LENAPE PARK
Pa. Route 52
Chester County, Pa.

**Phone:** 1-793-1986
**Open:** Mid-May to mid-September, daily 11 A.M.–9 P.M.
**Directions:** Schuylkill Expressway to U.S. Route 202 south to Pa. Routes 100 and 52
**Picnicking:** Areas provided

The Brandywine Creek runs through the Park. There are lovely old shade trees and picnic groves, but the main attraction is the amusements, among them giant swings and bumper cars. The marvelous merry-go-round is one of the few machines still in operation; it was built by pioneer carrousel builder Gustav Dentzel at the turn of the century. There are also canoes for hire and a large pool for swimming. Spectacular Fourth of July fireworks.

## SIX GUN TERRITORY
Easton and Moreland Roads
Willow Grove, Pa. 19090

**Phone:** OL 9-8000
**Open:** Mid-May–Labor Day, Sunday–Friday 12 noon–10 P.M., Saturday 12 noon–11 P.M.
**Admission:** Adults $4.35, children $3.25, includes everything
**Directions:** Pa. Route 611 (Broad Street) to Willow Grove
**Parking:** Free
**Public Transportation:** SEPTA Route 55 directly to Park

This is a "Western"-theme park at the location of the former Willow Grove Amusement Park. Many of the rides are the same as those in the old park, but some new things have been added. For the admission price you have unlimited privileges on thirty-seven amusements—staged gunfights, bank robberies, cancan dancers, and honky-tonk piano at the Palace Saloon (soft drinks only), picnic groves, and ball field. With the new admission policy, it is not the place to run to for an hour's entertainment; rather, make it an all-day outing.

# 7
# THE SURROUNDING COUNTRYSIDE

## Bucks County

For contrasts consider the rural and eclectic style of the New Hope area, the Fairless Steel Works and the adjoining community of Levittown. They all lie within diverse Bucks County. It's old and new, historic, and ultra-twentieth century. The area is vast, filled with antiquity, rich farmlands, museums, restorations, parks, and playgrounds—ideal for family exploration. It is easily accessible from Philadelphia via I-95 and connecting roads.

Here are some highlights; for more detailed information write to Bucks County Historical–Tourist Commission, Main Street and Locust Avenue, Fallsington, Pa. 19054 (phone 1-CY 5-5450).

### New Hope

**Directions:** I-95 north to Pa. Route 32, left into New Hope, Pa. *or* Route 611 north to U.S. Route 202 into New Hope.

Just walking around and taking in the natural scenery and beauty of the area are worthwhile. Wooded, rustic, and steeped in Colonial history, New Hope lies on the Delaware River. The center of town is full of every conceivable kind of shop—crafts, antiques, art galleries, toys—and restaurants for snacks or gourmet meals. Almost any interest can be accommodated here.

Over fifty years ago many noted artists settled in New Hope and established its fame as an art colony. Although today it is somewhat commercial and thousands of tourists overflow the narrow streets and walkways in any season, it is still an enjoyable day's outing. Try to avoid weekends in the summer when the crowds tend to peak. Parking is difficult; there are meters on the narrow main street and some public parking lots.

## BUCKS COUNTY PLAYHOUSE
South Main Street
New Hope, Pa. 18938

Phone: 1-862-2041
Open: Year-round
Parking: Paid parking available on grounds

Beautifully situated on the Delaware River in a converted mill
is the Bucks County Playhouse, one of the first summer theaters
in the United States. Since 1939 it has been presenting quality
theater—established plays as well as new productions headed for
Broadway. Recently it was rescued from the jaws of financial
disaster by a group of public-spirited New Hope citizens who
are continuing its tradition of presenting fine summer theater. It
has also been presenting repertory theater to Pennsylvania and
New Jersey students weekdays in the winter.

## MULE-DRAWN BARGES
New Street
New Hope, Pa. 18938

Phone: 1-862-2842
Open: April 1 through April 30 Wednesday, Saturday, and Sunday
1 P.M., 3 P.M., 4:30 P.M.; May 1 through Labor Day daily except
Monday, 1 P.M., 3 P.M., 4:30 P.M., and 6 P.M. (April schedule
resumes after Labor Day). Open all holidays during season.
Closed: November 1–April 1
Admission: Adults $1.25, children under 12 65¢
Parking: Free in barge parking lot

The Delaware Canal was completed in 1832 for the purpose of
bringing coal down from the mines in the Lehigh Valley area to
the limestone region between Easton and New Hope. Teams of
mules walking along a towpath pulled the large flat canal boats.

Today you can see what barge life was like 125 years ago by
taking a delightful hour-long trip on the Delaware Canal. The
awning-covered flat-bottom barge, drawn by mules as in bygone
days, takes you quietly through the town of New Hope and into
the countryside beyond. Groups: No special rate offered but you
can go at certain times (mornings) by reservation only. Private
parties can be arranged. Rental of large barge, which accommodates 80 people, $170; small barge (60 people), $125. Parties go

out anytime if time is available. Call ahead for arrangements. Peter Pascuzzo, owner and manager.

## PARRY BARN
Playhouse Plaza on Main Street
New Hope, Pa. 18938

**Phone:** 1-862-5529
**Open:** Monday to Saturday 11 A.M.–5 P.M., Sunday 1–5 P.M.

Topflight art exhibits and fine arts and crafts are displayed here.

## PARRY MANSION
Main Street at Mechanic Street
New Hope, Pa. 18938

**Phone:** 1-862-5529
**Open:** May, June, October, November: Friday, Saturday 11 A.M.–4
   P.M., Sunday 2–5 P.M.; July–September: Wednesday–Saturday
   11 A.M.–4 P.M., Sunday 2–5 P.M.
**Admission:** Adults $1
**Parking:** At the Logan Inn (across the street) for a fee

Built in the 1790s, the Parry Mansion has recently been restored by the New Hope Historical Society. It conveys an authentic picture of the life-style of a wealthy businessman's family from 1800 to 1900. Five succeeding generations are represented in the furnishings of the house, starting with late eighteenth century and going through the Federal, Empire, and late Victorian periods. Visually charming down to the smallest detail. Games, spittoons, children's rooms with appropriate books, washbasins, and the like make it seem as if the family is still living there.

GROUP TOURS

For further information, write New Hope Historical Society, New Hope, Pa. 18938.

## WASHINGTON CROSSING STATE PARK

. . . on the River Road just outside of New Hope. This 500-acre park commemorates the famous crossing of the Delaware by George Washington and his troops on Christmas night, 1776. Historic sights, Wild Flower Preserve, picnic grounds. For details see Chapter 1.

## Places of Interest around New Hope

### LAHASKA AND BUCKINGHAM
U.S. Route 202 and Pa. Route 263

These two villages are an antique collector's paradise. Both villages are filled with antique shops, art galleries, quaint old homes, and unusual shops. It's a pleasant day's outing, or stop in on your way to New Hope.

### PEDDLER'S VILLAGE
U.S. Route 202
Lahaska, Pa. 18931

Phone: 1-794-7051
Open: Year-round Monday–Saturday 10 A.M.–5 P.M., Friday 10 A.M.–9 P.M. (some shops are open on Sunday)
Restaurants: Monday–Thursday 11 A.M.–9 P.M., Friday and Saturday 11 A.M.–10 P.M., Sunday 12 noon–8 P.M.
Directions: Pa. Route 611 north to U.S. Route 202

For a pleasant outing that includes browsing and buying with lunch or dinner, Peddler's Village is an attractively maintained shopping complex with a variety of stores to tempt you: handcrafts, houseplants, dolls and toys, fabrics, children's clothes, and gourmet cookware, to mention only a few. Try the Cock 'n Bull Restaurant for lunch or dinner featuring homemade bread, rolls, and desserts. A special children's menu is available, and highchairs are provided. In the summer Pollywog's Porch offers ice cream, cokes, and hamburgers.

For information for charter groups call 1-794-7051.

### WILMAR LAPIDARY MUSEUM
P.O. Box 236
Pineville Road and Route 232
Pineville, Pa. 18946

Phone: 1-598-3572
Open: Tuesday–Saturday 10 A.M.–5 P.M., Sunday 1–5 P.M.
Closed: Christmas, New Year's Day
Admission: 50¢
Directions: U.S. Route 1 north to Pa. Route 413, west to junction with Pa. Route 232 and Pineville Road (just minutes from New Hope)
Parking: Free

Lapidary is the art of cutting, polishing, and engraving stones. The Wilmar Museum contains one of the world's largest private collections of carved stones, attractively displayed in a restored barn with rough stone walls. Mr. Kuhlman, the owner, is friendly and eager to share his knowledge with the visitor. Included in the collection are birds, animals, and carved figures from tourmaline, crystal, agate, ruby, and ivory; lovely cameos; and large polished stones, some cut to show the crystalline structure within. The collection is constantly growing. There is a small shop as you enter that sells tigereyes, jewelry, and semiprecious stones for craftsmen to set in their own jewelry. A nice memento of your visit is a bag of varied polished stones for 50 cents. Items for sale range in price from 50 cents to $100.

GROUP TOURS

Tours for schoolchildren can be arranged with eight days' notice. Group rate 35 cents; minimum number: 35. Write or call for further information.

**THE YARD**
U.S. Route 202 and Street Road
(Adjacent to Peddler's Village)

Fourteen attractive shops, many for special interests. Brakemans' Lantern for railroad buffs, lovely Swedish imports, and a wide selection of distinctive clogs for the whole family at W. Sk'old; Locktown Sweater Shop for woolen bargains. Try the Purple Plum for omelets, sandwiches, and salads at lunch; dinner menu also.

*About 15 Minutes beyond New Hope
on the Other Side of the Delaware*

**LIBERTY VILLAGE, LTD.**
2 Church Street
Flemington, N.J. 08822

**Phone:** 1-201-782-8550
**Open:** Monday–Saturday 10:30 A.M.–5:30 P.M., Sunday 11 A.M.–6 P.M.
**Admission:** Adults $2, senior citizens, students, and children under 12 $1.25. Group rates: Minimum number: 20, adults $1.50, children $1
**Directions:** Pa. Route 263 to Center Bridge; cross bridge to New Jersey and take N.J. Route 523 to Flemington. You will see

colored arrows indicating Liberty Village. If you are in New Hope, cross bridge to Lambertville and follow signs to Flemington.
Parking: Free

This growing complex already has a carpenter's shop, a "saltbox" house known for its button collection, gentleman's town house with an incredible collection of Boehm birds, a glassblower's workshop, a gunsmith's shop, a cabinetmaker's shop, and a blacksmith's forge. The costumed craftsmen inside each house perform their skills and explain what they are doing. These are not demonstrations. The working craftsmen are anxious to share their knowledge with you. Their products are for sale in Liberty Village Craft House. School groups are welcome.

HANDICAPPED

Most of the houses have only one step and are accessible by wheelchair. There are regular rest rooms that can accommodate wheelchairs.

## TURNTABLE JUNCTION
Adjacent to Liberty Village, Ltd.

Forty attractive Early American-style shops and restaurants are here. The emphasis is on trains, including a steam locomotive (runs April through November) that takes you on a one-hour trip to Ringoes, New Jersey, on the Black River & Western Railroad. Phone: 1-201-782-6622. Fare: Adults $2; children 5-12 $1, 3-5 50¢. Picnic area in Ringoes. Trains leave every hour and a half.

There's a Roundhouse Shop for train collectors with Lionel trains and every conceivable kind of souvenir with train motifs. The Choo-Choo Bakery sells gingerbread trains. For a light lunch try The Lunchbell, a charming eatery fashioned after a one-room schoolhouse, with desks for tables; hearty soups, sandwiches under $1, and don't miss the carrot cake and pumpkin nut bread. The Spread Eagle Inne serves more elegant fare in pleasant surroundings; the table tops are mounted on old treadle sewing machine bases; prices are fairly expensive.

NEARBY

... is the Raggedy Ann Antiques Doll and Toy Museum, located at 171 Main Street (closed Mondays). It's an old brick mansion, and the hundreds of dolls and toys are presented in a Victorian setting. Admission: Adults 75¢, children 50¢.

While you are in the Flemington area, stop at Stangl Pottery;

they have seconds here. The China Closet offers incredible savings on seconds in Spode—place settings, ornaments, ashtrays, etc. Don't miss this one.

## In the Doylestown Area

**CONTI CROSS KEYS INN**
Intersection of Pa. Routes 611 and 413
Doylestown, Pa. 18901

Phone: 348-3539

An elegant place for dining in the Doylestown area (see page 337).

**FONTHILL**
East Court Street
Doylestown, Pa. 18901
Phone: 1-348-4472

Open: Guided tours by appointment only; call ahead
Admission: Adults $1; children over 12 50¢, under 12 25¢
Directions: Pa. Route 611 north to Doylestown; at Court House (Court Street) bear right for four blocks to Fonthill
Parking: Free

It looks like a storybook castle complete with a tower and spinning wheel, but it was the home of Dr. Henry Mercer, archaeologist, collector, and pioneer in the making of tiles, as is evident throughout the house. Each room is a different size and shape, with tiles set into the walls, and with old books, furniture, and some antiques. The entire building is made of cement and is one of the three landmarks of Doylestown built by Dr. Mercer. The unusual and colorful guide is Mrs. Swain, Dr. Mercer's former housekeeper, who knows the house thoroughly and says she has "given it her life."

**MERCER MUSEUM**
Pine and Ashland Streets
Doylestown, Pa. 18901

Phone: 1-348-4373
Open: March–December, Tuesday–Saturday 10 A.M.–5 P.M.; April–October, Sunday 1–5 P.M.
Closed: January, February, all legal holidays
Admission: Adults $1, students 50¢, under 6 free

**Directions:** Pa. Route 611 north to Doylestown, turn right at first
traffic light (Ashland Street), then right on Pine Street
**Parking:** Free on street

The Mercer Museum contains one of the world's finest collections of early American tools and artifacts. It is a record of the
industrial and home life of the country between 1700 and 1860.
The building resembles a castle, and it was the first construction ever to be built of reinforced concrete. It was the inspiration
and gift of Dr. Henry Chapman Mercer, archaeologist, master
potter, and collector. The rooms of the museum are arranged
around a five-story open section where huge sleighs, old stage-
coaches, boats, looms, bicycles, cradles, chairs, and baskets are
suspended, creating an amazing effect. Winding stairs take you
from gallery to gallery, where there are collections of fine old
pottery, weather vanes, cigar-store Indians, confectioners' molds,
and tools. Every craft of earlier America is represented.

GROUP VISITS

Group rate, adults 75¢, children 25¢. Guided tours by appointment—write or call. Minimum age for tours: third grade. Minimum
number for tour: 10; maximum, 60. One adult for every 10 children. Length of tour: 1¼ hours.

The Gift Shop in the museum has interesting souvenirs for sale.
In good weather you may visit a restored eighteenth-century log
cabin and old horse-drawn vehicles from many periods of Pennsylvania history on the grounds of the museum.

In the adjacent Bucks County Historical Society, make arrangements to visit Fonthill, the home of Dr. Mercer.

**MORAVIAN POTTERY AND TILE WORKS**
Swamp Road
(Pa. Route 313)
Doylestown, Pa. 18901

**Phone:** 1-348-2911, ext. 479
**Open:** Wednesday–Saturday 10 A.M.–5 P.M., Sunday 12 noon–5
P.M.
**Closed:** Thanksgiving, Christmas
**Admission:** Adults $1, youths 4–18 25¢, family group $2
**Directions:** Pa. Route 611 north to Doylestown, turn right on Swamp
Road (Pa. Route 313) for about ½ mile
**Parking:** Plenty; free

In its heyday this world-renowned tile works produced over 400 tiles depicting the history of Pennsylvania for the State Capitol Building in Harrisburg, tiles for a gambling casino in Monte Carlo, and tiles for museums and private collectors all over the world.

Erected in 1910 in the Spanish mission style, the Tile Works was the second of three structures built of reinforced concrete by Dr. Henry Mercer. For many years no tiles were made here. Recently, however, they have begun reproducing for sale a selection of these famous tiles, using the original methods.

The tour is part guided and part on your own—it takes about ½ hour.

If possible, pick a warm and sunny day to visit. It can be damp and cold inside.

## SHRINE OF OUR LADY OF CZESTOCHOWA
Iron Hill and Ferry Roads
Doylestown, Pa. 18901

**Phone:** 1-345-0600
**Open:** Daily
**Admission:** Free
**Directions:** Pa. Route 611 north to Pa. Route 413, west (left) to Ferry Road (2½ miles), left to shrine

This is the counterpart of a twelfth-century shrine in a town of the same name in Poland. It is maintained by the Pauline Fathers, who established a monastery here in 1953. Organized pilgrimages come every Sunday by bus and car to this lovely 240-acre shrine. Everyone is welcome. It is also the site of the annual Polish Festival and Country Fair (page 267).

### *Lower Bucks County*

## GRUNDY HOUSE
610 Radcliffe Street
Bristol, Pa. 19007

**Phone:** 1-788-9432
**Open:** Tuesday, Thursday, Saturday 1–3 P.M.; other times by appointment
**Admission:** Free
**Directions:** I-95 north, south on Pa. Route 413 1 mile to Bristol.

This marvelous Victorian home belonged to Joseph Grundy,

wealthy manufacturer, powerful politician, and the founder of the Pennsylvania Manufacturing Association. It is completely furnished in high Victorian style—ponderous carved furniture, wood paneling, and stained glass windows. The back of the house overlooks the Delaware. It is a fine example of a rich man's life-style at the height of the Victorian era.

## HISTORIC FALLSINGTON
4 Yardley Avenue
Fallsington, Pa. 19054

Phone: 1-295-6567
Open: March 15–November 15, Wednesday–Sunday 1–5 P.M.
Admission: Adults $1, students 25¢, children under 12 free; group tours by appointment
Directions: I-95 north to Pa. Route 413 east on Pa. Route 413 1 mile to U.S. Route 13, north on U.S. Route 13 8 miles to Tyburn Road exit, west on Tyburn Road 1 mile to Fallsington.

Just minutes away from a highly urban part of lower Bucks County, surrounded by industry and housing developments, lies the quiet town of Fallsington, a beautiful and authentic pre-Revolutionary village. William Penn came here to worship when he was in residence at Pennsbury Manor.

Historic Fallsington was incorporated in 1953 as a nonprofit corporation to preserve the Colonial dignity and beauty of the area. Some of the properties are open to the public—the Burges-Lippincott House, the Stagecoach Tavern, the Moon-Williamson House, the Gambrel Roof house, and the Schoolmaster's house. Many privately owned Colonial houses lining Meetinghouse Square are occupied by descendants of the village's first families.

Don't miss Fallsington Day, the second Saturday in October (see Fairs and Festivals, page 263). The whole village comes alive with costumed residents demonstrating crafts, food, and flowers from the Colonial past.

## NEWTOWN
Directions: I-95 north, east on Pa. Route 332 to Newtown

This lovely pre-Revolutionary community served as County Seat of Bucks County until 1813, when it was moved to Doylestown. Newtown was a busy thoroughfare for two stagecoach lines, and several inns thrived for the lawyers, defendants, and plaintiffs from the Courts, in addition to the passengers from the coach lines. Four old taverns remain—the Brick Hotel, the Court Inn, Bird in Hand, and Temperance House—as do many private homes from the Colonial era. One of Newtown's most famous citizens, Edward Hicks (1780–1840), painted some of his world-famous *Peaceable Kingdom* canvases here.

The Court Inn at Court Street and Centre Avenue, built as a hotel in 1733, was a popular meeting place when Newtown was the County Seat. The Inn has been restored to its original appearance and houses lovely Colonial furnishings and historical items from the Newtown area. It is the headquarters for the Newtown Historic Association, Inc. Open to the public Sundays only 2 to 5 P.M.; groups by appointment. No admission charge. Call 1-968-4004 for information on their walking tours. For several years the Historic Association has sponsored a Christmas Open House Tour the first Saturday in December.

## PENNSBURY MANOR
Pennsbury Lane
Morrisville, Pa. 19067

**Phone:** 1-946-0400
**Open:** All year

The reconstructed country estate of William Penn overlooking the Delaware. Many outbuildings, antiques. Pennsbury Manor is described in detail in Chapter 1. Fallsington is 4 miles away.

### *Bucks County Parks and Camping Grounds*

Bucks County offers many excellent parks for recreation and quiet relaxation, open to both residents and nonresidents. For information on the following parks, write or call: Bucks County Department of Parks and Recreation, Cove Creek Park, Box 358, R.D. 1, Langhorne, Pa. 19047 (phone: 757-0571).

## CAMPING GROUNDS

Tinicum, Tohickon Valley, and Lake Towhee are fine camping grounds located just a couple of hours from Center City. Scenically located in Bucks County, they offer boating, fishing, ball fields, and playgrounds. For applications write Bucks County Department of Parks and Recreation, Cove Creek Park, Box 358, R.D. 1, Langhorne, Pa. 19047, or call 757-0571. There is a small fee.

## CHURCHVILLE PARK
Churchville Lane
Southampton, Pa.

At the site of the Philadelphia Suburban Water Company reservoir in Northampton Township. A forty-acre outdoor education center with museum, library, and the Florence W. Grintz Bittersweet Trail for the blind and physically handicapped. Nature hike or talk every Sunday at 2:30 P.M.; open to all. Group tours by appointment. Riding stables (on Holland Road) with class instruction programs.

## MILL CREEK VALLEY PARK

Includes Frosty Hollow Park, Silver Lake Park, and Black Ditch Park, with other areas under partial development.

### SILVER LAKE PARK

In Bristol Township on U.S. Route 13 and Bath Road. Phone: 1-785-1177. One hundred eighty acres with Olympic-size swimming pool open to the public in the afternoons. Small fee. Basketball court, fishing, boat rentals and dock, picnic areas with grills, hiking, playground, ball field, seasonal ice skating.

## RINGING ROCKS PARK
Bridgeton Township
(about 2 miles west of Black Eddy)
River Road
(Pa. Route 32)

This is an eight-acre field of primordial boulders of various sizes. The park is so named because the rocks are resonant when struck with a hard object. Be sure to bring a metal bar. There are walking trails to the boulder field, a lovely waterfall, and picnic tables and grills.

## TINICUM PARK
River Road in Tinicum Township
(Pa. Route 32)
Near Erwinna, Pa.

John J. Stover (1870–1958) bequeathed the house and the Park to Bucks County in May, 1955. The house, designed in the Federal period, has been restored and furnished. It is open on weekends for tours and other times by appointment. Donation (no fixed amount).

Tinicum Park has picnic areas with tables and grills, playground, ball fields, hiking and biking on the canal towpath, boat ramp to the Delaware River, and camping for families and groups.

## The Brandywine Valley—
### Chester County, Delaware County, and on into Delaware

Up until 1710 the Welsh formed the second largest group to emigrate to Pennsylvania. Many settled in the Brandywine Valley area, and their presence is felt in the many Welsh names they left behind—Uwchlan, Toughkenamon, and Tredyffrin, to mention a few. The Welsh plans to pay for their tract of land failed, and William Penn sold off portions of the original barony. Many Scotch-Irish also settled in the area. Chester County was one of the first three counties laid out by Penn, 40 miles long, 30 miles wide.

Today the Brandywine Valley still retains fertile farmlands, rolling hills, crossroads villages, and quiet woodlands. It is one of the fox-hunting centers of the country, national capital of the mushroom industry, full of antiquity, museums, restorations, gracious homes and estates, arboretums, and farm markets—in short, a delightful area for anyone young or old to explore.

Across the border in Delaware all state-owned historical sites and some major museums are open on the Monday holidays. For information on Delaware Triplet series write to Bureau of Travel Development, 45 The Green, Dover, Delaware 19901, or call 1-302-678-4254.

### *Chester County*

#### WEST CHESTER, THE COUNTY SEAT

**BRINTON 1704 HOUSE**
On U.S. Route 202
(1 mile north of U.S. Route 1)

**Phone:** 1-696-4755
**Open:** June–September, Tuesday, Thursday, Saturday 1–4 P.M.
**Closed:** Holidays
**Admission:** 50¢

Authentic Colonial architectural restoration, now a museum under the auspices of the Chester County Historical Society.
For further information on hours call: 1-696-4755.

## CHESTER COUNTY HISTORICAL SOCIETY
225 North High Street
West Chester, Pa. 19380

**Phone:** 1-696-4755
**Open:** Monday–Tuesday 1–5 P.M., Wednesday 1–9 P.M., Thursday and Friday 10 A.M.–5 P.M.
**Closed:** Holidays, August–Labor Day
**Admission:** Free
**Directions:** West Chester Pike (Pa. Route 3) takes you directly there; Schuylkill Expressway west to U.S. Route 202 south might be faster
**Parking:** Meters on street
**Public Transportation:** Market Street Subway to 69th Street and SEPTA Red Arrow West Chester Bus to High Street.

This is a friendly, warm museum staffed with highly informed people and full of priceless antiques and archives.

The basement is set up to re-create an old general store, a blacksmith's shop, an oldtime schoolroom complete with desks and books dating back to the early 1800s, and marvelous collections of tinware, glazed redware, stoneware, and early hardware. Recently added is the McKinstry Memorial Display, an esteemed collection which emphasizes minerals of the Delaware Valley region with comparative displays from other parts of the world.

The first floor houses museum-quality period furniture; tall clocks or grandfather's clocks; samplers; and a library for research. Upstairs are large cases of dolls from the very earliest china-head, wax, wood-head, and bisque dolls to a "Little Lulu," circa 1944. An elaborate dollhouse made by Voegler, an 1836 cabinetmaker, contains the original furnishings.

The archivist, Miss Dorothy Lapp, is eager to share her knowledge of the area and will bring out books dating back to 1699. One, a surveyor's book from the Chester County area, is handwritten with lists of bounties: "to Indian for one wolf's head—15 Shillings." There are clipping files on Chester County families from 1808 to the present and recipe books dating back to 1710.

School group visits can be arranged. Call ahead and make reservations. It's really worth the trip.

## DAVID TOWNSEND HOUSE
225 North Matlack Street
West Chester, Pa. 19380

**Open:** June–September, Tuesday, Thursday, Saturday 2–4 P.M.
**Closed:** October–May
**Admission:** Free

Townhouse of horticulturist and banker David Townsend. Furnished in Federal, Empire, and Victorian periods by Chester County Historical Society.
For further information on hours call: 1-696-4755.

### NEARBY PLACES OF INTEREST IN WEST CHESTER

## BALDWINS' BOOK BARN
865 Lenape Road
West Chester, Pa. 19380

**Phone:** 1-696-0816
**Open:** Monday–Saturday 10 A.M.–5 P.M., Sunday 12 noon–5 P.M.

For book browsing and bargains stop in at this West Chester landmark just a short ride from the center of town. Mr. Baldwin, the proprietor, is knowledgeable about books and the Chester County area. The barn contains three floors of volumes on every conceivable subject; rare books are also available here, In the children's collection you can find anything from the Rover Boys series published at the turn of the century to a bargain in a recent "series" book. If you have a love for books don't miss a visit here.

## MARSHALLTON INN
4 miles west of West Chester on Pa. Route 162

**Phone:** 1-692-4367
**Open:** Lunch Tuesday–Friday 11:30 A.M.–2 P.M.; dinner Tuesday–
Saturday 5:30–10 P.M., Sunday 4–9 P.M.

This charming inn, with warm old paneling, random plank floors, and numerous antiques, offers a sumptuous lunch or dinner and a welcome respite from a day of sightseeing in Chester County. Originally a country store, it eventually petitioned to become a tavern. In 1822 it received its license and has been flourishing ever since.
Attractive shops just adjacent to the Inn include Brandywine Candlecraft, with a good selection of molds and accessories, repli-

cas of old molds, and hand-dipped bayberry candles made in the shop. The Yellow Bow is an attractive craft shop with a wide variety of supplies.

## OTHER ATTRACTIONS IN CHESTER COUNTY

### BRANDYWINE RIVER MUSEUM
Chadds Ford, Pa. 19317

Phone: 1-388-7601
Open: Daily 9:30 A.M.–4 P.M. (summer until 4:30)
Admission: Adults $1, students 12–18 75¢, children (6–12) 50¢

A celebration of the Wyeths and other area artists in a converted gristmill overlooking Brandywine Creek. Environmental exhibits. For details see Chapter 2.

### LONGWOOD GARDENS
Kennett Square, Pa. 19348

Phone: 1-388-6741
Open: Every day of the year
Admission: Weekdays 50¢, weekends and holidays $1; children (6–12) 50¢, under 6 free

Outstanding gardens and horticulture displays. Covered in detail in Chapter 6. One-half mile south of Longwood Gardens is:

### PHILLIPS MUSHROOM PLACE
U.S. Route 1
Kennett Square, Pa. 19348

Phone: 1-388-6082
Open: Daily 10 A.M.–6 P.M.
Closed: Easter, Thanksgiving, Christmas, New Year's Day
Admission: Adults $1; children 50¢, under 6 free. Call for group rates.

Chester County is the mushroom capital of the world, and here is a chance to see and hear about them first hand. At Phillips Mushroom Place mushrooms can be seen growing in all their different stages; there are also a movie, dioramas, and exhibits. Gift shop sells mushrooms in all manner, shapes, and forms.

**PROJECT 400 (HILLENDALE MUSEUM)**
Hillendale Road
Mendenhall, Pa. 19357

**Phone:** 1-388-7393
**Open:** Monday–Saturday; tours (3 hours long) are scheduled to begin between 9:30 A.M. to 1 P.M. by reservation only
**Closed:** Holidays
**Admission:** Adults $3, students through senior high school $1.50 (includes loan of tape player and tape). No group rates; all visitors tour individually
**Restrictions:** Children under 16 must be accompanied by responsible adult and must have completed sixth grade. No cameras allowed in building. Reasonable standards of dress.
**Directions:** Schuylkill Expressway to City Avenue, U.S. Route 1 south to Pa. Route 52, left .8 mile to Hillendale Road, left .5 mile to Project 400. *Or* I-95 south to Del. Route 52 exit, right for about 10 miles, right on Hillendale Road to Project 400.
**Parking:** On grounds
**Picnicking:** Not permitted

If you are willing to conform, visit one of the newer and more elaborate museums in the area.

Four hundred years (1490–1890) of North American exploration have been condensed into a more than two-hour walking tour of Project 400. The idea is to show the influence of geography on the historical development of the continent through the use of dioramas, maps, and a taped descriptive narration (tapes in English only). However, political, social, and economic events are rarely mentioned, so that an appreciation of the museum's purpose really depends on your own knowledge of history. Almost all your favorite explorers—Columbus, Cabot, Cartier, Marquette, De Soto, Hudson, Balboa, Lewis and Clark—are there in highly detailed dioramas which show them struggling over mountains, deserts, and ·rivers.

NEARBY
Brandywine Battlefield State Park, where you can picnic.


**RED ROSE INN**
U.S. Route 1
West Grove, Pa.

**Phone:** 1-869-9964
**Open:** Year-round for lunch and dinner
**Closed:** Tuesdays

Named "Red Rose" by reason of the fact that the land on which the Inn stands was part of a grant from King Charles to William Penn, who deeded it to his grandson in 1731 with the provision that a yearly payment of one red rose should be made. This is done each September (the first Saturday after Labor Day) as part of a charming ceremony held at the Inn. Open to the public.

This delightful old Inn, always kept filled with flowers, is a fine place for lunch or dinner. Delicious honey-baked chicken and lots of dishes made with mushrooms grown right in the nearby Brandy-wine Valley. Combined with a visit to nearby Star Roses, it is a highly enjoyable outing.

## SAINT DAVID'S CHURCH
Valley Forge Road
Wayne, Pa. 19087

**Phone:** MU 8-7947
**Open:** Daylight hours. Anyone may attend services on Sunday at 8 A.M. and 11 A.M., Wednesday at 10 A.M.
**Directions:** Schuylkill Expressway to Valley Forge exit, U.S. Route 202 south to Devon exit, south to U.S. Route 30 (Lancaster Pike), left on Lancaster Pike to Dorset Road (which becomes South Valley Forge Road); church is on right

Almost untouched since Colonial days, this lovely old church with its closed pews was built in 1715 by Welsh Episcopalians. It is the final burial place of Anthony Wayne and was forever memorialized by Henry Wadsworth Longfellow in a poem:

> Here would I stay, and let the world,
> With its distant thunder, roar and roll. . . .

The churchyard is as quaint and beautiful as the church.

## SAINT PETERS VILLAGE
Saint Peters, Pa. 19470

**Phone:** 1-469-9301
**Open:** Daily. Shop hours: Tuesday–Friday 10:30 A.M.–5:30 P.M., Saturday 11:00 A.M.–6 P.M., Sunday 12 noon–6 P.M.
**Closed:** Mondays unless legal holiday
**Admission:** Free

**Directions:** Schuylkill Expressway to Pennsylvania Turnpike, to Downingtown exit (23), Pa. Route 100 toward Pottstown; then left on Pa. Route 23 (west) 4½ miles to Saint Peters Village. Approximate driving time from Center City: 1 hour.

**Parking:** Free in various lots throughout the village

In the mid-1800s David Knauer built this village to take care of the needs of his quarry workers. A general store, post office, bakery, livery stable, and more have been restored to their Victorian appearance. Now these buildings serve as small shops selling quilts, pottery, candles, dolls, and minerals and rocks, and there's also a livery stable with horses and burros for hire.

The best part of Saint Peters Village is what nature endowed it with. Sloping down behind the restored village is beautiful French Creek, wooded and fun for rock climbing and nature lovers.

You can eat lunch or dinner in the French Creek Falls Hotel in Victorian surroundings (prices fairly expensive) or try the Emporium for a reasonably priced hamburger or hot dog. Better still, spread out a picnic lunch or early evening supper on the massive granite boulders right in the middle of French Creek.

## STAR ROSES
U.S. Route 1
West Grove, Pa. 19390

**Phone:** 1-869-2426

**Open:** Year-round seven days a week 9 A.M.–6 P.M.

**Closed:** Thanksgiving, Christmas, New Year's Day

**Directions:** Schuylkill Expressway to U.S. Route 1, south to West Grove and follow signs

This is the country's outstanding and oldest rose grower. Thirty-five acres of rose fields containing over 400,000 varieties of plants. It is a breathtaking sight—and a special delight if you are a rose fancier. Many popular and unusual varieties to choose from: "Portrait," lovely peach roses, and "All American Winners." The height of bloom is the month of July, but remember that Star Roses is open all year long; check their garden center for unusual houseplants, poinsettias at Christmas, lovely lilies at Easter. In addition they have fine rhododendrons, azaleas, and many other varieties of shrubs.

Write for a free catalogue and you can order through the mail. For an added attraction combine your visit with lunch or dinner at the Red Rose Inn (see above).

HANDICAPPED
You can drive through the rose fields. Restrooms: one step.

## EVENTS IN CHESTER COUNTY

**BRANDYWINE POLO CLUB**
At General Richard King Mellon Memorial Polo Center off U.S.
  Route 1 at Toughkenamon
(Between Avondale and Kennett Square)
**Phone:** 1-268-8692
**Matches:** June–mid-October, Wednesday at 7:30 P.M., Sunday at
  3 P.M.
**Admission:** Adults $1, children under 12 free
**Directions:** Schuylkill Expressway, U.S. Route 1 south to Tough-
  kenamon, and follow the signs

Polo, an exciting spectator sport, is also a delightful summer afternoon or evening's entertainment. Various clubs in the area compete
in an outdoor arena with stands for viewing. Pack a picnic and
eat it in the stands or on the tailgate if you have a station wagon.
Snack bar.

**CHESTER COUNTY DAY**
Box 1
West Chester, Pa. 19380

**Phone:** 1-692-4322

If your interest is in historic homes and landmarks or if you're
curious to see the fantastic estates that lie behind the post-and-rail
fences at the height of the fall foliage season, definitely plan to go
to Chester County Day. For over thirty years the tour has attracted
a large following which looks forward to this annual event. There
are as many as fifty stops, so you must pick and choose. Snack
bars are strategically placed for lunch. Preview party Friday evening preceding Chester County Day at Longwood Gardens. It's a
kind of orientation—what houses are open, what is inside them,
color slides. This event is included in the price of the ticket. Chester
County Day also offers an opportunity to see a hunt, which begins
at 9 A.M. For further information call or write in September and
a detailed newspaper about the facts of the day will be sent to
you. The Chester County Hospital is the beneficiary.
   Tickets: $7.50 if you drive your own car; private charter bus
reservation, $10 (includes tour ticket). First Saturday in October,

rain or shine, 10 A.M.–5 P.M. This is really an adult tour. Unless your child has a real interest in antiques, better leave him home for this one.

## FARM CITY WEEK

One weekend in November the Chester County Farmers Association holds open house and invites you to visit working farms from 1 to 4 P.M. Visits usually include horse, dairy, and goat farms, greenhouses, and mushroom farms. There is no charge for these weekend visits. Program and tour map available. Write to Tourist Bureau, Room 108, Court House, West Chester, Pa. 19380, or call 1-696-4935.

## PENNSYLVANIA HUNT CUP

In November near Unionville, Pa. See page 186 for details.

## CHESTER COUNTY PARKS
Chester County Park and Recreation Board
Room 406
Court House
West Chester, Pa. 19380

**Phone:** 1-696-9100. Ask for Park and Recreation Board.

NOTE: Nonresidents in Chester County require special permission to use county park facilities. Call park you want to visit.

## HIBERNIA PARK
R.D. 2
Coatesville, Pa.

**Phone:** 1-384-0290
**Open:** Daily 8 A.M.–11 P.M.

Here are 721 acres for camping, hiking, trails, picnic and play area, fishing in the Brandywine (trout stocked annually). In winter, hiking and sledding.

## NOTTINGHAM PARK
Nottingham, Pa.

**Phone:** 1-932-9195
**Open:** Daily 8 A.M.–11 P.M.
**Directions:** Entrance off U.S. Route 1, 4 miles south of Oxford

For geology buffs, here are many unique rock formations—651 acres of them. Camping, hiking, boating, and fishing in three stocked (bass, bluegill) lakes. Winter hiking, sledding, and ice skating.

## WARWICK PARK
Pa. Route 23 south of Pottstown

**Phone:** 1-469-9461

Newest of the Chester County parks. Hiking, picnicking, fishing in French Creek.

## *Delaware County*

## BRANDYWINE BATTLEFIELD STATE PARK
U.S. Route 1
Chadds Ford, Pa.

Park open daily

The scene of an important battle of the American Revolution, this beautiful park offers picnicking facilities and a glimpse of history. For details see page 62.

## NEWLIN MILL PARK
U.S. Route 1
Box 307
R.D. 4
Glen Mills, Pa. 19342

**Phone:** GL 9-2359
**Open:** March–December 7 A.M. to dusk
**Admission:** Adults 75¢, children 25¢. No picnic fee if fishing. Reservations needed on weekends and holidays. Group rates available.
**Fishing Fee:** Adult or first child (under 16) fishing without an adult $1, additional children 50¢
**Directions:** Schuylkill Expressway to U.S. Route 1 south; it's about 18 miles from Center City Philadelphia, on the left
**Parking:** Facilities at park
**Picnicking:** Picnic groves with tables and fireplaces. Restroom facilities.

This is the place for the fisherman who wants to be sure of a catch. The mill race and ponds are heavily stocked with rainbow and brook trout in the spring and brown trout in the summer.

You can't miss—almost. Register at the office. No fishing license needed. Poles and bait available—and you must keep the trout you catch. Trout are $1.25 to $3.50, depending on where you fish. If you're lucky, someone will help you clean your fish at the cleaning bench. Then cook it over a fire at the picnic grove. Cool weather is best: March, April, May.

Nature trails, a baseball diamond, tennis courts, and an historic gristmill may eventually divert the enthusiastic junior fisherman.

HANDICAPPED
Call in advance. Assistance available.

## GOVERNOR PRINTZ PARK
Essington Township, Pa.

**Phone:** 586-7292
**Open:** Weekdays 8:30 A.M.–5 P.M.; Monday, Sunday 1–5 P.M.

New Sweden was founded in 1638, over forty years before William Penn established Pennsylvania. The purpose of the Swedish settlement was fur trade with the Indians. Johan Printz landed in 1643 to become the first royal governor and asserted the Swedish claim to a large trading area which today is near International Airport and the Industrial Highway. The old capital of New Sweden is an archaeological remain known as Governor Printz Park.

## PUSEY PLANTATION
10 Race Street
Upland
Delaware County, Pa. 19015

**Phone:** TR 4-0900
**Open:** Tuesday–Sunday 1–5 P.M.
**Closed:** Mondays
**Admission:** For the buildings: Adults 50¢, teenagers 25¢, children 10¢
**Parking:** On the grounds
**Directions:** Schuylkill Expressway to U.S. Route 1 south, left on Pa. Route 352 to Upland, then follow signs to Pusey Plantation.

The Caleb Pusey House, built in 1683, is reputed to be the oldest home of an English settler in Pennsylvania. Pusey came to Pennsylvania in 1683 to manage the first sawmill and gristmill set up by William Penn, and Penn was a frequent visitor.

The house has been restored with seventeenth-century furnish-

ings, some of which were still in the Pusey family. The Landing-
ford Plantation, site of the house, sawmill, barn, woodshed, and
toolshed, is part of a growing complex in the process of restoration.
Group visits: Schools and groups with over 30 children should make
advance arrangements.

## Delaware

### A DAY IN OLD NEW CASTLE

See Chapter 8.

### THE HAGLEY MUSEUM
P.O. Box 3630
Wilmington, Del. 19807

**Phone:** 1-302-658-2401
**Open:** Tuesday–Saturday, holidays 9:30 A.M.–4:30 P.M., Sunday
1–5 P.M.
**Closed:** Mondays (except holidays), Thanksgiving, Christmas, New
Year's Day
**Admission:** Free. Group visits: By reservation only. Telephone the
Tour Office two weeks in advance. Minimum age suggested:
Upper elementary school. Minimum number: 12; maximum num-
ber: 120. One adult with every 20 children. Length of tour:
2 hours.
**Directions:** I-95 south to exit 7 (Wilmington), Del. Route 52 north,
right on Del. Route 100, right on Del. Route 141 to Museum. *Or*
Schuylkill Expressway to U.S. Route 1 south, south on U.S.
Route 202 to Del. Route 141 to Museum
**Parking:** Free; at entrance to Museum
**Picnicking:** By reservation for sack lunches only. No food sold.
Picnic facilities also at nearby Longwood Gardens and Brandy-
wine Battlefield State Park.

The Hagley Museum was established to preserve the site of the
du Pont Company's original black powderworks, founded in 1802.
Various grades of military, sporting, and blasting powder were
produced here for over 100 years. Set in a deep ravine on the
banks of Brandywine Creek, the museum's parklike appearance
presents a sharp contrast with the original purpose of the entire
operation. An open-air jitney bus takes you on a 3-mile ride around
the complex, past the mill races, the powder mills, and the other
buildings rebuilt as exhibit halls with fascinating elaborate working
models and displays of flour, paper, iron, and textile mills—the

Colonial industries of the Brandywine. You can get on and off at exhibits along the way, continue on foot, or pick up the next jitney. In spring and in fall, "Eleutherian Mills," Mr. E. I. du Pont's residence on the hill, is open, as well as the adjacent buildings, including the Company office and the 1803 barn with its display of antique vehicles and farm equipment.

It's another well-done du Pont Production. The gardens are beautiful, the lawns immaculate, and the attendants helpful and polite. You can easily spend a couple of hours here. Even if you're not interested in gunpowder, the gardens and setting are worth the visit.

## MAGIC AGE OF STEAM
Del. Route 82
Yorklyn, Del. 19736

**Phone:** 1-302-239-4410
**Open:** Daily, July and August; Saturdays, Sundays, and holidays mid-April to mid-November. Museum may be visited by groups any day by reservation
**Admission:** Adults, grounds 25¢, miniature railroad 50¢, museum $1; children 2–12, grounds 25¢, miniature railroad 25¢, museum 50¢
**Directions:** Schuylkill Expressway to Route 1, to Kennett Square, left onto Pa. Route 82 to Yorklyn

The largest collection of Stanley Steamer cars in the world and a miniature steam railroad are here. The Auburn Valley Railroad carries passengers on its trains pulled by tiny coal-burning locomotives. Built on the scale of 1½" to the foot, it is the smallest railroad anywhere carrying passengers. Thirty people at a time can ride through the scenic grounds. Rides available: Stanley Steamer, a Toonerville trolley, miniature Ferris wheel, paddlewheel steamboat. All 25¢. Group rates available on request.

## WILMINGTON AND WESTERN RAILROAD
P.O. Box 1374
Wilmington, Del. 19899
(Near intersection of Del. Route 2 and Del. Route 41)

**Phone:** 1-302-998-1930
**Open:** May–October, Sundays and holidays
**Admission:** Regular run, adults $1.50, children 75¢. No reservations necessary; round-trip time about 1 hour.
**Directions:** I-95 south to exit 5, north on Del. Route 141 to Del.

Route 41, north to Greenbank Station (just beyond intersection with Del. Route 2)

For train buffs here is a fine day's outing. You can ride on an authentic turn-of-the-century steam train through the historic and beautiful Red Clay Valley.

### PARLOR CAR PARTIES

The Ex-PRR parlor car *Defender* may be chartered for parties. Rates on request.

### CABOOSE BIRTHDAY PARTIES

Two cabooses are available for birthday parties, including ice cream, cake, lemonade, and train ride. Prices on request.

## HENRY FRANCIS DU PONT WINTERTHUR MUSEUM
Del. Route 52
Winterthur, Del. 19735

One of the finest collections of Early American decorative arts to be seen anywhere. For details see Chapter 2.

Hex Signs on Pennsylvania Dutch Barn

## Pennsylvania Dutch Country

Although called Pennsylvania Dutch, the Mennonites, Dunkers, Pietists, Schwenkfelders, Moravians, and Church People (Lutherans and Reformed) spoke the German language. They came to the port of Philadelphia in great numbers in the early 1700s to avoid religious persecution. Some stayed in the city and acculturated;

most moved to the outlying counties—Montgomery, Berks, Lancaster, and Lebanon—to farm the rich lands. Today many of these people are still members of their respective sects and still work their farmlands, take their produce and handwork to Farm Markets, and ply their crafts in much the same manner as their ancestors did. Plain dress and no automobiles, tractors, mirrors, or electrical appliances identify the life-style of the "plain people."

The Church People, Lutheran and Reformed, were known for their decorative birth certificates (frakturs), and they too have maintained the culture, manners, and customs of their forefathers. This group is often referred to as the "fancy people" because of their love of color and decoration. Their folk art, identifiable by tulips, hearts, distelfinks, and peacocks often used in clusters of three, adorn barns, tool chests, hooked rugs, and pottery.

All the Pennsylvania Dutch are noted for their splendid cooking, though some people find it heavy. Try their smoked meats and sausages, corn pie, apple butter, funnel cake, and pretzels. There is evidence that the fruit pie, an American innovation, began with the Pennsylvania Dutch. True masterpieces are the apple tart, gooseberry tart, lemon sponge pie, and Montgomery pie.

A word of caution: Blatant commercialism has found its way into the Pennsylvania Dutch area, and it is often hard to separate the phony from the authentic. The best places to see and mingle with the people are at the Farm Markets and such fairs as the Goschenhoppen Folk Festival (see page 261). Leave U.S. Route 30 in Lancaster County and Pa. Route 29 in Montgomery County, and go off onto the back roads where you can glimpse the farms and the people dressed in their simple garb.

The Pennsylvania Dutch Tourist Bureau does not suggest travel in strictly Amish farm areas on Sunday because of possible interference with the people's way of keeping the Sabbath. Many places are closed. For complete information on places to see and things to do along with an excellent map of the area write to Pennsylvania Dutch Tourist Bureau, 1800 Hempstead Road, Lancaster Pa. 17601 (phone: 1-717-393-9705).

## AMISH FARM AND HOUSE
2395 Lincoln Highway East
(U.S. Route 30)
Lancaster, Pa. 17602

**Phone:** 1-717-394-6185
**Open:** Spring and fall, daily 8:30 A.M.–5 P.M.; summer 8:30 A.M.–8 P.M.; winter 8:30 A.M.–4 P.M., weather permitting

**Admission:** Adults $1.75, children (6–12) 50¢
**Directions:** U.S. Route 30 west to farm (6 miles east of Lancaster) *or* Pennsylvania Turnpike to Downingtown exit, Pa. Route 100 south to Pa. Route 113, right to U.S. Route 30, west to farm

The Amish Farm and House is an interesting replica of an Old Order Amish Farm. Hostesses take you through the house, which was built in 1805 and is furnished in typical Pennsylvania Dutch style. There are many outbuildings (blacksmith shop, barn, water-wheel, corncrib, tobacco shed), livestock, and crops to see. The last Thursday and Friday in April you can watch sheepshearing.

School and Scout field trips are welcome; it's a fine place for an annual class outing. Special group rates: 50¢, minimum 20 in group, 2 teachers free. Guides are furnished, and there are picnic facilities. Added attraction: Conestoga wagon rides 25¢. Homemade cookies, apricot-pecan bread, and soft drinks for sale.

## BAUM'S BOLOGNA
East High Street
Elizabethtown, Pa. 17022

**Phone:** 1-717-367-1552
**Open:** Monday–Friday (best Wednesday–Thursday). Preferable to write ahead.
**Admission:** Adults $1, children 12 and under free
**Directions:** U.S. Route 30 west to Pa. Route 283; Baum's Bologna is 2 miles east of Elizabethtown off Pa. Route 230

See bologna made the old-fashioned way, slowly smoked over hickory and oak wood fires in smokehouses. This family-owned and -operated organization has been turning out bolognas since 1920. They welcome visitors, and you can view the operation from meat on the hoof (choice Holstein bulls) to the slicing, packing, and packaging department. Different operations done on different days. Slaughtering Fridays only. The products are for sale. End-of-tour sample. Length of tour: about 20 minutes.

## DANIEL BOONE HOMESTEAD
Baumstown, Pa.
Off U.S. Route 422, just east of Reading

**Phone:** 1-582-4900
**Open:** April–October: weekdays 8:30 A.M.–5 P.M., Sunday 1–5 P.M.; winter: weekdays 9 A.M.–4:30 P.M., Sunday 1–4:30 P.M.
**Closed:** Good Friday, Easter, Election Day, Thanksgiving, Christmas, New Year's Day

**Admission:** Adults 50¢, under 12 free
**Directions:** U.S. Route 422 (Germantown Pike) to Daniel Boone
Homestead entrance road. *Or:* Pennsylvania Turnpike to Morgantown exit (22), Pa. Route 23 east to Pa. Route 345, north
past Hopewell Village to Pa. Route 742, left to Pa. Route 82,
right to U.S. Route 422; on U.S. Route 422 stay in left lane for
left turn at sign (not clearly visible) to Daniel Boone Homestead entrance road. About 1½-hour drive from Center City.
**Parking:** Free at Homestead and in picnic areas
**Tours:** Guided tours only at house
**Picnicking:** Tables, pavilions, grills

Your first sight of the Daniel Boone Homestead is somewhat startling: This two-storied structure is hardly one's idea of the rustic
life of that famous frontiersman. However, you quickly learn that
this is the site of the original log cabin in which Daniel Boone
was born in 1734. It was replaced by the present building some-
time during the eighteenth century, probably after the Boone
family moved to North Carolina in 1750. Restored and furnished,
the Homestead is administered by the Pennsylvania Historical and
Museum Commission as a "museum of the Pennsylvania Pioneer,"
portraying country life at that time. The furnishings are simple and,
to us, perhaps seem crude, but they evoke a picture of the hard-
ships of the frontier. Nearby are a smokehouse, blacksmith shop,
barn, and water-driven sawmill—all part of the growing complex
depicting pioneer life.

The Homestead is also a 600-acre sanctuary of the Pennsylvania
Game Commission, where wildlife wander about. Hiking trails
lead off into the woods, and there is a wayside lodge on the
grounds where organized youth groups can camp overnight.

NEARBY

Hopewell Village, Pottsgrove Mansion, French Creek State Park,
and Mary Merritt Doll Museum.

**BOYERTOWN MUSEUM OF HISTORIC VEHICLES**
P.O. Box 30
Reading Avenue and Warwick Street
Boyertown, Pa. 19512
(North of Pottstown)

**Phone:** 1-367-2091
**Open:** Monday–Friday 10 A.M.–4 P.M.; Saturday, Sunday by ap-
pointment
**Closed:** Legal holidays

**Admission:** Free
**Directions:** Schuylkill Expressway west to Pa. Route 363, north
to U.S. Route 422, west to Pa. Route 100, north to Pa. Route 73,
west to Pa. Route 562 (Reading Avenue), left to Warwick Street
**Parking:** Free at Museum

Wagons, carriages, sleighs, fire apparatus from 1790, a Conestoga
wagon, a mail coach, a doctor's carriage, a 1922 Daniels touring car
with a solid pewter radiator—they're all here, from the early 1700s
through the horse-and-buggy era to the Brass Age of Automobiles,
electric vehicles, and on. With the emphasis on vehicles produced
in the Boyertown, Fleetwood, Hamburg, Kutztown, and Reading
areas from the mid-1800s to the early 1920s, you'll be up to your
hubcaps in nostalgia.

ANNUAL EVENT
Duryea Day. Antique and classic auto meet. Saturday before
Labor Day, rain or shine. Flea market of old auto parts, open
9 A.M.–5 P.M.

TOURS
Tours of Boyertown Body Works available by appointment
(adults $1, children 50¢).

## COLONIAL VALLEY
Menges Mills, Pa. 17346

**Phone:** 1-717-225-4811
**Open:** May to November 9 A.M.–5 P.M.
**Admission:** Adults $1.25; children 50¢, under 16 free
**Directions:** Pennsylvania Turnpike west to York exit, Route I-83
to U.S. Route 30 west, interim bypass, and Menges Mills. Colo-
nial Valley is 6 miles east of Hanover on Pa. Route 116.

Colonial Valley is a Pennsylvania Dutch village begun in 1734
and containing some of the original buildings made of native stone,
bricks, and hand-hewn lumber. There are an operating water-
powered gristmill that has been in continuous use since 1740, a
blacksmith shop dating back to the American Revolution, one of
the very few up-and-down water-powered saws in the country still
in operation, a bake oven, an icehouse, and a hemp mill, along
with Loucks Museum, which is full of Pennsylvania artifacts.

The village is surrounded by meadows, streams, and places to
picnic and fish. Buggy rides are available (adults 50¢, children

25¢) Sundays only. There is a flea market on Sundays from 9 A.M. to 5 P.M.

Reasonably priced traditional Pennsylvania Dutch meals are served: baked and cooked potpie, country ham, homemade breads, apple dumplings, Montgomery pie, shoofly pie, and lemon sponge pie.

Special tour group rates available. Write or call Mr. Sterner for additional information.

## CORNWALL FURNACE
P.O. Box "V"
Cornwall, Pa. 17016

**Phone:** 1-717-272-9711
**Open:** April–October: Monday–Saturday 8:30 A.M.–5 P.M.; Sunday 1–5 P.M.; winter: Monday–Saturday 9 A.M.–4:30 P.M., Sunday 1–4:30 P.M.
**Closed:** Good Friday, Easter, Election Days, Thanksgiving, Christmas
**Admission:** Adults 50¢, under 12 free. Group rate 35¢.
**Directions:** Pennsylvania Turnpike west to Lebanon–Lancaster exit, north on Pa. Route 72 and follow signs to Cornwall Furnace
**Picnicking:** Allowed on the grounds

From 1742, when it was founded, to the discovery of the Mesabi range 150 years later, the Cornwall mine was considered the most important iron-ore deposit in North America. The mine was in operation long before the American Revolution, and iron from Cornwall went into the cannons, munitions, and equipment of George Washington's army. After more than two centuries of continuous operation the iron lode has finally been exhausted.

The original furnace, which was in operation from 1742 to 1883, is now a state museum and is one of the few early iron furnaces still intact. The structure, built into the side of a hill, contains a weighing room, a casting room, and, on the ground level, a steam engine and a giant wheel.

The picturesque village of Cornwall contains houses built more than a century ago in the style of an English mining community. Architects consider them classic examples of nineteenth-century stone houses in America.

Tours of the furnace are self-guided. For information on group visits write or call. It is suggested that schoolchildren be in the 3rd or 4th grade.

Cornwall Furnace is administered by the Pennsylvania Historical and Museum Commission.

## CRYSTAL CAVE
Kutztown, Pa. 19530

Phone: 1-683-3301
Open: Daily Washington's Birthday–November 1, 9 A.M.–6 P.M.;
during November open only Friday, Saturday, Sunday 9 A.M.–
5 P.M.
Closed: December 1–February 21
Admission: Adults $2, children 6–14 $1
Directions: Northeast Extension of Pennsylvania Turnpike to exit
33; U.S. Route 222 west to Kutztown and follow signs

Crystal Cave was discovered in 1871, and since then thousands of
tourists have come and marveled at the exquisite white dripstone
formations.
The tour is guided. You walk along sloping concrete walks,
guarded by steel railings, and observe the interesting formations
at every turn.
The cave grounds encompass 125 acres with free picnic park
and facilities. It's a fine day's excursion, especially in the heat of
the summer. The year-round temperature is 56 degrees F. Do
carry a sweater, wear sturdy shoes, and bring a camera.

NEARBY
Hawk Mountain.

## DUTCH WONDERLAND
U.S. Route 30
(4½ miles east of Lancaster)
Lancaster, Pa. 17602

Phone: 1-717-393-3846
Open: Easter weekend–Memorial Day: Saturday 10–6 P.M., Sun-
day 12 noon to 6 P.M., Memorial Day–Labor Day: Monday–Sat-
urday 10 A.M.–8 P.M., Sunday 11 A.M.–8 P.M.; day after Labor
Day–October: Saturday 10 A.M.–6 P.M., Sunday 12 noon–6 P.M.
Admission: Adults and children $1.50 (includes grounds, exhibits,
and dolphin show); rides about 30¢ each
Parking: Available

An enormous amusement park for children with a monorail, gift
shops, wax museum, and gardens. Bring your own picnic.

## THE EAGLE AMERICANA SHOP AND GUN MUSEUM
Pa. Route 741
West of Strasburg, Pa. 17579

**Phone:** 1-717-687-7931
**Open:** April, May, June, September, October: 10 A.M.–5 P.M.,
Saturday–Sunday 10 A.M.–7 P.M.; July–August: daily 9 A.M.–
8 P.M.; November: weekends only, weather permitting
**Admission:** Adults $1, children 11 and under free
**Directions:** U.S. Route 30 west to Pa. Route 896, left on Route 896
to Pa. Route 741 and follow the signs

The "Pennsylvania rifle"–also known as the "Kentucky rifle"–was
made in the Lancaster County area and reached its peak in the
era between 1725 and 1875. More than 300 gunsmiths followed
their trade in this area. It was the superior firepower and accuracy
from these guns that helped the Colonists win the Revolutionary
War.

The Eagle Americana Gun Museum houses one of the most
complete collections of Lancaster County (Kentucky) rifles in the
country. Weapons, firearms, and gun accessories from the crossbow
to World War II weapons are on exhibit. Also on display are fine
early glass, china, tin, toys, coins, and bottles.

The Americana Gift Shop has an unusual selection of gifts and
fine reproductions.

**EPHRATA CLOISTER**
632 Main Street
Ephrata, Pa. 17522
(About 12 miles northeast of Lancaster)

**Phone:** 1-717-733-6600
**Open:** April–October: weekdays 8:30 A.M.–5 P.M., Sunday 1–5
P.M.; winter: weekdays 9 A.M.–4:30 P.M., Sunday 1 P.M.–4:30
P.M.
**Closed:** Good Friday, Easter, Primary and General Election Days,
Thanksgiving, Christmas, New Year's Day
**Admission:** Adults 50¢, children under 12 free. Group visits: Rates,
35¢ by advance reservation only, at least one week in advance.
**Directions:** Pennsylvania Turnpike west to exit 21, south on U.S.
Route 222 to U.S. Route 322, left on Route 322 and follow
signs. Driving time from Center City under 2 hours
**Parking:** Area at entrance

In 1732 Conrad Beissel founded a religious society based on the
medieval concept of service to God through self-denial, meditation,
and a life of extreme simplicity. In addition to cultivating farms
and practicing the usual crafts of the time–basketmaking, car-

pentry, milling—the community developed a thriving press and revived the art of illuminated manuscripts. Membership declined after the Revolution, however, and in the early 1800s the society was incorporated into the Seventh Day German Baptist Church.

The Cloister has been extensively restored and is administered by the Pennsylvania Historical and Museum Commission. The surviving buildings, with narrow halls and low doorways symbolizing humility, contain the austere furnishings and utensils used by this religious sect: small bedrooms, board benches for sleeping, wooden pillows, wooden eating utensils. In the Chapel some of their magnificent illuminated songbooks and inscriptions are displayed.

Guides dressed in habits take you through the Cloister and explain the history and customs of this unique community. During the summer they bake pies and bread for sale in the bakehouse and demonstrate many of the crafts practiced by the community.

SPECIAL EVENTS

*Vorspiel,* a musical drama based on music of Conrad Beissel, Saturday evenings from the end of June until the first weekend in September and on several Sundays during the summer at dusk. Evening tours of the buildings on dates of performances begin at 6:30. Tickets: Adults $2, children 6 to 12 50¢. No reserved seats. For further information and group rates write: *Vorspiel* Chairman, Ephrata Cloister Associates, P.O. Box 155, Ephrata, Pa. 17522. Junior Guide Training Program and live-in; write for information.

## FARMERS MARKETS (LANCASTER)

The Lancaster Markets have been operating since 1742, when King George II established Lancaster as a borough and named the area as a perpetual market site. The Pennsylvania Turnpike west to Pa. Route 501 south takes you right into Lancaster.

CENTRAL MARKET
North Market and West Grant Streets
Lancaster, Pa.
Open: Tuesdays and Fridays 6 A.M.–5 P.M. (best hours 6 A.M.–2 P.M.)
This twice-weekly market held year round in a large mansard-roofed building is a good place to mingle with the Pennsylvania Dutch people in their traditional surroundings. They rise early and drive in from their farms in the surrounding countryside, bringing with them the freshest and most luscious produce, hickory-smoked meats, creamy longhorn home-cured cheese, corn relish, apple

butter, shoofly pie, and other baked goods. These delicacies are sold from the more than 200 stands within the marketplace.

GREEN DRAGON AUCTION MARKET
Crossroads of U.S. Routes 322 and 222
Ephrata, Pa.
Open: Fridays only 10 A.M.–11 P.M.
Indoor and outdoor shopping. Fresh meats, fruit, produce, baked goods, auction, livestock sales.

ROOTS COUNTRY MARKET AND AUCTION
On Pa. Route 72 between Petersburg and Manheim
Open: Tuesdays 5 P.M.–10 P.M.
Late afternoon and early evening auctions are held both indoors and outdoors. Depending on the time of the year, flowers, plants, shrubs, guinea pigs, and ducks are auctioned off. The very popular "Conestoga Auction" is a combination flea market and antique bric-a-brac auction.

SOUTHERN MARKET
Corner South Queen and Vine Streets
Lancaster, Pa.
Open: Saturdays only, 6 A.M.–2 P.M.

WEST END MARKET
501 West Lemon Street
Lancaster, Pa.
Open: Tuesday, Saturday 6 A.M.–12 noon; Friday 6 A.M.–5 P.M.

## GOSCHENHOPPEN FOLKLIFE MUSEUM
Red Men's Hall
Green Lane, Pa. 18054

Phone: 1-754-6013
Open: Sundays only, 1:30–4 P.M.
Closed: December 15–January 15
Admission: Free
Directions: Pa. Route 309 north to Pa. Route 73 west to Pa. Route 29 north. The Museum is at the intersection of Pa. Routes 29 and 63. *Or* Northeast Extension of the Pennsylvania Turnpike to Lansdale (exit 31), then north on Pa. Route 63 to Museum
Parking: Available and free

Montgomery County is just as rich in Pennsylvania Dutch culture as is Lancaster County—but less exploited.

On the second floor of Red Man's Hall in the heart of Upper Montgomery County is a charming museum dedicated to preserving and interpreting the folk culture of the oldest existing Pennsylvania Dutch Community.

An important part of their past is sustained in the furnished farmhouse rooms: a kitchen attic, bedroom (comer), stove room (stuba), blacksmith's, carpenter's, and weaver's shops, and a drugstore. Cookery is explored, and often you can taste a Pennsylvania Dutch specialty. Lovely quilts, frakturs, and other memorabilia are here in addition to a fine library with books and tapes devoted to the region. Group visits can be arranged by calling or writing in advance for appointment. Suggested minimum age for school groups: 3rd grade. See page 261 for information on the Goschenhoppen Folk Festival.

## GROFFS' FARM
R.D. 1
Mount Joy, Pa. 17552

**Phone:** 1-717-653-1520
**Open:** Lunch (Tuesday, Thursday, and Friday) and dinner; by reservation only
**Closed:** Sundays, Mondays
**Directions:** U.S. Route 30 past Lancaster to Pa. Route 283, to Pa. Route 230 Mount Joy; left on Marietta Avenue 4 blocks; left on Pinkerton Road; 4th farm on the left

It may be a bit of a trip—about two hours from Center City Philadelphia—but dining at Groffs' Farm is definitely worth it. The farmhouse is over 200 years old, the furnishings turn-of-the-century, and the food excellent Pennsylvania Dutch. Dinner includes four relishes, sweet pudding, and chocolate cake (to be eaten with the meal), appetizer, two or three meats, three vegetables—and then dessert (prices: lunch $3.75–$4.50; dinner $6.50; children under 10 half price). All served family style. Plan to arrive early: You can watch the cows being milked, and you may find Mrs. Groff in the barn shucking the corn for dinner. All year long Wednesday is Betty's surprise night. Dinner 5 to 7 P.M. ($8). Old Colonial recipes.

## HERSHEY, PA.
Hershey Estates
Hershey, Pa. 17033

**Phone:** 1-717-534-3172
**Directions:** Pennsylvania Turnpike to exit 20 (Lebanon–Lancaster), north on Pa. Route 72, west on U.S. Route 322, north on Pa. Route 743 (Cocoa Avenue) to Chocolate Avenue, right to factory. About a 2½-hour drive from Center City Philadelphia.
**Public Transportation:** Gray Line Motor Tours: see page 292; SEPTA Bus Rambles: see page 292.

## HERSHEY'S CHOCOLATE WORLD

**Phone:** 1-717-534-4900
**Groups:** Reservations not necessary
**Open:** Monday–Saturday 9 A.M.–5 P.M. Tours continuous (about 10-minute ride)
**Closed:** Sundays
**Admission:** Free

Where else but in this chocolate-lover's paradise would you find streetlamps shaped like Hershey kisses—both wrapped and unwrapped—a Chocolate Boulevard, a Cocoa Avenue? This monument to the world's sweet-tooth and to Milton Hershey, lord of the manor and founder of Hershey Company and Hershey, Pennsylvania, is one of the most popular tourist attractions in the country. If at all possible, avoid the summer months for this trip, because over 15,000 chocolate "nuts" pour through the world's largest chocolate factory each day to see the roasters, rollers, refiners, conching machines, gargantuan vats of chocolate, molds, conveyor belts, and packing machines. They have discontinued their regular factory tours and have instituted "Chocolate World," a simulation from bean to bar; you travel on an automated conveyance. No walking. Just sit in the car and off you go on a 10-minute tour from the cocoa bean plantations to the candy "kitchens" of Hershey. Efficient, effortless—a Disney-like production. Other Hershey "products" in the town are:

HERSHEY ROSE GARDEN AND ARBORETUM
April 15–November, daily 8 A.M.–dusk. Twenty-three acres of trees, shrubs, and flowers. Tulip display April and May; 1,200 varieties of roses in June; 200 varieties of chrysanthemums in September and October.

MILTON HERSHEY SCHOOL
Phone: 1-717-534-3500. Open: Monday–Friday 9 A.M.–4 P.M., Saturday and Sunday 10 A.M.–3 P.M. The elaborate domed Found-

er's Hall attracts quite a bit of attention as yet another testament to the man.

### HERSHEYPARK AND NEARBY AREA

Gardens, streams, an amusement park. Open: Mid-May to Labor Day 10:30 A.M.–11 P.M. Admission: One fee–adults $5.75; children 5–9 $3.75, 4 and under free

### HERSHEY MUSEUM

Phone: 1-717-534-3439. Open: Daily 10 A.M.–5 P.M. Closed: Thanksgiving, Christmas, New Year's Day. Admission: Adults $1; children 12–15 30¢, 6–11 25¢. The emphasis here is on Indian arts and Pennsylvania Dutch crafts. Groups: Bus tours adults 75¢, students 20¢.

### HIGHMEADOW CAMP AREA

Camp facilities open during camping season. Open: April 15–October 31. Fee: $5.50 per family per night; $33 per week plus utilities. Write for reservations to 1 Chocolate Avenue, Hershey, Pa. 17033.

### ANNUAL EVENT

Pennsylvania Dutch Days during either July or August. Phone 1-717-534-3172 for exact dates. This annual event has been going on for over twenty years: A five-day folk festival with craftsmen demonstrating early crafts of the country in Hershey Park. Admission: Adults $1.25, children under 16 free when accompanied by an adult.

### HERSHEY HOTEL

Stop by and take a look at this Old World hotel with its lovely grounds. It's from a bygone era.

## MARY MERRITT DOLL MUSEUM
R.D. 2
Douglassville, Pa. 19518
(About 10 miles east of Reading on U.S. Route 422)

Phone: 1-385-3809
Open: Monday–Saturday 10 A.M.–5 P.M., Sundays and holidays 11 A.M.–5 P.M.
Closed: Easter, Thanksgiving, Christmas, New Year's Day
Admission: Adults $1, children 12 and under 50¢
Directions: Pennsylvania Turnpike west to Morgantown exit (22),

I-176 north to U.S. Route 422 east. About 1½ hours from Center City Philadelphia.

**Parking:** Facilities at Museum

It's a veritable Lilliputian world at the Mary Merritt Doll Museum—over 1,500 dolls, rare, quaint, and beautiful, dating from 1725 to 1900; forty miniature period rooms furnished, papered, and inhabited by dolls of the appropriate time; furnished dollhouses, miniature china and tea services, a replica of a completely stocked Philadelphia toy shop of the mid-nineteenth century. If you have a fascination with minute detail, you might spend about an hour here.

GROUP VISITS

By reservation, preferably one week in advance. Minimum number: 10; minimum age suggested: 7. Group rate adults 50¢, children 25¢.

NEARBY

Daniel Boone Homestead, Hopewell Village, Pottsgrove Mansion, Boyertown Museum of Historic Vehicles.

## PENNSYLVANIA FARM MUSEUM OF LANDIS VALLEY
2451 Kissel Hill Road
Lancaster, Pa. 17601
(About 5 miles north of Lancaster)

**Phone:** 1-717-569-0401
**Open:** April–October: weekdays 8:30 A.M.–5 P.M., Sundays 12 noon–5 P.M.; winter: weekdays 8:30 A.M.–4:30 P.M., Sundays 12 noon–4:30 P.M.
**Closed:** Easter, Thanksgiving, Christmas, New Year's Day
**Admission:** Adults $1, children under 12 free
**Restrictions:** Strollers discouraged
**Directions:** Pennsylvania Turnpike west to exit 21 (Reading–Lancaster), south on U.S. Route 222 to Oregon Pike (watch for exit signs) to Valley Road, then follow signs to Pennsylvania Farm Museum. Driving time from Center City Philadelphia is under two hours.
**Parking:** Plenty of free space at entrance
**Picnicking:** Use the tables provided on the grounds or spread your blanket on the shady lawn

The Pennsylvania Farm Museum is a 100-acre complex of buildings depicting rural American life since the eighteenth century.

Some of the buildings have been restored, some re-created, and some moved here from the surrounding areas. Through furnishings, exhibits, and activities, many aspects of village life from farming to the trades and crafts of the time are explained. The Museum, administered by the Pennsylvania Historical and Museum Commission, includes an incredible collection of tools and artifacts all displayed in their appropriate setting—the gunsmith shop, the print shop, the tavern, the blacksmith shop, the barn, and the farmers' homes. The general store and post office has been carefully stocked with everything from buttons, calicos, and threads to some farm implements, kitchenware, and painted tin boxes—not for sale, just for looking. The one-room schoolhouse has books open on the desks and a lesson assignment on the blackboard. During the summer blacksmithing, spinning, and weaving are demonstrated. You can spend the better part of a day wandering through this picture of a vanishing world. It's a self-guided tour with people in each building to explain the contents and answer questions.

On the third weekend in June the Pennsylvania Farm Museum presents its annual Craft Days with a great variety of demonstrations: candle dipping, quilting, basketweaving, pottery making, etc. The annual Harvest Days exhibition is held the first weekend in October, with emphasis on eighteenth- and nineteenth-century harvesting techniques. They are both very lively events.

FOR ADULTS

Annual Institute of Rural Life and Culture. A workshop on folk life, music, and crafts taught by craftsmen and scholars. Write for information.

GROUP VISITS

By advance reservations only; 50 cents. Minimum number: 10.

TOURS

Guided tours available. Telephone reservations accepted. Minimum age suggested: 4th grade. Minimum number: 10; maximum number: 30. One adult with every 10 children. Length of tour: 1½ hours.

NEARBY

Ephrata Cloister and Cornwall Furnace.

## POLLOCK AUTO SHOWCASE I
70 South Franklin Street
Pottstown, Pa. 19464
**Phone:** 1-323-7108

**Open:** Hours vary. Call ahead.

**Admission:** Adults $1.50, children 12 and under 75¢

**Directions:** Pennsylvania Turnpike west to Downingtown interchange, Pa. Route 100 north to U.S. Route 422 (Business), which becomes High Street, to South Franklin Street

The antique and classic car collection of Pottstown steel magnate William Pollock includes an 1891 Peugeot, a Maxwell truck built in 1909, over sixty cars, thirty motorcycles, and the biggest attraction: *The Adams Probe 16,* the original spectacular sportscar from *A Clockwork Orange.*

## POTTSGROVE MANSION

U.S. Route 422

Pottstown, Pa. 19464

**Phone:** 1-326-4014

**Open:** April–October: Tuesday–Saturday 8:30 A.M.–5 P.M., Sunday 1–5 P.M.; winter: Tuesday–Saturday 9 A.M.–4:30 P.M., Sunday 1–4:30 P.M.

**Closed:** Mondays, Good Friday, Easter, Thanksgiving, Christmas, New Year's Day

**Admission:** 50¢; children under 12 free with adult. Senior citizens free. Guided tours only.

**Directions:** Pennsylvania Turnpike west to Downingtown interchange, then Pa. Route 100 north to U.S. Route 422 and follow signs

**Parking:** 20 cars

**Picnicking:** No eating facilities, but you can bring a picnic to nearby Daniel Boone Homestead

Built in 1750 by John Potts, a wealthy ironmaster, Pottsgrove Mansion even then drew visitors from miles around to view its size and elegance. This lovely Georgian house is still considered a work of art. Its large central hallway, corner cupboards, window seats, the beautiful Philadelphia Chippendale furniture, and the eighteenth-century flower and herb garden provide a picture of the prosperity of the ironmasters of the area. A tour of the house takes about 40 minutes. During the tourist season there may be a wait, so plan to make this one of your early stops if you're out for the day.

Pottsgrove Mansion is administered by the Pennsylvania Historical and Museum Commission.

### GROUP VISITS

By advance reservation, 35 cents. Maximum number on a tour: 15.

NEARBY

Hopewell Village, a restored iron-making community of the kind which gave rise to the magnificence of Pottsgrove Mansion. French Creek State Park, Daniel Boone Homestead, and Boyertown Museum of Historic Vehicles.

## RAILROAD MUSEUM OF PENNSYLVANIA
Pa. Highway 741
Strasburg, Pa. 17579

Open: April–October: Monday–Saturday 8:30 A.M.–5 P.M., Sunday 12 noon–5 P.M.; winter: Monday–Saturday 8:30 A.M.–4:30 P.M., Sunday 12 noon–4:30 P.M.
Directions: U.S. Route 30 west to Pa. Route 896, south on Route 896 to Pa. Route 741, turn left, and follow signs

One of the largest collections of locomotives, cars, artifacts, and exhibits to be seen anywhere. Indoor and outdoor displays, model trains, and full-scale equipment. Mid-nineteenth-century locomotives for inspection and boarding. The Museum has been developed by the Pennsylvania Historic and Museum Commission.

NOTE: Take a ride on the nearby Strasburg Railroad.

## STRASBURG RAILROAD
Pa. Route 741
P.O. Box 96
Strasburg
Lancaster County, Pa. 17579

Phone: 1-717-687-7522
Operating Schedule: December–March, Sunday afternoons only; April–mid-May, Saturday and Sunday afternoons; mid-May–October, daily; October–November, Saturday and Sunday afternoons. There are generally no trains running on weekends prior to and just after Christmas and New Year's Day.
Round Trip Fare: Adults $1.75, children under 12 75¢. Group rates available.
Directions: U.S. Route 30 west to Pa. Route 896 south, then turn left on Route 741 and follow signs to railroad

It's a 9-mile round trip to Paradise, Pennsylvania, on this steam railroad, with a stopover at a picnic grove. The coal-burning steam locomotive pulls an assortment of other old cars. Some have been featured in films; some are the last surviving models. The train clickety-clacks through the Amish farm country for about 45 minutes in a most leisurely fashion. Restrooms, gift shop, and snack bar at Strasburg depot.

## CONRAD WEISER PARK
R.D. 1
Womelsdorf, Pa. 19567
(West of Reading on U.S. Route 422)

Phone: 1-589-2934
Open: April–October: weekdays except Mondays 8:30 A.M.–5 P.M.;
Sunday 1–5 P.M.; winter: weekdays 9 A.M.–4:30 P.M., Sunday
1–4:30 P.M. Hours subject to change.
Closed: Mondays
Admission: 25¢
Directions: Pennsylvania Turnpike west to Morgantown inter-
change, I-176 north to U.S. Route 422, west to park
Picnicking: Tables

Conrad Weiser is best remembered for his role in keeping peace
between the Indians and white men; he had great knowledge of
Indian customs and languages and worked closely with the Iro-
quois League in maintaining peace from 1737 to 1750.

He built a simple home in 1729 consisting of one large room which
served as kitchen, dining room, and sitting room. Under the sloping
roof were sleeping quarters. These rooms are now a museum,
and some of the furnishings date back to Weiser's time. Also on the
grounds are a springhouse and a statue of Shickellamy with a peace
pipe, signifying the Indian gesture of friendship.

## WHEATLAND
1120 Marietta Avenue
Pa. Route 23
Lancaster, Pa. 17603

Phone: 1-717-392-8721
Open: March 15–November 30, Monday–Saturday 9 A.M.–5 P.M.,
Sunday 10 A.M.–5 P.M. Last tour 4:30 P.M.
Admission: Adults $1, children 12 and under free
Directions: Pennsylvania Turnpike west to Lancaster–Reading exit,
south on U.S. Route 222 into Lancaster to Pa. Route 23, right to
mansion

Wheatland is the home of James Buchanan, Pennsylvania's only
U.S. President (1857–1861). The lovely mansion, circa 1828, and
broad lawns are carefully preserved. You are shown about by well-
informed costumed guides. The house contains some of Buchanan's
original furniture, china, and silver. Wheatland has been designated
as a National Historic Landmark.

Group visits can be arranged by writing or calling in advance.

# 8
# FAIRS AND FESTIVALS

All year long the greater Delaware Valley is a never-ending spectacle of fairs and festivals. They celebrate almost anything—Scottish heritage, folk arts and crafts, expert horsemanship—or just provide an afternoon's entertainment. Almost every day some organization benefits from the months of planning required to stage these annual wingdings. We have therefore included some of the larger, or older, or somewhat out of the ordinary, ones both in the city and in the environs.

## BLACK EXPO
**Time:** Mid-August

For the past few years attendance has been growing at this showcase for black culture, business, and education. There are trade areas, business seminars, voter registration, and political education, but above all it is filled with music, dance, and traditional and native foods. Music from gospel and the blues to jazz and rock, soul food, and native African specialties cooked to order in the booths. Guest stars perform. There are areas especially for the kids. Come and see what all the excitement is about. Everyone is welcome and has a good time. Watch the papers for announcements.

## CHESTER COUNTY DAY
**Time:** First Saturday in October, rain or shine
**Phone:** 1-692-4322

Outstanding tour of historic estates and landmarks at height of fall foliage season (page 234).

## A DAY IN OLD NEW CASTLE
Box 166
New Castle, Del. 19720

**Phone:** 1-302-658-9251
**Time:** Annually, the third Saturday in May, 10 A.M.–5 P.M.

**Admission:** Adults $5; children (12–18) $2.50, under 12 free. Special group rates available.
**Directions:** I-676 to Walt Whitman Bridge, to I-295 south, cross Delaware Memorial Bridge, proceed south on Del. Route 9 to New Castle.

This lovely pre-Revolutionary town is built around a green. Once a year many of the private homes are open to visitors. New Castle was founded by the Dutch in 1651, but today the town decidedly reflects the British influence that followed after the Dutch. Home-cooked food is served at the parish house of Immanuel Church on the Green and at the New Castle Presbyterian Church. There are Continental troops in drill parade, costumed residents, and a fine Colonial atmosphere to the day. Don't miss a visit to the Amstel House and Buena Vista. For further information on events of the day call or write.

## DELCO SCOTTISH GAMES
Devon Horse Show Grounds
Devon, Pa. 19333

**Phone:** Delaware County Tourist Bureau, 565-3677 or 566-2572 (the chairperson of the event)
**Admission:** Adults $3; children $1 (6–12), under 6 free
**Directions:** Schuylkill Expressway west to U.S. Route 202 south, then Valley Forge Road to Devon Horse Show grounds
**Parking:** Available
**Public Transportation:** Paoli Local at Suburban Station (16th and John F. Kennedy Boulevard) to Devon Station. It's a short walk to the grounds just off Lancaster Avenue.
**Picnicking:** Pavilion with tables

The sound of bagpipes greets you on arrival, and you will hear their strains all day. This annual event in June, now several years old, attracts a colorful crowd, including many Scots dressed in full attire, but everyone is welcome.

Such festivities are not a new idea. They originated in Scotland to bring families together for visiting and choosing clan leaders.

The Delco Scottish Games provide a fascinating and fun-filled day for the whole family. You can watch the Highland fling, a tug-of-war, a stone throw, piping and drumming competitions. Sample a hot bridie, a meat pie, or fish and chips at the many booths selling Scottish foods. For the kids who don't like to experiment, there are hot dogs and hamburgers—or pack a picnic lunch. There's a pavilion with picnic tables.

There are grandstands for viewing exhibitions of Scottish dancing and some of the sporting events: caber toss, hammer throw, sheaf toss, and stone putt. There are junior competitions in many events.

Dress comfortably. If you are of Scottish descent, do come with your tartan. There are many in evidence in the crowd.

All kinds of Scottish food are for sale to take home. Also trinkets, jewelry, sweaters, even heather plants.

The Delco Scottish Games Association is a nonprofit organization of individuals seeking to provide events of interest to all. Watch the newspapers for the announcement in June.

HANDICAPPED

Call ahead for information. Big gate can be opened to let wheelchairs through.

## DEVON HORSE SHOW AND COUNTRY FAIR
Devon Horse Show Grounds
Devon, Pa. 19333

**Phone:** MU 8-2554 for tickets
**Admission:** $2, children 50¢
**Directions:** Schuylkill Expressway west to U.S. Route 202 south, then Valley Forge Road to Devon Horse Show grounds
**Parking:** On fairgrounds, $2
**Public Transportation:** From Center City take the Paoli Local at Suburban Station (16th and John F. Kennedy Boulevard) to Devon Station; it's a short walk to the grounds just off Lancaster Avenue.

For one week at the end of May and early June the Devon Horse Show attracts competitors and visitors from all over the world. The finest horses and equestrians meet at Devon each day and evening and compete in such events as jumping, the antique carriage–driving marathon, and a four-in-hand driving competition. Probably the most exciting events to attend are the championship jumping classes held the last couple of nights.

The Country Fair grounds offer a colorful variety of food and other goods. Many of the Philadelphia area's finest stores display their wares in a line of small shops with awnings painted Devon blue and white. You can buy anything from riding tack to haute couture.

There's plenty to eat . . . hot dogs and pizza at the refreshment stands, or a full-course roast beef dinner cafeteria style. Lots of picnic tables and a covered pavilion.

Wear comfortable shoes. It's loose gravel paths most of the way. Teenagers find the fair fun, a good way to meet and see their friends.

Bryn Mawr Hospital is the beneficiary of this unique and colorful event.

## FOLK FAIR
At Philadelphia Civic Center Convention Hall
34th and Civic Center Boulevard
Philadelphia

**Admission:** There is a charge. Group rates available. Call Nationalities Service Center for details, KI 5-6800.
**Directions:** Schuylkill Expressway to South Street exit, west on South Street to 34th Street, south to Civic Center
**Public Transportation:** SEPTA Routes D-1 (from Penn Central 30th Street Station), 40, 42

If you would like to eat, dance, and sing your way around the world but can't for various reasons, visit the Folk Fair sponsored by the Nationalities Service Center. Come early—and come very hungry—because there is marvelous food, a lot to do and see, and interesting things to buy. Craft demonstrations might include Ukrainian egg decorating, Dutch pottery making, and a lesson in origami by a lovely lady in her Japanese kimono. There are two-hour performances of folk dancing and folk singing for everyone. One of the big features of this fair is the food: Armenian shish kebab, Portuguese sausage sandwich, Puerto Rican pastries, and more. It's a gastronomic wonderland. Plan to spend several hours.

This biennial event occurs in even years, usually in the spring. Watch for the announcements or check with the Civic Center.

## GOSCHENHOPPEN FOLK FESTIVAL
East Greenville, Pa.

**Phone:** 1-754-6013
**Admission:** Adults $2, children (7th grade and under) free
**Directions:** On Pa. Route 29, 20 miles north of the Lansdale interchange of the Northeast Extension of the Pennsylvania Turnpike, *or* Pa. Route 73 west to Pa. Route 29 north to East Greenville. Approximate driving time from Center City Philadelphia, 1 hour.
**Parking:** Free under the direction of the Boy Scouts; you can make a small donation.

There are great charm and honesty about this annual festival held the second Friday and Saturday in August (no rain dates). Very little is for sale other than what you can enjoy on the spot. The Fair is held in a picnic grove covered with trees. More than 200 costumed craftsmen demonstrate their skills and chat with you about spinning, caning, making apple butter, dyeing, quilting, blacksmithing, hornsmithing, and more. Programs of Pennsylvania Dutch music, folklore, and humor are offered in a covered pavilion, and demonstrations of sheepshearing, flax breaking, and log splitting take place continuously throughout both days. Let the kids take a hayride for 25¢ while you sit in a haystack and wait for them.

The Pennsylvania Dutch love to eat, and the food alone is worth the visit. You can get a hot lunch prepared by country Dutch housewives or a great variety of soups, sandwiches, relishes, and salads cafeteria style. Try the chicken corn chowder or potato soup, both reasonably priced. The hot sausage sandwich or the ham-and-cheese on homemade bread are delicious. Funnel cake is made on the spot; there's always a line but it's worth waiting for. Also in the same area are homemade doughnuts, shoofly pie, and candy.

Most of the participants in this festival are the "plain people"— the Mennonites, the Schwenkfelders, and the Dunkers. They live close to the soil and make their wares in a timeless way that many young people can readily identify with.

## HEAD HOUSE SQUARE OPEN AIR MARKET
2nd and Pine Streets
Philadelphia

**Open:** Mid-June into September: Saturday 12 noon–midnight, Sunday 11 A.M.–6:30 P.M.
**Admission:** Free
**Public Transportation:** SEPTA Routes 5, 40, 90

This restored eighteenth-century marketplace in Society Hill is a kind of open-air street fair every weekend during the summer. It's not a flea market; it's a craft fair. Culinary and artistic craftsmen sell their own products, not imported crafts. You'll find a different craft demonstration each day; or maybe there'll be a puppet show or a concert. Anything from a rock group to a harp recital is possible here. And you'll be unable to resist the aroma of good food: *empanadas,* tacos, falafels, and stuffed grape leaves. It's a good place for the kids to break the pizza syndrome. Saturday evenings in the summer are delightful for a visit. Contact the Works Craft Gallery, 319 South Street (WA 2-7775) in February if you want a booth.

# HISTORIC FALLSINGTON DAY
4 Yardley Avenue
Fallsington, Pa. 19054

**Phone:** 1-295-6567
**Time:** Second Saturday in October annually—rain or shine
**Admission:** Adults $2.50; children 50¢, under 7 free (with an adult).
Fee includes all events and displays.
**Directions:** Pennsylvania Turnpike east to exit 29, north to U.S.
Route 13 for 5 miles, then follow markers (4 miles from Pennsbury Manor)
**Parking:** Free at nearby high school lot and on the street close by;
short walk to entrance

Hidden away in lower Bucks County, just minutes from busy U.S. Route 1 and the sprawling community of Levittown lies a beautiful historic restored eighteenth-century village known as Fallsington. Many of the original fine stone residences still line one side of Meetinghouse Square—some are being restored, some are occupied.

Once a year Historic Fallsington, Inc., an organization dedicated to the preservation of historic buildings, holds a gala eighteenth-century fair. All profits go toward further restoration. Not only is it fun and visually charming, it is a step back in history that is both enchanting and educational.

The day is jammed with events—a Colonial Musket Drill, puppet show, Colonial crafts, Grandmother's Trunk (specializing in small antiques), and tinsmithing demonstrations, visits to the Burges-Lippincott House, hot mulled cider at the Stagecoach Tavern (there is an Edward Hicks tavern sign here), pony rides, horse-drawn carriage rides, live and dried flowers, and plants for sale in large open sheds.

Outside snack tables serve hot dogs and homemade cakes and cookies. If you desire, a more leisurely lunch is served on a stone terrace overlooking many of the events. Tickets for this lunch are available in advance or on the day.

Nanny's Nursery is a place to leave your young one happily for a half-hour of storytelling and puppet making while you do some of the things that interest you; there's a charge.

The townspeople who participate in the fair are dressed in Colonial garb and the atmosphere is totally uncommercial. Allow yourself several hours to enjoy this fine reminder of our country's heritage.

## THE JUNE FÊTE
June Fête Fair Grounds
Edgehill Road
Upper Moreland Township, Pa.

**Phone:** 885-4000 (Abington Hospital will connect you with June Fête headquarters)
**Time:** The first Saturday in June
**Admission:** Adults $1; children 50¢, under 5 admitted free
**Directions:** Broad Street to Cheltenham Avenue; left to Easton Road right to Edgehill Road. Follow signs right on Edgehill Road to fairgrounds.
**Parking:** 50¢ (free buses from Abington Hospital take you to the fairgrounds that day)

June Fête is held the first Saturday in June regardless of the weather. In recent years the Friday night preceding, known as the June Fête Preamble, has become a tradition as well. All booths are open for both events.

This colorful event takes place on a beautiful permanent site donated by the Pitcairn family of Bryn Athyn. The Fête benefits Abington Memorial Hospital. Some of the outstanding activities include the Horse and Pony Show, the Dog Show sponsored by the Huntingdon Valley Kennel Club, the Automobile Show with modern, sports, and foreign cars, and a Classic Car Show where you might see a 1929 Rolls-Royce and a 1928 Mercedes-Benz.

There's a children's activity area with games, a Ferris wheel, lots of refreshments. On the midway are gaily decorated booths with everything from children's toys to gourmet foods. A lobster pot is a June Fête tradition.

## KUTZTOWN FOLK FESTIVAL
Kutztown, Pa. 19530

**Phone:** 1-717-683-8707
**Time:** Annually for eight days in late June and early July, with July 4 falling in the middle
**Hours:** 9 A.M.–7:30 P.M.
**Admission:** Adults $2, children under 12 50¢
**Directions:** Northeast Extension of the Pennsylvania Turnpike exit 33 (Lehigh Valley), then U.S. Route 222 west to Kutztown.
**Parking:** On the grounds, $1; free on the street a few blocks away

There are endless attractions at the Kutztown Festival. This annual eight-day event lures thousands of visitors to the area. Walk around the Commons and see their craftsmen, dressed in eighteenth-century attire, demonstrating their skills in quilting, horseshoeing, butter making, and canning. Artisans show how to work with pewter, vegetable dyes, and fraktur quills.

On the main stage watch a country auction, or listen to Pennsylvania Dutch music, folklore, and humor. Most of the participants at this festival are the "fancy Dutch" who love color, entertainment, and worldliness, as opposed to the "plain people," the Amish and Mennonites, who shun modern conveniences and regard such displays as sinful. The fancy Dutch act out some of the Amish traditions, such as a wedding ceremony and "barn raising."

There's lots to eat—all kinds of traditional Pennsylvania Dutch dishes, hot and cold—so leave the picnic lunch at home. Don't miss the funnel cake and soft pretzels.

You can buy many of the wares that you see being crafted. Beautiful quilts, tinware lanterns, woven baskets, frakturs, and stained-glass hex signs are just a few of the many items for sale. Although some aspects of the Festival seem a bit commercial, it's a fun-filled day and well worth a visit.

## THE MORGAN HORSE SHOW AND COUNTRY FAIR
Devon Horse Show Grounds
Devon, Pa. 19333

**Parking:** On the fairgrounds
**Directions:** Schuylkill Expressway west to U.S. Route 202 south, then Valley Forge Road to fairgrounds
**Public Transportation:** From Center City take the Paoli Local at Suburban Station (16th and John F. Kennedy Boulevard) to Devon Station. It's a short walk to the grounds just off Lancaster Avenue.

Held annually in August for three days and evenings. Over 100 events including Western, jumping, harness, and English classes. One of the highlights is a cavalcade of antique buggies with drivers in period costumes. The Morgan horse is one of the few native American breeds and is highly prized for its riding and jumping ability, its gentleness and stamina. Watch the papers for exact dates and ticket information.

## PENNSYLVANIA HOSPITAL DAY
Washington Square between Walnut and Locust Streets, 6th and 7th Streets
Philadelphia

**Public Transportation:** SEPTA Routes D, 42, 47, 50

Early in June the pigeons in Washington Square move aside for the annual fair held for the benefit of Pennsylvania Hospital. Wander among the booths featuring antiques, art shows, books, refreshments, and perhaps an auction. If you're not careful, you might come home with a player piano. All the activity is watched over by a statue of George Washington at the Tomb of the Unknown Soldier of the American Revolution near the fountain in the square.

## THE PHILADELPHIA FLEA MARKET
Independence Mall
(5th and 6th Streets between Market and Arch)
Philadelphia

**Phone:** WA 3-6415
**Open:** Spring–fall, occasional Sundays 12 noon–7 P.M. (rain or shine)
**Admission:** Adults $1, children 12 and under free (proceeds to local charities)
**Public Transportation:** Any bus on Market Street, Market Street Subway

For those who like browsing through flea markets, but don't like driving all over to find them, the Philadelphia Area Council on Tourism (PACT) has brought one to town, right in front of Independence Hall. Antiques, crafts, food, music, and entertainment. Have you been looking for a bubble-gum machine, an antique phonograph or music box, handcrafted toys? A bit of nostalgia? Watch the newspapers for dates.

## PHILADELPHIA FOLK FESTIVAL

**Time:** Last weekend in August. For information call or write Philadelphia Folk Festival, 7113 Emlen Street, Philadelphia 19119 (phone: CH 7-1300)

This is one of the larger festivals of its kind. It's been going on for over ten years and is efficiently run by a group of volunteers from the Philadelphia Folk Song Society. Held out in the country, it attracts people from all over for a weekend of folk, blues, and ethnic music and dancing under the stars. Each year is a bit different, depending on the performers, but the basic elements are constant: afternoon and evening concerts, folk dancing, afternoon workshops, folkcraft displays, and camping facilities and refreshments.

It's all outdoors and lovely when the weather cooperates. If you go, plan to start out early—traffic tends to pile up—and bring a picnic basket, a blanket, and insect repellent.

## POLISH FESTIVAL AND COUNTRY FAIR
Shrine of Our Lady of Czestochowa
Doylestown, Pa. 18901

**Phone:** 1-343-0600
**Time:** Annually over the Labor Day weekend and the preceding or following weekend
**Admission:** $2 per car (regardless of number of persons)
**Directions:** Pa. Route 611 to Doylestown, west on Pa. Route 313 (Ferry Road) about 2½ miles to well-marked sign, then left to Shrine

Vigorous polka bands, strains of the balalaikas, kishkies, pirogis— all these are part of the fun and gaiety that are becoming a traditional event over the three-day Labor Day weekend and the weekend that follows. On every day of the festival, Polish and Slavic dance groups perform, as does the Polish-American String Band.

Both Polish and American foods for snacks or full meals are available at many locations. Try a kielbasa sandwich with sauerkraut, colombki (stuffed cabbage), delicious kishkies (potato pancake roll) served with applesauce, and babka (cake). There are ample picnic tables, some in covered areas. You can bring your own lunch or dinner, but these homemade treats are well worth sampling.

In a covered pavilion with a big stage, Polish bands and dance groups perform traditional dances during the day. There is a large seating capacity.

An amusement area for children has a Ferris wheel, a merry-go-round, and the usual kind of midway entertainment. Rides are extra.

The Festival attracts thousands of people; the area is large and well laid out. The purpose of the Shrine and the event is to bring together people who wish to perpetuate Polish cultural traditions, but you don't have to be Polish to have a grand time.

## RITTENHOUSE SQUARE FLOWER MARKET
Rittenhouse Square
Walnut Street to Rittenhouse, 18th to 19th Streets
Philadelphia

**Public Transportation:** SEPTA Routes D, 17, 42, 90

Every May for just one day an indomitable army of ladies turns Rittenhouse Square into an outdoor flower market. Garden clubs from the Greater Philadelphia area participate, bringing you beautiful plants, flowers, and vegetables, delicious cakes, cookies, and breads—and that perennial favorite, lemon on a stick. There's a children's corner with pony rides and a carrousel. Proceeds go to various Center City charities. It's been going on for well over fifty years. When the weather cooperates, it is one of the prettiest sights around. Best to go early—that is, midmorning.

## SUPER SUNDAY
Benjamin Franklin Parkway

**Time:** A Sunday in October rain or shine, 12 noon–6 P.M.
**Parking:** Available

Super Sunday is a gala celebration sponsored by the cultural institutions along the Parkway. It's music, rides, movies, magicians, crafts, flea markets, food of every variety, and fun for the whole family. There are hundreds of stands and covered pavilions lining the streets from the Art Museum to Logan Circle and beyond. All auto traffic is diverted during the time of the festivities. The day attracts a tremendous crowd, and, astoundingly, the area readily accommodates the constant flow of people. Parking (normally not permitted on the grass) is allowed, and there seems to be space for almost everyone. Plan to spend a few hours. Each institution has free admission or reduced rates and special events such as puppet shows, concerts, art exhibits, and movies, so even if it rains there is plenty to do.

Rittenhouse Square Flower Market

# 9
# TOURS

Go "behind the scenes"—learn how a newspaper is put together or see coins minted. Satisfy that ageless curiosity—"How does it work?"—be it a bakery, a cattle ranch, a bottling company, or an airport.

A few words of advice: Many of the places listed in this section say "Group tours only." If you are not a "group" but a family or an individual, call and ask if you can join a scheduled group. Where a minimum age is given, it's their suggestion, and you may be able to negotiate if your group is a bit younger. Many places do have tours for school groups but prefer not to be listed. If you have a special interest, call the public relations department of the company. They may say, "Sorry"—but then again they may say, "Sure!"

## Sightseeing by Car: By Yourself or with a Group

### Civic

**CITY HALL**
Broad and Market Streets
Philadelphia 19107

**Phone:** MU 6-1776
**Open:** Monday–Friday 9 A.M.–5 P.M. Tower: Daily 9:30 A.M.–4 P.M.
**Closed:** Weekdays, holidays
**Parking:** Many Center City lots in the area
**Public Transportation:** Broad Street Subway, Penn Central Railroad to Suburban Station, Reading Railroad, SEPTA Routes, Shopper's Special, Mid City Loop bus, Cultural Loop bus

City Hall is an exciting place to visit. The building, once thought of as an eyesore, is now considered a masterpiece of Victorian architecture. The design by John J. McArthur, Jr., is based on the

William Penn Statue atop City Hall Tower

Louvre in Paris. Construction started in 1872 and was not completed until 1901. The tower and statue of William Penn atop are the work of Alexander Milne Calder. The statue, a monumental 37 feet high, is the largest sculpture on a building in the world. By custom no building in Center City can be taller than this statue.

How to See City Hall

*Guided Tours:* Free hour-long tours are available Monday through Friday at 10 A.M. Tours start promptly from Room 202 on the second floor, so be there a few minutes ahead of time. The tour includes a visit to the Mayor's Reception Room, City Council Chambers, and Courtrooms, and ends with a visit to the Tower. Uniformed Municipal Guides describe the history and background of City Hall.

*On Your Own:* If you should miss the guided tour or prefer to explore on your own, go to the Municipal Guides Office, Room 143, and pick up a sheet entitled "Do-It-Yourself Tour of City Hall." Special tours for large groups can be arranged by appointment. Call MU 6-3677 or MU 6-3678.

School visits to City Hall can be arranged from the 4th grade up; for the Tower from kindergarten up. High-school classes in American government may visit the courtrooms for a fascinating lesson in the judicial process.

*The Tower:* Open: Monday–Friday, 9:30 A.M.–4 P.M. Enter the northeast or northwest corner entrance of City Hall and take the elevator to the seventh floor. Follow the red lines on the floor to an elevator that will take you to the Tower. On a clear day the view from the Tower's observation platform is fantastic. All the city's landmarks come into perspective. William Penn's plan to build a city between two rivers is evident at a glance as you take in the Delaware to the east and the Schuylkill to the west.

*The Courts:* Open: Monday–Friday 10 A.M.–12 noon, 2 P.M.–4 P.M. The thirty-nine courtrooms contained in City Hall are usually open to the public. Should you want to see a court trial, go to one of the rooms lining the long corridors and look for a sign "Court in Session." You need only obtain permission from the court officer outside. He will usher you in to the Visitors' Gallery, where you may see the fascinating process of jury selection or the questioning of witnesses.

*Supreme Court of Pennsylvania:* The Supreme Court meets periodically in one of the stately courtrooms of City Hall. Call the office of the Prothonotary of the Supreme Court to determine when it is in session, and you can see the majesty of the judicial process. Seven judges sit at one time. It is the final court on all matters of Pennsylvania law that do not pose either Constitutional questions or questions under Federal law.

*City Council:* This is the legislative branch of Philadelphia's city government. It meets every Thursday. Although many of the questions deal with such items as zoning changes and ordinances, often there is lively debate on other controversial matters. The Visitors' Gallery is open when Council meets. Occasionally a highly charged issue arises or Council is on vacation, in which case the gallery is closed. Therefore, it is best to call ahead.

## NAVAL AIR DEVELOPMENT CENTER
Warminster, Pa. 19090

**Phone:** 672-9000; ask for Public Affairs Office
**Tours:** Group tours only, 10th grade and up. Thursdays 9:30–11:30 A.M. By reservation only at least two weeks in advance. Minimum number: 20; maximum number: 50. One adult for every 10 students.
**Restrictions:** No cameras
**Directions:** Pa. Route 611 (Broad Street) north to Pa. Route 132 (Street Road), turn right to Center
**Parking:** At Center
**Public Transportation:** Broad Street Subway north to Olney, then SEPTA Route 55 to Willow Grove; then SEPTA Route 6 to Johnsville, right to Center

The Naval Air Development Center can be toured only by groups with advance notice. These science tours take you through the centrifuge, the slide, and other facilities used in training astronauts. Demonstrations about related equipment are arranged for each group prior to the visit. Every third Saturday, a special one-hour Cub Scout tour is offered. Write to Public Affairs Office for information.

## NORTH PHILADELPHIA AIRPORT
Grant Avenue and Ashton Road
Philadelphia 19114

**Phone:** OR 3-4400
**Tours:** April–October, weekdays at 10 A.M. Group tours by appointment only one week in advance (call the Superintendent's office; minimum number 10, maximum number 50). Length of tour: 45 minutes.
**Directions:** Schuylkill Expressway to Roosevelt Boulevard to Grant Avenue, right to Ashton Road, then left to terminal
**Parking:** At airport
**Public Transportation:** SEPTA Route 20

It's often easier to understand the operation of an airport by visiting the smaller ones in the area. You can see the ramps, runways, and firehouse, but not the tower or the inside of a plane. Tours canceled in bad weather.

HANDICAPPED
Tours can be arranged.

NEARBY
Sightseeing flights (page 293).

## PENNSYLVANIA SOCIETY FOR THE PREVENTION OF CRUELTY TO ANIMALS
350 East Erie Avenue
Philadelphia 19134

**Phone:** 426-6300
**Tours:** Tuesday–Friday, 10 A.M. Group tours by appointment as far in advance as possible. Call Public Relations (426-6300). Minimum number: 10; maximum number: 70. Length of tour: 1–1½ hours.
**Directions:** Broad Street north to Erie Avenue, east to 350 (three blocks east of Front Street, between "B" and "D" Streets)
**Parking:** Lot next to building
**Public Transportation:** SEPTA Route 56 trolley to "C" Street

A tour of the headquarters includes the small-animal clinic, large dog kennels, small-animal facilities, kennel kitchen, ambulances and rescue equipment, horse stalls, bird sanctuary, and a chance to pet kittens, puppies, rabbits, a snake, a turtle, a guinea pig—or any other unusual pets available. Cameras and tape recorders are welcome. No live souvenirs.

PSPCA SERVICES
Adoptions: 10 A.M.–4 P.M. weekdays (cost is $20). Small-animal clinic: 10 A.M.–12 noon weekdays. Dog Obedience Training Classes: Call for information.

PSPCA JUNIOR CLUB
For school-age children interested in learning more about caring for pets.

## PHILADELPHIA DEPARTMENT OF SANITATION
Domino Lane and Umbria Street
Roxborough, Philadelphia
**Phone:** MU 6-5520

**Open:** Monday–Friday 8 A.M.–4 P.M.

**Tours:** For individuals and organized groups by appointment, preferably a day in advance. Minimum suggested age: 10. Maximum number: 40; 1 adult to 20 children. Length of tour: 1 hour.

**Directions:** Benjamin Franklin Parkway to East River Drive, to Ridge Avenue, left on Domino Lane

**Public Transportation:** SEPTA Route A north to 7200 Ridge Avenue, walk two blocks west

In this day of the ecology-minded, have you ever wondered just exactly what *does* happen to all that trash? How much is there? What is its ultimate destination? How does it get there? At the incinerator in Roxborough they'll show and tell you.

## PHILADELPHIA INTERNATIONAL AIRPORT
Philadelphia 19153

**Phone:** 365-5000, ext. 717

**Tours:** Tuesday and Thursday 10 A.M. and 12:30 P.M. Group tours by appointment two weeks in advance, preferably in writing to Office of Manager of Operations. Maximum number: 35. Length of tour: 1 hour.

**Directions:** Schuylkill Expressway east, follow signs to airport

**Parking:** At airport lots

**Public Transportation:** SEPTA Route M—Airport Bus at Broad and Snyder; SEPTA Airport Express makes several stops in Center City, including one near Reading Terminal, Suburban Station, and Penn Central 30th Street Station (fare: $1).

You tour the building, the observation deck, possibly an aircraft, and learn the inner workings of this sprawling, mind-boggling complex with its jet planes, Piper Cubs, jeeps, trucks, baggage carts, fire equipment, and nonstop activity. With or without a tour, the observation deck (10 cents) is a great spot: takeoffs, landings, fuel trucks scurrying about—even freighters in the distance slowly steaming up the Delaware.

HANDICAPPED

Building accessible via ramps and elevators. Restrooms accessible and some booths adapted to wheelchair size (symbol of access posted).

## PHILADELPHIA NAVAL SHIPYARD
Foot of South Broad Street
Philadelphia 19112

**Phone:** 755-3807

**Tours:** Monday–Sunday 9, 10, 11 A.M., 1 P.M. Guided tours only. By appointment at least a month in advance. Minimum age: 6. No minimum number; maximum number: 100. One adult for every 10 children.

A guide joins you in your car or bus and gives you a general tour of the base: ships in the Reserve Fleet (more generally known as the "mothball fleet"), dry docks, piers, and the battleship *Iowa*. If nothing else, the size of a battleship is overwhelming when seen up close.

ANNUAL EVENT
Open house during Armed Forces Week.

HANDICAPPED
The usual base tour in an automobile, excluding a visit to the *Iowa*.

## PHILADELPHIA WATER DEPARTMENT–WATER TREATMENT PLANTS

**Phone:** MU 6-3803, Plant Visits Secretary. Weekends: MU 6-1776; ask for plant.
**TORRESDALE:** 9001 State Road near Linden Avenue in Northeast Philadelphia on the Delaware River
**Directions:** I-95 to Linden Avenue exit, right on Linden Avenue, right on State Road
**Public Transportation:** SEPTA Route 66 at Frankford Avenue, walk six blocks
**QUEEN LANE:** 3545 Fox Street in East Falls
**Directions:** Schuylkill Expressway to Roosevelt Boulevard to Fox Street, left on Fox
**Public Transportation:** SEPTA Routes A, R, K
**BELMONT:** Ford Road and Belmont Avenue (off City Line Avenue)
**Directions:** Schuylkill Expressway to City Avenue (south)
**Public Transportation:** SEPTA Routes 38, 45, 85, E
**Tours:** For all three: Monday–Friday 10 A.M.–5 P.M., Saturday and Sunday 2–5 P.M. Groups and classes by appointment only at least three days in advance. Individuals and families weekends 2–5 P.M.; no appointment necessary. Length of tour: 1 hour.

Once upon a time water came out of the backyard pump. Now it comes out of a faucet and we just accept it. A tour of any one of these plants will show you where the water comes from, how it is stored, "washed," purified, and sent on its way, and how much is used. It's a far cry from Philadelphia's first reservoir (where the Art Museum now stands) and the elegant waterworks behind it.

## POLICE ACADEMY
State Road and Ashburner Street
Philadelphia

**Phone:** MU 6-3380 (Police Community Relations)
**Tours:** Monday–Saturday. Guided tours can be arranged by writing to: Commanding Officer, Police Academy, 8500 State Road, Philadelphia 19136. Minimum age: 3rd grade.
**Directions:** I-95 to Linden Avenue exit, State Road to Academy.
**Public Transportation:** SEPTA Routes T, Y

Both men and dogs are trained here, and you'll learn how.

## POLICE HEADQUARTERS
7th and Race Streets
Philadelphia 19106

**Phone:** MU 6-3380 (Police Community Relations)
**Tours:** Monday–Saturday. Guided tours can be arranged by writing in advance to: Commanding Officer, Police Community Relations Division, Southeast corner Broad and Grange Streets, Philadelphia 19141. Length of tour: 1 hour.
**Public Transportation:** SEPTA Routes 47, 61

The unique shape of this building has made it an architectural landmark.

Inside you'll see the police radio room (what happens when you dial 911 to report an emergency), the crime lab, the fingerprint section, and the police record room.

## SOCIETY FOR THE PREVENTION OF CRUELTY TO ANIMALS (WOMEN'S PENNSYLVANIA)
3025 West Clearfield Avenue
Philadelphia 19132

**Phone:** BA 5-4500
**Tours:** Monday–Friday at 10 A.M. Length: 1 hour. Group tours by appointment.
**Directions:** East River Drive to Nicetown cutoff onto Huntington Park, right on Clearfield Avenue (first traffic light)
**Public Transportation:** SEPTA Routes A local, 48, 60 trolley

There's a film and a tour of the kennels and a chance to see a variety of small animals.

ADOPTIONS

Monday–Saturday 10 A.M.–3:30 P.M., Tuesday–Thursday until 7:45 P.M., Sunday 12 noon– 4:45 P.M. (fee $5–15)

CLINIC

Monday–Saturday 9:30 A.M.–3:30 P.M.

OBEDIENCE CLASSES

Monday evenings. Call for information.

## UNITED STATES MINT
5th and Arch Streets
Philadelphia 19106

**Phone:** 597-7350
**Open:** Monday–Friday 9 A.M.–3:30 P.M.
**Closed:** Weekends, all national holidays, two weeks in the summer for inventory. You may walk through but the machinery is not operating. Call for specific dates.
**Admission:** Free
**Parking:** Underground across the street
**Public Transportation:** SEPTA Routes 48, 50 trolley, Cultural Loop bus, Mid City Loop bus

The building covers three city blocks and houses the most modern coin-making equipment in the world. The Mint grew from a small cluster of brick buildings dating from 1792 (the first public building erected by the United States Government) to the present ultramodern pink granite structure. There are only three mints in the entire country, and this is the largest.

The process of making coins is fascinating, and the tour is presented in a splendid manner. A large glass-enclosed gallery overlooks the entire operation. Push-button tape narrations placed at appropriate locations explain the various processes.

Commemorative and other special medals are also made here to honor a historic event, a President, or a spectacular achievement. No free souvenirs, but visit the attractive gift shop on the ground floor where old coins and commemorative medals may be purchased. It's a great tour for all ages. No advance notice needed for group visits.

HANDICAPPED

A sign at the front of the building indicates special ramps and elevators. Restrooms will accommodate wheechairs.

## UNITED STATES POSTAL SERVICE
30th and Market Streets
Philadelphia 19104

**Phone:** 597-5333
**Tours:** Throughout the year except December; preferably in the spring. Monday–Friday 9 A.M.–3 P.M. Group tours by appointment only, preferably in writing at least ten days in advance. Write to Public Information Office. Minimum age: 10. Minimum number: 5; maximum number: 30. One adult for every 10 children. Length of tour: 1 hour
**Parking:** Meters and public parking lots
**Public Transportation:** SEPTA Route buses on Chestnut Street, Market Street Subway, and 30th Street Station of Penn Central

How many pieces of mail move in and out and around Philadelphia each day? The idea is somewhat overwhelming. A tour of the post office will show you stamping machines, sorting machines, and all the other equipment needed to send your letters on their way.

HANDICAPPED
Tours can be arranged. Limited to 8 each time.

NOTE: Smaller children would be just as intrigued by a visit to the local post office. Call to arrange a tour.

## WILLOW GROVE NAVAL AIR STATION
Pa. Route 611 (Easton Road)
Horsham, Pa. 19044

**Phone:** OS 5-7070, ext. 203
**Tours:** Friday and Saturday only at 9:30 A.M. and 1:30 P.M.
**Directions:** Pa. Route 611 (Broad Street) north to Horsham
**Parking:** Free
**Public Transportation:** Broad Street Subway north to Olney; SEPTA Route 55 bus marked Doylestown to Willow Grove Naval Air Station

These popular tours of the Air Station must be booked well in advance. The tour includes an outside exhibit of World War II planes—some the only remaining examples—including a German *Messerschmitt* and a Japanese torpedo bomber. Present-day planes and operations are investigated. The tour lasts two hours, and there are no age restrictions. Maximum number: 40.

## Industrial

**ACME MARKETS, INC.**
(Bakery Division)
124 North 15th Street
Philadelphia 19101

**Phone:** 568-3000, ext. 455 or 495
**Tours:** Of bakery only: October–June, Wednesday 9:15, 10:15, 11:15 A.M., 1 and 2 P.M. For individuals and groups by appointment only, at least three weeks in advance. Contact Customer Service. Minimum age: 2nd grade. Maximum number: 100. Length of tour: 1 hour.
**Directions:** Shown on reverse side of admission ticket sent with confirmation
**Parking:** At bakery

A tour of this huge automated bakery shows the complete baking cycle from receipt of bulk flour to wrapping of completely processed baked goods. At the end you get a snack and a sample loaf to take home.

**BELL TELEPHONE COMPANY OF PHILADELPHIA**
**Tours:** Call your local business office to arrange a group tour. Minimum age: 5th grade. Minimum number: 10.

NOTE: Art Wire Program. The telephone company will supply free of charge unused wire for making jewelry and wire figures to organized groups and schools. Call 633-0050 and they will connect you with the business office for further information and supplies.

**BUCK AND DOE RUN VALLEY FARMS COMPANY**
R.F.D. 4
Box 242
Coatesville, Pa. 19320

**Phone:** 1-384-0106
**Tours:** May 20–October 1, Tuesday, Wednesday, and Friday 8–10 A.M., 1–4 P.M. Group tours only, by appointment two weeks in advance, preferably in writing. Minimum age: 12. Minimum number: 15; maximum number: 75. One adult for every 8 children. Length of tour: 2 hours.
**Directions:** Schuylkill Expressway to U.S. Route 1, south to Pa. Route 82, west on Pa. Route 82

There's a Texas ranch here in the suburbs of Philadelphia. The 10,000-acre Buck and Doe Run Valley Farms is a branch of the fabled King Ranch, cowboys, cattle "on the range," and all. Tour it —or just drive by. If the cattle are in the pastures near the road, you might think you're on the set of a Western.

## W. ATLEE BURPEE COMPANY
Fordhook Farms
Doylestown, Pa. 18901

**Phone:** 1-345-1072
**Tours:** July–August, Monday–Friday 8 A.M.–4 P.M. Guided tours by appointment for groups only, 2 or 3 weeks in advance. Minimum age: 12. Minimum number: 25; 1 adult for every 10 children. Length of tour: 1 hour
**Directions:** Pa. Route 611 north to Doylestown, left on West Court Street
**Parking:** At company
**Picnicking:** On lawn area

When anyone says "seeds," one of the first names that springs to mind is Burpee. On their Fordhook Farms you can take a guided walking tour of flower gardens and what Burpee refers to as American Flower Trials. Wear comfortable shoes. If the weather looks cloudy, call; tours cannot be given in rainy weather.

## CONOWINGO HYDROELECTRIC STATION
(Philadelphia Electric Company)
Conowingo, Pa. 21918

**Phone:** 841-4308 (Philadelphia Electric Company)
**Open:** Monday–Saturday 9 A.M.–4 P.M.
**Tours:** Minimum age: 4th grade. Length of tour, about 45 minutes; includes walking tour of hydroelectric plant, main control room, turbine floor, and fishing facilities.
**Directions:** Schuylkill Expressway to U.S. Route 1, south to Susquehanna River. About 1¾-hour drive
**Parking:** Facilities at Park and Station
**Picnicking:** Recreational area with tables and restrooms in Fisherman's Park adjacent to station; no fires permitted

For those not able to take a trip to Hoover Dam, a drive south to the Susquehanna River for a visit to the Conowingo Dam can be as educational, interesting, and enjoyable. The Conowingo Dam, built in 1928, is almost a mile in length. It backs up a reservoir 14 miles long and provides electrical power as well as boating and fishing facilities.

Not far from Conowingo Dam is Peach Bottom (page 285). Those who enjoy touring can visit the two places. Those who prefer sport can visit the dam and then do some fishing.

GROUP TOURS

By reservation only. Call or write. Minimum age: 4th grade. Maximum number: 60.

FISHING

All seasons. Everything from catfish to perch to shad and herring, pike and carp. Temporary Maryland license required. Can be picked up nearby. Information at the dam.

## CORSON'S QUARRY
Joshua Road and Stenton Avenue
Plymouth Meeting, Pa. 19462

**Phone:** 828-4300

**Tours:** School groups or private tours can be arranged by calling the main office. Available five days a week. Length of tour: about 45 minutes. For older groups two-hour tours are available, with greater attention paid to the scientific and geological aspects.

Dress for rocks and dust and rough walking; Corson's will supply a "hard hat" and safety glasses. It's a small child's dream tour with dump trucks, drills, giant rock-crushing machines, steam shovels, and conveyor belts in abundance. A spectacular sight and an exciting and informative trip. Best in the spring.

## DETRA FLAG COMPANY, INC.
Oaks, Pa. 19456

**Phone:** 666-5050

**Tours:** Monday–Friday 10 A.M. and 1 P.M. except the last week in July or the first week in August. Group tours only, by appointment. Call Plant Manager's office. Minimum number: 10; maximum number: 30. Minimum age: 11. One adult for every 10 children. Length of tour: 1 hour.

**Directions:** Schuylkill Expressway to King of Prussia exit, Pa. Route 363 across Betzwood Bridge, to Schrack's Corner, left to Oaks

How to make a flag—from the fabric till it's ready to run up the flagpole. They are all custom orders.

## EVENING AND SUNDAY BULLETIN
30th and Market Streets
Philadelphia 19101
**Phone:** 662-7550
**Tours:** Monday–Saturday (except holidays) at 9, 10, 11 A.M. For groups of 10 or more contact Tour Department (662-7377). Suggested minimum age: 8.
**Directions:** Schuylkill Expressway to 30th Street exit. Right at corner of 30th and Market.
**Parking:** Lots in vicinity are expensive; metered street parking or at 30th Street Station
**Public Transportation:** 30th Street Elevated Stop or 30th Street Station of Penn Central. SEPTA Routes D-1, 45, any Market Street bus.

The *Bulletin* has a three-story press which can run at 70 miles per hour and is a rather awesome sight even from the glass-enclosed visitors' gallery. Guided tours take you from the reporter's desk to the delivery truck and show you how those monstrous rolls of blank newsprint emerge as a newspaper all printed, folded, and ready for delivery. It's a 45-minute tour and along the way souvenirs are distributed: a special supplement, a mat, perhaps a slug of type.

There's a reasonably priced cafeteria in the building serving reasonably good cafeteria food.

## FRANKLIN MINT
U.S. Route 1
Franklin Center, Pa. 19063
**Phone:** 459-6168
**Tours:** Monday–Friday all year except for two weeks in July. Hours vary; call Tour Office for times. Group tours preferably September–May. Minimum number: 15; maximum number: 50. Minimum age: 4th grade. One adult for every 10 children.
**Directions:** Schuylkill Expressway to U.S. Route 1, go south, Mint is on the left approximately 17 miles from Philadelphia
**Parking:** Adjoining building

The Franklin Mint is the world's largest private mint. From a glass-enclosed visitors' gallery you can follow the whole minting process—all previously explained at the start of the tour in a special film, *The Art of Minting*. Next to their headquarters is a Museum of Medallic Art, containing displays of personal effects, photographs, artifacts, and memorabilia related to the Franklin Mint's Commemorative Medal Series. Collectors of the mint's commemorative medals and coins find a tour an interesting experience.

## LANKENAU HOSPITAL "CYCLORAMA OF LIFE"
Lancaster and City Line Avenues
Philadelphia 19151

**Phone:** MI 9-1400, ext. 213 or 369
**Open:** Daily 9 A.M.–5 P.M.
**Closed:** Good Friday, Memorial Day, Fourth of July, Labor Day, Thanksgiving, Christmas, New Year's Day
**Directions:** Schuylkill Expressway to City Avenue (U.S. Route 1), south to Lancaster Avenue (U.S. Route 30), right for about a block, and left at hospital entrance.
**Parking:** Use front area; Cyclorama just inside main entrance. Parking fee 50¢.
**Public Transportation:** SEPTA Red Arrow Bus G

The life cycle from fertilization of the egg to maturity in photographs, drawings, and diagrams, with push-button exhibits on dominant and recessive genes, the nervous system, how the eye functions. And a section on drugs, alcohol, and smoking. It's a bit "preachy," but everyone from the age of 5 up is bound to learn something in the hour or so that it takes you to go through. There's a coffee shop.

GROUP TOURS
Of Cyclorama, not hospital. Maximum number: 30. Minimum age: 3rd grade. Call Health Education Department, preferably a week in advance.

HANDICAPPED
Ramp at main entrance.

## LINVILLA ORCHARDS
137 West Knowlton Road
Media, Pa. 19063

**Phone:** TR 6-9047
**Open:** Daily including Sunday, summer 10 A.M.–8 P.M., winter 10 A.M.–6 P.M.
**Closed:** Thanksgiving, Christmas, New Year's Day
**Tours:** September–November, weekdays 9 A.M.–4 P.M. Guided group tours by appointment only as far in advance as possible. Minimum number: 10; maximum number: 50. Minimum age: kindergarten. Individuals and families welcome to visit the orchards and salesroom any time. Length of tour: 45 minutes.
**Directions:** Schuylkill Expressway to U.S. Route 1, south to Pa.

Route 352 south (2nd exit) on 352 to second traffic light, right on Knowlton Road ½ mile
**Parking:** On grounds

Linvilla Orchards, on 285 acres, is one of the few remaining large fruit and vegetable farms in suburban Philadelphia. Group tours are taken to the orchards and follow the apples from there to the

Octagonal Barn at Linvilla Orchards

loading area, apple-grading room, cold storage, cider press, and into the octagonal barn, where everyone gets a drink of cider and an apple—and a chance to buy pumpkins or candied apples. They also sell several varieties of apples, pears, pies, preserves, dried leaves and plants for round-the-year and seasonal decorations, and special firewood. Near the barn, deer, rabbits, turkeys, pheasants, bulls, sheep and horses wander about in large open pens. Allow additional time for wandering about and dress warmly even though the day seems mild.

## MARTIN'S AQUARIUM
6900 Old York Road
Philadelphia 19126

**Phone:** LI 9-7050
**Tours:** Monday–Friday 11 A.M.–5 P.M. School groups by appointment only. Call for reservations at least a week in advance. Minimum age: nursery school. Maximum number: 25. Length of tour: ½ hour.

**Directions:** Broad Street (Pa. Route 611) north to Old York Road

This mecca for amateur ichthyologists (page 392) offers weekday tours which introduce the group to their collections of freshwater and saltwater fish, their birds, snakes, guinea pigs. Everyone leaves with a free fish certificate toward a future purchase.

## NABISCO, INC.
Roosevelt Boulevard and Byberry Road
Philadelphia 19115

**Phone:** OR 3-4800
**Tours:** October–April, Tuesday and Wednesday at 1 P.M., Thursday at 10 A.M. Individuals and groups by appointment only. Write or call Personnel Office at least one week in advance. Minimum age: 10. Maximum number: 20. Length of tour: 1 hour
**Directions:** Roosevelt Boulevard (U.S. Route 1) north to Byberry Road
**Parking:** In front driveways

It's just a bit different from mixing up a batch of cookies at home. This is the main plant of this biscuit, cookie, and cracker company. The tour takes you through the whole baking process from the receipt of those tons of ingredients—flour, sugar, shortening, eggs, flavoring—through the mixing, baking, and wrapping of the seemingly endless stream of cookies. Everyone leaves with a sample of the day's baking. Included in the tour is a lot of walking and steps, so wear comfortable low-heeled shoes. No high heels permitted.

## PEACH BOTTOM ATOMIC INFORMATION CENTER
(Philadelphia Electric Company)
R.D. 1
Delta, Pa. 17314

**Phone:** 1-717-456-5101
**Open:** Wednesday–Sunday, holidays 10 A.M.–4 P.M.
**Directions:** South on U.S. Route 1, cross Conowingo Dam, right on Maryland Route 623 and follow signs. About a two-hour drive.
**Parking:** At Center
**Picnicking:** Facilities at Muddy Run Recreation Park and Conowingo Dam Fisherman's Park (page 280)

Twelve miles upstream from the Conowingo Dam is the Peach Bottom Atomic Power Station. The power station is not open to visitors, but in the Information Center next door there are pushbutton exhibits, slides, films, and scale models to explain this newest form of energy: how the atom is split, how an atomic reactor works and how electricity is made from atomic power. The Atomic Power Station isn't doing all this yet, but it may be someday soon. The process doesn't look as exciting as water rushing over a dam, but in its own way it is more impressive. You can learn it all in about 1½ hours.

GROUP TOURS

By advance reservation to Information Center Director, preferably in writing. Minimum age suggested: 4th grade level.

HANDICAPPED

Ramp available for access to building. Exhibits are all on one floor.

NEARBY

Muddy Run Recreation Park, R.D. 1, Holtwood Pa. 17532. Phone: 1-717-284-4325. Another part of the Philadelphia Electric Company complex on the Susquehanna River, the Park contains a 100-acre manmade lake and 500 acres of woods for fishing, camping, boating, and picnicking.

## PHILADELPHIA–BALTIMORE–WASHINGTON STOCK EXCHANGE
17th and Stock Exchange Place
(At Sansom Street)
Philadelphia 19103

**Phone:** LO 3-4700
**Open:** Monday–Friday 10 A.M.–3 P.M.
**Tours:** Group tours by appointment only, 10:30 A.M. and 2:00 P.M. Requests in writing should be sent two weeks in advance. Minimum age: 14. Minimum number: 10. Maximum number: 25. One adult. Individuals may watch trading on the floor from a special visitors' gallery. Length of tour: 45 minutes.
**Public Transportation:** SEPTA Routes D, 2, 42

The Philadelphia–Baltimore–Washington Stock Exchange, founded 1790, is the oldest and third largest exchange in the country. A film describes the intricacies of the exchange, and you have an opportunity to watch the floor activity from the gallery.

## PHILADELPHIA COLLEGE OF TEXTILES AND SCIENCE
School House Lane and Henry Avenue
Philadelphia 19144

**Phone:** VI 3-9700
**Open:** September–December, February–May, Monday–Friday 10
A.M.–4 P.M.
**Tours:** By appointment only three weeks in advance, preferably
in writing to Department of Institutional Advancement. Mini-
mum age: 3rd grade. Minimum number: 10; maximum number:
50 plus 2 adults.
**Directions:** East River Drive to Wissahickon Drive, right on Gypsy
Lane to School House Lane, left to Henry Avenue
**Parking:** On campus
**Public Transportation:** SEPTA Route A to School House Lane and
Henry Avenue

Founded in 1884, the Philadelphia College of Textiles and Science
is the oldest college of textiles in the country. Students come from
around the world to study all aspects of the textile industry. The
hour-and-a-half tour includes the laboratories for raw-fiber processing, handweaving and power-weaving demonstrations, and exhibits of textile processes: design, weaving, and knitting of fabric.
It is next to impossible to find factories willing to give tours; groups
interested in seeing how fabric is manufactured should plan a trip
to the college. They have all the necessary equipment and can
show you the whole process.

**PHILADELPHIA FRESH FOOD TERMINAL**
3301 South Galloway Street
Philadelphia 19148

**Phone:** DE 6-3003
**Tours:** Guided group tours are by appointment. Minimum age:
14. Minimum number: 10. One adult to every 10 children.
Length of tour: 1½ hours
**Directions:** South on Broad Street, east on Pattison Avenue
**Parking:** At Terminal
**Public Transportation:** SEPTA Route 4 to Galloway Street

In the early morning hours this is where you find retailers and
restaurant owners buying for their customers. Starting about midnight, it's a busy place of trucks and stalls, cartons of lettuce, sacks
of potatoes, eggplants, onions—and restaurateurs. A guided tour isn't
really necessary. Put on comfortable shoes and go watch the
activity some morning. This building under the Walt Whitman
Bridge is a vital part of the life of the city.

## SEVEN UP BOTTLING COMPANY, INC.
1103 Ridge Pike
Conshohocken, Pa. 19428

Phone: 828-7700

Tours: Monday–Friday 10:30 A.M. and 1:30 P.M. Group tours only by appointment ten days in advance; preferably in writing to Manager, Cold Drink Department. Minimum age: 7 years. Minimum number: 40; maximum number: 80. Length of tour: 1 hour.

Directions: Schuylkill Expressway to Conshohocken interchange, cross river, take Fayette Street to Ridge Pike

There's a movie about carbonated beverages and a tour of the plant where visitors see columns of containers marching along, being filled, sealed, and packed—ready to quench the thirst of thousands. Souvenir: complimentary package.

## SOMMER MAID CREAMERY, INC.
Swamp Road
Doylestown, Pa. 18901

Phone: 1-345-6160

Tours: Monday–Friday 10 A.M.–3 P.M. By appointment only 1 week in advance for individuals or groups. Minimum age: grammar school. Maximum number: 25. One adult for every 10 children. Length of tour: ½ hour.

Directions: Pa. Route 611 (Broad Street) north to Doylestown, west on Pa. Route 313 (Swamp Road) to plant

Have you ever seen an egg candled? It's a simple, fascinating, and essential step in processing eggs for distribution. The Sommer Maid Creamery also packages butter. Giant hunks of butter are cut and wrapped by machines for various distributors and price ranges.

## WILLET STAINED GLASS STUDIOS
10 East Moreland Avenue
Chestnut Hill, Philadelphia 19118

Phone: CH 7-5721

Tours: Call for appointment. Minimum age: 5th grade. Maximum number: 40. Length of tour: 1 hour.

Directions: East River to Wissahickon Drive to Lincoln Drive to Allens Lane, right to Germantown Avenue, left to Moreland Avenue

**Public Transportation:** SEPTA Route 23 trolley

Here they practice the art of making stained-glass windows. It's a complicated, fascinating, precise process to make those cathedral windows we admire.

## *Architecture*

From its beginning Philadelphia has been a center for notable architecture: the distinctive row houses of Society Hill, the small "Trinity" houses (3 stories high, one room to a floor), the private mansions, and the civic, cultural, and educational institutions. The Delaware Valley contains many examples of important and unusual buildings. In addition to the places mentioned throughout the book, here are a few tours of buildings interesting from an architectural point of view.

### ACADEMY OF MUSIC
Broad and Locust Streets
Philadelphia 19102

**Phone:** KI 5-1535
**Tours:** October–May, Monday afternoon 2–4 P.M. By advance reservation only. 75¢. Groups of 25 or more 50¢. Minimum age: elementary school. Length of tour: 45 minutes
**Public Transportation:** SEPTA Routes A, C, 38, 90, Broad Street Subway

Patterned after La Scala in Milan, this Registered National Historic Landmark now offers tours depending upon the performance schedule. You can visit backstage, the pit, the ballroom, and learn why and how its architectural features make this an acoustically perfect concert hall (page 152).

### AMERICAN BAPTIST CHURCHES IN THE U.S.A.
Pa. Route 363 and First Avenue
Valley Forge, Pa. 19481

**Phone:** 768-2000

Near Valley Forge State Park is this interesting circular office building designed by Vincent Kling. Tours, primarily for adults, can be arranged by calling for an appointment.

## BETH SHOLOM SYNAGOGUE
Old York Road and Foxcroft Road
Elkins Park, Pa. 19117

**Phone:** TU 7-1342
**Tours:** Monday–Thursday, Sunday 12:30–3:30 P.M. Groups by appointment, preferably in writing, giving number, age, number of adults, date, and an alternative date three weeks in advance.
**Directions:** Broad Street (Pa. Route 611) via Old York Road to the Synagogue
**Public Transportation:** SEPTA Route 55, Broad Street Subway to Olney

This is the only synagogue designed by Frank Lloyd Wright, one of America's greatest architects, and it represents Mount Sinai. Wright designed the interior color and seating as well as the building. Individuals may visit Friday night during services. Prior arrangements are necessary for groups.

## BRYN ATHYN CATHEDRAL
2nd Street Pike and Paper Mill Road
Bryn Athyn, Pa. 19009

**Phone:** WI 7-0266
**Open:** Daily 9 A.M.–noon, 2 P.M.–5 P.M. except Friday; Saturday 9 A.M.–noon. Guided tours on Sunday 2:30–5 P.M.
**Closed:** Fridays
**Parking:** Visitors' lot on grounds
**Group Visits:** Write or call in advance
**Directions:** Broad Street (Pa. Route 611) to Old York Road (611) to Meetinghouse Road in Elkins Park, turn right and proceed until Meetinghouse Road ends at Huntingdon Pike (Pa. Route 232), then turn left and continue to Bryn Athyn and Cathedral at Paper Mill Road

This cathedral–church at Bryn Athyn, an outstanding example of Gothic architecture, stands majestically on a knoll overlooking Huntingdon Valley. The raw materials used to build the church, begun in 1914, came from the countryside. During its construction the designers and craftsmen were grouped together around the building in workshops similar to the medieval guilds. The fine craftsmanship is in evidence throughout the Cathedral. The exquisite stained glass windows were handmade in Bryn Athyn also.
Spring or fall are ideal for a visit when you can walk around the

beautifully kept grounds. Bring your camera. The Cathedral and castlelike homes on the preserve belong to the descendants of John Pitcairn, friend of Andrew Carnegie and founder of the Pittsburgh Plate Glass Company, who was a philanthropist of the Swedenborgian faith.

## PENNSYLVANIA HOSPITAL
8th and Spruce Streets
Philadelphia 19107

**Phone:** 829-3251
**Historical Tour:** By appointment only
**Public Transportation:** SEPTA Routes 47 and 90

Founded in 1751 largely through the efforts of Benjamin Franklin, this hospital—the oldest in the United States—is an excellent example of Colonial architecture and contains many interesting artifacts. This tour is popular with children.

GROUP VISITS

By appointment only, preferably Monday or Wednesday. One adult to every 10 children. Length of tour: 30 minutes (page 42).

## PRINCETON UNIVERSITY
Princeton, N.J.

**Phone:** 1-609-452-3603 for tours. The Orange Key Guide Service is a free year-round student guide service. If possible, call three days in advance for a tour.
**Directions:** U.S. Route 1 to U.S. Route 206 into Princeton

Princeton University is one of the outstanding college campuses in the country. Nassau Hall, built in 1756, is now a national monument. The University Chapel, a modern treatment of traditional Gothic architecture, contains features of fourteenth-century English churches and interesting stained-glass windows. The Princeton Art Museum (Tuesday–Saturday 10 A.M.–4 P.M., Sunday 1–5 P.M.) has a comprehensive art collection and outstanding loans. The McCarter Theater, the University's center for the performing arts, features a fine program of plays, films, concerts, and dance. The Harvey S. Firestone Memorial Library (open daily, Sunday at 2 P.M. except during vacations) has an interesting collection, from Egyptian papyri to the papers of Booth Tarkington, F. Scott Fitzgerald, Woodrow Wilson, John Foster Dulles, and Adlai Stevenson.

## LIBERTY TRAIL TOURIST MAP

Mentions highlights for historic tours in the five-county area. It is available at the Convention and Visitors Bureau, 16th and John F. Kennedy Boulevard.

# Sightseeing by Bus

## THE GRAY LINE OF PHILADELPHIA
16th and John F. Kennedy Boulevard
Philadelphia 19103

**Phone:** LO 9-3666

Main starting point is the Convention and Visitors Bureau. Sight-seeing bus tours of historic Philadelphia, cultural institutions, day trips to the environs: Valley Forge, Pennsylvania Dutch Country, Bucks County, Gettysburg, Kutztown. You can leave the driving to them—and you will get a lecture en route. Student tours available from grammar school up. Call for details.

## SEPTA BUS RAMBLES
Throughout the year SEPTA offers trips to various places of interest in Philadelphia and the surrounding countryside (page 394).

# Sightseeing by Boat

## PHILADELPHIA HARBOR TOURS, INC.
Pier 11 North
Delaware Avenue and Race Streets
Philadelphia 19106

**Phone:** WA 5-7640
**Open:** Early May–Labor Day; May–June primarily for school groups (minimum number: 20); from July 1, Monday–Saturday at 11 A.M. and 2 P.M., Sundays 1 and 3:30 P.M.
**Admission:** Adults $2.50, children under 12 $1.50. Group rates available.
**Parking:** On Delaware Avenue
**Public Transportation:** SEPTA Routes 17, 33 to Front and Market Streets, then one block east to Delaware and two blocks north

This two-hour cruise on the Delaware River on an old-fashioned paddle-wheel boat is a pleasant way to learn a lot of facts about Philadelphia, which is the largest freshwater port and the third busiest seaport in the world. The captain points out sights and fills your head with interesting bits of information as you sail down the Philadelphia side and up the Jersey side, under bridges, past tugboats, freighters, and tankers from faraway places and the Philadelphia Naval Shipyard. Snack bar aboard.

HANDICAPPED

For those in wheelchairs, it's a good idea to check in advance— admission depends upon sailing conditions.

## Sightseeing by Air

**DOWNTOWN AIRLINES, INC.**
221 South Delaware Avenue
(Foot of Walnut Street at Penn's Landing)
Philadelphia 19106

**Phone:** WA 3-0750

These seaplanes fly to Wall Street in New York, but they also take passengers on a tour of the Philadelphia area. It's a 15-minute flight at $8 per person with room for five people plus the pilot on these planes. They operate all year.

**MONTGOMERYVILLE AIRPORT**
Pa. Routes 309 and 202
Montgomeryville, Pa. 18936

**Phone:** 1-855-7171
**Open:** Daily
**Cost:** $3 per person, half price for children under 10

A ten-to-twelve-minute ride.

**NORTH PHILADELPHIA AIRPORT**
Grant Avenue and Ashton Road
Philadelphia 19114

**Phone:** HO 4-1600 (ask for Flight Department)
**Open:** Sunday afternoon sightseeing flights
**Cost:** $5 per person; minimum number: 2

The 15-minute ride usually goes over the city and across to New Jersey (see page 272).

## PERKIOMEN VALLEY AIRPORT
Collegeville, Pa. 19426

**Phone:** 1-489-6011
**Open:** Daily sightseeing flights lasting 10–15 minutes.
**Cost:** Adults $5, children $3

Longer flights available. Call in advance.

## POTTSTOWN MUNICIPAL AIRPORT
Pottstown, Pa. 19464
(Actual location: Glasgow Street, Stowe, Pa.)

**Phone:** 1-327-0200
**Open:** Any clear day
**Cost:** $3 per person (minimum number 2) for a 15-minute ride

Flight instruction for ages 14 and up.

## PROFESSIONAL PILOT SERVICE
West Chester Airport
Airport Road
West Chester, Pa. 19380

**Phone:** 1-696-9659
**Cost:** $10 per hour for 5 passengers, $7.50 for 3

Sightseeing flights over Philadelphia, the Brandywine, and Valley Forge. Minimum flight 15 minutes. They also offer flight instructions. You can start as soon as you can reach the rudder pedals (about 12 or 13), solo at 16, and get a private license at 17.

## TURNER AIRPORT
Horsham and Lower State Roads
Prospectville, Pa. 19002

**Phone:** MI 6-2255
**Cost:** $3 per person, $5 minimum

Sightseeing flights call ahead. Flight training available at 15.

## WINGS FIELD
Stenton Avenue
Blue Bell, Pa.

**Phone:** MI 6-1800
**Cost:** $10 for 3 people ($5 minimum) for an 18-minute flight

Weekends may be crowded, so call in advance.

# 10
# CLASSES, CLUBS, AND HOBBIES

Do you want to fly a plane? learn to sew? take a computer course? This section is by no means a definitive listing, but it provides a selection of various classes and groups that merit consideration either because of an unusual offering or a long tradition of excellence. It may help you pursue your special interests—or perhaps find a new one.

Art Class at Samuel S. Fleisher Art Memorial

296 BICENTENNIAL PHILADELPHIA

# Art and Cultural Centers

The many centers in the area offer a wide selection of classes and courses for all ages and at all levels of proficiency.

**ALLENS LANE ART CENTER**
Allens Lane and McCallum Streets
Philadelphia 19119

Phone: CH 8-0546

In addition to their arts program they have a nursery school, a kindergarten, a day camp, and a counselor-in-training program.

**CHELTENHAM ART CENTER**
439 Ashbourne Road
Cheltenham, Pa. 19012

Phone: ES 9-4660

Pottery and ceramics classes for children and teenagers, plus a full range of programs in the arts.

**HERITAGE HOUSE EDUCATIONAL AND CULTURAL CENTER**
1346 North Broad Street
Philadelphia 19121

Phone: CE 2-1700

African–American cultural center offering classes in art, music, dance, drama, and history.

**ILE-IFE HUMANITARIAN CENTER**
2544 Germantown Avenue
Philadelphia 19144

Phone: BA 5-7565

Cultural arts program for children and adults, administered by Arthur Hall (page 97).

**JEWISH Y's AND CENTERS OF GREATER PHILADELPHIA (JYCs)**
401 South Broad Street (Broad and Pine)
Philadelphia 19147

**Phone:** KI 5-4400

The Jewish Y's and Centers of Greater Philadelphia (JYCs) have extensive programs for recreation, informal education, cultural interests, and athletic programs for all age groups. Programs vary somewhat from branch to branch and year to year. *Nursery schools* for children 3 to 5 are held at some of the branches. *After-school activities* normally include arts and crafts, dance, drama, sports, science. Call for brochures. The Neighborhood Center at 6600 Bustleton Avenue (Philadelphia 19149; DE 8-9800) has a special Tiny Tots physical education program for children 2 to 3.

*Summer Programs* include overnight camps and a counselor-in-training camp, day camps, half-day nursery camps, traveling Teen Tours. For information on the overnight camps call KI 5-4400, on the day camp and counselor-in-training camp in Bucks County call DE 8-9800. The Western Branch (896-7770) at City Line Avenue and Haverford Road also has a day camp and Teen Leadership Institute.

Teen Tours, a summer program for junior high students (6th to 9th grades), includes day trips to parks, theater, cities, and some overnight trips. For further information on high-school activities call KI 5-4400.

Children's concerts, including special entertainment such as storytelling, magicians, dancers, and audience participation, are held several times during the year in the Center City and the Northeast branches. Call for information.

## OLD YORK ROAD ART GUILD
Alverthorpe Manor
515 Meetinghouse Road
Jenkintown, Pa. 19046

**Phone:** TU 4-9327

Classes in all the arts.

## SOCIETY HILL SCHOOL OF MUSIC AND ART
506 South 5th Street
Philadelphia 19147

**Phone:** TE 9-3136

Classes for young children and their parents.

## SOUL SHACK
122 Ardmore Avenue
Ardmore, Pa. 19003

**Phone:** MI 2-9657

Art classes by the Philadelphia Museum of Art Department of Urban Outreach. Everyone welcome. Call for information.

### YMCA OF ROXBOROUGH
Ridge Avenue and Domino Lane
Philadelphia 19128

**Phone:** IV 2-3900

An excellent children's swimming program.

### YWCA OF GERMANTOWN
5820 Germantown Avenue
Philadelphia 19144

**Phone:** GE 8-6266

Children's programs (infants to 12); nursery school; Fun Days for girls 6 to 12 on Saturday mornings, including arts and crafts, dance, trips, drama, swimming. For teenagers (7th to 12th grade), there can be modern dance, African dance, handicrafts, sewing, pottery. You name it; they'll try it. Classes in adult section open to young adults (18 to 35). Family swims. Summer day camps: boys and girls ages 4 and 5, girls 6 to 10, 11 to 16. Specialized instruction in gymnastics, tennis, typing, sewing, weekly trips. For ages 11 to 16 coed: biking, hiking, sightseeing, canoeing.

### YWCA—MID-CITY AREA
2027 Chestnut Street
Philadelphia 19103

**Phone:** LO 4-3430

All racial, economic, religious, and cultural groups are welcome. *Chestnut House* is a nursery school for children 1 year to kindergarten. Applications and interviews from August 1.

A wide variety of activities are available at the YWCA: arts, dance, scuba diving, folk dancing, synchronized swimming, sewing (for children and adults), aquatics for children 2 years and up. *Town House* provides an after-school program for children 6 to 12, including creative arts, performing arts, physical recreation, and homework tutoring. The Day Camp is for children 6 to 11 during the summer from 9 A.M. to 5 P.M. For the benefit of the working parent there is supervision from 8:30 to 9 A.M. and from 5 to 5:30 P.M.

# Art Classes

Classes in various media are available at the Department of Recreation Centers (MU 6-1776; see page 168), the neighborhood Y's, and several cultural and art centers in the area (page 296).

## SAMUEL S. FLEISHER ART MEMORIAL
715 Catharine Street
Philadelphia 19147

**Phone:** WA 2-3456

Free art classes for children and adults (page 95).

## MOORE COLLEGE OF ART
20th and Race Streets
Philadelphia 19103

**Phone:** LO 8-4515

Young People's Art Workshop has Saturday morning classes for boys and girls grades 1 to 6.

## THE PHILADELPHIA MUSEUM OF ART

. . . has classes for children ages 6 to 15 during the winter on Saturdays, weekdays during the summer. Courses in filmmaking are available for young people 14 to 22. Adult classes and workshops (page 108). Phone: PO 3-8100.

## PRINTS IN PROGRESS WORKSHOPS

. . . are held by The Print Club (PE 5-6090) in various locations throughout the city (page 117).

## WOODMERE ART GALLERY
9201 Germantown Avenue
Philadelphia 19118

**Phone:** CH 7-0476

Saturday morning classes for children in drawing and painting (page 127).

# Archaeology and Anthropology

**UNIVERSITY MUSEUM**
33rd and Spruce Streets
Philadelphia 19174

**Phone:** EV 6-7400

Their workshops for children and teenagers are open to members only. Call or write the Department of Education at the Museum (page 123). The Ethnic Arts Division runs a series of workshops in the music, dance, and ceremonies of non-Western civilizations. High-school and college music students are repairing many of their ancient instruments. Call ext. 309.

# Bicycling

**AMATEUR BICYCLE LEAGUE OF AMERICA**
921 Delmont Drive
Wynnewood, Pa. 19096

**Phone:** MI 9-3209

Bicycle races in Fairmount Park in front of Memorial Hall every Sunday into April (9 A.M.–12 noon). Events for all classes: midget, intermediate, junior men, senior men, women, and veterans. Spring training races for members only. Membership fee nominal. Contact C. J. Harper, Jr.

**AMERICAN YOUTH HOSTELS, INC.**
4714 Old York Road
Philadelphia 19141

**Phone:** GL 7-5700

Bicycling trips for a day or a weekend with longer trips during the summer with an experienced leader. Family trips: A special program for families with children 1 year and older, including 5-mile hikes and 30-mile bicycling trips at a leisurely pace. Instructions: Courses for beginners.

# Dance Instruction

There are many schools of dance and dance classes in the art centers throughout the city and surrounding area. Those listed below are affiliated with a professional or semiprofessional dance company.

**BALLET DES JEUNES**
7596 Haverford Avenue
Philadelphia 19151

**Phone:** GR 3-2253

Young dancers perform at the Civic Center and other places in the community. Classes for children and adults.

**ILE-IFE HUMANITARIAN CENTER**
2544 Germantown Avenue
Philadelphia 19133

**Phone:** BA 5-7565

The center is under the administration of Arthur Hall of the Afro-American Dance Ensemble (page 97).

**PENNSYLVANIA BALLET COMPANY, SCHOOL OF THE PENNSYLVANIA BALLET**
2333 Fairmount Avenue
Philadelphia 19130

**Phone:** 232-1500

The official school of the Pennsylvania Ballet Company. Professionally oriented. Admission by audition only, minimum age 8. Barbara Weisberger is the inspiration, founder, and director of this nationally acclaimed company.

**PERFORMING ARTS SCHOOL, PHILADELPHIA DANCE ACADEMY**
1035 Spruce Street
Philadelphia 19107

**Phone:** WA 2-0533

An academic education as well as instruction in dance, music, theater. Classes for preschool and adults also.

**PHILADELPHIA CIVIC BALLET**
School of the Philadelphia Civic Ballet
277 South 11th Street
Philadelphia 19107

**Phone:** WA 5-4405

Members of the company perform throughout the city. Classes for children and adults.

**JEAN WILLIAMS SCHOOL OF BALLET**
5555 Germantown Avenue
Philadelphia 19144

**Phone:** VI 4-0233

Jean Williams is the founder and artistic director of the Germantown Dance Theater, a member company of the National Association of Regional Ballet.

## Flying Lessons

Flight instruction is available at many nearby airports: Perkiomen Valley Airport at Collegeville, Pottstown Municipal Airport, Turner Airport at Prospectville and West Chester Airport (see page 294).

## Music Instruction

**JENKINTOWN MUSIC SCHOOL**
547 Washington Lane
(On Abington Friends School campus)
Jenkintown, Pa. 19046

**Phone:** TU 7-3677

A nonprofit community music school with a variety of classes in percussion and string instruments, ballet, and modern dance. Scholarships available.

**SETTLEMENT MUSIC SCHOOLS**
6128 Germantown Avenue
Philadelphia 19144
**Phone:** GE 8-4955 (main office)

416 Queen Street, Philadelphia 19147
Phone: DE 6-0400

9230 Bustleton Avenue, Philadelphia 19155
Phone: HO 4-4740

The Settlement Music School was founded in 1908 to give children the finest musical education possible regardless of color, religion, or ability to pay. It has been doing this ever since. Individual instruction on all orchestra instruments. Fees are on a sliding scale.

## Nature and Science

### ACADEMY OF NATURAL SCIENCES
19th Street and Benjamin Franklin Parkway
Philadelphia 19103

Phone: 567-3700

Classes on Saturdays during the winter, week-long sessions during the summer (page 76), Expeditions for Everyone (page 77).

### AMERICAN YOUTH HOSTELS, INC.
4714 Old York Road
Philadelphia 19141

Phone: GL 7-5700

Biking, hiking, canoeing, horseback riding, sailing, and ski trips—throughout the year for a day or a weekend—with an experienced leader. Longer trips during the summer. Family trips: A special program for families with children one year and older, including 5-mile hikes and 30-mile bicycling trips at a leisurely pace. Courses for beginners in bicycling, canoeing, sailing, riding, skiing.

### DELAWARE MUSEUM OF NATURAL HISTORY
Del. Route 52
Greenville, Del. 19807

Phone: 1-302-658-9111

Shell Club meets the first Monday of every month (page 85).

### FRANKLIN INSTITUTE
Benjamin Franklin Parkway at 20th Street
Philadelphia 19103

**Phone:** 448-1287

Science workshops on Saturdays in spring and fall and weekdays during the summer for kindergarten through 12th grade. The workshop in airplanes includes radio-controlled planes. For information write or call Workshop Registrar (page 87).

## PENNSYLVANIA HORTICULTURAL SOCIETY
325 Walnut Street
Philadelphia 19106

**Phone:** WA 2-4801

A summer workshop for the 10-to-14 age group at the Morris Arboretum (page 202). Summer gardening program for ages 4 through 14 held throughout the city. For detailed information write or call the Society. They also have programs throughout the year for the public (free plant clinic, etc.) and are happy to answer your horticulture questions.

## PHILADELPHIA ZOOLOGICAL GARDENS
34th Street and Girard Avenue
Philadelphia 19104

**Phone:** BA 2-5300

High-school girls with an interest in animals work as hostesses at the Children's Zoo during the summer. For information call Superintendent at the Children's Zoo early in February (page 113).

## SCHUYLKILL VALLEY NATURE CENTER
8480 Hagys Mill Road
Philadelphia 19128

**Phone:** 482-7300

The "Spider's Web": family-oriented Saturday and Sunday nature walks and programs (page 204).

## SIERRA CLUB
6923 Greene Street
Philadelphia 19119

**Phone:** VI 8-3268

For information on their outings, activities, and membership write or call. Hikes, canoe trips, both long and short. Publications.

# Obedience Classes (For Dogs, Not for Children)

## PENNSYLVANIA SOCIETY FOR THE PREVENTION OF CRUELTY TO ANIMALS
350 East Erie Avenue
Philadelphia 19134

Phone: 426-6300

See page 273.

## SOCIETY FOR THE PREVENTION OF CRUELTY TO ANIMALS (WOMEN'S PENNSYLVANIA)
3025 West Clearfield Avenue
Philadelphia 19132

Phone: BA 5-4500

See page 276.

# Puppetry

Classes are held at the centers of the Department of Recreation (page 168).

## MARTHA MARY KEARNS
515 Carpenter Lane
Philadelphia 19119

Phone: VI 8-2591

This charming lady teaches puppetry at centers throughout the city and has given performances at libraries and in the park. If children, parents, teachers, or group leaders are interested in a short workshop or a performance, she will be happy to discuss it. Rates vary.

# Sailing and Boating Courses

Starting in September, courses are given in various locations throughout the Greater Philadelphia area. Instruction is usually free, with a nominal charge for books, charts, etc., if you don't already have them. Call for detailed information and locations:

## AMERICAN RED CROSS
23rd and Chestnut Streets
Philadelphia 19103

Phone: 561-8200

National Aquatic School holds a 10-day sailing course in June at
Camp Towanda in Honesdale. Minimum age: 17. Fee: $80.

## AMERICAN YOUTH HOSTELS, INC.
4714 Old York Road
Philadelphia 19141

Phone: GL 7-5700

Instructions for beginners in canoeing and sailing.

## DELAWARE RIVER NAVIGATION COMMISSION

Phone: 521-3675

Motorboating course: family oriented. Minimum suggested age: 8.

## DELAWARE RIVER POWER SQUADRON
(Of U.S. Power Squadron)
2707 South Marvine Street
Philadelphia 19148

Phone: 334-0611

Classes start in September and January. Notices in the newspapers
one or two Sundays before. Minimum suggested age: 12.

## UNITED STATES COAST GUARD
Gloucester, N.J.

Phone: 597-4355

Suggested minimum age: 14. Regular and family plan classes.

# Workshops

## PHILADELPHIA COLLEGE OF TEXTILES AND SCIENCE
School House Lane and Henry Avenue
Philadelphia 19144

Phone: VI 3-9700

Free summer workshops in textile design, engineering, and chemistry for high-school students. Call in April for information.

## PHILADELPHIA FOLK SONG SOCIETY
7113 Emlen Street
Philadelphia 19119

Phone: CH 7-1300

A nonprofit education group which sponsors concerts, workshops, the Philadelphia Folk Festival (page 266), and group sings. Monthly meetings September through June, second Sunday of the month. Membership: families $10, individual $8, students $6.

## SOLEBURY SUMMER INSTITUTE OF CHINESE AND JAPANESE
New Hope, Pa. 18938

Phone: 1-862-5261

For high-school students. No previous experience in either language required. Students live on campus of Solebury School. In addition to classes all other activities, games, hikes, and special projects are conducted in desired language.

# Theater Workshops

## ABBEY STAGE DOOR
6615 Rising Sun Avenue
Philadelphia 19111

Phone: PI 2-8324

Summer workshop for teenagers. Weekly acting classes for teenagers during the winter. Admission by interview. Fee.

## CHILDREN'S MUSICAL COMEDY WORKSHOP
485 General Muhlenberg Road
King of Prussia, Pa. 19406

Phone: 265-1580

Musical comedy workshops for children ages 4 through 14, including singing, dancing, and acting.

## CHILDREN'S REPERTORY THEATER
1134 Western Savings Bank Building
P.O. Box 1222
Philadelphia 19105

**Phone: LO 3-2050**

Performances at Mandell Theater, Drexel University. Paid apprenticeship program for ages 8 through 14. Admission by audition only. Watch papers for notice or call.

## PHILADELPHIA YOUTH THEATER
Society Hill Playhouse
507 South 8th Street
Philadelphia 19147

**Phone: WA 3-0210**

Susan Turlish directs a summer workshop as well as a winter program for young people ages 15 through 18 in all aspects of theater: acting, costumes, makeup, production, lighting, and set design and construction. The programs conclude with a PYT production. No previous experience necessary. Admission is by interview only. They don't necessarily look for the "star" of the school play, but for people interested in learning theater. Small registration fee. Scholarships available.

# 11
# THE HANDICAPPED

We have accumulated a list of museums, theaters, parks, arboretums, tours, some with facilities designed especially for the handicapped, others where ramps, special parking, and restrooms can accommodate wheelchairs. Details of these places are covered in other sections of the book.

International Symbol of Access for the Handicapped

The International Symbol of Access for the handicapped was designed for display on public buildings, hotels, motels, theaters, restaurants, stores, parking lots, conveniences, and transportation facilities of all kinds which are fully accessible for use by wheelchair users and other handicapped persons with limited mobility. The places mentioned in this section do not necessarily meet all the criteria of architectural specifications. They have been included because some of their facilities, events, or exhibits are accessible depending upon a person's particular disability.

"Handicapped" obviously means many different things. It is, therefore, advisable to call in advance. Successful outings require thought and planning. To help you check the facilities and plan your trips, we include the list of criteria that must be met by all buildings that display the Symbol of Access:

| | |
|---|---|
| ENTRANCE | No steps. If ramp is used, slope should not exceed 5 percent. |
| DOORWAYS | Width not less than 32 inches |
| PASSAGES AND CORRIDORS | Width not less than 45 inches |
| TOILETS | When provided for public use, doorways not less than 32 inches. At least one toilet each must be provided for men and women. |
| ELEVATORS | Width of entrance not less than 30 inches with sliding doors; all others 32 inches wide. |
| PARKING | If available, must be on same side of street and adjacent to building. Parking space for handicapped drivers should be at least 10 feet wide to enable driver to transfer to wheelchair. These spaces should be marked with a displayed symbol. |
| OTHER | In the case of restaurants and places of worship or entertainment, there must also be facilities not only to enter the building, but also to enjoy the amenities provided. |

Some additional information which may be useful for your outings: A sturdy leather belt or strap can make a wheelchair an inch or two smaller to get through a narrow door—or the same result can be achieved by twisting a coat hanger around the rear extensions. If possible, carry a portable ramp.

The Easter Seal Society publishes a list of highway restroom stops and a guide to motels with wheelchair units. Here are a few of the motels in Philadelphia and eastern Pennsylvania with these units: PHILADELPHIA: *Holiday Inns* at 4th and Arch Streets (WA 3-8660); Penn Center, 18th and Market Streets (561-7500); City Line Avenue and Monument Road (TR 7-4900); *Marriott Motor Hotel,* City Line Avenue and Monument Road, Bala-Cynwyd (MO 7-0200); *Holiday Inns* at Philadelphia International Airport; 45 North Governor Printz Boulevard, Essington (521-2400) and 260 Goddard Boulevard, King of Prussia (265-7500). ALLENTOWN: *Holiday Inn,* U.S. Route 22 and Pa. Route 309 (1-395-3731). LEVITTOWN: *Holiday Inn,* 6201 Bristol Pike (946-9100). LANCASTER: *TraveLodge,* 2101 Columbia Avenue (1-717-397-4201); *Holiday Inn East,* U.S. Route 30 Bypass and Hempstead Road (1-717-299-2551). NEW HOPE: *Holiday Inn,* U.S. Route 202 (1-862-5221).

There are several publications by and for handicapped people with many interesting articles, information, and valuable contacts not only for those with limited mobility but for their families as well:

*Accent on Living,* P.O. Box 726, Gillum Road and High Drive, Bloomington, Ill. 61701

*Achievement,* 925 Northeast 122nd Street, North Miami, Fla. 33161

*The Caliper,* 153 Lyndhurst Avenue, Toronto, Ontario M5R 3A2, Canada

*The Cord,* International Journal for Paraplegics, Stoke Mandville Hospital, Aylesbury, Bucks, England. Subscription ( £1) to Miss D. French.

*National Hookup,* Indoor Sports Club, 9536 Mason, Riverside, Calif. 92503

Our aim in this chapter is to provide information for outings which not only take into consideration the limitations of the handicapped but can also be enjoyed by the whole family. If you have suggestions of additional places, events, or other information, they are most welcome. Write to us at: J. B. Lippincott Company, East Washington Square, Philadelphia, Pa. 19105.

## Museums and Historic Sites

### ACADEMY OF NATURAL SCIENCES
19th Street and Benjamin Franklin Parkway
Philadelphia

**Phone:** 567-3700

The 19th Street entrance has one step. Call in advance so the door can be opened. Elevator available inside building. The Mineral and Gem Collections are not accessible to a person in a wheelchair.

### ATWATER KENT MUSEUM
15 South 7th Street
Philadelphia

**Phone:** WA 2-3031

This Museum, which traces the growth of Philadelphia from earliest times through its fascinating collection of artifacts, is accessible through the rear entrance. One step. All but one section of the museum can be reached by elevator. Restrooms totally accessible. Parking adjacent.

## BRANDYWINE RIVER MUSEUM
U.S. Route 1
Chadds Ford, Pa.

Phone: 1-388-7601

Paintings by the Brandywine artists and a charming Christmas exhibition are features of this Museum converted from an old mill. Wheelchair parking is clearly marked near the rear of the building. No steps at this entrance. Elevators to all levels. Restrooms on second floor; booth doors are narrow. Tearoom and bookshop on main floor.

## CHRIST CHURCH
2nd and Market Streets
Philadelphia

Phone: WA 2-1695

This church is both historically and architecturally significant. One step at the entrance. Off-street parking nearby. If attending services, person may remain in wheelchair.

## DELAWARE MUSEUM OF NATURAL HISTORY
Del. Route 52
Greenville, Del.

Phone: 1-302-658-9111

This is the newest natural history museum in the area. It contains three sections—Sky, Land, Sea—of beautifully mounted exhibits. The Museum is all on one floor, and there is a ramp at the entrance.

## FRANKLIN INSTITUTE AND FELS PLANETARIUM
20th and Benjamin Franklin Parkway
Philadelphia

Phone: 448-1000

A fascinating museum of science and technology. Use the entrance at 21st and Winter Streets. There are elevators to all floors, but because of stairs only a portion of the Institute is accessible for a person in a wheelchair. Restrooms are accessible, but booth doors are narrow. Person may remain in wheelchair at the Fels Planetarium. Parking lot adjacent. Guided tours for the blind can be arranged, preferably in the afternoon; call 448-1111 or 448-1346.

## FREE LIBRARY
Logan Square
19th and Vine Streets
Philadelphia

**Phone:** MU 6-5322

Once inside the Library, practically everything is accessible by elevator. However, there are two sets of steps (about four each) at the front entrance.

## GETTYSBURG NATIONAL MILITARY PARK
Gettysburg, Pa. 17325

**Phone:** 1-717-334-1124

The Visitors Center, except for the Cyclorama, and a portion of the walking tour are accessible to those in wheelchairs. Also, arrangements can be made for a guide to join you in your car.

## HOPEWELL VILLAGE
Elverson, Pa.

**Phone:** 1-582-8783

An eighteenth- and early nineteenth-century iron-making village. Visitors Center and museum accessible for those in wheelchairs. Arrangements can be made to tour the Village either by auto or by wheelchair to the bottom of the hill and then return by auto, both with a park ranger.

## INDEPENDENCE NATIONAL HISTORICAL PARK
Philadelphia

**Phone:** MA 7-1776

The entire park is accessible to those in wheelchairs if the curb can be negotiated. However, the only building accessible in the Park is Independence Hall, 5th and Chestnut Streets, the first floor only. The best entrance is from Independence Square (three steps). Call in advance and they will put down a ramp.

## NEW JERSEY STATE MUSEUM
205 West State Street
(Cultural Center Complex)
Trenton, N.J.

Phone: 1-609-292-6464

A museum, auditorium, and planetarium. The Natural Science Hall has exhibitions relating to New Jersey (Pine Barrens, Lenni-Lenape Indians, etc.). Museum and restrooms accessible.

## OLD FORT MIFFLIN
Island Avenue
Philadelphia

Phone: WA 2-8399

The ramparts and buildings are not accessible, but you can watch the "militia."

## PERELMAN ANTIQUE TOY MUSEUM
270 South 2nd Street
Philadelphia

Phone: WA 2-1070

One step to enter. Elevator to upper floors, and restroom in basement.

## PHILADELPHIA CIVIC CENTER AND CIVIC CENTER
   MUSEUM
34th Street and Civic Center Boulevard
Philadelphia

Phone: EV 2-8181

Museum is accessible to wheelchairs on ground and first floors. Special restrooms on the ground floor. Civic Center accessible through level entrance to left of front entrance. Elevators to all levels. Restrooms accessible, but booth doors are narrow. Parking adjacent.

## PHILADELPHIA MUSEUM OF ART
26th Street and Benjamin Franklin Parkway
Philadelphia

Phone: PO 3-8100

One of the leading art museums in the country, it contains treasures from the pre-Columbian era to modern times, from both Eastern and Western civilizations. There are also many special exhibitions, concerts, films, and workshops. There is a street-level entrance through the tunnel on the north side of the building. All levels in the Museum can be reached by elevator. The new restaurant is completely accessible to those in wheelchairs, as are the new restroom facilities. The parking lot is on the west side of the building with a long driveway down to the north entrance. The Volunteer Guides Office can provide guides for the deaf. Guides for the blind can be arranged through the Division of Education.

## PHILADELPHIA ZOOLOGICAL GARDENS
34th Street and Girard Avenue
Philadelphia

**Phone:** BA 2-5300

The oldest zoo in the United States. Most buildings accessible. Many have ramps. Restrooms have one step at entrance; booth doors are narrow. Wheelchairs available at main gate for minimal fee. Parking adjacent.

## UNIVERSITY MUSEUM
University of Pennsylvania
33rd and Spruce Streets
Philadelphia

**Phone:** EV 6-7400

One of the largest and finest archaeological collections in the country. Kress Wing makes this museum accessible to people in wheelchairs. Enter from Spruce Street. Announce yourself at the entrance for school buses and they will raise the yellow barrier for you to drive to the entrance. Restrooms accessible to those in wheelchairs. Elevators to second and third floors. Restaurant on second floor. Nevil Gallery for the Blind and Sighted is a permanent section of the exhibits for visually handicapped. Braille and large-print labels identify the objects, which are mounted for touching.

## VALLEY FORGE STATE PARK
Valley Forge, Pa.

**Phone:** 783-0177

Over 2,200 acres for picnicking and sightseeing. The Valley Forge Park Commission is restoring one area to show how it looked during Washington's encampment. You can rent a tape cassette at Reception Center at junction of Pa. Routes 23 and 363 and tour the park in your car. Restrooms accessible.

## Arboretums, Sanctuaries, and Parks

### BRIGANTINE NATIONAL WILDLIFE REFUGE
P.O. Box 72
Oceanville, N.J. 08231

**Phone:** 1-609-641-3126

This 20,000-acre refuge for waterfowl along the Atlantic Flyway has an 8-mile road with stopping points along the way. Restrooms have one small step; booth doors are narrow.

### CHURCHVILLE PARK
Churchville Lane Southhampton
Bucks County, Pa.

The Florence W. Grintz Bittersweet Trail has been adapted as a nature trail for the blind and physically handicapped. A Braille Walk Book is available for sightless visitors.

### LONGWOOD GARDENS
Kennett Square, Pa.

**Phone:** 1-388-6741

Considered one of the outstanding display gardens in America, this former Du Pont estate has almost 1,000 acres of beautifully maintained gardens, trees, and trails. Throughout the Gardens there are wide paths and ramps. A fully accessible restroom in the basement of the conservatory is entered from the fountain level. Wheelchairs available at the Superintendent's office on a first-come, first-served basis.

#### GARDEN FOR THE BLIND
Adjacent to the building containing the scale model of Longwood is a very small garden for the blind. From mid-April through the summer they plant about twenty different species such as mint geranium, licorice—those with a distinctive smell—all labeled in Braille. The walled-in garden may be a bit uncomfortable on a warm day. (Nearby John J. Tyler Arboretum and Ridley Creek State Park have more extensive trails for the blind.)

### NEWLIN MILL PARK
U.S. Route 1
Glen Mills, Pa.

**Phone:** GL 9-2359

Picnic area and stocked pond for fishing. Call in advance. Assistance available.

## PICNICS

Along the Schuylkill when the cherry blossoms are out and weekends during regattas. Valley Forge State Park. Washington Crossing State Park. Old Fort Mifflin.

## RIDLEY CREEK STATE PARK
Main entrance on West Chester Pike (Pa. Route 3)
Media, Pa. 19065

**Phone: LO 6-4800**

A 2,500-acre park with a mile-long nature trail constructed especially for the blind and handicapped and landscaped to accommodate wheelchairs. The trail is marked with Braille signs and has a handrail all along the way. Restrooms are accessible to those in wheelchairs.

## SCHUYLKILL VALLEY NATURE CENTER
Hagys Mill Road
Philadelphia 19129

**Phone: IV 2-7300**

In upper Roxborough, about twelve miles from Center City, is the Schuylkill Valley Nature Center—acres of open fields, woodlands, streams, and ponds.

They are constructing a paved nature trail accessible to the handicapped and the blind at the Nature Center. The quarter-mile-long trail has benches, no rails but a curb, a wildlife observation deck, and a small pond. Plantings along the trail have been selected to attract wildlife. A description of the trail, available at the Education Building, is contained in a small special portable radio which can be carried very easily. The trail is designed as a self-guided tour, but guides are available. There is a reserved parking area. Restrooms, the museum, bookstore, and auditorium accessible. It is preferable to call in advance. Classes can be arranged for handicapped groups.

## ARTHUR HOYT SCOTT HORTICULTURAL FOUNDATION
Swarthmore College
Swarthmore, Pa.

**Phone: KI 3-5380**

Asphalt paths throughout the campus. A person in a wheelchair may need some help on some of the hills, but they can be negotiated. Restrooms in Du Pont Science Building (two steps) to the right of the auditorium. Open all day.

## STAR ROSES
West Grove, Pa.

**Phone:** 1-869-2426

Acres of rose gardens. Space for wheelchairs along the paths, or you can drive through the rose fields. Restrooms in main building accessible.

Garden for the Blind at John J. Tyler Arboretum

## JOHN J. TYLER ARBORETUM
515 Painter Road
Lima, Pa.

**Phone:** LO 6-5431

They have established a Fragrant Garden especially for the blind with guide-rail and labels in Braille.

## Theaters and Stadiums

Most movie theaters are accessible, but some request that a person transfer to a regular seat from a wheelchair. Drive-in movies are always good. Theaters generally request that a person transfer to a regular seat. It is always wise to make necessary arrangements in advance, preferably when purchasing tickets.

**ABBEY STAGE DOOR**
6615 Rising Sun Avenue
Philadelphia

**Phone:** PI 2-8324

**ACADEMY OF MUSIC**
Broad and Locust Streets
Philadelphia

**Phone:** Ticket Office: PE 5-7379

Proscenium box seats are best. Call Manager's Office (KI 5-1535) the morning of the performance for permission to drive in South Alley off Broad Street. There is a ramp at this entrance and assistance is available.

**ANNENBERG CENTER**
3680 Walnut Street
Philadelphia

**Phone:** Box Office: 594-6791; Executive Office: 594-6701

The Zellerbach Theater, the Studio Theater, and the Annenberg Auditorium can accommodate persons in wheelchairs. Call in advance to reserve convenient seating. There are a limited number of spaces available for those who need to remain in wheelchairs. Assistance is available. Wheelchair entrances are marked. Restroom facilities are available but not readily accessible.

**BANDBOX THEATRE**
30 Armat Street
Germantown, Philadelphia

**Phone:** VI 4-3511

Restrooms inaccessible.

### CHERRY HILL ARENA
Berlin and Brace Roads
Cherry Hill, N.J.

Phone: 1-609-795-1275

Level entrance. Assistance available. Restroom booth doors are narrow. Parking adjacent.

### CINEMA 19
19th and Chestnut Streets
Philadelphia

Phone: LO 9-4175

Level entrance with section where person may remain in wheelchair. Restrooms inaccessible. Parking nearby.

### CITY LINE CENTER MOVIE
77th Street and City Line Avenue
Philadelphia

Phone: GR 3-2045

Person may remain in wheelchair. Restrooms accessible, but booth doors are narrow. Parking adjacent; curb to sidewalk.

### COLLEGE THEATER
Chester Road and Fairview Avenue
Swarthmore, Pa.

Phone: KI 3-2290

Accessible, with special section for wheelchairs. Restrooms accessible, but booth doors are narrow. Parking available at the rear.

### DEVON HORSE SHOW GROUNDS
Devon, Pa.

Big gate can be opened to let wheelchairs through. Paved roads.

### DREXEL UNIVERSITY MANDELL THEATER
32nd and Chestnut Streets
Philadelphia

Phone: 895-2000

Concerts, theater, lectures. Children's Repertory Theater. Level entrance and ramps at Chestnut Street entrance. Special seating for wheelchairs with advance notice. Restrooms fully equipped for handicapped.

## DUKE AND DUCHESS THEATERS
1605 Chestnut Street
Philadelphia

**Phone: LO 3-9881**

Theaters are adjacent with the same accommodations. It is best to transfer to regular seat. Restrooms inaccessible. Parking nearby on 16th Street between Market and Chestnut Streets.

## SAM ERIC THEATRE
1908 Chestnut Street
Philadelphia

**Phone: LO 7-0604**

Person may remain in wheelchair in side aisles.

## FORREST THEATRE
1114 Walnut Street
Philadelphia

**Phone: WA 3-1515**

Level entrance. Person must transfer to regular seat. Restrooms inaccessible. Parking nearby.

## FRANKLIN FIELD
33rd and Walnut Streets
Philadelphia

**Phone: EV 6-0961**

Use "Pass Gate" entrance to field level section. Limited seating. Restrooms not readily accessible. Parking adjoining.

## GOLDMAN THEATER
15th and Chestnut Streets
Philadelphia

**Phone: LO 7-4413**

Person may remain in wheelchair. Restrooms inaccessible. Parking nearby.

## JOHN B. KELLY PLAYHOUSE IN THE PARK
Belmont Mansion Drive
West Fairmount Park
Philadelphia

**Phone: GR 7-1700**

This summer theater has ramped entrance and ramps to seating. Call ahead for special section for those in wheelchairs. Restrooms outside are accessible. Parking adjacent.

## LA SALLE MUSIC THEATRE
20th Street and Olney Avenue
Philadelphia

**Phone: VI 8-8300**

Restrooms inaccessible.

## MILGRAM THEATER
1614 Market Street
Philadelphia

**Phone: LO 4-5868**

Level entrance. Room for person to remain in wheelchair. Parking nearby.

## NEW LOCUST THEATER
1411 Locust Street
Philadelphia

**Phone: PE 5-5074**

Level entrance. Person may remain in wheelchair in side aisle or transfer to regular orchestra aisle seat. Assistance available. Restrooms inaccessible. Parking nearby.

## ORLEANS THEATER
Bustleton and Bleigh Avenues
Philadelphia

**Phone: RA 8-7575**

Person may remain in wheelchair. Restroom booth doors are narrow. Parking adjacent.

**THE PALESTRA**
33rd Street between Walnut and Spruce Streets
Philadelphia

**Phone:** EV 6-0961

Special section for four persons to remain in wheelchairs. Main entrance level and ramps available. Restrooms accessible.

**RITTENHOUSE TWINS**
19th and Walnut Streets
Philadelphia

**Phone:** LO 7-4986

Elevator to restroom, but booth doors are narrow.

**ROBIN HOOD DELL**
East Fairmount Park
Philadelphia

**Phone:** LO 7-0707

Level section at rear of amphitheater.

**SHUBERT THEATER**
250 South Broad Street
Philadelphia

**Phone:** PE 5-4768

Level entrance. Person may transfer to orchestra seat or remain in wheelchair. Restrooms inaccessible. Parking nearby.

**SPECTRUM**
Broad and Pattison Streets
Philadelphia

**Phone:** DE 6-3600

Ramps on Broad Street side. Request tickets for special section for wheelchairs. Restrooms accessible via elevators, but booth doors are narrow. Parking lot adjacent.

**TEMPLE UNIVERSITY MUSIC FESTIVAL**
Meetinghouse Road and Butler Pike
Ambler, Pa.

Phone: CE 5-4600

Special section for wheelchairs. Person may remain in wheelchair, but assistance is available if the person prefers to transfer to a regular seat. Outdoor snack bar, gift shop, and sculpture garden all accessible to person in wheelchair. Restroom booth doors narrow.

**THEATER 1812**
1812 Chestnut Street
Philadelphia

Phone: LO 3-7100

Person may remain in wheelchair.

**TLA CINEMA, INC.**
334 South Street
Philadelphia

Phone: WA 2-6010 for recording of schedule

Limited space for wheelchairs. Restrooms accessible but narrow booth doors.

**UNIVERSITY OF PENNSYLVANIA CLASS OF 1923 ICE SKATING RINK**
3130 Walnut Street
Philadelphia

Phone: EV 6-0961 (Franklin Field)

Skating events. Walnut Street entrance has a ramp. Spaces available for persons who must remain in wheelchairs, and assistance available for those able to transfer to regular seats. Restrooms accessible but booth doors narrow.

**VALLEY FORGE MUSIC FAIR**
Routes U.S. 202 and Pa. 363
Devon, Pa. 19333

Phone: 644-5000

Year-round theater. Use ramp near main entrance. Space for wheelchairs in rear of theater. Restrooms accessible; booth doors are narrow.

**VETERANS STADIUM**
Broad and Pattison Streets
Philadelphia

**Phone:** Call Eagles HO 3-5500, Phillies HO 3-1000 for information
and assistance at their events. For other special events call
Veterans Stadium (MU 6-1776, ext. 84201, 84202). Use Stadium
parking entrance on Broad Street below Hartranft. Inside parking
area request Handicapped Parking

Ramps to wheelchair area and restrooms. Assistance available.

**WALNUT STREET THEATRE**
825 Walnut Street
Philadelphia

**Phone:** 629-0700

Accessible entrance. Wheelchair accommodations can be made by
advance request. Restrooms inaccessible.

## Tours

**CITY HALL**

For help call Room 121 (MU 6-1776). Elevators. Restrooms on
street floor with room for wheelchairs. Elevator, ramp, and fourteen steps to Tower.

**HARBOR TOURS**
Depending on sailing conditions.

**LANKENAU HOSPITAL "CYCLORAMA OF LIFE"**

**LINVILLA ORCHARDS**

**NORTH PHILADELPHIA AIRPORT**

**PEACH BOTTOM ATOMIC INFORMATION CENTER**

**PENNSYLVANIA SOCIETY FOR THE PREVENTION OF
CRUELTY TO ANIMALS**

**PHILADELPHIA INTERNATIONAL AIRPORT**

**PHILADELPHIA NAVAL SHIPYARD**

**UNITED STATES MINT**

# Restaurants

## ASIA
4746 North Broad Street
Philadelphia

Phone: DA 9-3843

Level entrance.

## BELMONT MANSION
Next to John B. Kelly Playhouse in the Park
West Fairmount Park
Philadelphia

Phone: TR 7-4830

Open summers. Outdoor terrace.

## BOOKBINDERS, OLD ORIGINAL
125 Walnut Street
Philadelphia

Phone: WA 5-7027

Parking lot across the street. Level entrance through exit door. Ample room for wheelchairs. Restrooms inaccessible.

## CONTI CROSS KEYS INN
Intersection of Pa. Routes 611 and 413, 1 mile north of center of Doylestown, Pa.

Phone: 1-348-3539

Call in advance. You can enter by a special door—one step. Assistance available.

## DOWNINGTOWN 1796 HOUSE
U.S. Route 30
Downingtown, Pa.

Phone: 269-1000

Parking; curb at sidewalk. Side entrance is level. Restrooms accessible.

**DRAGON GATE**
913 Race Street
Philadelphia

**Phone:** MA 7-5767

**FISHER'S RESTAURANT**
3545 North Broad Street
Philadelphia

**Phone:** BA 5-7591

Reasonably priced seafood restaurant near Temple Hospital. One step at entrance. Narrow doors. Room for wheelchairs. Restrooms inaccessible.

**HAPPY GARDENS**
134 North 10th Street
Philadelphia

**Phone:** WA 2-9603

One step at entrance. Restrooms accessible but small. Parking nearby.

**HEAD HOUSE TAVERN**
2nd and Pine Streets
Philadelphia

**Phone:** MA 7-9469

One steep step. Room for wheelchairs at table. Restrooms inaccessible.

**HOLIDAY INNS**

Most of these inns are equipped for visitors in wheelchairs.

**HOUSE OF PAGANO'S**
3633 Walnut Street
Philadelphia

**Phone:** EV 2-4105

Level entrance and ample room for wheelchairs. Restrooms inaccessible. Parking nearby.

## KUM LIM
2417 Welsh Road
Philadelphia

**Phone:** OR 3-3909

One step at entrance.

## LONGHORN RANCH
U.S. Route 1
(Baltimore Pike)
Glen Mills, Pa.

**Phone:** GL 9-3600

One step at entrance. Restrooms accessible, but booth doors are narrow. Parking adjacent.

## MARRIOTT MOTOR HOTEL AND RESTAURANTS
City Line Avenue and Monument Road
Bala-Cynwyd, Pa.

**Phone:** MO 7-0200

All restaurants very accessible. Public restroom booth doors are narrow, but person in a wheelchair may ask desk clerk for key to special rooms for handicapped. These rooms available for overnight stay.

## OPEN HEARTH RESTAURANT
City Line and Belmont Avenues
Philadelphia

**Phone:** TR 7-0345

No steps at motel entrance. Room for wheelchair at the table. Restrooms accessible, but booth doors are narrow. Parking lot adjacent.

## LE PAVILLON
203 South 12th Street
Philadelphia

**Phone:** WA 2-1319

Not *the* most expensive French restaurant in the city, but close. Restrooms accessible, but booth doors are narrow.

## PHILADELPHIA MUSEUM OF ART
Phone: PO 3-1600

Restaurant, cafeteria, and adjacent restrooms accessible. Entrance either through Museum or restaurant entrance on south side of building adjacent parking lot.

## PUB TIKI
1718 Walnut Street
Philadelphia

Phone: KI 5-4200

Level entrance. Ample room for wheelchair at the table. Restrooms accessible, but booth doors are narrow.

## RALPH'S
760 South 9th Street
(9th and Catharine Streets)
Philadelphia

Phone: MA 7-6011

One step at entrance.

## RED ROSE INN
West Grove, Pa.

Phone: 1-869-9964

There are a few steps at the main entrance, but assistance is available. Room for wheelchair at the table. Restrooms accessible but booth doors are narrow (page 231).

## SMITHVILLE INN
Historic Smithville, N.J.

Phone: 1-609-641-7777

See page 392.

## STOUFFER'S RESTAURANT
1526 Chestnut Street
Philadelphia

Phone: LO 3-4260
Entrance through large single door next to revolving door. Restrooms inaccessible. Parking nearby on 16th Street between Chestnut

and Market Streets, and Sansom Street between 16th and 17th
Streets (same side of street).

**SUGAR CONE**
414 South 2nd Street
(Head House Square)
Philadelphia

**Phone:** WA 3-8376

One step at entrance. Restrooms on first floor, but entrance is
narrow.

**SUMNEYTOWN HOTEL**
Main Street
Sumneytown, Pa.

**Phone:** 1-234-4091

Level entrance, restrooms on same floor, room for wheelchair at the
table.

**VALLE'S STEAK HOUSE**
9495 Roosevelt Boulevard
(In Northeast near North Philadelphia Airport)
Philadelphia

**Phone:** OR 6-9910

Curb from parking area. Level entrance. Room for wheelchair at
the table. Restrooms on same floor, but booth doors are narrow.

**WALBER'S ON THE DELAWARE**
Taylor Avenue
Essington, Pa.
(South of Philadelphia International Airport)

**Phone:** SA 4-1232

Overlooks the Delaware River. Level entrance. Room for wheelchairs at the table. Restrooms accessible; booth doors open out but
are narrow. Parking adjacent to restaurant.

**WILLIAMSON'S RESTAURANT**
(Top of the GSB Building)
City Line and Belmont Avenues
Bala-Cynwyd, Pa.

**Phone:** TE 9-7946

Room for wheelchair at the table. Restrooms accessible, but booth doors are narrow. Parking adjacent.

**ZUM-ZUM**
1527 Chestnut Street
Philadelphia

**Phone:** 563-8588

Side entrance. No steps. Call in advance and they will open the door for you.

Drive-in restaurants are, like drive-in movies, always comfortable for those in wheelchairs.

## Shopping

**CHERRY HILL MALL**
Haddonfield Road and Route 38
Cherry Hill, N.J.

**Directions:** Cross Benjamin Franklin Bridge, then take U.S. Route 30 to N.J. Route 38

This indoor shopping mall has many stores opening into the mall area. Restrooms accessible, but booth doors are narrow. Parking area adjacent, but there is a curb to sidewalk.

**MOORESTOWN MALL**
Route 38 and Lenola Road
Moorestown, N.J.
**Directions:** Take I-95 to Tacony–Palmyra Bridge, then N.J. Route 73 to N.J. Route 38

Indoor shopping mall. Parking adjacent.

**PLYMOUTH MEETING MALL**
Germantown Pike and Hickory Road
Plymouth Meeting, Pa.

Large indoor shopping mall on two levels. Elevators in department stores. Adjacent parking with curb. Level entrance at truck entrance near Lits.

## READING TERMINAL MARKET
12th and Filbert Streets
Philadelphia

The best entrance to this market is on Arch Street, where there is a
small ramp. Parking lot across the street. Restrooms inaccessible.
Fridays may be crowded (page 377).

## SHOPPING VILLAGES

Historic Smithville N.J. (page 392); Liberty Village, Flemington,
N.J. (page 219); Peddler's Village in Bucks County (page 218)

## STRAWBRIDGE & CLOTHIER and LITS
8th and Market Streets
Philadelphia

Both of these department stores are accessible at various levels
directly from the parking lot at 8th and Filbert Streets.


# Especially for the Handicapped

## CAROUSEL HOUSE
Belmont and Parkside Avenues in West Fairmount Park
Philadelphia 19131

**Phone:** MU 6-1776, ext. 81366

Year-round free programs provide recreation and camping programs
for children, teens, and adults, mentally or physically handicapped
or both. Activities include music, sports and games, storytelling,
singing, arts and crafts, cooking, sewing, fishing, gardening, and
trips to places of interest. Trained and skilled recreation leaders.
All facilities are on one level: Library, craft room, stage, large social
hall, game room. The Carousel Recreation Center for the Handicapped is the first of its kind to be operated and sponsored by a
municipality.

### CAROUSEL DAY CAMP FOR RETARDED CHILDREN
. . . is held at Carousel Recreation Center. The camp is designed
for retarded children ages 5 through 18. There are three three-week
sessions during the summer, $6 a session. It is sponsored by the City
of Philadelphia Department of Recreation and the Kiwanis Clubs
of Philadelphia in cooperation with the Fairmount Park Commission.

## LIBRARY FOR THE BLIND AND PHYSICALLY HANDICAPPED

Free Library of Philadelphia
919 Walnut Street
Philadelphia 19107

**Phone:** WA 5-3213
**Open:** Monday–Friday 9 A.M.–5 P.M.
**Parking:** Public lots nearby
**Public Transportation:** SEPTA Routes D, 42, 47, 61

Talking books, large-print material, Braille, cassette books, and open reel tapes. All books can be mailed to the reader and returned to the library postage free. This branch of the Free Library, with an entrance on street level, has a reading room with browsing and reference collection, audio and study carrels with cassette machine, talking-book machines, and open-reel tape recorders. Their collection also contains spoken-word records (plays, poetry, and prose), a display of aids and appliances used by the blind (such as alarm clocks, canes, Braille materials, and kitchen aids), and can supply information about ordering these items. The Student Service Center provides information and location of textbooks available in Braille and on tape. The Library for the Blind will arrange to transcribe or tape materials not already available. Restrooms accessible. Special telephones and water fountains for the handicapped are here. For information on the Vacation Reading Club, check your local library branch. All services of the Library are free.

## SWIMMING

**Memorial Hall Pool in West Fairmount Park.** Call Carousel House for information (MU 6-1776, ext. 81366).

**YWCA Mid City area,** 2027 Chestnut Street, Philadelphia. Phone: LO 4-3430. For children and adults.

## TRAVEL INFORMATION CENTER–MOSS REHABILITATION HOSPITAL

12th Street and Tabor Road
Philadelphia 19141

**Phone:** 329-5715

A free service of the Moss Rehabilitation Hospital, the Travel Information Center has assembled a library of facts for travelers with physical disabilities: which hotels or motels have wheelchair ramps, which airlines make the extra effort to accommodate the disabled, which sites are accessible and suitable. Call or write, outlining the cities or countries you plan to visit and your special interests. They will send you the available information. An invaluable service for vacation-bound handicapped people.

## Calendar of Events

Among the events listed in the Calendar (Chapter 14), many are readily accessible to the handicapped. The Civic Center and the Spectrum almost always have something scheduled and are among the most comfortable places for those with limited mobility. Here are some suggestions:

### JANUARY

Mummers' Parade; Kite-flying Contest; Frostbite Sailing Competition (continues into March)

### FEBRUARY

Ice Capades

### MARCH

Flower Show; Philadelphia String Bands Show of Shows; visit Brigantine National Wildlife Refuge

### APRIL

Cherry blossoms and regattas along the Schuylkill

### MAY

Rittenhouse Square Flower Market; boating regattas (continue through the summer); Devon Horse Show and Country Fair; Azalea Festival; dogwoods in bloom in Valley Forge State Park; Monkey Island Day at the Zoo

### JUNE

Washington Square Fair; Clothesline Exhibit; Festival of Fountains; Head House Square Open Air Market runs into September; *A Nation Is Born*, Sound and Light Show evenings at Independence Hall through Labor Day; summer evenings at Rittenhouse Square; Scottish Games at Devon Horse Show grounds

## JULY

July 4 at Independence Hall; Longwood Gardens colored fountain displays; Star Roses

## AUGUST

Morgan Horse Show at Devon Horse Show Grounds

## SEPTEMBER

Thrill Show at Kennedy Stadium

## OCTOBER

Super Sunday; Philadelphia Horse Show and Jumping Competition; Dog Show at Rittenhouse Square

## NOVEMBER

Thanksgiving Day Parade; Brigantine Wildlife Refuge

## DECEMBER

Amateur Figure-Skating Show; Christmas City Hall Tree-Lighting; Christmas activities at the department stores in Center City; Brandywine River Museum Annual Christmas Exhibit

# 12
# RESTAURANTS

This is not intended for gourmet dining around Philadelphia but rather as a brief guide to restaurants where families feel comfortable. Dining out with children does not have to be only at fast-food counters—nor must it be approached with apprehension. It can be as much fun, and as much of an adventure, as a visit to a museum or a picnic in the park. And it requires the same kind of planning and thought.

Everyone has his favorite neighborhood seafood, Italian, or delicatessen spot. The restaurants included in this section were specifically chosen for atmosphere or proximity, or because they welcome children, offer an opportunity to enjoy a foreign cuisine, or are reasonably priced.

However, what may be reasonable for a family of three may be expensive for a family of seven. Then again, if you order carefully, an "expensive" restaurant may cost no more than a "reasonably priced" one. Some restaurants have a children's menu, some charge a bit less for a child's portion, some will give you a plate for a small child. Don't hesitate to ask, but be sure to inquire when making a reservation or before ordering. Finally, go early—if possible, call for a reservation—and ask for help when ordering new or strange dishes.

## American

**BELMONT MANSION**
Next to John B. Kelly Playhouse in the Park
West Fairmount Park
Philadelphia

**Phone:** TR 7-4830
**Open:** Summers only: Dinner; lunch on Wednesday

With its proximity to Playhouse in the Park, its outdoor terrace, and delightful view of Philadelphia, this is a pleasant place for dinner during the summer theater season.

## CONTI CROSS KEYS INN
Intersection of Pa. Routes 611 and 313
1 mile north of center of Doylestown, Pa.

**Phone:** 1-348-3539
**Open:** Lunch and dinner
**Closed:** Sundays

This inn, which dates back to 1758, has been added to over the years and serves some of the best food in the Delaware Valley. The extensive menu contains a large selection of seafood. They enjoy having children here; platters are usually half price. This is a good place for a special family dinner.

## GREEN PEPPER
8515 Germantown Avenue
Chestnut Hill
Philadelphia 19118

**Phone:** CH 7-6700
**Open:** Lunch and dinner
**Closed:** Mondays

An attractive addition to the Chestnut Hill shopping area. Try it if you're planning to shop and want a leisurely lunch.

## HEAD HOUSE TAVERN
2nd and Pine Streets
Philadelphia

**Phone:** MA 7-9469
**Open:** Daily lunch and dinner

This restored Colonial tavern in the heart of Society Hill serves sandwiches and supper platters.

## INGLENEUK TEAROOM
120 Park Avenue
Swarthmore, Pa.

**Phone:** KI 3-4569
**Open:** Lunch and dinner
**Closed:** Mondays

An old-fashioned tearoom serving good food, plain and plentiful, and homemade baked goods. No liquor. Call for reservations.

## SMITHVILLE INN in HISTORIC SMITHVILLE, N.J.

You can combine dinner here with an outing to this re-created historic village (page 392).

## 21 WEST
21 West Highland Avenue
Chestnut Hill
Philadelphia 19118

**Phone:** CH 2-8005
**Open:** Lunch and dinner
**Closed:** Sundays

It started as an omelet place but became so popular they expanded the menu. The omelets are still good, and so is the rest of the menu. Combine a special lunch here with a shopping trip to Chestnut Hill.

## VALLEY GREEN INN
In the Wissahickon (page 149)

## WALBER'S ON THE DELAWARE
Taylor Avenue (Pa. Route 420)
Essington, Pa.

**Phone:** SA 4-1232
**Open:** Lunch and dinner
**Closed:** Mondays

The accent here is on seafood and the setting—the Delaware River. The extensive menu includes seafood, shellfish, beef, and fowl. It's just a few miles south of the Philadelphia International Airport and not far from Governor Printz Park. Sunday is family day from 1 to 9 P.M. Children under 12 (up to three in a family) free from children's menu.

## WILLIAMSON'S RESTAURANT
Top of the GSB Building
City Line and Belmont Avenues
Bala-Cynwyd, Pa.

**Phone:** TE 9-7946
**Open:** Lunch and dinner
**Closed:** Sundays

American food served up with a spectacular view of Philadelphia.

**H. A. WINSTON**
50 South Front Street
(Front and Chestnut Streets)
Philadelphia
Phone: 928-0660
Open: Daily lunch and dinner

812 Lancaster Avenue
Bryn Mawr
Phone: LA 5-1900
Open: Daily lunch and dinner

There is more than one way to cook a hamburger. Here the popular dish is a gourmet meal: French (sauce béarnaise), Mexican (chili and chopped onion), Israeli (sour cream and caviar), Hawaiian (pineapple and coconut). There are plain ones for the unsophisticated palate, and room for exploration by the more daring members of the group. Onion soup, antipasto, sangría, and penny candy are among other items available.

# Chinese

Chinese restaurants abound along Race Street between 9th and 10th Streets and around the corners. China Gate, China Castle, China City, China Village, Lotus Inn, and Happy Gardens all have their devoted following. They are relatively inexpensive, and you can share the dishes. The atmosphere is informal, and they are open on Sundays. Go early; they tend to be crowded.

**ASIA**
4746 North Broad Street
Philadelphia

Phone: DA 9-3843
Open: Daily lunch and dinner

A long-time family restaurant serving Cantonese and Mandarin, including Szechwan food.

**JADE PALACE**
2222 Cottman Avenue
Philadelphia

Phone: FI 2-6800
Open: Daily dinner

Yes, you *can* have a good Chinese dinner without going to Race Street. Head for the Great Northeast and you won't be disappointed—as a matter of fact, you'll be delighted.

## THE MAYFLOWER
220 North 10th Street
Philadelphia

**Phone:** WA 2-9119

The Mayflower has, in addition to its Mandarin food, an interesting and extensive Szechwan menu—hot and sweet, spicy dishes that are becoming popular. Like most Chinese restaurants, this one is no place for a leisurely meal. It is small, crowded, inexpensive. Ignore the decor and concentrate on the food.

Restaurants in Chinatown

# Dairy

## AMBASSADOR DAIRY
700 West Girard Avenue
Philadelphia

**Phone:** WA 3-6172
**Open:** Daily breakfast, lunch, and dinner

There aren't many dairy restaurants left in Philadelphia. Come here for blintzes, borscht, fish—Jewish specialties of a "meatless" sort.

# French

**LA BANANE NOIRE**
534 South 4th Street
Philadelphia

**Phone:** 627-9429
**Open:** Dinner and Sunday brunch
**Closed:** Mondays

Informal, with a French flavor, this is one of the many interesting restaurants to have opened during the South Street Renaissance.

# German .

**OTTO'S**
233 Easton Road
Hatboro, Pa.

**Phone:** OS 5-1864
**Open:** Lunch and dinner
**Closed:** Sundays

Family dinners with bountiful portions of German specialties.

**SCHWARZWALD INN**
2nd Street and Olney Avenue
Philadelphia

**Phone:** HA 4-9653
**Open:** Daily lunch and dinner

German specialties such as sauerbraten, Schnitzel *à la* Holstein, spaetzle, in this old German neighborhood. Extensive American menu also. Delicious lemon meringue pie. Children's full-course dinners about half price.

# Greek

**KONSTANTINOS**
2nd and South Streets
Philadelphia

**Phone:** MA 7-0650
**Open:** Daily dinner

Greek food in a very pleasant, attractive *taverna* atmosphere, including Greek music. Walk through the bar to the dining room in the rear and order some *spanikopita*, moussaka, or shish kebab. It's expensive, so save it for a special family occasion.

# Italian

Italian restaurants are favorites. There is always something on the menu which will appeal to the varying tastes of a family: a piece of salami from the antipasto, a plate of spaghetti, or a bowl of mussels. Many platters are large enough to be shared. The atmosphere is informal; children are welcome and the total bill need not be exorbitant.

**DANTE AND LUIGI**
762 South 10th Street
Philadelphia

**Phone:** 922-9501
**Open:** Daily lunch and dinner

An oldtime favorite South Philadelphia Italian restaurant whose fame has spread.

**MAMA LOMBARDO'S**
745 Oak Lane Avenue
Philadelphia

**Phone:** WA 4-5836
**Open:** Daily dinner

The decor at Mama Lombardo's must be seen to be believed. No amount of description can do justice to this collection: flowers, travel posters, colored lights, birds, fans, parasols, plus red-checkered tablecloths. It keeps everyone occupied. The food is good neighborhood Italian—the portions big enough for two, maybe three.

**MARRA'S**
1734 Passyunk Avenue
Philadelphia

Phone: FU 9-9042
Open: Lunch and dinner
Closed: Mondays

Pizza, sausage, and pasta always, but squid on Fridays for those who know or care. If the children are getting restless by dessert time, stop in at LaRosa Pastry at 1721.

**RALPH'S**
760 South 9th Street
Philadelphia

Phone: MA 7-6011
Open: Daily lunch and dinner

This old established neighborhood restaurant has children's portions.

**STROLLI'S**
1528 Dickinson Street
Philadelphia

Phone: DE 6-3390
Open: Lunch and dinner
Closed: Sundays

Once you've found the street (a small one below Washington Street), you have to find the door. Use the "Ladies' Entrance" around the corner. Their specialties are pasta: spaghetti, ravioli, gnocchi. Call for reservations on the weekends.

**VICTOR'S CAFÉ**
1303 Dickinson Street
Philadelphia

Phone: HO 8-3040
Open: Dinner
Closed: Sunday

For opera with your lasagna. The extensive collection of opera recordings adds a certain atmosphere. And one of the waiters or customers may even break into an aria. . . .

## VILLA DI ROMA
934 South 9th Street
Philadelphia

**Phone:** MA 7-9543
**Open:** Daily dinner

In the heart of the Italian market. The menu is posted on the wall
for all to see.

# Japanese

## BENIHANA OF TOKYO
2 Decker Square (behind Saks Fifth Avenue)
Bala Cynwyd

**Phone:** MO 7-7773
**Open:** Dinner Tuesday–Sunday 5:30–11 P.M.; lunch Monday–
Friday

In a Japanese steak house the grill is part of your table. The chef
cooks your shrimp, chicken, or steak with much rapid flourishing of
knives—and everyone watches in mute astonishment. The food is
good, the surroundings and atmosphere not so exotic as to make
anyone feel uncomfortable.

## CHOCHO
1824 Ludlow Street
(Between Market and Chestnut Streets)
Philadelphia

**Phone:** 567-9679
**Open:** Daily dinner, lunch weekdays

At this small restaurant you have an opportunity to enjoy reasonably
priced Japanese cooking. It's often crowded, so plan to make an
early reservation.

## HOUSE OF JAPAN
1119 Walnut Street
Philadelphia

**Phone:** WA 5-5536
**Open:** Daily dinner

Here you can introduce the family to Japanese food served Japanese style (assuming everyone is limber enough). Make a reservation for their tatami room. Be sure the ladies in your group aren't wearing very short or straight skirts; you sit shoeless on the floor at low tables. They also have regular tables in another room. There's more to Japanese food than raw fish, and most of it is cooked right at your table by a kimono-clad waitress.

## Mexican

**TIPPY'S TACO HOUSE**
1218 Pine Street
Philadelphia

**Phone:** PE 5-1880

415 East Lancaster Avenue
Devon, Pa.

**Phone:** 687-5822
**Open:** Daily from 11 A.M.

It's casual, informal, and inexpensive. Burritos, enchiladas, tostadas, tacos, and other Mexican foods can be eaten here or taken out.

## Middle Eastern

**MIDDLE EAST**
126 Chestnut Street
Philadelphia

**Phone:** WA 2-1003
**Open:** Daily dinner, lunch weekdays

Shish kebab for dinner, baklava for dessert, lively Arabic music, and some mild belly dancing—nothing too exotic.

## Pakistani and Indian

**MAHARAJA**
110 South 40th Street
Philadelphia

**Phone:** 222-2245
**Open:** Daily lunch and dinner

If you have no Pakistani or Indian friends to invite you to dinner, go here. Not for the timid and cautious, but for those who are adventurous about trying new dishes, some of which (here) are rather hot and spicy. Ask for help in ordering; they are most willing to advise. Reasonable prices.

**MAHARAJA II**
237 Chestnut Street
Philadelphia

**Phone:** MA 7-3020
**Open:** Daily dinner; lunch Monday–Saturday

They've opened a branch in Society Hill. Similar menu, slightly higher prices.

# Pennsylvania Dutch

**GROFF'S FARM**
R.D. 1
Mount Joy, Pa. 17552

**Phone:** 1-717-653-1520
**Open:** Lunch and dinner, by reservation only
**Closed:** Sundays, Mondays

It's beyond Lancaster, but worth planning a trip to the Pennsylvania Dutch Country just to end up at the farm for a marvelous Pennsylvania Dutch meal (page 250).

**SUMNEYTOWN HOTEL**
Main Street
Sumneytown, Pa.

**Phone:** 1-234-4091
**Open:** Dinner Thursday–Saturday 4:30–9; Sunday 11–9
**Closed:** Monday–Wednesday
**Directions:** Northeast Extension of Pennsylvania Turnpike to Pa. Route 63 (exit 31) west to Sumneytown

If you don't want to drive to "Pennsylvania Dutch Country" but want Pennsylvania Dutch food, try the specialties here. Children's portions.

## Polynesian

### KONA KAI
Marriott Motor Hotel
City Line Avenue and Monument Road
Bala-Cynwyd, Pa.

**Phone:** MO 7-0200
**Open:** Daily dinner 5 P.M., Sunday 3 P.M.

Bogus Polynesian, but nevertheless effective surroundings. Children love the waterfalls and the exotic flora and fauna. The food is expensive and elaborately presented. Fun for a special occasion.

### PUB-TIKI
1718 Walnut Street
Philadelphia

**Phone:** KI 5-4200
**Open:** Daily lunch and dinner

It's dressed up Chinese, but kids like the overdone South Seas atmosphere. Moderate to expensive, depending on what you order. Children's portions.

## Seafood

### BLUE POINT CRAB HOUSE
Harbison and Tulip Streets
(At Bridge Street exit of Delaware Expressway)
Philadelphia

**Phone:** PI 3-8838
**Open:** Lunch and dinner
**Closed:** Sundays

Strictly for seafood lovers. Come for fresh seafood, not for atmosphere. They have steamed clams, mussels, crabs, corn on the cob (always), soft drinks, lots of paper napkins, and beer. No salad, no coffee, no desserts. There's also a takeout counter.     •

## BOOKBINDERS, OLD ORIGINAL
125 Walnut Street
Philadelphia

**Phone:** WA 5-7027
**Open:** Daily lunch and dinner; family dinners Sunday

If you say "Philadelphia" to an out-of-towner he'll say "Bookbinders." This famous institution has been feeding visitors and residents for over 100 years. The rooms are hung with old pictures and prints. There is the usual enormous lobster tank and much to look at while waiting for your order. Seafood is the specialty, and some of it is very good. Most of it is very expensive. Free parking.

## BOOKBINDERS SEAFOOD HOUSE
215 South 15th Street
Philadelphia

**Phone:** KI 5-1137
**Open:** Daily lunch and dinner

This is not the original Bookbinders Restaurant, but the original Bookbinder family's restaurant. It's good food with the emphasis on seafood—all very expensive.

## BOOTHBY'S OYSTER HOUSE
3700 North Randolph Street
(On Erie between 5th and 6th Streets)
Philadelphia

**Phone:** BA 9-2095
**Open:** Lunch and dinner Wednesday–Sunday
**Closed:** Mondays, Tuesdays

This old-fashioned oyster house has been serving seafood since 1880: fried oysters, baked and broiled seafood. Steaks for those who insist.

## SNOCKEY'S OYSTER HOUSE
532 South 8th Street
Philadelphia

**Phone:** 627-9416
**Open:** Daily lunch through late dinner

Down the street from the Society Hill Playhouse. Crabs when available—you'll more than likely see a sign in the window. Seafood appetizers, soups, and platters. This neighborhood oyster house draws its patronage from all of Philadelphia.

## Smorgasbord

**COLLEGEVILLE INN**
Germantown Pike and Ridge Pike
Collegeville, Pa.

**Phone:** 1-631-0700
**Open:** Daily except Christmas

Reasonably priced smorgasbord. Children's prices for those under 7.

**VIKING INN**
128 East Lancaster Avenue
Ardmore, Pa.

**Phone:** MI 2-4360
**Open:** Daily dinner (Sunday 12 noon–8 P.M.)
**Closed:** Mondays

A smorgasbord is good for small children. They can see what is available, pick and choose small quantities, and keep getting up to go back for more. There is a wide variety here in this cheerful restaurant. Special prices for children under 6.

## Lunch and Snacks

**CHOCK FULL O'NUTS**
1338 Chestnut Street
Philadelphia

**Closed:** Sundays

Fast counter service, reasonable prices, and Center City location. For a quick snack or lunch.

**LA CRÊPE**
1425 Chestnut Street
Philadelphia

**Phone:** 665-9828
**Open:** Monday–Saturday lunch and dinner
**Closed:** Sundays

Crêpes—from the simplest to the most elaborate—onion soup, quiches. For a full meal, a snack, or a dessert.

## FAMOUS DELICATESSEN
700 South 4th Street
(4th and Bainbridge Streets)
Philadelphia

Phone: MA 7-9198
Open: Daily from early morning; weekdays until 6 P.M., Saturday until 7 P.M., Sunday until 3 P.M.

If you don't care about atmosphere and want an enormous delicatessen sandwich (hot corned beef or pastrami), this is the place. Down the street from TLA Cinema.

## LATIMER DELICATESSEN
15th and Latimer Streets
Philadelphia

Phone: 545-9244
Open: Opens early, closes late daily

Around the corner from the Academy of Music. Strictly delicatessen atmosphere, service, and good—meaning good-tasting—substantial sandwiches and platters. Its convenient before or after a performance at the Academy.

## LEE'S HOAGIE HOUSE
1906 West Cheltenham Avenue
Philadelphia

Phone: LI 9-7600
Closed: Mondays

Their delicious freshly made hoagies and steak sandwiches come in two sizes: halves and giants. If you can eat one of the giants, you must be one too. Mostly for takeout.

## MAGIC PAN
1519 Walnut Street
Philadelphia

Phone: 563-4756
Open: Daily

Crêpes for lunch, dinner, or dessert.

## OLD ORIGINAL LEVIS
507 South 6th Street
(6th and Lombard Streets)
Philadelphia

**Phone:** MA 7-9311
**Open:** Daily early morning to late night

Famous hot dogs eaten standing up; secret-formula cherry soda from the oldest working soda fountain in the country. A few tables in the rear, or take your hot dog across the street to the Star Playground—imaginative equipment and comfortable benches.

## READING TERMINAL
12th and Market Streets
Philadelphia

**Closed:** Sundays

Good soup, reasonable hearty sandwiches, and the best ice cream in town—at various counters in the market (page 377).

## THE SUGAR CONE
414 South 2nd Street
(Head House Square)
Philadelphia

**Phone:** WA 3-8376
**Open:** Daily

The atmosphere is "old-fashioned ice-cream parlor"—tile floor, Tiffany lamp shades, old pictures and accessories. You can find a variety of sandwiches under a dollar. Also foot-long hot dogs, hamburgers, and waffles, twenty-four flavors of ice cream, whopping sundaes, milk shakes, and sodas. Homemade soups in the winter and an outdoor dining area in the summer. If you're in the mood for an ice-cream cone, just step in the front door to their take-out counter.

## TAYLOR'S COUNTRY STORE
1609 Sansom Street
Philadelphia

**Phone:** LO 3-7627
**Open:** Monday to Saturday for lunch

This gourmet food store also makes delicious sandwiches, which can be eaten right there—turkey and Gruyère is their most popular —or taken out.

## JOHN WANAMAKER
13th and Chestnut Streets
Philadelphia

The Crystal Room on the ninth floor is Old World elegant and a lovely traditional spot for lunch or afternoon tea. Children love tea parties, so instead of having lunch why not stop in here for afternoon tea?

## ZUM-ZUM
1527 Chestnut Street
Philadelphia

Phone: 563-8588
Open: Monday–Saturday lunch and dinner
Closed: Sundays

A link in the chain of snack bars featuring Bavarian sausages in sandwich form: frankfurters, bierwurst, plockwurst, and touristen-wurst.

# Ice Cream

## AU NATUREL
133 South 18th Street
Philadelphia

Phone: 563-1106
Open: Monday to Saturday
Closed: Sundays

Goat's-milk ice cream made with natural ingredients—naturally. Bulk only.

## BASSETT'S ICE CREAM
Reading Terminal Market
12th and Market Streets
Philadelphia

Phone: WA 2-1771
Closed: Sundays

Philadelphia's most famous name in ice cream—and rightly so. For over 100 years, Bassett's has been making their delicious, rich, creamy product. Have a cone or plate at the counter, or buy it packed to take home.

## JUST ICE CREAM
1141 Pine Street
Philadelphia

**Phone:** WA 2-9633
**Open:** Daily

Enormous, delicious cones, sugar or plain, with chocolate "irvings" —"jimmies" or just plain "sprinkles" to the rest of the world—should you so desire. Wide selection of flavors, starting with black raspberry and working in both directions. Buy a cone, then work the pinball machines or wander on Pine Street. Open late.

## LORE'S CHOCOLATE SPOT
34 South 7th Street
(Independence Hall Area)
Philadelphia

**Phone:** MA 7-3233
**Closed:** Sundays

It's really a candy store, but they have homemade ice cream too. Buy a cone to eat immediately and some of their special chocolate for later.

## NOBODY'S
2018 Walnut Street
Philadelphia

This "after-school hangout" of the forties and fifties has a jukebox, a pinball machine, and penny candy. Egg creams, shakes, splits, sodas, sundaes, and cones. Wide choice of flavors. And good tea.

## THE SUGAR CONE
414 South 2nd Street
(Head House Square)
Philadelphia

**Phone:** WA 3-8376
**Open:** Daily

An old-fashioned ice-cream parlor serving more than just ice cream. A good place to stop while visiting the Historic Area.

### Italian Water Ices

All those handy carts on street corners around town during the summer offer a refreshing change from the ice cream on a stick, and it's easier to manage.

### Soft Ice Cream

**RIDGE AVENUE ICE CREAM DRIVE-IN**
5461 Ridge Avenue
Roxborough, Philadelphia

**Phone:** IV 3-3368
**Open:** May–Labor Day

They come from miles around to the stand at this busy intersection.

## Soft Pretzels

Philadelphia is famous for ice cream, pepper pot soup, and scrapple, but above all else the soft pretzel reigns supreme. There's hardly a street corner without a vendor. Try them plain or with mustard. Other cities imitate, but the soft fresh pretzels in Philadelphia are the best.

NOTE: In Chapter 1 there is a list of restaurants in the historic area (page 49).

# 13
# SHOPS AND SERVICES

If you can't find it in Philadelphia, you haven't looked hard enough. There is an astounding array of stores to fill your needs and feed your interests in the Delaware Valley area. Perhaps you shop only for what you need; maybe it's a way to pass the time of day. Buying vegetables can be a family outing if you try one of the "pick your own" farms. Children's clothes are available at the most elegant of shops—or you can go to a factory outlet for brand-name apparel. If you're tired of insipid department-store greeting cards, visit the museum shops. There are many ways to shop and many places to visit in order to accommodate your life-style. Our emphasis here is on children—their hobbies, clothing, books, and toys. At the end of the chapter are listed some helpful and unusual services.

## Bicycle Shops

Besides conserving gasoline these days many people are discovering it's faster to get some places on a bicycle than in a car, and for recreation the whole family seems to be infected with the bicycle craze. No longer is it a simple two-wheeler—there are three-, five-, and ten-speed bikes with every conceivable accessory available. For advice on picking out the right bicycle for you and the children try these reputable shops.

**THE BICYCLE SHOP**
4040 Locust Street
Philadelphia
**Phone:** EV 2-1363

**HILL CYCLE SHOP**
8135 Germantown Avenue
Chestnut Hill, Philadelphia
**Phone:** CH 7-1502

**KESWICK CYCLE COMPANY**
408 Easton Road
Glenside, Pa.

**Phone: TU 4-6996**

**WARMINSTER BICYCLE SHOP**
298 York Road
Warminster, Pa.

**Phone: OS 5-1739**

**WOLFF CYCLE**
4311 Lancaster Avenue
Philadelphia

**Phone: BA 2-2171**

Try the bicycle paths in Fairmount Park. If you don't own a bike or prefer not to drag it in the car, rent one at:

**FAIRMOUNT BICYCLE RENTAL**
East River Drive
(Behind the Art Museum)

**Phone: PO 5-9076**

## Birthday Parties

Instead of the usual party games, clown act, or Saturday matinee at the movies, take the group to one of the many cultural institutions or special museums described in detail elsewhere in the book. Many have facilities for lunch or ice cream and cake on the premises. Some are free; some have group rates. It is best to call ahead. Try:

**ACADEMY OF NATURAL SCIENCES**
19th Street and Benjamin Franklin Parkway
Philadelphia

**Phone: LO 7-3700**

**ATWATER KENT MUSEUM**
15 South 7th Street
Philadelphia

**Phone:** WA 2-3031

Free

**FRANKLIN INSTITUTE**
20th Street and Benjamin Franklin Parkway
Philadelphia

**Phone:** 448-1201

**JOHN B. KELLY PLAYHOUSE IN THE PARK**
West Fairmount Park, Philadelphia

**Phone:** GR 7-1700

Summer only

**PERELMAN ANTIQUE TOY MUSEUM**
270 South 2nd Street
Philadelphia

**Phone:** WA 2-1070

**PHILADELPHIA FIRE DEPARTMENT MUSEUM**
2nd and Quarry Streets
Philadelphia

**Phone:** 922-9844

Free

**PHILADELPHIA MUSEUM OF ART AND PARK HOUSES**
26th Street and Benjamin Franklin Parkway
Philadelphia

**Phone:** PO 3-8100

**SMITH MEMORIAL PLAYGROUND**
East Fairmount Park
Philadelphia

**Phone:** PO 9-0902

Free

## UNITED STATES MINT
5th and Arch Streets
Philadelphia

Phone: 597-7350

Free

## U.S.S. OLYMPIA
Pier 11 North
Delaware Avenue and Race Street
Philadelphia

Phone: WA 2-1898

## VALLEY FORGE MUSIC FAIR
Routes U.S. 202 and Pa. 363
Devon, Pa.

Phone: 644-5000

# Books

The following are bookstores with a good supply of children's books—hardback, paperback, or both. These stores merit your attention not only for their juvenile sections but for their overall quality in adult books also.

## *Philadelphia*

## DAVID'S BOOKSHELF
205 South 38th Street
Philadelphia

Phone: BA 2-4422

In the University of Pennsylvania area—hobby and craft books, posters, hardback and paperback juveniles.

## FIRESIDE BOOKS
8523 Germantown Avenue
Chestnut Hill, Philadelphia 19118
Phone: CH 2-1442

186 East Evergreen Avenue
Chestnut Hill, Philadelphia
Phone: CH 8-3122

Both stores have new titles and old favorites of children; no juvenile paperbacks in the Evergreen Avenue store, but lots of quality toys with the hardbacks.

## JOSEPH FOX
1724 Sansom Street
Philadelphia

**Phone:** LO 3-4184

Small personal bookstore. Choice selection in most fields. Particularly strong in art and architecture.

## THE FRIGATE BOOK SHOP
16 East Highland Avenue
Philadelphia

**Phone:** CH 8-1065

Wide selection in hardback and paperback. Lending library of current novels and nonfiction. Arranges school book fairs.

## HOW-TO-DO-IT BOOK SHOP
1526 Sansom Street
Philadelphia

**Phone:** LO 3-1516

Books on how to do almost anything.

## LEAVES OF GRASS BOOKSTORE
5600 Greene Street
Germantown

**Phone:** VI 9-9872

Offers paperbacks and hardbacks in most areas, including juveniles.

## MIDDLE EARTH BOOKS
1134 Pine Street
Philadelphia

**Phone:** WA 2-6824

The children's section is small, but there is plenty for the here and now generation on poetry, ecology, the occult, and Mother Earth.

## PENN CENTER BOOKS, INC.
Penn Center Concourse
Suburban Station, 16th and John F. Kennedy Boulevard
Philadelphia

Phone: LO 3-0868

One of the best selection of adults' and children's paperbacks in Center City.

## THE SCARLET LETTER
222 West Rittenhouse Square
Philadelphia

Phone: 732-6222

They pride themselves on carrying "nonsexist" children's books.

Sessler's Book Store

## SESSLER'S BOOK STORE
1308 Walnut Street
Philadelphia

Phone: PE 5-1086

One of Philadelphia's finest traditions. This quality store has been serving the city's book-lovers for over ninety years. They maintain an excellent selection of books for adults and children. Whatever your interest, chances are you'll find it here. Rare collector's items. Helpful staff.

## UNIVERSITY OF PENNSYLVANIA BOOK STORE
3729 Locust Street
Philadelphia
**Phone:** 594-7595

Excellent paperback and hardback titles for adults and children, including foreign-language books for young readers in French, Italian, and Spanish. One of the most complete bookstores in the city.

## U.S. GOVERNMENT PRINTING OFFICE BOOK STORE
Room 1214
Federal Office Building
600 Arch Street
Philadelphia 19106
**Phone:** 597-0677

Reasonably priced publications on thousands of subjects: Cooking, camping, games, sports, crafts, history. Almost any subject you can think of—from Aztec ruins to flights into space. You no longer have to write to Washington because it's all here on Independence Mall.

**JOHN WANAMAKER, GIMBELS, AND STRAWBRIDGE & CLOTHIER** all have book departments in their main stores and branches handling a variety of hardcover and paperback for both adults and children. Of them Wanamaker's has the most extensive selection in their downtown store.

### *Suburbs and Surrounding Area*

## B. DALTON BOOKSELLER
282 Exton Square
Exton, Pa.
**Phone:** 1-363-9636

The first in this area of a large chain of fine bookstores carrying a wide selection of adult and children's books.

## BRADD ALAN BOOK STORES
Cheltenham Shopping Center
Cheltenham, Pa.
**Phone:** TU 6-3675

Bucks County Mall
Feasterville, Pa.
**Phone:** 357-4222

4652 Frankford Avenue
Philadelphia
**Phone:** CU 8-2828

Huntingdon Valley Shopping Center
Huntingdon Valley, Pa.
**Phone:** RA 2-5560

Leo Mall Shopping Center
Bustleton and Hendrix Avenues
Philadelphia
**Phone:** 934-5363

Few hardbacks, but an excellent selection of paperbacks, including the hard to find "young adult" titles.

## THE BOOK HOUSE OF SUBURBAN SQUARE
Suburban Square Building
Ardmore, Pa.

**Phone:** MI 2-4915

Wide selection of both hardback and paperback juveniles. You will get helpful and enthusiastic assistance.

## THE BOOKSTORE
Leedom Street and Greenwood Avenue
Jenkintown, Pa.

**Phone:** TU 4-3134

Fine selection of new adults' and children's titles along with old favorites. They do a brisk business in book fairs with knowledgeable people to handle them.

## CEDARBROOK BOOKS
Cedarbrook Mall
Cheltenham Avenue and Easton Road
Wyncote, Pa.
**Phone:** CA 4-6362

Red Lion Shopping Plaza
Red Lion Road and Roosevelt Boulevard
Philadelphia
Phone: HO 4-1313

A large select inventory of adults and children's paperbacks, well arranged and easy to find. Hardback books here also.

**CHERRY HILL BOOKS, INC.**
Cherry Hill Mall
Cherry Hill, N.J.

Phone: 1-609-665-5412

A fine selection of adults' and children's books in hardcover and paperback on the other side of the Delaware River.

**COUNTRY BOOK SHOP**
28 Bryn Mawr Avenue
Bryn Mawr, Pa.

Phone: LA 5-2218

Well-selected and good variety of hardback titles. Small but choice paperback section.

**DAVID'S BOOKSHELF**
Morrisville Shopping Center
Morrisville, Pa.

Phone: 295-4405

This is a branch of the store in West Philadelphia. They carry a greater variety of children's books here.

**DOUBLEDAY BOOK STORES**
Bala-Cynwyd Shopping Center
105 East City Line Avenue
Bala-Cynwyd, Pa.
Phone: MO 4-3603

Benjamin Fox Pavilion
Jenkintown, Pa.
Phone: TU 7-6632

These stores are part of the Doubleday chain emphasizing current fiction, nonfiction, and gift books. Hardback and paperback juveniles available.

## FARLEY'S NEW DELAWARE BOOKSHOP
44 South Main Street
New Hope, Pa.

**Phone:** 1-862-2452

Books of local historical interest. Newest hardback titles are available here along with a strong assortment of old favorites and "easy-to-reads." Many paperback titles also. Old and rare upstairs.

## NOOK OF KNOWLEDGE
Oak Lane Shopping Center
53 West Cheltenham Avenue
Cheltenham, Pa.
**Phone:** ME 5-2855

Davisville Shopping Center
Warminster, Pa.
**Phone:** 355-6313

Woodbury Shopping Center
N.J. Route 45
Woodbury, N.J.
**Phone:** 1-609-848-5404

Klein Shopping Center
Cherry Hill, N.J.
**Phone:** 1-609-667-5414

Korvette Shopping Center
(Across from Moorestown Mall)
N.J. Route 38 and Lenola Road
Moorestown, N.J.
**Phone:** 1-609-234-3094

Gateway Shopping Center
Valley Forge, Pa.
**Phone:** 687-4298

This growing chain has a good selection of hardbacks and paperbacks for adults and children.

## SANFORD BOOKS
King of Prussia Plaza
King of Prussia, Pa.

**Phone:** 265-5075

A wide selection in all categories: current fiction, nonfiction, technical, crafts, juveniles, special selection of sale books year round. In February and July there are "hurt" book sales with amazing buys in adult and juvenile hardbacks. Knowledgeable staff.

**F. A. O. SCHWARZ**
Suburban Square
Coulter Street and St. James Road
Ardmore, Pa.

**Phone:** MI 9-0600

Primarily a toy store but with a small choice selection of children's books emphasizing the classics and old favorites.

**STACKS, INC.**
932 West Lancaster Avenue
Bryn Mawr, Pa.

**Phone:** LA 5-9820

This paperback bookshop has a wide selection because it caters to the colleges and schools in the area. It also carries a fairly extensive stock of paperback juveniles, with a good group for those young teenagers.

**WALDENBOOKS**
Neshaminy Mall
Cornwells Heights, Pa.
**Phone:** 355-1850

Plymouth Meeting Mall
Plymouth Meeting, Pa.
**Phone:** 282-2678

Echelon Mall
Cherry Hill, N.J.
**Phone:** 1-609-722-1703

A growing chain of fine bookstores offering good selections in paperback and hardback children's books.

*Books—Used, Out of Print, Bargains*

## BALDWIN'S BOOK BARN
865 Lenape Road
West Chester, Pa. 19380

**Phone:** 1-696-0816

For browsing, bargains, rare books, and a real treat, take yourself to this book lovers mecca. A whole barn—three floors—full of books (page 229).

## ENCYCLOPEDIA DISCOUNT CENTER
38 South 19th Street
Philadelphia

**Phone:** LO 3-9340
**Open:** Monday–Friday 11 A.M.–5 P.M., Saturday 11:30 A.M.–3 P.M.

Britannica World Book, Americana. Used encyclopedias and reference sets at greatly reduced prices, and knowledgeable people to advise you on your needs. Many of the sets are in their original cartons.

## GWYNEDD VALLEY BOOK STORE
Plymouth Road
Gwynedd Valley
(Between Ambler and North Wales via Pa. Route 73 right on U.S. Route 202)

**Phone:** MI 6-0881

Used, rare, hard-to-find, and out-of-print books by categories in various rooms. It is pleasant to browse here, especially if you have a particular interest. They are open every day from 9 A.M. until 11 P.M.—believe it or not.

## THE OWL
Morris Avenue and Yarrow Streets
(On the Bryn Mawr campus)
Bryn Mawr, Pa.

**Phone:** LA 5-6117
**Open:** Tuesday and Thursday 1–6 P.M., Saturday 10 A.M.–1 P.M.
**Closed:** July, August

Out-of-print, rare, and used books all at bargain prices, including a large selection of new and used children's books. The shop is run by volunteers and all proceeds from the sale of these donated books go to the Bryn Mawr Alumnae Scholarship Fund.

## SALVATION ARMY
4555 Pechin Street
Roxborough, Philadelphia

Phone: IV 2-9622

Among the furniture, clothes, and other items there is a book section featuring recent best-sellers at bargain prices. Currently popular cookbooks often show up here.

## THE THRIFT SHOP
1213 Walnut Street
Philadelphia

Phone: WA 2-9526

It's a small area of books, but you'll find slightly old best-sellers, occasional rare books, and out-of-print books at great savings.

# Children's Clothing

These shops are mentioned for their fine quality and unusual merchandise:

## CALLIOPE
229 South 20th Street
Philadelphia

Phone: LO 3-8646

Attractive, durable, classic children's clothes made to last.

## CHILDREN'S BOUTIQUE
Yorktown Inn Mall
York and Church Road
Elkins Park, Pa.

Phone: TU 6-2122

18th and Sansom Streets
Philadelphia

Phone: LO 3-3881

Everything in the shops reflects the owner's good taste. A large selection of Florence Eiseman, Fischer coats, imports; good depth in boys' clothing, Mighty-Mac outerwear. Hard to find "preteens." Individual attention. Semiannual sales.

## ELDER CRAFTSMEN
1628 Walnut Street
Philadelphia

Phone: KI 5-7888

Hand-smocked dresses, hand-knitted sweaters, afghans, patchwork quilts, reasonably priced and made by people over sixty. It is merchandise of a quality rarely seen in this day of mass production, and you perform a real service to the elder craftsmen, who receive 25 percent of the selling price.

## MES ENFANTS BOUTIQUE
5 East Gravers Lane
Chestnut Hill, Philadelphia
Phone: CH 2-1661

Merion and Morton Avenues
Bryn Mawr, Pa.
Phone: LA 7-4330

Beautiful and elegant clothes for infants, boys, and girls with prices to match.

## PACAYA
10 Fetters Mill Square
Huntingdon Valley, Pa.

Phone: WI 7-1158

Unusual Mexican and Guatemalan clothes and trinkets, pierced earrings, colorful ponchos all sizes.

## RODEO BEN'S
6240 North Broad Street
Philadelphia

Phone: WA 4-4200

Jeans and Western clothing. Well-fitting jeans in small sizes: boots, jodhpurs, riding coats, hunt hats for the whole family.

**W. SK'OLD**
"The Yard"
Lahaska, Pa.

Phone: 1-794-8138

Swedish imports, including distinctive clogs for the whole family.

**WOMEN'S EXCHANGE**
109 South 18th Street
Philadelphia

Phone: LO 3-1882

Here are lovely smocked dresses, hand-knitted booties, caps, and dresses for the youngest ones; rag dolls. Delicious brownies and cakes here also. Closed July and August.

**WOMEN'S EXCHANGE**
429 Johnson Street
Jenkintown, Pa.

Phone: 885-2470

Each Women's Exchange is distinct, although they belong to the same Federation of Women's Clubs. At this one you'll find lovely knitted caps and sweaters for infants and charming patchwork stuffed toys, all hand done. They also have the best cookies in town. Closed July and August.

## *Bargains*

It's best to check hours, especially with "factory outlets." Some stores will accept charges, but with most it is cash-and-carry.

**ARTIE'S**
Main Store: 1601 East Wadsworth Avenue
Philadelphia
Phone: CH 7-5084

365 North Easton Road
Glenside, Pa.
Phone: TU 4-5400

Feasterville Shopping Plaza
Feasterville, Pa.
Phone: 357-4358

1437 York Road
(Sears Shopping Center)
Abington, Pa.
**Phone: TU 7-7770**

174 Butler Pike
Ambler, Pa.
**Phone: MI 6-4533**

Discount prices on children's underwear, socks, name-brand snow-
suits, slacks, shirts, and bathing suits; you'll find Danskins and Chips
'n Twigs here for less.

**BEE EM**
525 North 11th Street
Philadelphia

**Phone: PO 5-0828**

Boys' wear, raincoats, suits, sportcoats, and outerwear at tremendous
savings. Sizes 8 to 18. Saturday mornings 9 A.M. to 12 noon.

**BROWNIE'S**
6722 Bustleton Avenue
Philadelphia

**Phone: MA 4-9994**

Teenage girls and their mothers will find name-brand sportswear
at outlet prices.

**FACTORY OUTLET (Infanta)**
309 Huntingdon Pike
Rockledge, Pa.

**Phone: FI 2-8500**

Factory outet for Infanta, a top-quality brand of children's knitwear. Slacks, tops, dresses. Closed Mondays.

**GASTWIRTH BROTHERS**
350 North 16th Street
Philadelphia

**Phone: LO 3-3104**

Factory outlet of one of the finest makers of girls' coats, which are
available here at tremendous savings. They prefer that you bring
the child along. Best time Saturday morning 8 A.M.–12 noon.

## GENERAL SALES DEPARTMENT STORE
995 North 2nd Street
(2nd Street below Girard)
Philadelphia

**Phone:** MA 7-6080
**Parking:** Available

This is a full discount department store with savings from 33⅓ to 60 percent. Children's clothes and shoes plus top name-brand men's and women's wear, furniture, pet supplies, bicycles, appliances, typewriters. The merchandise changes from week to week. Some groceries.

## I. GOLDBERG'S
902 Chestnut Street
Philadelphia

**Phone:** WA 5-9393

Good selection on outerwear coats for boys and girls size 12 and up; pea jackets and Army-style field jackets at discount prices. Free catalogue. Write or call.

## HOUSE OF BARGAINS
724 Adams Avenue
Philadelphia
**Phone:** JE 5-6929

7116 Ridge Avenue
Philadelphia
**Phone:** IV 3-5752

3142 Willits Road
Philadelphia
**Phone:** HO 4-4219

Irregulars of better clothing for boys and girls and samples at 50 percent off. Also underwear and socks.

## LOCKTOWN SWEATER SHOP
Sergeantsville Road
Stockton, N.J.
(Less than 15 minutes from New Hope off N.J. Route 523)

**Phone:** 1-201-996-2960

Knitwear for the whole family at great savings. Sweaters of every variety, knit dresses; the trip is definitely worth it. Branch at "the Yard," Lahaska, a much smaller operation with no children's merchandise.

## PHIL'S
Anchor Street and Loretta Avenue
Philadelphia

Phone: PI 3-9848

Children's shoes, name brands at a good savings.

## PORTEN'S
605 South 4th Street
Philadelphia

Phone: WA 5-0498

Name-brand clothing for children sizes 2 to 14. Sportswear and good selection of outerwear at 20 to 40 percent off. Such brands as Chips 'n Twigs, Gastwirth coats.

## RUBIN'S
191 West Roosevelt Boulevard
Philadelphia

Phone: GL 7-0800

Teenage girls and their mothers will appreciate the savings—up to one-half regular price—on sportswear, lingerie, and coats.

## SANTARIAN'S
14 East Moreland Road
Hatboro, Pa.
Phone: OS 5-1442

Bucks County Mall
Feasterville, Pa.
Phone: 355-5535

South Line Street and Penn Street
Lansdale, Pa.
Phone: 1-855-0700

It's a family department store: shoes, underwear, sportswear, slacks, tops, for everyone in the family, including layette items. Name brands and everything at a discount.

**WISSAHICKON SKATING CLUB SKATE SHOP**
Willow Grove Avenue and Cherokee Street
Philadelphia

**Phone: CH 7-1907**

Good used ice skates at reasonable prices.

## Children's Furniture

**IT'S A SMALL WORLD**
8042 Gemantown Avenue
Chestnut Hill, Philadelphia

**Phone: CH 7-7929**

Attractive children's furniture, mostly imports.

**KARL'S**
724 Chestnut Street
Philadelphia

**Phone: MA 7-2514**

Highchairs, car seats, strollers, and infant's furniture in quantity.
Most is very conventional, but here also you will find English
prams and armoires for baby's room. Teenage-furniture department.

**THE WORKBENCH**
1709 Walnut Street
Philadelphia

**Phone: LO 3-9393**

Beautifully designed and functional children's furniture, modestly
priced considering the quality of workmanship.

## Christmas Cards

Wherever there is a line of stores, you can be pretty sure a
greeting card shop is among them—with the usual fare. However,
unusual and especially attractive Christmas cards can be found at:

**FREE LIBRARY**
Logan Square
19th and Vine Streets
Philadelphia

**Phone:** MU 6-5416

Illustrations from their rare book department. For the literature buff or anyone else who appreciates books.

## PHILADELPHIA MUSEUM OF ART
26th Street and Benjamin Franklin Parkway
Philadelphia

**Phone:** PO 3-8100

Many attractive Christmas cards with some reproductions of their own collection. Proceeds benefit the museum.

## ROSENBACH MUSEUM FOUNDATION
2010 Delancey Place
Philadelphia

**Phone:** 732-1601

Delightful Christmas cards by Maurice Sendak and Marianne Moore, both of whose collected literary works reside here.

## UNICEF GREATER PHILADELPHIA AREA COMMITTEE
1218 Chestnut Street
3rd floor
Philadelphia

**Phone:** WA 2-2265

Every year outstanding artists design the UNICEF Christmas cards. They can be purchased here and at outlets around the city and suburbs. Call for locations. Plain greeting cards are available here all year long. For the benefit of the United Nations International Children's Emergency Fund.

## Craft Supplies and Materials

Most local hobby shops have supplies to meet your varied interests. Some tend to be more toy- than craft-oriented despite their names. Here are a few that might further your hobby—or stimulate you to consider a new one. Sears, Roebuck has a special catalogue devoted solely to arts and crafts.

## General Craft Supplies

**AMERICAN HANDICRAFT COMPANY**
1206 Walnut Street
Philadelphia

Phone: 735-7929

**PHILADELPHIA ART SUPPLY COMPANY**
25 South 8th Street
Philadelphia

Phone: 627-6655

## Leathercraft

Do you want to make sandals, pocketbooks, belts, or jackets? Start here:

**TANDY LEATHER COMPANY**
124 South 13th Street
Philadelphia

Phone: 735-7582

**CHARLES A. TOEBE**
149 North 3rd Street
Philadelphia

Phone: 627-0649

## Needlepoint

It's very popular now and there is more than one shop in every neighborhood, but look into:

**SAWYER NEEDLEPOINT**
8611 Germantown Avenue
Chestnut Hill, Philadelphia

Phone: CH 8-4660

Grace Sawyer is the owner and inspiration behind this tasteful and creative shop. She encourages children in the popular art of needlepoint. If you buy a piece, she will patiently teach you the stitches. Mrs. Sawyer says that boys as well as girls enjoy this craft.

*Scientific Supplies*

## EDMUND SCIENTIFIC COMPANY
101 East Gloucester Pike
Barrington, N.J. 08007

**Phone:** 1-609-547-3488
**Open:** Monday–Thursday 8 A.M.–6 P.M., Friday and Saturday 8 A.M.–9 P.M., Sunday 11 A.M.–6 P.M.; November 16–December 30, Monday–Saturday 8 A.M.–9 P.M.
**Directions:** Cross Benjamin Franklin Bridge, U.S. Route 30, pass under I-295 overpass in Barrington, turn right at third traffic light to Gloucester Pike.

Scientific toys and kits, lenses, magnets, telescopes, gyroscopes, terraria, lapidary tumblers, a 3-foot (when inflated) balloon, a weather-station kit. Science items for the scientific and not-so-scientific from $1. A good place for stocking stuffers at Christmas. Send for their catalogue or take a trip to see for yourself.

To show what can be done with their lighting equipment, they have mounted a multimedia light show on a 96 foot × 8 foot 180-degree screen. Free. Once an hour.


# Food—Marketplaces, Specialties, and Farms and Orchards

## *Marketplaces in Philadelphia*

### ITALIAN MARKET
9th Street between Washington Avenue and Christian Street

**Parking:** On street, or on lot on Carpenter Street between 9th and 10th Streets
**Public Transportation:** Any bus east on Market Street and transfer to SEPTA Route 7 at 8th Street

Stretching along 9th Street between Washington and Christian Streets is the open-air Italian market—lively, noisy, crowded, bustling, and a world away from the plastic, prepackaged, Muzak'd supermarkets. It's almost a way of life, and all ages enjoy the festive atmosphere. The open stalls piled high with vegetables, fruits, canned foods, and eggs line the curb. In the windows of the butcher shops hang whole animals (dressed and not), sides of beef, and hogs' heads. There are live chickens, ducks, turkeys, pigeons, and, at Eastertime, rabbits. You'll find mussels by the bushel, crabs and snails climbing around in baskets, squid and fresh tuna in season, as well as dried fish. Spice shops, cheese shops, bakeries, and pasta stores offer irresistible goodies. And in the midst of all this is Fante's, carrying an astounding assortment of cooking equipment.

It's best to go at the end of the week—Thursday to Saturday (early Saturday, that is). Take a shopping bag or a collapsible shopping cart. Don't buy immediately; do some comparison shopping first.

The Italian Market

## THE READING TERMINAL MARKET
12th Street between Market and Filbert Streets
Philadelphia

**Open:** Monday–Saturday

**Parking:** Several public lots in the area (most stalls will stamp your ticket for free parking with a purchase); *or* "Take a ride on the Reading"—to some children a train ride is a treat in itself, and this is the last stop for all Reading commuter lines

Stalls of food in its beautiful nonpackaged state, all under one roof. Bring your shopping list and plan to eat lunch or snack at the many counters serving a variety of appetizing dishes at reasonable prices. The Market is in full swing on Fridays and Saturdays when the farmers come in from the Lancaster area with their specialties—meats, produce, or baked goods. Some stalls are always open. The following are a sampling:

## L. D. Bassett

Philadelphia is known as the ice-cream capital of America, and Bassett's is the most esteemed name. *The New York Times* sent down a group of ice-cream experts, and they agreed unanimously —it's the best. For over 100 years Bassett's has been making rich creamy ice cream—dark chocolate, Irish coffee, French vanilla— but don't overlook the ices (the strawberry and orange are fantastic). You can sit at the counter and have a dish, take out a cone, or ask them to pack it in dry ice for the trip home; it will keep for two to three hours. Bassett's also has a branch at Spring House Village Center, Spring House, Pa.

## William B. Margerum and Pierce and Schurr

Prime meats: two-inch-thick lamb chops and delectable steaks competitively priced. Margerum's has an old-fashioned corner with open canisters full of black-eyed peas, cranberry beans, whole buckwheat groats, and pinto beans. Indians and Pakistanis find their cooking ingredients here.

## Franklin H. Field & Son

Well known for their considerable variety of spices. They grate horseradish and coconut for you. Take home some peanut butter that you can watch them prepare on the spot, and taste the difference.

## Dorothy Herman

Marvelous selection of cheeses, imported and domestic; homemade chowchow; and German potato salad.

## Pearl's Seafood Bar

Oysters and clams on the half shell, shucked on the spot; snapper soup, steamed mussels, and oyster or clam stew. The prices are reasonable, the seafood delicious.

## Produce

There are many stalls full of the finest specimens of fresh fruit and vegetables. Out-of-season items such as asparagus and rhubarb in the middle of winter.

## H. Schmalenback

Delicatessen to take home or eat at their old-fashioned tile counters. Ham sandwiches are the specialty—delicious and reasonable.

## Terminal Sea Food

Jumbo shrimps that are colossal, fresh fish, and lobster tails. Great display of seafood.

## *Farmers' Markets*

Lancaster County is noted for its rich farmlands, and the Pennsylvania Dutch bring their produce, meats, smoked sausages, and baked goods to markets in the Philadelphia area. These Lancaster County farmers' markets can be found in the following locations:

150 East Lancaster Avenue, Wayne, Pa.; Wednesday and Saturday
19 West 7th Street, Chester, Pa.; Wednesday and Saturday
5317 North 5th Street, Philadelphia; Wednesday and Saturday
5942 Germantown Avenue, Philadelphia; Tuesday and Friday

If you are going out into Lancaster County, however, visit the marketplaces listed in the section on Pennsylvania Dutch Country in Chapter 7.

## *Food Specialties: Sweets*

**KIPSELY'S SWEET SHOP**
212 South 11th Street
Philadelphia

**Phone:** WA 5-2535

Delicious Greek pastries—*baklava*, *floyeres*, and *galactobouriko*. *Filo* dough (strudel leaves for making pastries).

**WILLIAM PENN SHOPS**
1520 Chestnut Street
Philadelphia
**Phone:** 561-5400

Fox Pavilion
Jenkintown, Pa.
**Phone:** TU 7-8334

2 Decker Square
Bala-Cynwyd, Pa.
**Phone:** 4-1200

6515 Castor Avenue
Philadelphia
**Phone:** 831-0100

The William Penn Shops carry a fine selection of choice meats, fruit, and cheeses all year, but they are mentioned in this section because of a "sweet" specialty. Once a year, around June 1, gigantic chocolate-covered strawberries appear. These strawberries are especially grown in California for this event and flown in daily to the William Penn Shops, where they are dipped into the most luscious chocolate imaginable. You can watch them being hand-dipped in the window of the Chestnut Street store. They are available at all their stores for only two weeks. It is an eagerly awaited annual happening.

## SWISS PASTRY SHOP
35 South 19th Street
Philadelphia

**Phone:** LO 3-0759

Homemade ice cream and cakes.

## WOMEN'S EXCHANGE
429 Johnson Street
Jenkintown, Pa.

**Phone:** 885-2470

The best cookies in town: thin sand tarts, nut bars, choclate chip, and chocolate swirls. Their beautiful birthday cakes must be ordered at least a week in advance.

## ZUND'S SWISS BAKERY
1916 Welsh Road
Philadelphia

**Phone:** OR 6-6592

Especially recommended: chocolate leaves and homemade thin chocolate mints. Birthday cakes are a specialty.

## Orchards and Farms

The rich farmlands of Pennsylvania are easily accessible to city residents and offer a fine way to buy fresh fruits and vegetables in the summer and early fall. There's the added attraction at some of them that you can "pick your own."

### FOX HILL FARMS
249 Smithbridge Road
Elam
Glen Mills, Pa.

Phone: 1-459-3448
Directions: Schuylkill Expressway to U.S. Route 1 (south) to U.S. Route 202, south on U.S. Route 202 for 1.8 miles, left on Smithbridge Road 1 mile to farm

Pick your own peppers, corn, tomatoes, and beans. All crops here are grown for "pick-it-yourself" customers. A recorded message will tell you when they are open and which crops are in, or you can write and ask to be put on their mailing list. They will send you a card telling when vegetables are ready for picking. It's less than 20 miles from Center City Philadelphia. Crops begin in early June. Bring your own containers.

### HIGHLAND ORCHARDS

One mile north of Marshallton on Thorndale Road. Take Pa. Route 162 and follow the signs out of West Chester. Pick your own fruit in season: peaches, apples, fresh vegetables, sweet corn, and tomatoes, strawberries the first week in June. Bring your own containers. Open Monday through Saturday 9 A.M. to 8 P.M., Sunday 12 noon to 6 P.M.

### LARCHMONT FARMS
N.J. Route 537
Moorestown, N.J.

Phone: 1-609-235-0400
Directions: East on N.J. Route 38, turn left at second traffic light after crossing the New Jersey Turnpike, turn left again after you cross railroad tracks, ½ mile down the road on right-hand side is Larchmont Farms

From July 22 throughout the summer and early fall you can pick your own fruit. Bring a basket or buy one. You ride to the field in red-and-white-striped canopied wagons. Picnic tables available, so pack a lunch. Hours: Saturday 9 A.M. to 5 P.M., Sunday 11 A.M. to 5 P.M., Monday 9 A.M. to 5 P.M.

## LINVILLA ORCHARDS
137 West Knowlton Road
Media, Pa.

**Phone:** TR 6-9047
**Open:** Daily year-round including Sunday, July–November 10 A.M.–8 P.M.; rest of year 10 A.M.–5:30 P.M.
**Closed:** Thanksgiving, Christmas, New Year's Day
**Directions:** Schuylkill Expressway to U.S. Route 1, south to Pa. Route 352 south (second exit) on 352 to second traffic light. Right on Knowlton Road ½ mile.
**Parking:** On the grounds
**Picnicking:** Picnic tables; no charge

Fall is the most popular time of year to visit Linvilla Orchards. With its 285 acres, it is one of the few large fruit and vegetable farms left in suburban Philadelphia. What is your favorite apple? Turley? Crandall? Jonathan? Grimes? They have more than ten varieties, as well as cider, fresh vegetables, pies (place your order for the holidays), dried leaves and plants, and autumn decorations. Outside their large octagonal barn from October 1 they have an enormous stock of pumpkins.

Near the barn, deer, rabbits, turkeys, pheasants, bulls, sheep, and horses wander about in large open pens, much to the delight of the children. Dress warmly even though the day seems mild and allow a couple of hours for walking, watching, and buying.

## Magic Shops

It's surprising how many young magicians are around these days entertaining at children's parties and for their friends. To increase their repertoire, try these shops. Tricks vary in price from very little to costly. They make a welcome gift to the budding conjurer.

## CHANIN'S STUDIO OF MAGIC
1212 Walnut Street—2nd floor
Philadelphia

**Phone:** KI 5-5452

**KANTOR'S MAGIC SHOP**
200 South 13th Street
200 South 13th Street—2nd floor

Phone: KI 5-4033

Professionals and amateurs buy here.

**MAGIC FUN SHOP**
109 South 11th Street
Philadelphia

Phone: WA 5-3400

Novelties, gags, and magic.

## Musical Instruments

Both of these places come highly recommended by professionals:

**ALBERT A. KNECHT**
24 South 18th Street
Philadelphia
Phone: 561-0820

118 South Bellvue Avenue
Langhorne, Pa. (Bucks County)
Phone: 757-7666

A fine old reputable name in musical instruments. Quality is here. Also sheet music, song albums, orchestra/band arrangements.

**ZAPF'S**
Main Store
5421 North 5th Street
Philadelphia
Phone: WA 4-8736

Baederwood Shopping Center
Jenkintown, Pa.
Phone: TU 7-1447

300 West Johnson Highway
Norristown, Pa.
Phone: 277-4481

New and used instruments. Rental plan with option to buy. Wide variety of selections.

## Museum Shops

If you want to find unusual items not ordinarily seen in gift departments, try the museum shops of these institutions. They have many reasonably priced objects for the disciminating buyer.

### ACADEMY OF NATURAL SCIENCES
19th Street and Benjamin Franklin Parkway
Philadelphia

**Phone:** LO 7-3700

Geodes, fossils, Eskimo sculpture, jewelry, and books. Everything related to their overall interest: animal, vegetable, or mineral.

### BRANDYWINE RIVER MUSEUM
Route 1
Chadds Ford, Pa.

**Phone:** 1-388-7601

Wyeth reproductions, books, ecology kits.

### FRANKLIN INSTITUTE
20th Street and Benjamin Franklin Parkway
Philadelphia

**Phone:** 448-1000

Ben's Shop: For the scientifically minded. Books, models, chemistry sets, telescopes, and gyroscopes. Reasonably priced.

### PHILADELPHIA ART ALLIANCE
251 South 18th Street
Philadelphia

**Phone:** KI 5-4302

Atttractive one-of-a-kind craft items; juried pieces.

### PHILADELPHIA MARITIME MUSEUM
321 Chestnut Street
Philadelphia

**Phone:** WA 5-5439

Interesting nautical items, including authentic scrimshaw.

**PHILADELPHIA MUSEUM OF ART**
26th Street and Benjamin Franklin Parkway
Philadelphia

**Phone: PO 3-8100**

Enormous selection of books on art and architecture; art books for children, puzzles, notepaper, jewelry, and sculpture. A shop with reasonably priced items especially for children in separate location.

**PRINT CLUB**
1614 Latimer Street
Philadelphia

**Phone: PE 5-6090**

Contemporary prints and graphics.

**UNITED STATES MINT**
5th and Arch Streets
Philadelphia

**Phone: 597-7350**

Medals and commemorative medallions made on the premises.

**UNIVERSITY MUSEUM**
33rd and Spruce Streets
Philadelphia

**Phone: EV 6-7400**

Museum shop and Pyramid Shop for children. Unusual crafts and exquisite jewelry from around the world. Wide selection of books, toys, kites, puzzles, and jewelry in the Pyramid Shop to fit a child's budget.

## Party Supplies

Most gift and card shops sell party supplies. The following is a list of stores that offer more unusual fare or extensive stock.

**COMERS**
Germantown Avenue and Washington Lane
Philadelphia

**Phone: GE 8-5400**

From children's parties through golden wedding anniversaries, every conceivable kind of party need. You'll find a wide assortment; everything at a slight discount.


## DECKER'S STATIONERY STORE
1216 Chestnut Street
Philadelphia

**Phone: WA 3-1644**

Cherry Hill Mall
Cherry Hill, N.J.

**Phone: 1-609-663-8622**

Decorative and coordinated items; good place to look for needs of "theme party." Centerpieces made to order.


## ETC. ETC.
234 Bala Avenue
Bala-Cynwyd, Pa.

**Phone: MO 4-8234**

Unusual greeting cards, invitations, decorations, and party supplies.


## PAPER BOUTIQUE
Yorktown Inn Mall
York and Church Roads
Elkins Park, Pa.

**Phone: TU 6-0805**

Party goods, unusual quality stationery, invitations, and gifts picked with discrimination.


## SOFFER'S
7709 Germantown Avenue
Philadelphia

**Phone: CH 7-5140**

Great quantities of paper goods of all kinds for entertaining; inexpensive party favors.

# Plants

In the ecology-minded world of today many young people have become interested in plants and gardening. There are many notable florists, greenhouses, and gardens in and around Philadelphia. Here are just a few your child might enjoy visiting and where he might develop an interest in horticulture.

**THE GREENERY**
1114 Pine Street
Philadelphia

Phone: MA 7-6322

Terraria (gardens under glass), hanging pots, exotic plants. Plant advice to the novice.

**MEADOWBROOK FARMS**
1633 Washington Lane
Meadowbrook, Pa.

Phone: 885-2693

The greenhouses and shop are on the magnificent estate of the owner, J. Liddon Pennock. Visitors and buyers are welcome. Of special interest are potted topiaries, hanging baskets, and outstanding terra-cotta containers priced from very reasonable to very expensive. Mr. Pennock supplies the White House at Christmas. The sign for Meadowbrook Farms is easy to miss. It's the first driveway on the right beyond Meadowbrook Road.

**A NEW LEAF**
8111 Germantown Avenue
Chestnut Hill, Philadelphia

Phone: CH 8-0377

Small shop with a large variety of plants, pots, and greenery.

## Stamps and Coins

There are many stamp and coin dealers in the Delaware Valley. This partial list has been compiled with the help of people who are collectors and have found these dealers to be reputable and helpful in starting a collection or adding to an established one.

**EARL P. APFELBAUM**
1420 Walnut Street
Philadelphia

Phone: 985-1550

For the beginning and advanced collector. Unique stamp auctions. Come in and browse.

**C. E. BULLOWA**
1616 Walnut Street, Suite 1006
Philadelphia

Phone: PE 5-5517

Coin-hunter for the advanced collector. Anyone looking for unique coins and rarities, try here.

**DAVE'S NORTHEAST MINT**
1825 Cottman Avenue
(In the Northeast)
Philadelphia

Phone: PI 5-4900

David Gorlin is the proprietor, and he specializes in United States coins. Stamps here also. Numismatic supplies.

**DOROTHY GERSHENSON**
129 South 16th Street
Philadelphia

Phone: LO 3-4232

Coins for the beginner and advanced collector. Rare autographs and documents.

**PENN VALLEY COIN SHOPPE**
22 East Lancaster Avenue
Ardmore, Pa.

**Phone:** MI 9-7255

Coins for the beginner and advanced collector. Collector's supplies.

**WILLARD P. SNYDER**
26 South 18th Street
Philadelphia

**Phone:** LO 4-2191

An old standby for the new collector and good finds for the established collector.

## Toys and Play Equipment

Many well-advertised discount toy operations abound. Here are some quality retail toy stores you may not know about, all staffed with helpful salespeople.

**BAYNE'S TRAINS**
4327 Main Street
Philadelphia

**Phone:** MO 4-4259
**Open:** Hours vary so it is best to call ahead

Lionel and American Flyer, repairs and parts. Used trains bought and sold. Young and old train collectors come from all over the Delaware Valley to this cluttered shop overflowing with trains, tracks, stations, transformers, cranes, whistles, trestles—and good advice.

**FIRESIDE**
186 East Evergreen Avenue
Chestnut Hill, Philadelphia

**Phone:** CH 8-3122

"Creative Playthings" are on sale here and a wide selection of imaginative toys. Also children's records, books, and games for all ages. Helpful personnel.

## HARLEQUIN MARIONETTES
2013 Moravian Street
Philadelphia 19103

Phone: LO 7-0468

Hal Taylor will take orders for his hand-carved marionettes and puppets. He also produces a half-hour Punch and Judy show ($50) for birthday parties.

## IT'S A SMALL WORLD
8042 Germantown Avenue
Chestnut Hill, Philadelphia

Phone: CH 7-7929

Toys and accessories and children's furniture, mostly imports.

## THE KITE STORE
39 Maplewood Mall
(Between Germantown Avenue and Greene Street, one block south
   of Chelten Avenue)
2nd floor
Germantown

Phone: 842-3620

Kites from all over the world. Nothing but kites. Everything from simple cutter kites to a spectacular 45-foot dragon. Airplanes, butterflies, birds, boxes. They all fly. Or use them as handsome decorations. Kite flying: Sundays 2–4 P.M. (weather permitting), Chestnut Hill Academy Field, 500 West Willow Grove Avenue, Chestnut Hill

## BILL MULLER WOODEN TOYS
100 Main Street
Souderton, Pa. 18964

Phone: 1-723-8103

In these days of "hard sell" and mass-produced toys, it is a pleasure to see the simple but fine handcrafted and designed toys of Bill Muller. Cars, trucks of every variety, toy trains, rocking horses, doll cradles are available. The toys are made of the finest sugar pine assembled with wooden dowels and nontoxic glue. No metal parts or fasteners are used. All toys are hand sanded to a natural finish. Each toy is guaranteed against breakage: You can return a broken toy, and it will be repaired or replaced. Write for illustrated catalogue: 87 Commerce Drive, Telford, Pa. 18969. Christmas orders must be received by November 15. Freight in continental United States is paid by Bill Muller Wooden Toys.

## PLAY-ART
20 West Armat Street
Germantown, Philadelphia

**Phone:** VI 8-0200

Play-Art caters to schools, but you are welcome to buy and it's definitely worth a visit. Sturdy outdoor equipment, seesaws, slides, merry-go-rounds, and swings. Educational toys and aids such as flash cards, preprimers and primers, and art supplies of all kinds.

## L. PONNOCK
1012 Chestnut Street
Philadelphia

**Phone:** WA 3-1310

If you heard it advertised on TV, it's probably here. Large selection of mass-market toys in huge quantities, games, puzzles, packaged dolls, and trains. You can also find many "Creative Playthings." Also party goods, bicycles, and toddler equipment. Some items are discounted; "Creative Playthings" are not.

## F. A. O. SCHWARZ
Suburban Square
Coulter Street and Saint Georges Road
Ardmore, Pa.

**Phone:** MI 9-0600

Quality toys, Madame Alexander dolls, and anything from a modest squeeze toy to an elaborately furnished dollhouse. Good book department with emphasis on classics and old favorites. Fine variety of children's records. They have Caedmon-Stratford records, an excellent but expensive series for children, along with Sesame Street and Mr. Rogers. Ask to be put on their Christmas catalogue mailing list. The selection is astounding.

## VENDO NUBES
1929 Chestnut Street
Philadelphia

**Phone:** 561-3377

Kite-flying enthusiasts check here. Large stock of unusual kites: Indian fighter, Japanese centipede, West German condor, mylar dragon, English box, and Chinese butterfly kites. Also imaginative line of toys from baby's things to a computer to put together.

# Tropical Fish

**MARTIN'S AQUARIUM**
6900 Old York Road
Philadelphia 19126

**Phone:** LI 9-7050
**Open:** Every day, including Sunday

This is the supermarket of aquariums. Tremendous collection of freshwater and saltwater fish, fish supplies, bonsai trees, cactus, fossils, and minerals, all at discount prices. The young staff are helpful with children.

# Shopping Villages

**HISTORIC TOWNE OF SMITHVILLE**
New York Road
(U.S. 9)
Smithville, N.J. 08201

**Phone:** 1-609-641-7777
**Open:** Daily 10:30 A.M.–9:30 P.M.
**Admission:** Free
**Parking:** Free
**Directions:** 12 miles north of Atlantic City on U.S. 9

The restored village of Smithville resembles a crossroads community of the early nineteenth century. The present village is created around the historic Smithville Inn and was the brainchild of Fred and Ethel Noyes. It consists of thirty-four completely restored buildings moved from all sections of New Jersey, including shops, homes, a gristmill, and a smokehouse with imported cheeses and smoked meats for sale.

Many special events are held here throughout the year: antique auto shows, band concerts, old-style costume shows, and the like.

There are three inns for lunch and dinner, all with different menus; men must wear coats at the large Smithville Inn. The decor and menu have an early American flavor. Group visits should be planned in advance. For further information write or call.

NEARBY:
Brigantine National Wildlife Refuge (see page 193).

These shopping villages are mentioned in other sections of the book:

Lahaska and Buckingham
Peddler's Village
Saint Peter's Village
Turntable Junction and Flemington

## Services

### *Important Information*

EMERGENCY SERVICES
Philadelphia Police Department: To stop a crime . . . save a life 911; other emergencies 231-3131
Philadelphia Fire Department and Rescue: 563-6700
Poison Information Center: 922-5523
Doctor's Emergency Service: 563-2500
Office of Mental Health: MU 6-4958; after 5 P.M. MU 6-4420
Dental Emergency Service: LO 8-1668
Veterinary Emergency: 594-8881

HANDY NUMBERS: TRANSPORTATION
City Transit (SEPTA): DA 9-4800
Pennsylvania Railroad: EV 7-6600
Reading Railroad: WA 2-6530
Taxi Service—Yellow Cab: WA 2-8400
General Information on City: Philadelphia Convention and Visitors Bureau: 864-1976
Mayor's Office for Information and Complaints: MU 6-9700

CURFEW LAWS

Children under seventeen are forbidden in public places or streets after 10:30 P.M. or before 6 A.M.; Friday and Saturday extended to midnight. This does not apply if the child is accompanied by parent, is sent on an errand, or is employed during curfew hours.

## Public Transportation around the City

**SEPTA**
(Southeastern Pennsylvania Transportation Authority)
200 West Wyoming Avenue
Philadelphia 19140

For information on how to get anywhere in greater Philadelphia by public transportation, call DA 9-4800. Bus schedules, routes, and the SEPTA Map can be obtained by writing to SEPTA at the above address. The map is also available at many newsstands.

### SEPTA Bus Rambles

From May through Christmas on almost any Saturday SEPTA features a trip to outlying points of interest such as Longwood Gardens, Kutztown Folk Festival, New Hope, and Hershey. No advance reservations are needed. Prices vary with length of the trip. Call DA 9-4800 for list of rambles, or write for brochure.

### Cultural Loop Bus

The historic and cultural areas of the city from Independence Hall to the Benjamin Franklin Parkway area to the Philadelphia Zoo are linked by a one-fare low-cost (50¢) bus. This fare entitles you to "on and off" privileges all day and special discount admissions at the various stops. Check SEPTA for schedule.

### Mid City Loop Bus

For short rides on Market and Chestnut Streets between 5th and 17th Streets, SEPTA provides a Mid City Loop Bus (15¢).

### SEPTA Airport Express

It starts at 5th and Market Streets and makes several stops in Center City including Reading Terminal, Suburban Station, and Penn Central Station at 30th Street. One-way fare $1. A transfer is available for an additional 5¢ on the trip from the airport. With a transfer in downtown Philadelphia the fare to the airport is 65¢.

## Helpful Sources for Current Happenings

Every Friday the *Evening Bulletin, Daily News,* and *Inquirer* devote space to entertainment, cultural, and sporting events over the weekend. *Philadelphia Magazine, Metropolitan Magazine,* and *WFLN Guide* are also excellent sources. Suburban newspapers, mostly weeklies, provide information on neighborhood events with coverage of school and community activities.

# TOURIST INFORMATION
Tourist Center
1525 John F. Kennedy Boulevard

**Phone:** 864-1976

Thirty-minute free parking on 16th Street side of building (parking places are at a premium). Maintained by Convention and Visitors Bureau. Free brochures and information. Call or stop in.

# LEAGUE OF WOMEN VOTERS
11th Floor
Strawbridge & Clothier
8th and Market Streets
Philadelphia

**Phone:** MA 7-7937

Nonpartisan political information on state and local government. When you want to know who is your state senator and how to get in touch with him, where to register to vote, how to obtain an absentee ballot, call here. They are also an invaluable source of publications on national, state, and local issues.

## *Baby-Sitting*

# UNIVERSITY HOME SERVICES
6 Aldwyn Center
Villanova, Pa. 19085

**Phone:** LA 5-8580

The neighborhood teenager may fill the bill for Saturday night, but what do you do when you have a trip in the offing, without children, and have no one to leave them with? A happy combination of intelligent young married couples (many of them graduate students) who need extra income, plus your need for someone to care for your home and children has been realized with University Home Services. You may interview them in advance and then go away with an easy mind. The cost is not nominal, but it is worth looking into.

## Doll Hospital

### ANN'S DOLL REPAIR AND BOUTIQUE
6324 Rising Sun Avenue
Philadelphia

**Phone:** FI 2-7085
**Open:** Tuesday–Thursday 1–6 P.M., Friday 1–9 P.M., Saturday 10
A.M.–6 P.M.

This is the only doll hospital in Philadelphia. People come from
great distances for the repair of favorite dolls in need of new hair,
eyes, or limbs, or suffering cracks and bruises.

## International Services

### ETHNIC HERITAGE AFFAIRS INSTITUTE, INC.
Fellowship Commission Building
260 South 15th Street
Philadelphia

**Phone:** KI 5-6600

They have a bulletin, *Ethnic Philadelphia*, focusing on various
ethnic and cultural backgrounds in films, fairs, etc.

### INTERNATIONAL HOUSE
3701 Chestnut Street
Philadelphia

**Phone:** EV 7-5125

This center of activities on the Penn campus for foreign students
has a gift shop and dining room open to the public. Both are
worth a visit. The building itself is architecturally quite interesting.

### NATIONALITIES SERVICE CENTER
1300 Spruce Street
Philadelphia

**Phone:** 545-6800

If you are interested in meeting people from other countries, or if
you are a visitor or a student from a foreign land, call here and find
out about language lessons, international meetings, social gather-
ings, and interpreters' services. Help is available in finding schools,
housing, medical care, and legal aid.

## PHILADELPHIA COUNCIL FOR INTERNATIONAL VISITORS

34th Street and Civic Center Boulevard
Philadelphia

**Phone:** MU 6-1776, ext. 21261

Tours with bilingual guides. Introductions and appointments arranged with the visitor's professional counterpart and visits with American families in the Philadelphia area. Residents interested in entertaining foreign visitors call for information about the CIV program.

## TRAVELER'S AID SOCIETY

1 North 13th Street
Room 1100
Philadelphia
**Phone:** 665-0280

Penn Central Station
**Phone:** EV 6-0845

Philadelphia International Airport
**Phone:** 365-6525

## *Volunteer Work*

## CONVENTION AND VISITORS BUREAU

1525 John F. Kennedy Boulevard
Philadelphia

**Phone:** 864-1976

Volunteers 16 years of age and older man the Summer Information Booth across from Independence Hall. It's open seven days a week to aid visitors. Call for further information.

## COUNCIL ON VOLUNTEERS

Health and Welfare Council, Inc.
7 Benjamin Franklin Parkway
Philadelphia 19103

**Phone:** LO 8-3750

Volunteer jobs in hospitals, day nurseries, Head Start, and YMCAs are among those available all year for youths 14 and over in all areas of the city and suburbs. A fine directory put together by the Council on Volunteers explains the types of work available. Write or call for further information.

# 14
# CALENDAR OF EVENTS

Throughout the year annual holidays, notable events, sports tournaments, and fairs and festivals take place in the Delaware Valley. Here is a month-by-month description of these celebrations.

Dates of events sometimes vary by a week or so and may fall in a month other than the one listed here. For the exact dates and times check the local papers, *Philadelphia* Magazine, *Metropolitan* Magazine, and the *WFLN Guide*. The Convention and Visitors Bureau also has the latest schedules and is delighted to answer your questions.

Mummers' Parade

# January

*Mummers' Parade.* Broad and Snyder to Broad and Arch Streets, Philadelphia. Starts at 8 A.M. on January 1 and runs until it's over—usually around dusk. Reserved seat tickets $2, available early in December for section near City Hall adjacent to judging area at Tourist Center, 16th Street and John F. Kennedy Boulevard, or Mayor's Office of Information, Room 121, City Hall; free tickets in preferred area through your city councilman. But it's more fun to just dress warmly and join the crowds along the route. This annual strut of fancy feathers, antics, and string bands takes its name from Momus, the Greek god of ridicule. In Philadelphia the 100-year-old institution had its origins in the city's earliest days: the Swedish settlers had neighborhood parties and parades at Christmastime; the English added their traditions of costumes and pantomime. Gradually clubs and parades evolved, ending at Independence Hall, where they shot off pistols at midnight on New Year's Eve. There's no more pistol shooting, but the name New Year's Shooters and Mummers Association survives, and they've been marching up Broad Street annually since 1901.

*Annual Kite-Flying Contest.* To celebrate Benjamin Franklin's birthday. Held annually on the Saturday nearest January 17, 11 A.M. to 1 P.M., at Independence Mall. Prizes for highest flyer, best decorated, and most original in each of three age divisions: under 13, 13 to 19, and over 19. For information about the competition call City Representative's Office (MU 6-1776); Convention and Visitors Bureau (864-1976); or Department of Recreation (MU 6-3600). Other activities related to Franklin's many interests. Check with Convention and Visitors Bureau.

*Frostbite Sailing Competition.* Late January through mid-March. Every Sunday on the Schuylkill River between the Columbia Avenue and Dauphin Street bridges.

*United States Professional Indoor Tennis Championships.* Leading professional male tennis players of World Championship Tennis compete for top prize money at the Spectrum.

*New Year's* comes two more times: Chinese, and Russian.

# February

*Frostbite Sailing Competition* continues through mid-March; Sundays on the Schuylkill.

*Sport, Camping, and Vacation Show* at the Civic Center.

*Philadelphia Boat Show* at Civic Center.

*Washington's Birthday Observation* at Old Fort Mifflin; call WA 3-8299 for information (page 68).

*Chinese New Year.* Parades, firecrackers, dragons, lots of noise. Watch papers for exact date. Late January or early February.

*Ice Capades* at the Spectrum.

*Philadelphia Track Classic.* Scholastic, collegiate, and individual entries in this international field and track competition at the Spectrum (page 191).

# March

*Philadelphia Flower and Garden Show.* At the Civic Center. Mid-March for one week. Probably the largest and finest flower show on the East Coast. When you can't wait for spring, take the family in hand to a spectacular glimpse of woodland scenes, gardens for every taste and age, glorious specimen flowers, ponds, and pools. For sale are bulbs, just the kind of flower container you never had but always wanted, tools, and small plants which made fine souvenirs for the children. It's a good place for strollers and cameras too. Parking at the exhibition hall. Cafeteria and dining room. Elevator for wheelchairs.

*Saint Patrick's Day Parade.* Sunday closest to March 17.

*Philadelphia String Bands Annual Show of Shows.* At Civic Center. A portion of the Mummers' Parade, but indoors where it's warmer and you can sit down.

*Brigantine National Wildlife Refuge.* Peak of northbound waterfowl migration starts March 20 (page 193).

*Frostbite Sailing Competition* continues to middle of the month.

# April

*Cherry Blossoms.* Watch for them along the East and West River Drives.

*Brigantine National Wildlife Refuge.* Northbound migration of waterfowl continues until April 15 (page 193).

*Easter Promenade.* Rittenhouse Square, Walnut to Rittenhouse, 18th to 19th Streets. Easter Sunday strollers. Fashions for everyone. Music, entertainment.

*Penn Relays.* Franklin Field. For over 75 years this major classic track-and-field event has been drawing top contestants from high schools and colleges (page 191).

*University Hospital Antique Show,* 103rd Engineer's Armory, 33rd Street north of Market. One of the finest antique shows in the East. Not so much for children as for parents who appreciate exquisite antiques. Many items of museum quality. Go to look even if you can't afford to buy.

*Earth Week.* Learn how to help save our planet. Local ecology-minded institutions participate.

*"A" Day,* Delaware Valley College of Science and Agriculture, Pa. Route 611 north to U.S. Route 202, 1 mile west of Doylestown, Pa. Phone: 345-1500. Flower show, livestock judging, contests, entertainment, food. No admission charge. Bring strollers for little ones. Last weekend in April or early in May.

*Philadelphia Virginia Slims Tennis Classic.* In April at the Palestra. Women's professional tournament.

*Valborgs Celebration.* Annual welcome to spring at American Swedish Historical Museum (see page 77).

# May

Go see the Azalea Garden behind the Art Museum. Presented by the Pennsylvania Horticultural Society, it has 125 different varieties, examples of azaleas growing in this area. Special ceremonies second Sunday in May.

*Monkey Island Day at the Zoo.* A Sunday in May. Contests, prizes, to celebrate the monkeys' move to their summer home (page 113).

*Wissahickon Day.* At Valley Green. A Sunday early in May, 1 to 3 P.M. Riders, drivers, horses, buggies; competition, entertainment, and a colorful parade. Free.

*Rittenhouse Square Flower Market,* Rittenhouse Square, Rittenhouse to Walnut 18th and 19th Streets. Since 1914 this pretty annual event has been attracting hundreds of people to the Square. Go early to admire and buy (resist if you can) beautiful flowers, plants, vegetables, delicious baked goods, and Philadelphia's lemon on a stick.

*Regatta Time* on the Schuylkill. Weekends from now until September. Call National Association of Amateur Oarsmen (PO 9-2068).

*Dad Vail Regatta.* Usually second weekend in May. Largest collegiate regatta in the country—about 1,000 oarsmen from U.S. colleges compete. Hunting Park Avenue to Columbia Avenue bridge. Take a picnic and watch Thomas Eakins's paintings come alive.

*Old Fort Mifflin* reopens on a daily basis on Memorial Day with appropriate ceremonies (page 68).

*Colonial Mansions in the Park Auto Rambles.* May through October (page 131).

*Devon Horse Show and Country Fair.* One week, end of May into June (page 260).

*Philadelphia Flea Market,* Independence Mall, occasional Sunday afternoons into the fall (page 266).

*Annual Bach Festival* in Bethlehem. Two weekends of Bach's music. Concerts are held in the Packer Chapel at Lehigh University. For information write Bach Choir Office, Main and Church Streets, Bethlehem, Pa. 18018, or phone 1-866-4382. Information about tickets and concerts is usually sent out late in February.

*Ringling Brothers Barnum & Bailey Circus* due in town last week in May or early June.

*Walking Tour of Colonial Germantown.* For exact date and information call Germantown Historical Society (VI 4-0514).

*A Day in Old Newcastle,* Newcastle, Delaware. Third Saturday in May. Once a year this pre-Revolutionary town opens its private homes, its residents put on Colonial dress, and much Colonial activity and atmosphere prevail (page 258).

*Annual Spring Festival* sponsored by the Greater Philadelphia Cultural Alliance. Week-long celebration of the arts—music, theater, dance, art, films—throughout the city.

# June

*Elfreth's Alley Day.* First Sunday in June. Open house on a Colonial street (page 36).

*Pennsylvania Hospital Day at Washington Square.* Early in June. Art exhibits, books, antiques, refreshments (page 265).

*June Fête,* first Friday night and Saturday in June. Edge Hill Road, Abington, Pa. One of the big ones in the area. Horse and pony show, dog show, classic and modern cars, children's area with games, Ferris wheel—and good food for all (page 264).

*Attention, Candy Lovers!* Chocolate-covered strawberries make their annual appearance at the William Penn Shops (page 379).

*Clothesline Exhibit.* Rittenhouse Square, Rittenhouse to Walnut, 18th to 19th Streets. Outdoor art show and sale. Works of professionals and students of local art schools selected by a jury.

*Old Swedes' Church Fair.* Gloria Dei Church grounds, Delaware and Christian Streets, Philadelphia (FU 9-1513). Festival in honor of Swedish settlers. Folk dances, pageant, food.

*Devon Horse Show and Country Fair* continues into first week of June.

*Delco Scottish Games.* The gathering of the clans, but everyone is welcome for this annual day of bagpipes, drums, dances, games, and food (page 259).

*Flag Day Parade,* evening of June 14. Annual salute to the flag. Benjamin Franklin Parkway to Independence Hall. Additional ceremonies at Betsy Ross House.

*Head House Square Open Air Market.* Mid-June into September, Saturday 12 noon to midnight, Sunday 11 A.M. to 6 P.M. Music, crafts, exotic foods from around the world in an eighteenth-century setting in Society Hill (page 262).

*Old Newsboys' Day.* Parades, marching bands, floats, and fun. Proceeds for the handicapped.

*Batsto Annual Arts and Crafts Day* (page 61).

*Craft Days at Pennsylvania Farm Museum of Landis Valley* (page 253).

*Freedom Week.* Week-long celebration of Fourth of July. Check papers or call Visitors Bureau for activities.

*Festival of Fountains.* 8 P.M. Logan Square, 19th Street and Benjamin Franklin Parkway. String bands, fireworks, dancing waters, and colored lights. Bring a blanket.

*"A Nation Is Born."* Sound and light show 9 P.M. at Independence Square (page 29).

*Philadelphia Fling.* June to September. Free entertainment. Noon at John F. Kennedy Plaza weekdays. Evenings at Independence Mall, Rittenhouse Square, Kennedy Plaza, and Art Museum Terrace: string bands, dance, theater, opera, concerts. For program call Tourist Center 864-1976.

# July

*Freedom Week* continues to Fourth of July. Special ceremonies at Independence Hall on Fourth of July at 11 A.M.: a nationally known speaker, a reading of the Declaration of Independence, music, and parade of flags.

*July 4 Annual Independence Day Bus Tour of Society Hill* sponsored by Strawbridge & Clothier.

*Old Fort Mifflin.* Take a picnic lunch on Fourth of July and hear a reading of the Declaration of Independence (page 68).

*Independence Day Regatta* on the Schuylkill.

*Kutztown Folk Festival,* Kutztown, Pa. First week in July. One of the biggest and most popular of the Pennsylvania Dutch festivals (page 264).

*Star Roses,* U.S. Route 1, West Grove, Pa. Roses at their height (page 233).

*Mifflin Day* at Old Fort Mifflin, July 18 (page 68).

*Hopewell Village.* Candlelight Program. One evening in July and again in August; whole village is lit by candlelight. Call 1-582-8773 for exact day (page 65).

*Ephrata Cloister.* Vorspiel performances weekends, end of June to September (page 247).

*Longwood Gardens.* Colored fountain display (page 199).

*Head House Square Open Air Market, Philadelphia Flea Market at Independence Mall, Philadelphia Fling* all continue.

## August

*Head House Square Open Air Market, Philadelphia Flea Market at Independence Mall, Philadelphia Fling* all continue.

*Colonial Mansions in the Park Auto Rambles* continue (page 131).

*Hopewell Village.* Candlelight Program one evening in July and August; whole village is lit by candlelight. For exact dates call 582-8773. Also Establishment Day, first Sunday in August (page 65).

*Philadelphia Folk Festival.* Last weekend in August (page 266).

*Goschenhoppen Folk Festival,* East Greenville, Pa. The second Friday and Saturday in August (no rain date). In a tree-covered picnic grove more than 200 costumed craftsmen demonstrate spinning, making apple butter, basketry, caning, etc. Pennsylvania Dutch music, humor, folklore, and delicious food. It's very friendly and noncommercial (page 261).

*The USLTA National Girls 18 (Grass) Championships.* At the Philadelphia Cricket Club. Call CH 7-6001 for information.

*Pennsylvania Lawn Tennis Championships.* At the Merion Cricket Club. For information call MI 2-5800.

*Morgan Horse Show* at Devon Horse Show Grounds (page 265).

*Black Expo.* Showcase of black culture, business, and education. Good music, good food, and a good time for everyone (page 258).

*Pennsylvania Dutch Days,* Hershey, Pa. A five-day folk festival with craft demonstrations and good food (page 252).

# September

*Annual Hero Scholarship Fund Thrill Show,* John F. Kennedy Stadium. Precision riding and acrobatics by the motorcycle drill team, music, and fireworks. A queen and her court rule over it all. Proceeds from this long-standing annual event go to the scholarship fund for children of police and firemen killed or disabled in the line of duty. Tickets from local police district or firehouse. For groups: Room 497, City Hall, Hero Scholarship office (MU 6-3400).

*Steuben Day Parade*

*Puerto Rican Day Parade*

*Victorian House Tour* in Germantown. Call the Germantown Historical Society for exact date and details (VI 4-0514).

*Polish Festival and Country Fair.* On the grounds of national Shrine of Our Lady of Czestochowa in Doylestown, Pa. Largest show of Polish culture, food, entertainment, and fun (page 267).

*Duryea Day.* Saturday before Labor Day, Boyertown Museum of Historic Vehicles. Antique and Classic Car Meet. 9 A.M.–5 P.M. Flea Market of old car parts. Rain or shine (page 243).

*Hawk Mountain Sanctuary.* From mid-September through November birds of prey fly over in great quantities (page 197).

*Red Rose Inn,* U.S. Route 1, West Grove, Pa. First Saturday after Labor Day. Ceremony marking yearly payment of one red rose (page 231).

*Fairmount Fall Festival.* Two weeks of sightseeing, cycling, hiking, sports events, concerts, boat races, exhibitions—something for everyone—in Fairmount Park, culminating in Super Sunday on the Parkway.

# October

*Pulaski Day Parade*

*Columbus Day Parade*

*Super Sunday.* A Sunday in October. Rain or shine, 12 noon to 6 P.M. Sponsored by the cultural institutions along the Benjamin Franklin Parkway. The Parkway becomes a giant midway: music, games, crafts, puppets, exhibits, food. From Logan Circle to the Art Museum (page 268).

*Philadelphia Horse Show and Jumping Competition* at the Spectrum.

*Harvest Days* at Pennsylvania Farm Museum of Landis Valley (page 253).

*Chester County Day.* First Saturday in October. Rain or shine. Open house at historic homes, landmarks, and estates. Not particularly for children (page 234).

*Historic Fallsington Day,* Fallsington, Pa. The second Sunday in October, rain or shine. This historic restored village holds an eighteenth-century fair: musket drills, glassblowing, mulled cider (page 263).

*Hawk Mountain Sanctuary.* See the hawks, bald eagles, etc. (page 197).

# November

*Brigantine National Wildlife Refuge.* November 1–10. Ducks, geese brant are here in spectacular numbers (page 193).

*Old Fort Mifflin.* Salute to Men of Mifflin. Anniversary of Battle of Fort Mifflin. Celebrated on Sunday closest to November 16 (page 68).

*Farm City Week.* One weekend in November some of the working farms in Chester County hold open house: orchards, greenhouses, mushroom houses, horse, goat, and dairy farms. Free. For program, date, and map call or write Tourist Bureau, Court House, West Chester, Pa. 19880. Phone: 696-4935.

*Thanksgiving Day Parade.* Christmas Season officially opens with the arrival of Santa Claus. Presented by Gimbels, it's the oldest parade of its kind in the country.

*Army–Navy Game.* John F. Kennedy Stadium, 11th Street and Pattison Avenue. This annual clash is full of color and tradition (page 185).

*Pennsylvania Hunt Cup,* near Unionville, Pa. Cross-country races. Long-standing annual event (page 186).

# December

*Amateur Figure-Skating Show.* University of Pennsylvania Class of 1923 Ice Skating Rink. First weekend in December. Leading competitors from around the country in a benefit performance.

*Philadelphia Flyers Annual Hockey Clinic* at the Spectrum. Call HO 5-4500.

*Philadelphia Dog Show* at Civic Center.

*Mummers' Parade.* Tickets for seats in reserved section go on sale early in December at Tourist Center, 16th Street and John F. Kennedy Boulevard, and Mayor's Office of Information, Room 121, City Hall (page 399).

*Ice Follies* from end of December into January.

*Reenactment of Washington Crossing the Delaware.* December 25 at 2 P.M., Washington Crossing State Park, Pa., Routes 32 and 532, Washington Crossing, Pa. At the Memorial Building. Retreat service and flag ceremony. Two Durham boats, the type Washington used, cross with about thirty men each in Colonial garb. Come early for parking and a good vantage point to see the "Crossing." At 1 and 3 P.M. half-hour sound and color film, *Washington Crossing the Delaware,* in the Memorial Building.

# Especially for Christmas

*City Hall Tree-Lighting Ceremony,* City Hall Courtyard. The Mayor presides, police and firemen's bands play. Second Wednesday in December at dusk. Free.

*Lucia Festival* at Gloria Dei Church (page 38). Also at American Swedish Historical Museum (page 77).

*The Nutcracker* by Pennsylvania Ballet Company at the Academy of Music.

*Medieval Illuminated Manuscripts* from Rare Book Department on display in Central Lobby of the Free Library, Logan Square.

*Ebenezer Maxwell Mansion,* Greene and Tulpehocken Streets, Germantown. Annual Dickens Christmas Party. Second Sunday of the month. Celebrate the holidays nineteenth-century style.

*Colonial Mansions* in Fairmount Park featuring eighteenth-century decorations. Call Park House Office at Art Museum (PO 3-8100).

*SEPTA Bus Rambles.* Christmas Tour of Longwood Gardens (page 394).

*Brandywine River Museum.* "A Brandywine Christmas" (page 82).

*Morris Arboretum.* Annual sale of fresh holly and Christmas greens. Call for exact date: CH 7-5777.

*Newtown Historic Association House Tour* early in December. Call 1-968-4004 for information (page 224).

*At the Department Stores in Center City.* Santa with breakfast, Santa with lunch, theater, ballet, lights, and music. Wanamaker's for years has been presenting its spectacular show of fountains, lights, and music in the Grand Court.

*Pennsylvania Horticultural Society*, 325 Walnut Street. Annual display of Christmas decorations made from natural dried materials—tree ornaments, mobiles, kissing balls, outdoor trees for birds—done by local garden clubs. Also open house following Society Hill Christmas Walking Tour. Open to the public. Call WA 2-4801 for exact dates.

# INDEX